INTERCONNECTIONS

....

Interpersonal Communication Foundations and Contexts

JONATHAN M. BOWMAN

University of San Diego

 CENGAGE

Australia • Brazil • Mexico • Singapore • United Kingdom • United States

Interconnections: Interpersonal
Communication Foundations
and Contexts
Jonathan M. Bowman

Content Development Manager: Janine Tangney

Senior Content Developer: Leslie Taggart

Product Assistant: Camille Beckman

Marketing Manager: Allison Moghaddasi

Content Project Manager: Dan Saabye

Manufacturing Planner: Doug Bertke

IP Analyst: Ann Hoffman

IP Project Manager: Kathryn Kucharek

Production Service: MPS Limited

Compositor: MPS Limited

Art Director: Marissa Falco

Text and Cover Designer: Chrissy Kurpeski

Cover Image: Chrissy Kurpeski

For product information and technology assistance, contact us at
Cengage Customer & Sales Support, 1-800-354-9706.

For permission to use material from this text or product,
submit all requests online at **www.cengage.com/permissions.**
Further permissions questions can be emailed to
permissionrequest@cengage.com.

Library of Congress Control Number: 2017941443

Student Edition:
ISBN: 978-1-285-44933-3

Loose-leaf Edition:
ISBN: 978-1-337-55505-0

Cengage
20 Channel Center Street
Boston, MA 02210
USA

Cengage is a leading provider of customized learning solutions with employees residing in nearly 40 different countries and sales in more than 125 countries around the world. Find your local representative at **www.cengage.com.**

Cengage products are represented in Canada by Nelson Education, Ltd.

To learn more about Cengage platforms and services, visit **www.cengage.com.**

Purchase any of our products at your local college store or at our preferred online store **www.cengagebrain.com.**

Printed in the United States of America
Print Number: 01   Print Year: 2017

This book is dedicated to Mike, Sherri, Stanley, Arline, Trudy, and Martha, who collectively modeled interpersonal relationships in an authentic and loving way and who enabled all around them to pursue their potential.

About the Author

Jonathan M. Bowman

Jonathan M. Bowman (Ph.D., Michigan State University) is Professor of Communication Studies at the University of San Diego. His primary identity is as a teacher, and he finds no greater thrill than seeing students apply classroom knowledge in practical contexts. He has received the highest teaching awards in his discipline, including the National Communication Association's (NCA's) Ecroyd Award for Outstanding Teaching in Higher Education and the Western States Communication Association's Distinguished Teaching Award, among others. Bowman's program of research includes articles and books that investigate interpersonal and small-group communication processes in a variety of contexts, with an emphasis on the revelation of unknown information (i.e., "self-disclosure" in the interpersonal literature; "discussion of unshared information" in the small-group literature). In addition to his scholarly publications, Bowman has contributed his expertise to multiple national media outlets, including *The Boston Globe* and *Good Morning America*. He has served on the executive committees for multiple NCA divisions and participates in a variety of professional organizations within and beyond the field of communication.

Bowman loves to connect directly with students, something that allows him to write for undergraduates while remaining pedagogically relevant. He has directed a social justice learning community and also completed a four-year stint as a Faculty-in-Residence, living in the core residential area of his university and serving as a mentor and adviser to undergraduates. He has been an adviser and/or volunteer for multiple campus student organizations, including a national fraternity, a national honor society, and a national faith-based organization. Dr. Bowman was given a national award for his work with the National Communication Association's Honor Society, Lambda Pi Eta. Bowman is known on campus for his direction of undergraduate research in communication and is an instructor in the Honors Program.

Contents

8

Relational Difficulties 175

PART THREE UNIQUE INTERPERSONAL COMMUNICATION CONTEXTS

9

Romantic Relationships 203

10
Families 229

11
Workplace Interactions 259

List of Boxes

Communication Currents

Let's Get INTRApersonal

InterConnect

iPersonal

Commendable Connections

InterFace

Preface

With the rise of communication technologies like social media and smartphones, social change can occur at breakneck speeds. Students and faculty sometimes feel left behind because of these rapid shifts in culture. As the primary social process, interpersonal communication is uniquely positioned as a comprehensive way to understand how lives and cultures are impacted by the manner in which we now interact with each other as diverse individuals. As unique perspectives and distinctive styles of the millennial generation are shared in our classrooms and are influenced by the professoriate, it is important to address and support students' current lived experiences. In conversations about how to best teach today's students, it's not at all unusual for faculty to mention two concerns: first, faculty feel that students don't relate well to a traditional textbook structure, with students often eschewing the purchase of a book altogether if they don't immediately find a point of connection during their quick bookstore perusal; second, faculty often want a textbook that uses narrative to further students' understanding by addressing the complex challenges of their diverse social interactions. The goal of this textbook is to engage students by meeting them in the contexts of their daily experiences with stories of people that they may encounter in their everyday life.

THE APPROACH: CROSS-CULTURAL NARRATIVES IN DIVERSE INTERPERSONAL CONTEXTS

Interconnections: Interpersonal Communication Foundations and Contexts incorporates core content of the basic interpersonal communication course while also arranging contemporary scholarship in a student-friendly way. After receiving a solid foundation in theory in Parts 1 and 2, students are able to approach the study of interpersonal communication similarly to how they actually contemplate and process the communication field in their own lives: by scrutinizing their specific relationship contexts. Part 3 of the text is devoted to these relationship contexts. By moving through the variety of family relationships, to casual romantic encounters or early dating partners, to long-term committed partners, to a variety of workplace relationships, this portion of the text allows the specific application and explication of theory together within contexts that students can understand. For example, discussions of physical attraction, the courtship model, and the cultural proscriptions regarding premarital sex—within the context of a friends-with-benefits encounter—allow students to draw theory-driven connections between the behaviors that often underlay such a casual relational pairing. Instead of *just* organizing concepts by relational stage as some texts do, *Interconnections: Interpersonal Communication Foundations and Contexts* makes these connective cross-linkages more salient for both the student and the instructor. At the same time, Parts 1 and 2 of the book can serve as a comprehensive stand-alone text in a traditional course structure, and Part 3 can then be used as either supplemental chapters or as reference materials and further readings for students.

THE ORGANIZATION: FOUNDATIONS AND CONTEXTS

Interconnections: Interpersonal Communication Foundations and Contexts capitalizes on that unique three-part organizational structure, with distinct sections and scaffolded chapters that allow faculty to customize their classroom experience according to the needs of the students:

- Part 1 discusses *interpersonal communication foundations*. Chapter 1 lays the groundwork for an understanding of the models and principles of interpersonal communication interactions. Chapter 2 focuses on cognitions about the self in relation to identity and self-perception, and Chapter 3 locates those concepts within the motivations for interpersonal communication and the environments in which they occur. Taken together, the first three chapters give students the language and perspective to begin critically engaging the relationships in their social world.

- Part 2 focuses on *interpersonal communication in action*. Chapter 4 focuses on the nature of verbal communication and message construction. Chapter 5 covers listening, providing students with a clear understanding of how to best engage diverse others. Chapter 6 looks at the basics of nonverbal communication, with attention to the main codes in which that communication occurs. Chapters 7 and 8 both focus on the changing nature of significant relationships, with an emphasis on theories about relationship building, relational maintenance, and relational transgressions that shape the interpersonal relationship environment.

- Part 3 highlights the variety of *unique interpersonal communication contexts* that individuals encounter, beginning in Chapter 9 with romantic relationships and love, highlighting seminal relationship research. Chapter 10 takes a turn toward families and the diversity of structures and challenges that individuals engage throughout the life span. Finally, Chapter 11 highlights other significant interpersonal relationships that might occur in the workplace, focusing on theory that adds to our understanding of how individuals might manage interpersonal communication within the career context.

THE FEATURES: STUDENT ENGAGEMENT AND REFLECTION ACROSS CONTEXTS

Stories are at the root of interpersonal relationships, and throughout every chapter of *Interconnections,* students read relatable anecdotes about diverse people in engaging communication situations that they may encounter in their own social world. In addition to the ongoing narrative style of the book, six types of boxes featured in every chapter offer more examples of interpersonal concepts in action in everyday life. Boxes engage human diversity, address the impact of technology on relationships, explore ethical dilemmas, help students gain insight into their personal relationships via questionnaires and journal writing, and use current media depictions of interpersonal relationships to illustrate key concepts.

Key Concepts Illustrated by Current Media Depictions

Communication Currents boxes use current electronic media clips to further expand on chapter content. These media selections briefly illustrate key theories or concepts in an accessible, student-centered way. Embedded links in the e-book on MindTap allow one-click access to short clips from these television episodes.

Personal Insights Using Key Interpersonal Research

Let's Get INTRApersonal boxes include scholarly questionnaires that students can use to gain insight into their own personal experiences. These reflective self-assessments use the scales and measures associated with key interpersonal research to allow students to get unbiased behavioral data about themselves that they can then process at their own leisure or during class discussion.

Journal Topics for Qualitatively Inclined Students

InterConnect boxes share lay prompts to allow more qualitatively inclined students to reflect in writing on their communication patterns and behaviors. By responding to journal prompts, an engaged student can consider the topic of each chapter from a more personal perspective.

The Impact of Technology on Relationships

iPersonal boxes highlight the role of technology in shaping our interpersonal interactions. Each iPersonal box discusses the implications of an innovative communication technology—such as emojis, electronic calendaring, or social media use—on human interaction in an increasingly mediated social environment.

Interpersonal Ethical Dilemmas

Commendable Connections boxes discuss ethical issues that are widely known yet rarely discussed in a modern classroom context. This boxed feature provides an extended example of an interpersonal communication dilemma, asking probing questions to encourage the exploration of ethical communication.

Diversity on Campus and in Community

InterFace boxes focus on specific praxis-based behaviors that can be applied directly to interactions with diverse others, combining scholarship and practical advice to highlight some of the common challenges that an engaged student may face in an increasingly complex social world.

By adopting features with reflective opportunities and contemporary references, the course facilitator can focus class discussion and bring student perspectives directly into the classroom. Discussions in the classroom can include the interconnected topics of personal life, theory, influences, scholarship, and peer analysis/application.

THE PEDAGOGY: DISCUSSION AND REVIEW

The book also includes important features to help instructors facilitate their courses while also helping an independent reader grasp key concepts and remain engaged with the text.

Each chapter begins with anecdotes and guiding questions, allowing an instructor to tie real-world examples in diverse contexts to the lived student experience. The guiding questions help to prompt classroom discussion and preview upcoming material, while a chapter summary with discussion questions at the end of the chapter allows for either group discussion or a facilitated classroom overview of the chapter as a whole.

For students studying on their own, both marginal definitions and an end-of-book glossary provide a place for students to refer throughout the chapter. Key terms also provide a prompt for students to query their overall knowledge about the material, while a comprehensive quiz ensures that students assess their own ability to engage with the learning outcomes of each chapter.

Finally, each chapter includes extensive references that provide the opportunity for the instructor to assign a deeper read of concepts while also allowing the independent reader to explore additional literature about the discussion topic at hand.

THE TECHNOLOGY: INNOVATIVE AND ACCESSIBLE CONTENT DELIVERY

The Speech Communication MindTap for *Interconnections: Interpersonal Communication Foundations and Contexts* is a fully online, easily customizable learning experience built upon the core text. MindTap combines student learning tools—chapters, videos, activities, and assessments—into a Learning Path that guides students through the course. Instructors can personalize the experience by combining authoritative Cengage Learning content and learning tools with their own content in the Learning Path via apps that integrate into the MindTap framework.

- **Learning Path.** The MindTap experience begins with the chapter-specific Learning Path built with key student objectives. This intuitive navigator guides students to mastery of the subject matter and provides immediate access to the resources they need along the way. You can use it as is or match it to your syllabus exactly. MindTap delivers a suggested Learning Path right "out of the box," ready for you to personalize for your course. Customize your Learning Path by

  - changing due dates
  - reordering content
  - renaming course sections
  - moving or hiding chapters you don't use
  - removing unneeded activities
  - engaging students by inserting campus- or course-specific resources, like handbooks, school catalogs, and web links, your favorite videos, activities, current events materials, or any other resource you can upload to the Internet

  Students see "Counts for a grade" flags to alert them to assignments due, and personalized resources you add appear online for a seamless experience that keeps students focused while they are in your course.

- **MindTap Reader.** The MindTap Reader is more than a digital version of a textbook. It is an interactive learning resource built to create a digital reading experience based on how students assimilate information in an online environment. Videos and activities bring the book concepts to life. The robust functionality of the MindTap Reader allows learners to make notes, highlight text, and even find a definition right from the page.

- **First-Person Video activities,** unique to *Interconnections*, feature real-life communication scenarios that students can watch and analyze based on chapter concepts.

- **Flashcards and Chapter Quizzes.** After completing the reading, students can review vocabulary with the flashcards and check their comprehension with auto-graded versions of the chapter quizzes found at the end of each chapter.

- **MindApps.** Each MindTap course is enriched through a comprehensive library of learning tools called MindApps. MindApps give instructors the ability to manage and customize their course and students the tools they need to prepare for a course or exam—all from a single platform.

  - **ReadSpeaker**® is an online text-to-speech application that vocalizes, or "speech-enables," the MindTap content.

  - **YouSeeU** presents a variety of authentic assessment opportunities that allow students to respond to assignments individually or in groups using video.

  - **The Merriam-Webster MindApp** allows students to look up a word simply by highlighting it and selecting "Dictionary" on the contextual menu.

  - **The Notebook App** captures the notes and highlights that the student creates in the MindTap Reader, and it links to the popular Evernote web-based note-taking platform.

  - **The ConnectYard App** allows you to bring in "virtual speakers" to discuss important issues with students. You can even invite other classes— even outside your school—to join in a discussion.

  - **The RSS Feed App** can be used to bring current event topics into the classroom, making book content even more relevant!

  - **MindTap Analytics**, a visual dashboard fueled by powerful analytics, allows educators to track learner engagement and class progress while empowering students with information on where they stand and where they need to focus. Instructors can instantly access an in-depth analysis of students to understand how engaged they are in the course, how often they're accessing the solution, and what progress they've made within the course activities. Students can quickly see where they stand.

Acknowledgments

THE TEAM: PROFESSIONAL AND PRECISE DIRECTION

I would like to thank the team at Cengage for their enthusiasm for the project. Throughout the project, Monica Eckman and Dr. Brooke Barbier have proven invaluable friends and cheerleaders on the Cengage team. Kate Scheinman and Leslie Taggart refined the content to a smooth finished product, and Kelli Strieby ensured the book reached completion. In addition, I would like to thank the following reviewers who contributed to—and challenged—the process through which the book broke new ground and moved the conversation forward:

Donald Abel, Amarillo College
Courtney Allen, University of Florida
Angie Anderson, Anoka-Ramsey Community College
Brenda Armentrout, Central Piedmont Community College
Jacob Arndt, Kalamazoo Valley Community College
Aarti B. Arora, Bloomsburg University of Pennsylvania
Cameron Basquiat, College of Southern Nevada
Constance Berman, Berkshire Community College
Angela Blais, University of Minnesota–Duluth
Anthony Boehler, South Central College
Aaron Brown, Hibbing Community College
Kara Burnett, Sinclair Community College
Ken Bush, Norwich University
Chantele Carr, Estrella Mountain Community College
Rod Carveth, Morgan State University
Janet Colvin, Utah Valley University
Diana Cooley, Lone Star College–North Harris
Dona Coultice-Christian, The George Washington University
Anita Croasmun, North Carolina State University
Amanda Denes, University of Connecticut
Leonard "Larry" Edmonds, Arizona State University
Karen C. Engels, Waukesha County Technical College
Michael Fleming, Mt. San Jacinto College
Karyn Friesen, Lone Star College–Montgomery
David S. Fusani, Erie Community College–North Campus
Bonnie Gabel, McHenry County College
Rosemary Gallick, Northern Virginia Community College
Ann Gardner, Central Baptist College
Karen Hamburg, Camden County College
Meredith Harrigan, SUNY Geneseo
Brittany Hochstaetter, Wake Technical Community College

Ronald Hochstatter, McLennan Community College
Elizabeth Robertson Hornsby, Southeastern Louisiana University
Susan Huckstep, Averett University
Jessica Hurless, Casper College
Rae Ann Ianniello, Chabot College
Jacob Isaacs, Purdue University
Candace Lester Jones, Louisburg College
Charles J. Korn, Northern Virginia Community College Manassas Campus
Scott Ku, North Seattle College
Sandra Lakey, Pennsylvania College of Technology
Cynthia Langham, University of Detroit Mercy
Dianna Laurent, Southeastern Louisiana University
Cindy Leonard, Bluegrass Community and Technical College
Victoria Leonard, College of the Canyons
Julie Mayberry, North Carolina State University
Mingsheng Li, Massey University
Connie McKee, West Texas A&M University
Delois Medhin, Milwaukee Area Technical College
Alan Mikkelson, Whitworth University
Mark Morman, Baylor University
Amy Morrison, Angelina College
Creshema Murray, University of Houston–Downtown
Johnny Parrish, Tarrant County College
Perry Pauley, San Diego State University
Frank Perez, University of Texas at El Paso
Jennifer L. Peterson, Mount Mary University
Narissra Punyanunt-Carter, Texas Tech University
Jon Radwan, Seton Hall University
Rasha Ramzy, Georgia State University
Amber Reinhart, University of Missouri–St. Louis
Todd Rendleman, Seattle Pacific University
Sarah Riley, Bluegrass Community and Technical College
Loretta Rivers, New Orleans Baptist Theological Seminary
Richard Rogers, Northern Arizona University
Kay Rooff-Steffen, Muscatine Community College
Sudeshna Roy, Stephen F. Austin State University
Mollye Russell, Baton Rouge Community College
B. Christine Shea, California Polytechnic State University–San Luis Obispo
Pavica Sheldon, The University of Alabama in Huntsville
Kirt Shineman, Glendale Community College
Julie Simanski, Des Moines Area Community College
Gregory Smith, Stephen F. Austin State University
Christina Stansell-Weaver, Eastern Michigan University
Stephanie K. Van Stee, University of Missouri–St. Louis
Debra White, Moreno Valley College
Michael Woeste, University of Cincinnati
Jonathan Zilliox, Aiken Technical College

PERSONAL ACKNOWLEDGMENTS

Jonathan would like to first thank his family. His parents Michael and Sherri instilled a love of education from the earliest days growing up on a college campus, and he is forever grateful to these two loving, brilliant, caring individuals who sacrificed so much of their personal lives to ensure his success. He would also like to thank additional family who provided support during the writing of the book, grandparents Mema and Papa, and aunts Trudy and Martha; without the four of them his life would be much lacking in fun and ridiculousness. He has had the opportunity to witness some amazing professors in action over the years, and thanks them all, including Gwen Wittenbaum, Frank Boster, Sandi Smith, Kelly Morrison, and Steve McCornack. He appreciates the brotherhood of the NCA Posse, Drs. Hesse, Floyd, Mikkelson, Morman, Pauley, and Schrodt. Dr. Bowman would also like to take the time to thank all of his former undergraduate students and advisees over the years, each of whom taught him something about being a professor, being a mentor, and being a man of character; specifically, those former students who deserve special acknowledgment include A. Morris, A. Breaux, A. Feld, A. Pavlovic, A. Lords, B. Seguin, B. Compton, B. Carava, B. Abraham, C. Dake, C. Torrey, C. Tushaus, C. Hanneke, C. Sullivan, C. Phillips, D. Brink, D. Caminite, D. Rayburn, D. Feeney, D. Tschetter, D. Contreras, E. Pippert, E. Prickett, E. Forster, G. Wiebe, J. Williams, J. Bennett, J. Marshall, J. D. Rees, J. Day, J. Whelan, J. McSorley, J. Noerenberg III, K. Bryce, K. Lovel, M. Toyama, M. Harris, M. Baird, M. Schwanke, N. Heinz, N. Nelson, N. Baig, R. Safar, R. Sidhoo, S. Mehltretter, S. MacDonald, S. Mariucci, S. Shepherd, T. Machado, T. Gatlin, W. Newman, and W. Schmidt. Finally, Bowman's colleagues at USD have created a warm and supportive environment, particularly faculty in the Communication Studies Department (including mentors like Drs. Chung, Huston, Moran, Pace, Stern, and Williamson), the Unreasonables (Drs. Meter, del Rio, Fisher, Guerreri, and Williams), and the CAS Team (Deans Din, Kauffman, Myers, and Powell), as well as Noelle Norton who was a rock of support during difficult times. Thanks to dear campus friends like A. Phukan, B. Bond, D. Dickson, D. Keeling, E. Fritsvold, G. Lew, J. Tullis, L. Nunn, M. Lovette-Colyer, T. Eves, T. Clark, and V. Attisha. Finally, thanks to Bowman's oldest friends: A. Anderson, A. Pellegrin, B. Parineh, Dr. B. Barbier, C. Elges, C. Bradt, D. Bradt, H. Hall, J. Law Hall, J. MacDonald, J. Lauka, K. Parineh, N. Pelsma, P. Larimer, P. Bunge, R. Shelton, T. Eckerle, and W. P. Craig Filar. 1 Corinthians 15:57

Interpersonal Communication Overview

skynesher/Getty Images

Allison encounters a wide variety of people in her daily life. From responding to the shouted commands of her gym's boot camp instructor every morning to purchasing her daily steamed soy latte at the local coffee shop, Allison has interacted with a range of individuals before she even "starts" her day as a commuter student at her local college. As she texts her mother while waiting for her professor to start class, Allison's best friend Chantelle tosses her bag down in the chair next to her and complains about her weekend. Reflecting on Chantelle's story, Allison is grateful for her boyfriend, Andrew, whom she plans to see this evening after finishing up a group project in the library. She and Andrew have tickets to a comedy show and are attending with a few of Andrew's friends from work. Allison hardly has time to think about the event, though, because her Philosophy 101 professor starts class with a loud greeting, immediately filling the whiteboard with the backgrounds and dates of famous thinkers. With such a wide range of people in her everyday life, it can sometimes be difficult for Allison to keep track of all the names and relationships as her social connections grow and grow.

What are the different types of relationships that people may encounter?

How do people communicate across a range of relationships?

MindTap®

Review the chapter's learning objectives and **start** with a quick warm-up activity.

Learning Objectives

After you finish reading this chapter, you will be able to:

Identify the necessary components of interpersonal communication.

Compare different models of communication.

Explain the key principles of interpersonal communication.

Analyze the process of using channels to communicate in interpersonal relationships.

MindTap®

Read, highlight, and take notes online.

What are the different types of relationships that people may encounter? How do people communicate across a range of relationships? Every part of daily life is influenced by one's own individual experience of communication. Sending and receiving messages are basic units of social interaction, and much of the success of the human race is based on the ability to send and receive messages about objects, people, attitudes, values, and beliefs of individual beings and groups.[1] In fact, many scholars argue that society cannot be understood apart from the communicative acts of its members.[2] Indeed, without the ability to send messages to one another, people cannot work, or love, or reproduce, or survive, or thrive as a species; as the primary social process, throughout the years communication has allowed us to live in community with one another. Communication, therefore, is what makes us truly human.

Fast-forward many thousand years, and a complex and highly structured set of norms allows us to understand both how—and to whom—we send messages among ourselves. From the sophisticated communication rules that allow us to survive the turmoil of middle school, to the basic prohibition of information-sharing implied by the phrase "What happens in Vegas, stays in Vegas...," people are constantly managing their understandings of the communication patterns and content that allow for the most basic to more complex ideas to be shared with relative ease.

One student, Feng, has just moved halfway around the world to attend college for the first time. As a traditionally aged first-year student, Feng is acutely aware that he doesn't know what to expect out of the college experience. Because neither his parents nor siblings ever considered attending college, most of his cultural "experience" with college has been gleaned from television programs and novels about the college life. Picturing a stereotypical

valentinrussanov/Getty Images

combination of crazy seniors partying and high-end learning with intense peers, Feng was surprised to find that the people in his residence hall seemed just as concerned and confused about how to navigate life as he. The one exception, of course, is his residence hall's peer mentor, a sophomore barely months older than Feng himself. Somehow, this mentor was able to make the transition from "terrified newbie" to "composed veteran" in just under one year; by paying careful attention to his surroundings, Feng hopes to do the same.

INTERPERSONAL COMMUNICATION DEFINED

What is interpersonal communication? The easiest way to develop an understanding of interpersonal communication is to look at the different parts of the words: *inter-* (meaning between or among), *-personal* (meaning that people are involved), and *communication* (which gets at the sending and receiving of messages.) From this, we can probably assume that interpersonal communication has something to do with the sending and receiving of messages between two people. However, such a limited definition does not fully reflect the complexity of the ways in which we will discuss interpersonal communication in this book. If we were to accept this basic definition, we could say then that someone like Gertie is engaging in interpersonal communication with the driver when she pays her bus fare each morning, or perhaps that Clark is communicating interpersonally when he thanks the person who holds the elevator door open at the mall, yet both these interactions seem to lack depth or quality as a characteristic. Technically, yes, these could be traditionally defined as interpersonal interactions. However, communication scholars typically refer to this more basic form of sending and receiving messages between two people as **dyadic communication**, reflecting the fact that these two people (a **dyad**) are simply engaged in messaging of some sort—regardless of quality.

   Instead, from the early days of the field, scholars like G. R. Miller and Mark Steinberg would assert that there is an important distinction between this type of **impersonal communication** and the interpersonal communication that happens when we can use our understanding of the other person to predict the impact of our messages with one another.[3] In fact, most communication textbooks[4] reflect an even broader understanding that includes the importance of **uniqueness**, or treating the other person as somehow different from how you treat other people. **Interpersonal communication**, therefore, is messaging between two people who use knowledge they have derived from their unique relationship to predict the impact of those messages. For example, when Makaio orders a drink at the local coffee shop, she spends a great amount of time explaining what size and how much skim milk and sugar and which type of flavoring she wants added to her particular blend of decaf iced coffee. However,

Dyadic Communication
The sending and receiving of messages between two people.

Dyad
Two people who interact.

Impersonal Communication
Messaging between two people that is not characterized by the reliance on a unique relationship.

Uniqueness
A relational characteristic demonstrated by treating a relational partner differently than other individuals.

Interpersonal Communication
Messaging between two people who use knowledge they derived from their unique relationship to predict the impact of those messages.

Jacob Lund/Shutterstock.com

Linear Model of Communication
The noninteractive process of sending and receiving messages from one person directly to one or more other persons.

Transactional Model of Communication
The interactive process of creating meaning and shared understanding among two or more people.

Rawpixel.com/Shutterstock.com

Monkey Business Images/Shutterstock.com

when her office mate Carl offers to drop by that same coffee shop after an on-site meeting with a client to pick Makaio up a drink, Makaio simply has to ask, "Can you get me *my* coffee *my* way?" to know that she is going to end up with the perfect combination. Because Makaio and Carl have a special relationship with one another and share insight into one another's lives that isn't readily available to everyone, they engage in both *interpersonal communication* and the basic *impersonal messages* that are a part of almost every interaction between people.

MODELS OF COMMUNICATION

Not all communication looks the same, and people may send messages from a lectern in front of thousands, from a chair around the family dinner table, by tapping a thumb on a smartphone in the back of a classroom, or through a furtive whisper on a quiet dusky park bench. Regardless of the context or format of communication processes, there are a few key components that shape and structure the ways that scholars have developed an understanding of human communication, in general, and of interpersonal communication specifically. Depending on the basic form of the communication environment, one of two key communication models may be best suited for understanding how messages get from one person to another person (or persons). The older of these two models is known as a **linear model of communication** and reflects an early understanding of how one person best packages information in order to successfully deliver a message to another. The later model—a **transactional model of communication**—reflects the interaction and sharing that occurs as two people cocreate meaning with one another.

Linear Model of Communication

Scholars Shannon and Weaver first popularized the linear model of communication in the middle of the 20th century, focusing the attention of researchers on the elements of communication interaction that occur as one person sends a message directly to another person or persons.[5] As seen in Figure 1.1, the linear model of communication highlights the process through which the **sender** converts his or her own thoughts or ideas into a **message** through the process of **encoding**. When someone encodes a message, she is creating a representation of thoughts or ideas with verbal or nonverbal language to share with another person or persons. That message is then sent through one or more **channels** of communication, which is one of many means of transmission like a text message or telephone call, a news report on television or a podcast, or even a visual image from the face-to-face interaction when they spend time with another person. The person who hears or sees the message is the message **receiver**, who then tries to discover the intent of the message sender by converting the language or symbols into understanding through a process known as **decoding**.

This early linear model of communication was particularly useful when thinking about media messages like broadcasts and political propaganda, as the model highlighted the idea of taking a concept and packaging it in a way that encouraged a receiver to interpret or decode the intended message in a certain way. The linear approach to communication also encouraged people to consider the **context** in which a message was sent, whether that context

Sender
The originator (or creator) of a verbal or nonverbal message.

Message
The intentional and/or unintentional verbal and nonverbal content that is transmitted during a communication interaction.

Encoding
Creating a verbal or nonverbal message that represents the sender's idea (i.e., through language/expression/gesture).

Channel
The mechanism through which a message is transmitted, whether using sight, sound, taste, touch, or smell.

Receiver
The recipient of a verbal or nonverbal message.

Decoding
To interpret a sender's idea based on a verbal or nonverbal message.

Context
The physical or conceptual environment in which a communication message is transmitted.

A and N photography/Shutterstock.com

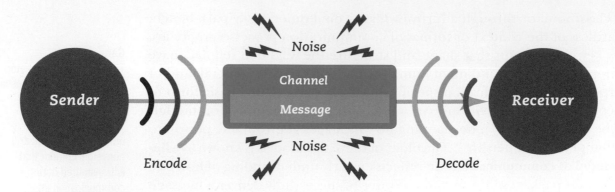

FIGURE 1.1
The Linear Model of Communication

Noise
A physical or psychological barrier to the process of perceiving a communication event.

Physical Noise
Any sound that stops someone from accurately perceiving the full extent of a verbal or nonverbal message.

Psychological Noise
Any mental state of being that stops someone from accurately perceiving the full extent of a verbal or nonverbal message.

Physiological Noise
Any physical state of being that stops someone from accurately perceiving the full extent of a verbal or nonverbal message.

Semantic Noise
Any word choices or pronunciations that stop someone from accurately perceiving the full extent of a verbal or nonverbal message.

Feedback
Verbal and nonverbal responses in reaction to a message that influence or alter future messaging pattern among or between people.

was the physical environment (i.e., outside, or in a church, in a small group of people, etc.) or the conceptual environment (i.e., in a relationship, or among sworn enemies, or during times of jubilation, etc.). Each context can influence the ability of both parties to ensure that a message is correctly perceived. Additionally, **noise** within that environment can distract or prevent people from fully perceiving the intended message, such as when **physical noise** (i.e., a gardener's leaf blower, the loud music at a concert, or a dripping faucet, etc.), **psychological noise** (i.e., biases and stereotypes or the stress of an upcoming exam, etc.), **physiological noise** (i.e., feelings of exhaustion or hunger or the pain from an injury, etc.), and **semantic noise** (i.e., hearing an accent, or trying to understand words with multiple meanings, etc.) cause someone to be unable to correctly perceive the intended content of a message. As our understanding of human messaging continued to evolve, though, scholars began to realize that a linear model did not sufficiently explain the intricacies of the interpersonal communication process. And, while a more interactive model was developed to highlight the importance of audience response,[6] the transactional model of communication began to be held as the best model of human interaction, reflecting greater complexity within the human system.

Transactional Model of Communication

The linear model of communication fairly accurately represents a one-way form of message delivery, like when someone records a video and posts it to YouTube but never goes back online. However, if you've ever followed any creative persons who regularly upload their videos in that sort of online platform, you quickly realize that most artists constantly check the comments section and attend to the **feedback** or responsive interactions of their audience. What happens when someone reads a message that criticizes or encourages his work? Often, the artist or content provider will respond accordingly. The give-and-take nature of many online communication platforms allow for quick feedback to occur, making it very similar to most

other forms of human communication. Instead of assuming that communication is only **unidirectional** and reliant upon turn-taking, it becomes helpful to move toward a more transactional model of communication like the one depicted in Figure 1.2.

This transactional perspective on human communication highlights the way that interpersonal interaction *typically* occurs, with people able to continuously send and receive messages—about a topic of discussion or more

Unidirectional
A communication pattern in which messages only flow in one direction, from a sender to a receiver, with no feedback to that original sender from his or her audience.

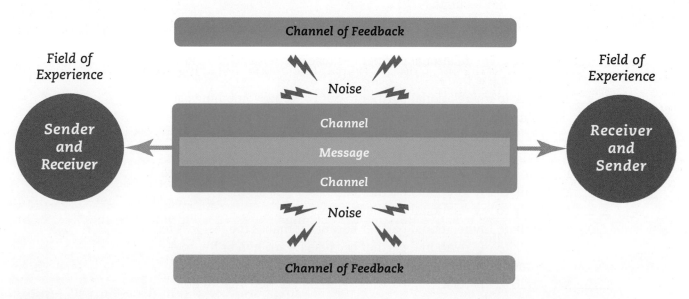

FIGURE 1.2

The Transactional Model of Communication

BOX 1.1: Let's Get INTRApersonal

Interpersonal Communication Motives Scale[7]

People interact with one another for a variety of motives, and sometimes our motivations for communicating with a relational partner can provide us with some helpful insight into ourselves. For some, interpersonal communication is about enjoying time with one another. For others, it helps you to feel like you are a part of something bigger and less alone. Why do you think that you are likely to interact within one of your significant relationships? Are there one or more things that motivate you to communicate?

Scholars have found six main motives for interpersonal communication, and you can use this self-assessment to gain insight into your own motivation(s). This is a modified and shortened version of the Interpersonal Communication Motives Scale that was created by the original researchers (Rubin, Perse, & Barbato) in 1998 to help people understand why they communicate.

INSTRUCTIONS: Think carefully about one of your close relationships. Using the 5-point scale below, please indicate your agreement with the statement about this relationship.

1	2	3	4	5
Strongly Disagree	Disagree	Neutral	Agree	Strongly Agree

_____ 1. I talk to my relational partner to have a good time.

_____ 2. I talk to my relational partner because it peps me up.

_____ 3. I talk to my relational partner because I enjoy it.

_____ 4. I talk to my relational partner to show encouragement.

_____ 5. I talk to my relational partner because I'm concerned about him or her.

_____ 6. I talk to my relational partner to let him or her know that I care about his or her feelings.

_____ 7. I talk to my relational partner because it makes me feel less lonely.

_____ 8. I talk to my relational partner because I need someone to talk to or be with.

_____ 9. I talk to my relational partner because it is reassuring to know someone is there.

_____ 10. I talk to my relational partner to put off doing something I should be doing.

_____ 11. I talk to my relational partner to get away from pressures and responsibilities.

_____ 12. I talk to my relational partner because I have nothing better to do.

_____ 13. I talk to my relational partner because it relaxes me.

_____ 14. I talk to my relational partner to unwind.

_____ 15. I talk to my relational partner because it makes me feel less tense.

_____ 16. I talk to my relational partner because I want him or her to do something for me.

_____ 17. I talk to my relational partner to tell him or her what to do.

_____ 18. I talk to my relational partner to get something I don't have.

Now, look at your answers. Separately add up your scores for items 1–3, items 4–6, items 7–9, items 10–12, items 13–15, and items 16–18. Look over your totals. If you scored highest on items 1–3, you probably tend to communicate with others for pleasure or fun. If you scored highest on items 4–6, you more likely to want to demonstrate affection for your interaction partner. If you scored highest on items 7–9, you use interpersonal communication to make you feel included in a relationship or a group. If your highest scores were items 10–12, you use conversation as a way to escape boredom. And, if you scored highest on items 13–15, you likely find that conversing with your partner is an opportunity to relax. Finally, if you scored highest on items 16–18, you likely prefer to use interaction as a method of control, hoping that conversational partner would meet your needs.

Do you agree with the scoring listed above? How would you characterize your motives? Were you surprised by the results? Remember, these are general tendencies *about this specific relationship*.

generally about the interaction—at all times. As each person receives this feedback, she is able to adapt the message to fit an intended audience. Carla is planning to ask her father if she can travel out of the country on a Spring Break service trip with her university. Knowing her father's hesitation about flying, his protective attitude toward Carla, and his relative frugality with money, Carla is sure to pay attention to the tone and tenor of the conversation. Each time her father's eyebrow begins to twitch or he sucks in a breath of air, she is quick to point out a benefit of the trip (Carla knows that these are her father's indicators of anxiety). She treads lightly around each topic until she begins to notice her father becoming more resigned to the trip, using his resignation to manipulate him even further into a formal agreement. Having been used to this sort of attempt before, however, Carla's father secretly believed from the beginning that the idea was a good one but wanted to make her "work for it." He was careful to be responsive to Carla as well, looking at her feedback cues to know how she was feeling about the interaction and whether he was taking the "game" too far.

Purestock/Getty Images

Both the linear and transactional models of communication lend insight into the process by which humans communicate in general. However, the transactional model of communication better exemplifies a process that we will call "interpersonal communication" because of the interactive nature of feedback that occurs within close relationships. The **communication climate** or relationship tone (e.g., "friendly" or "cold") that is created as a result of these interactions serves to influence future interactions among participants, shaping the ways that individuals think about, interact with, and approach one another.[8,9] A natural part of daily life, these sorts of interpersonal encounters allow us to live interconnected and interactive lives with the various individuals and communities that we encounter and experience regularly.

Communication Climate
The tone of an interpersonal relationship, often discussed using emotive terms.

FOUNDATIONAL PRINCIPLES OF INTERPERSONAL COMMUNICATION

Interpersonal communication is a process that accomplishes many unique goals within a relationship, and as such it is characterized by at least five different important principles. Much research demonstrates the important distinguishing characteristics of the interpersonal communication process, and those key characteristics include the origin of interpersonal messages and what they convey, the impact of those messages, and the changing nature of the process of interpersonal communication.

Principle 1: Interpersonal Messages Are Omnipresent

In his early work, scholar Paul Watzlawik famously claimed that people are constantly and consistently communicating a message, regardless of their intention to do so.[10] By pointing out that messages are perceived regardless of the intent of the sender, Watzlawik drew attention to the widespread and ubiquitous nature of communication messages, emphasizing the idea that people ascribe meaning to both carefully planned communication attempts as well as accidental behaviors that were not meant to send a message. Interpersonal relationships are especially complicated by intentional and unintentional messaging, as individuals may make assumptions about one another as they become aware of the subtleties of their relational partners' behaviors. Anton and Jack have been together for years and are often expected to attend the social gatherings associated with their workplaces. Whenever Jack notices that Anton gets fidgety and begins to check his phone more frequently than normal, Jack realizes that Anton is having a difficult time and is ready to go. Even though Anton does not mean to send a message about his discomfort, Jack has noticed Anton's eagerness to leave and begins to make an early—and unwanted—exit from the event. Although he's pleased that they have left, Anton doesn't understand the chilly reception he receives from Jack as they drive home, since Jack is irritated by an unintended message.

Do you think that Jack's communication during the drive home in the above example was intentional or unintentional? People are motivated to create both intentional and unintentional messages for a variety of reasons, and Box 1.1 highlights some research by Rubin, Perse, and Barbato that helps us better understand the motivations for which we engage our relational partners. Whether our communication is motivated by a desire to get to know one another better, to meet needs, or simply for the sheer pleasure of communicating with a partner, the questions in Box 1.1 help shed light on the omnipresent messages that surround us in everyday interactions.

Principle 2: Interpersonal Messages Follow Rules

Not only are people constantly sending and receiving messages regardless of their intent; they are also engaging in messaging in ways that follow very sophisticated rules in their culture. As we grow up, each of us becomes aware

Heather Shimmin/Shutterstock.com

of communication rules during our earliest developmental stages,[11] and an understanding of our own cultural proscriptions helps create an understanding of communication competence that may be quite different than those in other contexts and communities. Uriah grew up in a family with little to no money and didn't even start a formal education until after the age when he should have entered high school. His speech patterns fit right in with his rural upbringing, and as is the norm, elders in his community expect to be addressed in a formal way that he also uses in his childhood home and with friends' families. However, once Uriah begins taking courses at a community college near his cousins' house in the city, he notes that the formal way of addressing his elders is very different from the manner that his professors and career counselors expect to be treated. As his relationship with these mentors grows and develops and deepens over time, Uriah is even more surprised to see an increasing informality emerge between them, and Uriah has to relearn once again how to behave in each new setting. Each person brings to the communication context a set of norms and rules and exceptions that is based on his own experiences, and these mutually negotiated rules (rules figured out with one another) eventually become a part of the way that people act—or intentionally avoid—during a variety of interpersonal experiences.

Principle 3: Interpersonal Messages Contain Both Substance and Nuance

Not only might rules constrain communication, but there are also messages within the communication interactions that may give hints about the general communication context. Paul Watzlawik and his colleagues were among the first to point out the multiple dimensions of each communication interaction,[12] specifying that each

BOX 1.2: Commendable Connections

Ethics and Connectivity

Interpersonal relationships span the breadth of our everyday lives. Indeed, from the moment we awake each day we can engage in interpersonal communication regardless of the distance between us and our relational partners, thanks to a variety of communication technologies that increase our ability to connect with one another. In fact, there are a variety of things that we use to form these interpersonal connections: social media like Instagram and Twitter, smartphones with the ability to video chat or text message with ease, or even apps like Tinder or LinkedIn

Justin Horrocks/Getty Images

that allow us to pursue a new relationship or a new professional connection. Our increasingly mediated environment allows us to engage in multiple communication interactions at the same time.

However, sometimes we can offend or discourage a relational partner because of our seeming lack of interest in the immediate conversation. Constantly checking a phone for new messages while hanging out with a girlfriend or boyfriend may send the message that you are unengaged or disinterested. Answering the phone during a particularly intimate conversation or in a private setting may cause the other person to feel like you are bringing an unwanted other into the experience. Given the widespread nature of our technological connectivity, however, what is a person to do?

In an increasingly tech-focused culture, it can be difficult to even imagine disconnecting from technology for a moment, but there are a variety of reasons why it may be not only wise—but also ethical—to turn off or even not bring digital technology. If your conversational partner is likely to be offended by your distraction or if there is something that needs your undivided attention, it may be wise to keep the phone (or other digital technology) off. Should you interact with someone who isn't used to technology, that person may also be unable to understand the "demands" that such connections put on an individual and may interpret your behavior as an indicator of disinterest. And before posting any pictures or quotes of some other person, our modern culture now encourages asking that person for permission to display his or her identity in an electronic forum. Respecting others is essential despite our culture's increasing variety of media and communication technology outlets.

INSTRUCTIONS: Consider your recent interactions in public spaces. Did you make anyone feel like her voice didn't matter, or that you did not acknowledge her as a person? Have you ever felt like you were invisible or unseen because of the technology use of the people around you? Did you let that person know how they made you feel? Has anyone ever confronted you about a similar situation? How would you imagine each person likely feels after such an encounter?

interpersonal communication message contains both *content* information and *relational* information.

Content information is simply the verbal basics of a message. When Clara tells Brian, "Clean your room, now!" the content information is simply that there is a time-specific request to clean up a particular location within a house. However, the relational information contained in such a message gives a greater amount of context and understanding to an outside observer. For example, the manner in which the statement is said could indicate that Clara is exasperated with Brian's unwillingness to do his chores, or perhaps that she is panicked because the realtor is at the front door with prospective buyers for the home. Additionally—and even more significantly—the fact that Clara can give direct orders to Brian establishes her as occupying a higher level on the hierarchical chain, such that Clara has some position or experience that makes us believe that Clara has power over Brian to some degree. Ask yourself: What was the automatic assumption that you made in the preceding example? Are Clara and Brian mother and son? Or perhaps siblings, or spouses? Hearing the statement spoken aloud by Clara may have provided additional insight to nuance our understanding of the relational information contained in the interpersonal message beyond the basic content information contained in those four words.

BOX 1.3: Communication Currents

Nuanced Relationships in Current Television

House of Cards, Season 1 Trailer, "Lift the Veil" http://bit.ly/2n7PYkX

The Internet sensation *House of Cards* has redefined Internet viewing. In the online-only drama, a congressman (Frank Underwood) tries to manipulate both media coverage and public perception through his use of interpersonal relationships. Each episode of each season portrays Frank manipulating people around him through both overt and subtle suggestions about what may result in a desirable outcome for all parties involved. As he serves as a veritable "puppet master" in the Washington, D.C., area, Frank watches his career advance as those of his enemies crumble.

In the video clip, we see brief glimpses of many of the individuals who are being subtly played through Congressman Underwood's suggestions and manipulations. From his sexual relationship with a young reporter to his use of his wife's power in the nonprofit and art worlds, we see Frank carefully shaping the future of his—and the United States'—enmeshed destinies.

INSTRUCTIONS: Watch the video again, paying careful attention to the types of relationships depicted throughout the clip. How many different relationship contexts can you identify? How does the clip portray the subtle nuances (and not-so-subtle communication patterns) of Congressman Underwood's communication style? Do you recognize patterns or attempts to influence other characters?

Principle 4: Interpersonal Messages Permanently Impact Relationships

Another important principle is relatively simple, so don't let the short space allotted to this topic undermine the great importance placed on the content of this simple message: Interpersonal communication impacts one's relationship experience and is irreversible. Each time that an individual sends a message by making a statement or creating a nonverbal gesture of some sort, that message cannot be taken back once it is processed by a receiver. Every romantic comedy film seems to have a moment of conflict where something, once spoken, dramatically impacts the trajectory of the relationship between the two main characters. Indeed, if you have ever fallen in love or ended a close friendship or experienced a tumultuous relationship, you likely know the impact of phrases like "I don't like you anymore" or "I've found someone else" or "I know what happened, and this changes everything." A phrase or a sentiment or even a particularly poignant facial expression can change the course of an individual's relational experience.

Principle 5: Interpersonal Messages Vary Widely

Our final principle of interpersonal communication covers the varying meanings and understandings across a wide variety of messages. In addition, interpersonal messages are subject to interpretation and may change over time. Have you ever said something that was misinterpreted, only to discover that the person who heard the message assumed quite the opposite of the message that was intended? In a classic comedy, *Dumb and Dumber,* the main character wants to know his chances of getting to date the romantic lead in the

JGI/Tom Grill/Getty Images

BOX 1.4: InterFace

Interpersonal Encounters with Diverse Others

Casey was always told to look everyone directly in the eye and to give a firm handshake when meeting new people. However, he's just started a study-abroad program in Latin America and has found that the native college students at his host university jokingly call him "the creepy staring guy." He feels at a loss, because how is he supposed to meet people and make friends if he doesn't take the first step?

JGI/Jamie Grill/Getty Images

Evelyn has been meeting lots of interesting women using a dating app on her smartphone. Although she is the queen of casual online interaction, Evelyn finds herself unable to carry a conversation once she actually meets up with these women in local coffee shops. She begins to wonder whether she's destined to never be able to move beyond that dreaded "first date" stage of relationships.

On his first day of class, Cameron worked hard to try to seem funny and engaging. In fact, he consistently was able to use humor to crack the class up with laughter during the first day's interactive lecture. However, the professor of the course clearly doesn't take Cameron seriously anymore and she has interpreted Cameron's efforts to be social as a lack of respect and diligence. Cameron can't figure out how to "win back" his professor so that the next 10 weeks aren't a miserable exercise in futility.

Abdul is the "new guy" at his place of employment, and he knows that all the other young employees meet together for happy hour after work. When Abdul was in the military, it seemed natural to invite himself anywhere because there seemed to be an open invitation to camaraderie. However, no matter how hard he tries, he can't seem to feel included with the young men and women at his new job, and he feels more discouraged each day.

Although everyone has experienced miscommunication or the discomfort that comes when someone doesn't "get" him or her, the discomfort that comes from rejection may be increased when that rejection is caused by a seeming lack of understanding of a person's motives or behaviors. In each of the above examples, you may find yourself sympathizing with one of the people and disregarding the perspectives of the other. However, cultural differences cause both perspectives in each scenario to make sense or seem ludicrous depending on one's background. Before you react to your interaction partners in daily life, consider what they may understand about *your* style. You may be surprised that most behavior makes sense to the person doing it, and this impacts their defensiveness and the ways that people relate to one another.

INSTRUCTIONS: How would you respond if you were the main character in each of the above scenarios? Can you think of a possible reason for the behavior of the other people in the story? Do you find yourself identifying more strongly with any of the people more than the others?

mouse	coke	gay
court	cell	fantastic
awesome	bump	cloud

FIGURE 1.3
Common Words Whose Meanings Have Changed over Time

movie. When she claims that the chance is one in a million, Jim Carrey's lovably awkward character proclaims that at least she's "saying there's a chance!!!" Despite her intention to indicate that they wouldn't end up together, the exact opposite statement was (arguably intentionally) perceived by the receiver of the message.

Each time that we send a message, we may also rely on words or ideas that may change over time. Your grandparents may have used words like *wild* or *sick* to indicate negative concepts, while your parents may have used the exact same phrasing to highlight a particularly excellent experience or opportunity. Indeed, depending on where you live you may currently have either one of the meanings for those words in your common usage, or possibly even a third interpretation. In Figure 1.3, we highlight a list of common words that have recently "changed" meaning. Not only do existing words change, but also rules for phrases and contexts can change over time as well. People throw around words like *love* to describe their romantic partner, but then they also "love" their favorite hobby or even "love" a particularly delicious burrito.[13] Funerals used to be characterized by black apparel and somber moods, but now people are often encouraged to wear bright colors and feign happiness to celebrate the life of the dearly departed. The very message that could have inspired outrage or horror or joy or sadness only a generation ago can now cause a wide range of different emotions depending on the receiver's perspective and the context in which that interpersonal message is delivered.

INTERPERSONAL COMMUNICATION CHANNELS

There are many different channels of interpersonal communication, and the selection of each channel has great impact on the nature of the communication between two people. From the most complex channels like face-to-face interpersonal communication to the least complex like leaving a partner a note, interpersonal communication can occur across a wide variety of ways of messaging. Alicia, for example, was able to sit down and talk with her partner before deployment so that they could fully discuss the fears and issues they wanted to talk through before they lived in different cities. Octavio, however, didn't have a productive conversation with his boss about his workplace behavior because he kept misunderstanding the tone that his employer was using to send a message.

Each time that you choose how to communication with a partner, you are also choosing the default characteristics of that conversation. Each specific way that you send a message may influence that message in a variety of ways:

Channel Richness
The degree to which a communication attempt relies on a variety of channels in order to send a message.

- **Channel richness** refers to the number of channels that one can use to send a message, like sight, sound, or touch.[14,15]

- **Channel immediacy** refers to the interest and attention that the channel demands based on the specific characteristic of the channel. It is easy to throw junk mail on the kitchen counter and forget about it, but a salesperson knocking at your door more likely demands a response.[16]

- **Channel synchronicity** refers to the ability of a message to be received and responded to in real time.[17,18] When Phil texts his wife, he knows he'll hear back from her almost immediately; when he sends an old friend a postcard, however, he is expecting a response time of days, if he hears back at all.

Channel Immediacy
The degree to which the channel through which a message is conveyed can gain interest and attention.

Channel Synchronicity
The degree to which the channel through which a message is conveyed can be received and responded to in real time.

Face-to-Face Communication

Face-to-face communication is the most complex of all forms of communication, as it allows for the greatest channel richness between two people. When in close proximity to one another, communication partners can see, touch, taste, smell, and hear the verbal and nonverbal messages of their conversation partner. The combination of these multiple channels allows for each channel to confirm or deny the meaning of the message and gives the message receiver greater opportunity to make an informed decision about the intent of the message sender.

Having a conversational partner physically present also causes both parties to pay greater attention to one another than they might if the other person is not watching them. Both parties quickly understand whether or not the interaction feels immediate. Additionally, face-to-face communication is real time, and messages are sent and received instantaneously and are therefore the most synchronous of the channels of communication.

Stuart Jenner/Shutterstock.com

Video Chatting

Using digital forms of communication that rely on real-time video feeds is another type of communication that allows for greater channel richness than just the spoken or written word. FaceTime, Google Chat, Skype, video chatting, and even some forms of online webinar platforms allow you to both see and hear a message simultaneously. Although there is often a slight delay in message relay because of the minor limitations of technology, video chatting is almost as synchronous as face-to-face conversations, even if the communication medium does not offer as much richness as an in-person interaction. Video chatting's major drawback when compared to face-to-face conversation is that the viewing capacity is limited to the area that the camera can capture, so (1) not all nonverbal cues are able to be picked up by the interaction partner, and (2) interaction partners can be doing things "off screen" that limit their general immediacy. For example, when Steffanie went off to be a counselor at a remote summer camp, she asked to Skype with her best friend, an avid video game player named Morton. Morton regularly made himself available for conversation, but what Steffanie didn't realize was that Morton also had another computer screen open for gaming and was distracted by role-playing games while he was chatting with her.

Phone Conversations

Having a conversation by telephone, whether a mobile phone or a landline, has a moderate level of channel richness. Verbal and nonverbal messages can still be sent through a single auditory channel, but that channel allows for people to hear tone, loudness, pitch, and a variety of other vocal characteristics that add depth and complexity to a message. Although it does not offer the richness of our previously discussed communication options, phone

Franek Strzeszewski/Getty Images

BOX 1.5: iPersonal

Use of Communication Channel and Technology[19]

As discussed, interpersonal communication can occur across a wide variety of communication channels. The smartphones that you see in people's hands every day can allow someone to engage in a wide variety of communication interactions across multiple channels. Indeed, that smartphone can facilitate telephone conversations, video chats, emails, text messages, taking and posting photographs, or even applications that allow for a variety of other ways of sending a message that change with every new update.

Often, people make highly sophisticated choices about communication medium without seeming to consider the implications of that choice. If you are upset with a romantic partner, should you call him to talk it through, or send him a picture message of you making some interesting gestures in a photo? What about the increasingly complicated arena of social media, where it is easy to post a message for public consumption that can make or break a relationship? In an instant, a seemingly simple choice can have far-reaching implications. Consider the tweets of recent celebrities and politicians that have gotten them into trouble. Is there an easy way to avoid such exposure?

Unfortunately, in an increasingly digital age, most forms of communication can leave a digital footprint that can be accessed later in life. How might you want to engage in communication in a way that both capitalizes on the incredible advances in human communication technologies and also protects you from either the immediate or long-term pain associated with messaging that you wish you could erase?

Interestingly, governments are beginning to consider allowing people to clean up their digital footprint. Although a picture or a voicemail or a message may be forever accessible to authorities, at least some of these communication channels may not appear on search engines and websites with the request of the individual depicted. Stay tuned to legal rulings about communication technologies, but in any case, be sure to treat mediated communication as a permanent record, from the note you passed in third grade to the sexy photo you may be tempted to tweet to your current romantic interest.

INSTRUCTIONS: Consider your common channels of communication within your interpersonal relationships. Are you making wise choices about what you send? About what you post? About what statements you make about the people in your daily life? Sometimes, as relationships change, it may be easy for embarrassing information to reach a wider audience. What steps can you take to make sure that you are sending messages that are not only ethical but also present you and your future self in the best way possible? (As the saying goes, "Once online, always online!") Carefully consider what steps you might take to more critically create and send interpersonal messages through technology.

conversations are relatively synchronous (with only the incredibly small delays associated with routing, signal distance, and/or satellite relay). Because people often find it difficult to ignore a ringing (or vibrating) mobile phone or landline, telephone conversations are often initially immediate and also offer the immediacy associated with real-time conversations. However, because *none* of the behaviors accomplished by a conversational partner can

Rob Van Petten/Getty Images

Jordan Siemens/Getty Images

be seen, it is not unusual for people to talk on the phone while doing other things, a phenomenon that has been cited time and time again as a factor in the lessened focus and attention that occur during distracted phone conversations.[20,21,22,23]

Text Messaging and Email

One of the least channel-rich mediums for communication is text-based verbal communication, which is discussed in great detail in Chapter 4.

Jupiterimages/Getty Images

Although people may use rudimentary **emoticons** or **emojis** to stand in for an additional channel (see Chapter 6),[24] text-based messages are generally considered to utilize only one channel: seeing the written word. Historically, text messages have been thought of as a moderately synchronous form of verbal messaging, as people tend to respond relatively quickly to text messages as compared to email messages, which had been considered to be a much less synchronous form of communication.[25] Because one used to have to log on to a computer or a general server, email messages were often delivered in batches, and the user made the decision about how to prioritize each batch upon receipt. However, the movement of email messaging to smartphones has made many people consider text messages and emails to be relatively similar forms of communication.[26] Text messages, however, are much more likely to convey immediacy as there are often notifications immediately given to the message recipient (i.e., a banner on a home screen or a special tone or vibration) while emails often have no special alert set up on the typical smartphone.[27]

Notes, Letters, and the Written Word

Finally, handwritten or typed notes or letters that are delivered in physical form are among the least channel-rich and least synchronous forms of messaging. Sharing very similar channel-richness characteristics with the verbal messages involved in text messaging and email, notes and letters are considered relatively **asynchronous** and do not always ensure a response. In fact, some people don't even check their mailboxes weekly, much less daily, and often throw physical mail onto a countertop to sort through on a rather sporadic basis. Interestingly, though, people often report enjoying

Emoticon
A "nonverbal" symbol used in text-based channels to represent emotions or facial expressions (i.e., an emotion icon) or alter the meaning of a message (e.g., using ;) to indicate a wink).

Emoji
A small graphic image used in text-based channels to nonverbally alter the meaning of a message (e.g., using ☺ to indicate happiness).

Asynchronous
A description of messages that are not sent or received in a timely fashion and do not afford either interaction partner the opportunity to create an immediate response.

receiving personal mail and letters, and often hold on to such items with much greater sentiment than they do with similar messages sent electronically or spoken aloud.[28]

BOX 1.6: InterConnect

What Relationships Do You Now Have? Which Are Most Important?

Who are your interpersonal partners? There are many different relationship types that may be considered interpersonal. Although people are tempted to think of interpersonal communication as communication among romantic partners, in fact there is a huge variety of relational types that satisfy the key conditions to be able to engage in interpersonal communication.

> Craig and BJ met during an after-party for a major marathon in their hometown. Now, Craig and BJ get together regularly to go for long runs and talk about life. Interestingly, they find they are very similar, and often go to each other for advice not only about running but also about daily life.

> Kimpton and Sara barely knew each other when they graduated from college, yet they both accepted entry-level positions at the same consulting firm and now share an office. Because they spend so much time together during the workday, it seems only natural to them that they hang out constantly after work and on the weekends.

> Gertie and Martha experienced a flash of attraction across the room at a crowded college party, but neither thought they'd get a chance to meet because they each came with someone else. Fast-forward a couple years, and they have a friends-with-benefits relationship that they keep coming back to, time and time again.

> When Sylvana left the military, she wasn't sure that she'd ever feel as close to a group of people again. However, she has since had two children, and her niece has moved in with the family to help out; now, Sylvana cannot imagine a life without her favorite three young people.

INSTRUCTIONS: Think carefully about *your* significant relationships. What characteristics make them interpersonal? What types of communication do you engage in with each of those individuals? Do you ever find yourself concerned that you may have too many or too few interpersonal interactions with those around you? What steps might you consider to more carefully manage the significant people in your everyday life? Is this something that you think is important? Why or why not?

Chapter Summary

As the primary social process, human communication has been important in the development of our social system. Over the years, scholars have become increasingly more skilled at explaining the complex process of sending and receiving messages. We know that a variety of things influence our understanding of messaging, from the way that we package a message to the channel that we use to send that message from one person to others. Each type of interpersonal communication shares some common characteristics, however, including that we are always communicating to one another—whether we know it or not—and are using a rule-based system to do so. Indeed, those messages may look different from one another, but they often impact our personal relationships in a variety of ways.

First-Person Video   MindTap˙

Coming Home for the Holidays

Apply what you've learned in this chapter by analyzing the "Coming Home for the Holidays" video, using the accompanying questions as a guide. This video and these questions are available online with your MindTap Speech for *Interconnections: Interpersonal Communication Foundations and Contexts.*

Key Terms   MindTap˙

Asynchronous	**Emoji**	**Physical Noise**
Channel	**Emoticon**	**Physiological Noise**
Channel Immediacy	**Encoding**	**Psychological Noise**
Channel Richness	**Feedback**	**Receiver**
Channel Synchronicity	**Impersonal**	**Semantic Noise**
Communication	**Communication**	**Sender**
Climate	**Interpersonal**	**Transactional Model**
Context	**Communication**	**of Communication**
Decoding	**Linear Model of**	**Unidirectional**
Dyad	**Communication**	**Uniqueness**
Dyadic	**Message**	
Communication	**Noise**	

Use flashcards to learn key concepts and take a quiz to test your knowledge.

Discussion Questions

1. What close relationships do you have, and how does your interpersonal communication with those people look different from other forms of interaction that you might have?

2. Have you ever felt like an interaction partner wasn't fully engaging you? How did that impact your future feelings or messages with them?

3. Discuss a time when a person switched from being a casual acquaintance to a "unique" communication partner. How did your attitude toward that person change?

4. Think about your close personal relationships. What communication channels do you typically engage with each person?

5. Pick up your phone and look over the recent text messages that you have sent. What is the content of each? What is the relationship message that is implied by each type of content?

Making Connections

Consider the introduction to interpersonal communication from this chapter. How does the material in this chapter connect to the material in other courses that you have taken? In what manner do you expect to apply this material to your daily life?

Chapter Quiz

1. Which of the following elements of the communication process best describes the selection of an auditory message over a visual message?

    a. Noise   d. Encoding
    b. Channel   e. Feedback
    c. Sender   f. None of the above

2. Which of the following models of the communication process best highlights the process of verbally and nonverbally responding to a message from another person?

    a. Transactional model   d. Intrapersonal model
    b. Linear model   e. All of the above
    c. Automobile model   f. None of the above

3. Charisse is excited to get to interact with her relational partner after a long summer vacation. She plans to use the richest communication channel possible. As such, Charisse is likely to select which of the following communication channels?

    a. Email   d. Text message
    b. Phone   e. Postcard (written word)
    c. Face-to-face   f. Video chat

4. Elizabeth wants to break up with Blake but hopes to leave for her Peace Corps trip before he gets a chance to respond. She plans to use one of the most asynchronous communication channels possible. As such, Elizabeth is likely to select which of the following communication channels?

    a. Email   d. Text message
    b. Phone   e. Postcard (written word)
    c. Face-to-face   f. Video chat

5. Nico wants to make sure that his friend Wendy knows how special she is to him, so when they go out to dinner he holds the door open for her and pulls out her chair when they sit down, leading Wendy to comment that Nico treats her far better than their other friends. Because their relationship has uniqueness compared to other relationships, we can say that their relationship has an important component of which of the following forms of communication?

    a. Impersonal communication

    b. Intrapersonal communication

    c. Noninterpersonal communication

    d. Interpersonal communication

    e. All of the above

    f. None of the above

6. T/F Verbal communication is sometimes reversible.

7. T/F Content information demonstrates to observers the often-unspoken relative relationship between two people.

8. T/F The linear model of communication best demonstrates the give-and-take of interpersonal communication processes.

9. T/F Interpersonal messages are sent and received regardless of the intent of the sender.

10. T/F In order for interpersonal communication to occur, a person must be able to somewhat predict the impact of their words or behaviors on the other interaction partner.

Endnotes

1. For a discussion, see Hauser, M. D. (1996). *The Evolution of Communication*. Cambridge, MA: MIT Press.

2. For an example, see Habermas, J. (1979). *Communication and the Evolution of Society*. Boston, MA: Beacon Press.

3. Miller, G. R., & Steinberg, M. (1975). *Between People: A New Analysis of Interpersonal Communication*. Chicago, IL: Science Research Associates.

4. For a review of these discussions, see Adler, R. B., Rodman, G., & du Pre, A. (2014). *Understanding Human Communication* (12th ed.). New York, NY: Oxford University Press.

5. Shannon, C. E., & Weaver, W. (1949). *The Mathematical Theory of Communication*. Urbana: University of Illinois Press.

6. Schramm, W. (1954). *The Process and Effects of Communication*. Urbana: University of Illinois Press.

7. Rubin, R. B., Perse, E. M., & Barbato, C. A. (1988). Conceptualization and measurement of interpersonal communication. *Human Communication Research, 14*(4), 602–628.

8. Adler, R. B., Rosenfeld, L. B., & Proctor, R. F. (2013). *Interplay: The Process of Interpersonal Communication*. New York, NY: Oxford University Press.

9. For an example of climate in an office environment, see Reed, K., Goolsby, J. R., & Johnston, M. K. (2016). Extracting meaning and relevance from work: The potential connection between the listening environment and employee's organizational identification and commitment. *International Journal of Business Communication, 53*(3), 326–342. doi:10.1177/2329488414525465

10. Watzlawick, P., Beavin, J. H., & Jackson, D. D. (1967). *Pragmatics of Human Communication: A Study of Interactional Patterns, Pathologies, and Paradoxes*. New York, NY: Norton.

11. Hauser, M. D. (1996). *The Evolution of Communication*. Cambridge, MA: MIT Press.

12. Watzlawick, P., Beavin, J. H., & Jackson, D. D. (1967). *Pragmatics of Human Communication: A Study of Interactional Patterns, Pathologies, and Paradoxes*. New York, NY: Norton.

13. Obviously, the passion associated with a good burrito far surpasses such a basic term as *love...*

14. Daft, R. L., & Lengel, R. H. (1984). Information richness: A new approach to managerial behavior and organizational design. *Research in Organizational Behavior, 6,* 191–233.

15. Lind, M. R. (2001). An exploration of communication channel usage by gender. *Work Study: A Journal of Productivity Science, 50*(6–7), 234–240. doi:10.1108/00438020110403338

16. For a review of related concepts, see Walther, J. B., Van Der Heide, B., Ramirez, A., Burgoon, J. K., & Peña, J. (2015). Interpersonal and hyperpersonal dimensions of computer-mediated communication. In S. S. Sundar (Ed.), *The Handbook of the Psychology of Communication Technology* (pp. 3–22). Hoboken, NJ: Wiley-Blackwell.

17. Swaab, R. I., Galinsky, A. D., Medvec, V., & Diermeier, D. A. (2012). The communication orientation model: Explaining the diverse effects of sight, sound, and synchronicity on negotiation and group decision-making outcomes. *Personality and Social Psychology Review, 16*(1), 25–53. doi:10.1177/1088868311417186

18. For an example, see Westerman, C. K., Heuett, K. B., Reno, K. M., & Curry, R. (2014). What makes performance feedback seem just? Synchronicity, channel, and valence effects on perceptions of organizational justice in feedback delivery. *Management Communication Quarterly, 28*(2), 244–263. doi:10.1177/0893318914524060

19. Arthur, C. (2014, June 24). Google removing 'right to be forgotten' search links in Europe. *The Guardian*. Retrieved from http://www.theguardian.com/technology/2014/jun/26/google-removing-right-to-be-forgotten-links

20. Bowman, J. M., & Pace, R. (2014). Dual-tasking effects on outcomes of mobile communication technologies. *Communication Research Reports, 31*(2), 221–231.

21. Craig, R. T. (2007). Mobile media and communication: What are the important questions? *Communication Monographs, 74,* 386–388.

22. Katz, J. E. (2007). Mobile media and communication: Some important questions. *Communication Monographs, 74,* 389–394.

23. Sullivan, C., Bowman, J. M., & Pace, R. (2014, February). *Effects of Partner Distraction and Amount of Individual Information on Task and Relational Achievement.* Paper presented at the Western States Communication Association Annual Convention, Anaheim, CA.

24. For an overview, see Highfield, T., & Leaver, T. (2016). Instagrammatics and digital methods: Studying visual social media, from selfies and GIFs to memes and emoji. *Communication Research and Practice, 2*(1), 47–62. doi:10.1080/22041451.2016.1155332

25. For a general discussion, see Austin, R. (2013). An investigation of the use of synchronous text-based communication technologies by undergraduate university students. *Dissertation Abstracts International Section A, 74.*

26. For an example, see Haller, D. M., Sanci, L. A., Patton, G. C., & Sawyer, S. M. (2009). Text message communication in primary care research: A randomized controlled trial. *Family Practice, 26*(4), 325–330. doi:10.1093/fampra/cmp040

27. For a higher education example, see Brett, P. (2011). Students' experiences and engagement with SMS for learning in higher education. *Innovations in Education and Teaching International, 48*(2), 137–147. doi:10.1080/14703297.2011.564008

28. For an overview of the role of such letters, see Dindia, K., Timmerman, L., Langan, E., Sahlstein, E. M., & Quandt, J. (2004). The function of holiday greetings in maintaining relationships. *Journal of Social and Personal Relationships, 21*(5), 577–593. doi:10.1177/0265407504045888

Africa Studio/Shutterstock.com

Stephen has always thought of himself as "above average" because his high school years were marked by a lot of playing time on the field and a consistent appearance in the top 10 percent of his class. However, those accolades faded away once he arrived at college and met his new set of friends. Although most of his free time in the past was spent volunteering and building a résumé to get into college, Stephen now devotes most of the hours of his day to playing multiplayer video games and working out at the campus gym. Stephen didn't think about this change in lifestyle until the weekend he visited home and met up with his high school girlfriend, Becca. Although they seemed to have a pleasant evening sharing college stories, at the end of the night she told him that he seemed to have changed since high school—and not in a good way. At that moment, Stephen wrote off Becca's comment as coming from her envy of his new social group, but now that Stephen has received a failing midterm grade, he really wonders whether Becca might have been right. As Stephen sits in the empty lecture hall waiting for his next class to begin, he questions his identity in ways that he hasn't in years. "Who am I?" "What am I doing with my time and energy?" "What kind of person do I want to become?" Stephen has a lot to ponder.

How do we develop an understanding of our identity?

What factors influence the ways that we present ourselves to others?

MindTap®

Review the chapter's learning objectives and **start** with a quick warm-up activity.

Learning Objectives

After you finish reading this chapter, you will be able to:

Identify the elements of self-identity.

Describe schemata and how they relate to our understanding of self.

Analyze the ways that others influence perceptions of self.

Correctly identify different examples of how we manage identity.

Compare our online and in-person self-portrayals.

MindTap®

Read, highlight, and take notes online.

IDENTITY

How do we develop an understanding of our identity? What factors influence the ways that we present ourselves to others? The average college student might say that she knows herself well. Each person has a set of perceptions or ideas about who she is, and the combination of those perceptions forms a relatively stable or unchanging **identity** (or **self-concept**). By exploring the individual ideas that each person holds about herself, a person can come to a clearer understanding of her sense of self, including how each person evaluates her identity (i.e., **self-esteem**). The things that we think about ourselves often impact how we relate to—and interpret—the world around us.

Common Influencers of Identity

We have a variety of influences that help to form and shape our understanding of the self, and it is not easy to pinpoint or narrow down how much influence each single experience may have on our own personal identity. Although there are almost limitless factors that may or may not influence each person's identity, a few main factors are widely believed to have an impact on *most* people's identity. As seen in Figure 2.1, some common influencers of identity include family background, early experiences with sex and gender, race and/or ethnicity, religiosity, and group membership. In addition, other people's reactions to an identity also influence an individual's future portrayals of that identity.

Family

One of the earliest influences on our sense of self is derived from our family and early attachment experiences.[1] As we develop an understanding of ourselves as a son or a daughter, as a grandchild, as a sibling or cousin, or even as a member of a larger extended family unit, we begin to locate ourselves within

Identity
The relatively unchanging set of ideas and/or perceptions that one holds about oneself.

Self-Concept
See Identity.

Self-Esteem
The positive or negative evaluation that each individual forms about his own identity.

FIGURE 2.1
Influencers of Identity Are Limitless

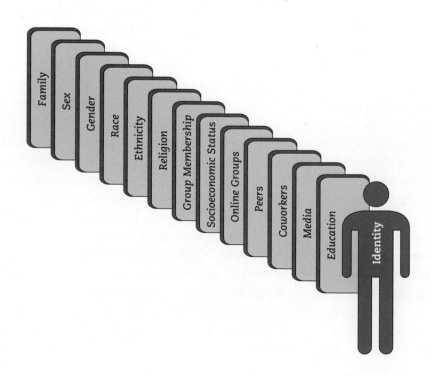

fstop123/E+/Getty Images

that group of individuals. This family background helps to construct and to reflect ideas and attitudes toward the self,[2] and we use our family experiences to explore and practice a variety of possible "identities" as we witness the reactions to the portrayals that others have within our interpersonal relationships.

Sex and Gender

Not only is family an early influence on the self, but also the family attitudes toward **biological sex**—as well as the cultural views toward this characteristic—are highlighted from the moment of birth. Entire industries thrive around the "It's a boy!" and "It's a girl!" celebration of sexual identity. Because most of us are born with a sexual designation so clearly highlighted throughout American culture, people often consider their biological sex to be a key component of their identity. Although people often confuse the terms *sex* and *gender*, **gender** is something that is culturally-learned as both men and women discover the norms that are expected of individuals behaving in a variety of manners—including **masculine**, **feminine**, or **androgynous**—as they enact social roles.[3] From the earliest interaction experiences, people learn that behaviors and attitudes about their gender displays will influence their actions, often through seemingly innocuous phrases like "boys don't cry" or "girls can't throw well." Steph and Kirk were born as fraternal twins, and Steph always outperformed Kirk in her favorite subject: their shared science classes throughout elementary and middle school. By high school, however, Kirk noticed that Steph didn't talk about her love for science anymore. When Kirk brought it up, she acted amazed that he hadn't yet learned that "girls don't talk about science, silly." As a result, Kirk wondered whether he had been taught not to follow any of his hopes and dreams. For many such men and women, much effort is spent in carefully adhering to traditional sex roles.[4] More so, individuals who believe that their gender identity is not defined by—or correctly assigned to—their biological sex (often referred to as **transsexual** or

Biological Sex
The genetic continuum established at birth that includes genital, hormonal, and chromosomal displays of maleness and femaleness.

Gender
The cultural continua learned over time that include social, preferential, and constructed displays of masculinity and femininity.

Masculinity
The culturally determined norms for what is considered the set of social roles associated with biological males.

Femininity
The culturally determined norms for the set of social roles associated with biological femaleness.

Androgyny
The norms associated with someone displaying approximately equal amounts of masculinity and femininity.

Transsexual
The experience of identifying completely with the opposite biological sex.

Transgender
The experience of not completely identifying with one's own culturally proscribed gender roles.

Gender Expression
An individual's binary gender presentation as male or female based on social behaviors and/ or external appearance.

transgender individuals) typically experience difficulties when others refuse to acknowledge an identity separate from the more normative biological definition of sex.[5] As such, one's **gender expression** is often characterized by an individual's binary gender presentation (as either male or female) based on the behaviors and/or external appearance that they choose to maintain.

Race/Ethnicity

People often form an impression of themselves based on their racial and/ or ethnic heritage, identifying with the people around them who look or

---

BOX 2.1: Commendable Connections

Ethics and Gender Identity[6,7]

Cultural norms clearly identify patterns of acceptable behavior for a variety of situations and contexts. As such, people often establish an understanding of competence or "goodness" with being able to conform to those patterns of acceptability. However, what happens when someone doesn't feel that they can be true to themselves while also following such rules? Individuals who struggle with cultural norms of gender identity often experience discrimination or social pressure to conform to traditional gender roles.

Current legal issues revolve around such concepts, as employers and educational institutions attempt to figure out how to treat people similarly regardless of gender identity. Conflict can arise around access to sex-based facilities (e.g., locker rooms or bathrooms) or to official regulations in the workplace like dress codes and other codes of conduct. For example, for someone born biologically male who identifies more with female gender roles, an employer needs to carefully consider what accommodations are necessary for that employee.

However, not all ethical issues revolve only around formal institutions. For example, you may find yourself in situations where you or someone you know is treated differently because of not fitting the norms of biological sex. Young boys are often teased for owning dolls or for "playing house," while young girls may find themselves socially ostracized because they don't fit norms of social or physical femininity. Adults often self-report that they have difficulties socially when others refuse to respect their displays of their own gendered selves.

Anatoliy Karlyuk/ShutterStock.com

Some people claim that it is difficult to know the appropriate response when dealing with someone who has a gender identity different than the one typically expected. When interacting with new people, often a good strategy is to engage conversationally before assigning any labels.

INSTRUCTIONS: Consider your assumptions about being male or female. Have you ever felt like someone didn't consider you to be "acting like a man/woman should"? What did that feel like? Have you recently caused others to feel discomfort about their own behaviors? What can you do to affirm or respect the feelings or decisions of the people around you? Why do you think you might feel the way you do?

behave similarly to them. People in a majority culture in which they have a similar heritage to the people they see in everyday life may not consider their race or ethnicity as a major component of their identity. However, for those people who have experiences as one of the only people who look or act the way they do, these markers of racial or ethnic heritage become a core part of their identity. For Susan, her biracial background seemed relatively typical in the northwestern city where she was raised; however, when she moved to a small town in the middle of the country, Susan suddenly became very aware that she was the only woman in her area with Asian features. Her identity—though relatively stable in all other ways—suddenly seemed strongly influenced by her sense of "Asian-ness," where before she hardly noticed or acknowledged race and biraciality as a part of her daily lived experience.

Religion

Many people have a complicated relationship with religion, one formed by years of instruction and observation and awareness. Regardless of one's adherence to a specific tradition, religion may influence each person's identity in both

Tuul & Bruno Morandi/Corbis Documentary/Getty Images

anticipated and surprising ways. Whether you consider yourself to be "very spiritual" or "not at all," most people derive some understanding of themselves based on three main factors associated with religion:

- We form a religious identity based on our primary religion (or the fact that we do not practice a religion at all).

- We also gain an understanding of whether we "fit" into our local culture as a whole, based on whether we practice the majority religion that we encounter within that context.

Religiosity
The degree of adherence to the teachings of a particular religious tradition.

Social Identity Theory
The idea that people often form an understanding of the self based on the group memberships in which they select or find themselves.

Looking-Glass Self
The understanding of the self that is derived from testing and observing the reactions of others who view an identity portrayal.

- And finally, we adapt our identity based upon **religiosity**, or the degree to which we practice our particular religion, if any.[8]

For example, Andrew's experience as a nonpracticing atheist who grew up in a devout Catholic family in Boston looks very different from that of Ryan, an Orthodox Jew in the predominantly kosher Brookline neighborhood on the edge of that same city. Each man forms part of his identity based on his view of how he fits in to the practices of those individuals who surround him.

Group Membership

In addition to demographic characteristics, a major set of memberships may also be related to formal groupings of people like those found in clubs, activities, Greek-letter organizations, or teams. **Social identity theories** highlight that people often form an identity based on their membership in such groups, and that people particularly define their own identity based on those people that they can identify as members of their same groupings.[9] When Malcolm joined a Greek-letter organization, he immediately began to draw a distinction between his fraternity brothers and those wearing T-shirts from other campus organizations, subconsciously forming a focused identity as *different* from those members of the other groups.

Fuse/Corbis/Getty Images

Looking-Glass Self

Scholars often highlight this back-and-forth of trying out social identities as essential to the process of forming an understanding of self. As each of us portrays a role, we look to others' responses as a way of determining whether our behaviors and identity fits the needs and goals that we consider appropriate. In his discussion of the **looking-glass self**, sociologist Charles Cooley explains that we use others' reactions as a reflection of our own identity, giving us essential feedback about the quality of our self-presentation.[10] Just as we look to a mirror to gain a greater understanding of the success of our attempt to look a certain way physically, we also scrutinize the reactions of our interaction partners to gain an understanding of the way we present our social self.

COGNITION AND SCHEMATA

Not only do people develop a complex understanding of themselves as they create and live out their identity in the presence of others, but they also continue to fine-tune that identity over the course of their life span. Indeed, each of us creates a mental model of both ourselves and the world around us. As we observe and try to create an understanding of how we relate to the people we encounter, each of us uses **cognition** or higher-level thinking to consider the relationship to our social world. As we continue to create an understanding of ourselves and of the social world around us, we use **schemata** as the mental framework to define concepts and "hold" our understanding of these concepts in order to reason quickly and interpret experiences. For example, when Francis was in her first dating relationship, she thought she was in love. Because of all the romantic comedies that she had seen and each of the conversations that she had participated in over the years, Francis had a relatively complex set of characteristics that helped her to define what love was supposed to feel like. She believed that sweaty palms, butterflies in her stomach, difficulties speaking, and a hot nervous flush were the perfect indicator of true romance. However, looking back on her relationship, Francis is now convinced that her schemata for "being in love" and "having food poisoning" may have been too conceptually similar to one another. Regardless, as she experiences more and more romantic interactions she has been able to more clearly define and locate an understanding of love and can use that moving forward.

Cognition
The process associated with thinking, learning, and applying logic to observations and experiences.

Schemata
The mental framework of experience, consisting of defining characteristics used to understand and quickly process new information.

Johari Window

As we interact with others and think about our experiences, sometimes we learn things about ourselves that we never knew before. Indeed, we all are constantly discovering new preferences, beliefs, and attitudes that we may

WAYHOME studio/Shutterstock.com

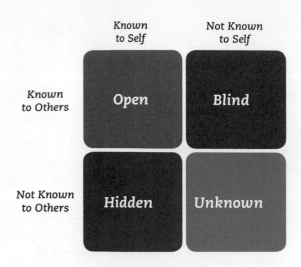

FIGURE 2.2

The Four Quadrants of the Johari Window

Johari Window
A graphic representation of the knowledge that we may access about ourselves, as well as the knowledge that others may access in evaluating us.

Open Quadrant
This quadrant of the Johari Window can be used to describe information that we know about ourselves and of which others also have awareness.

Blind Quadrant
This quadrant of the Johari Window can be used to describe information that we do not know about ourselves but of which others have awareness.

Hidden Quadrant
This quadrant of the Johari Window can be used to describe information that we know about ourselves and of which others have no awareness.

Unknown Quadrant
This quadrant of the Johari Window can be used to describe information that we do not know about ourselves and of which others have no awareness.

hold about the world around us. Psychologists Luft and Ingham found a way to describe this continual shifting of information about ourselves called the **Johari Window**, a visual representation of the knowledge that we and others possess about ourselves.[11] In Figure 2.2, we see that there are four combinations of knowledge about ourselves:

- In the first of these quadrants, the **open quadrant**, are all of those things that we understand about ourselves and that other people can know about us as well. These can be attitudes like a favorite sports team or deeply held beliefs like a religious identity that you proclaim through actions and artifacts. Idil is a staunch vegan and not only watches her own diet but also the diets of her friends and family; for her birthday, friends even bought her a shirt that said "Rabid Vegan," which she wears proudly and frequently.

- In the **blind quadrant**, there are things about ourselves that we simply do not know but that seem obvious or at least somewhat accessible to those around us. Chet, for example, has relatively low self-esteem; other people recognize his skills at drawing and think he is a good listener, and so they are aware of positive traits that he has never considered.

- In the third area known as the **hidden quadrant**, secrets or private self-information is known by the individual but not by those around the individual. Carlos finds himself attracted to men yet for some reason doesn't want to express that sexual identity; because his friends assume that he is sexually interested in women, that part of Carlos remains hidden to those around him.

- Finally, the last area is called the **unknown quadrant** because neither the person nor others know the information held in that box. Items in the unknown quadrant may never be discovered or may transition toward any of the other three quadrants over the course of the life span. Stephanie makes a variety of surprising choices based on her "gut" instincts about romantic partners, often without knowing why; because these characteristics are unknown, her friends and family are also frequently surprised by her motivations and behaviors.

The Johari Window is helpful in thinking about self-identity, particularly because it allows us to recognize and acknowledge the complexities of how information causes people to form an understanding of one another in a variety of complex ways.

Attribution

One interesting aspect of our identity involves our willingness to use cognition and schemata to interpret our own behavior and the behaviors of those

BOX 2.2: Communication Currents

The Inner Life in Current Television

Scandal, Season 4 Finale, "You Can't Take Command"
http://abc.go.com/shows/scandal/video/PL55126743/VDKA0_xdhlw7i2

One of the most-discussed television shows in recent years, *Scandal* follows a Washington, D.C., "fixer" who manages the image and identity of some of the most powerful and wealthy players in American politics. Each episode highlights Olivia Pope as she negotiates the lives of a veritable *Who's Who* list of politicians and celebrities. Unfortunately for Olivia (but fortunate for the viewing audience), her father is also the head of a super-secret spy organization operating far beyond the boundaries of law and common decency.

In this clip, we watch Olivia's father describing his feelings of imprisonment in the clandestine organization that he started. Regardless of his own complicity in creating the culture that now ensnares him, Olivia's father, Eli Pope, believes that he has no ability to effect change and leave the life of crime in which he participates. When Olivia tries to shut down his spy organization, her father monologues about his feelings of freedom from obligation.

INSTRUCTIONS: Watch the video again, noting how Eli describes being choiceless in his life and in his profession. How do people "back themselves into a corner" where they feel that they aren't responsible for their own decisions? Have you ever felt that you were trapped into making a difficult choice? How might reflection and introspection change that feeling?

around us through a process known as **attribution**, where we often create complex explanations for behaviors that we enact or observe. For example, if we see Sarah take an entire hamburger and throw it into a nearby garbage can, we might wonder why she engaged in that behavior. Perhaps she is on a diet and is trying to remove the temptation to eat a second burger, or maybe she noticed that the meat in her sandwich was uncooked and doesn't want to upset her sensitive stomach. Either way, each attribution influences our understanding and helps us to try to make sense of Sarah's unexplained behavior. We often make an **internal attribution** when we think that the person is responsible for the behaviors that she enacts, while an **external attribution** describes a belief that something in the situation has caused a person to behave in a certain manner. Interestingly, two key issues emerge as a result of the attribution-making process: the *correspondence bias* and the *actor–observer effect*.

Attribution
The process of assigning an explanation for an observed or enacted behavior.

Internal Attribution
Assigning responsibility for a specific behavior to the decision making of an actor.

External Attribution
Assigning responsibility for a specific behavior to the context in which an actor finds him- or herself.

Guas/Shutterstock.com

Correspondence Bias (the Fundamental Attribution Error)

Correspondence Bias
Assuming that the behavior of others is due to individual choice or personality rather than external or contextual factors.

Fundamental Attribution Error
See Correspondence Bias.

The **correspondence bias** (sometimes called the **fundamental attribution error**) is the natural tendency of people to assume that the behavior of others is caused by individual choices made by each person rather than taking into account the possible impact of the context or situation in which those others find themselves.[12,13] For example, when Diane sees Brad driving in the rain with his driver's side window open, she assumes that he arrogantly wanted to draw attention to himself rather than considering that he may have been the victim of a vehicle break-in that caused him to have a smashed window.

Actor–Observer Effect

Actor–Observer Effect
Assuming that negative experiences in one's own life are the result of external or contextual factors rather than caused by individual choice or personality.

On the other hand, people tend to assume that their own "bad" behavior is caused by an external force rather than being the result of their own choices—resulting in what is known as the **actor–observer effect**.[14] Instead of admitting that she caused everyone to be late to the movie by not correctly figuring out how long it would take her to get ready, Gerrie instead blamed the group's tardiness on the traffic and the stoplights that she encountered along the way, not to mention the "surprising" need to stop and get gasoline in her car.

IDENTITY MANAGEMENT

Although we may develop an identity or self-concept based on a variety of influences and factors in our everyday lives, we are also just as likely to try to manage our identity in our interactions with other people. By paying attention to the ways that we present ourselves, we may subtly influence the attitudes and interests of the people with whom we interact, as well as

BOX 2.3: InterFace
· ·
Attributions with Diverse Others

Ricky has just discovered ska music, a few decades too late. For some reason, his interest in the genre is insatiable, and his new roommate José is having difficulty adjusting to college in general and the musical tastes of his roommate specifically. The night before a midterm exam, Ricky returns from the gym and turns on his iPod to his current favorite tune, and José has had enough. He is sick and tired of making hints about his distaste for the music, and José picks up the iPod from Ricky's desk and throws it out the residence hall window.

Erica and Ken text back and forth regularly, often flirting with one another despite an explicit decision to keep their relationship casual. During the long holiday weekend, Erica sends Ken a text wishing him a safe flight and a fun time with his family. After not hearing from Ken for almost two days, Erica decides that Ken doesn't really appreciate her like he should and blocks his number on her phone. Ken may never know the truth, though, because he accidentally left his phone in the airport shuttle.

kurhan/ShutterStock.com

Jericho and Alan have been neighbors for years but rarely talk. In an effort to get rid of a particularly large crop of zucchini, Jericho puts bags of the homegrown vegetable on the front porches of every single home in his neighborhood. Alan is touched when he opens his door and sees the harvest and immediately invites Jericho to attend a local sporting event.

Although people may interact in unique ways based on a variety of backgrounds and perspectives, we often are tempted to make sense of each other's behavior using our own cultural lens. Whether we interpret communication based on our sense of morality, the ways that we were taught to respect privacy or invite interaction, or even our own assumptions about right and wrong behavior, it is easy to misinterpret what the people around us do (or notably do not do) as we relate to one another. Each time we are tempted to blame someone for a specific behavior within a specific interaction, first we must check our own cultural assumptions while also looking at the context in which people are likely to find themselves and the ways that each situation may guide their behavior.

INSTRUCTIONS: How would you respond in each of these situations? Do you find yourself willing to "cut people some slack," or are you more likely to jump to conclusions about people's behaviors? How might you make attributions that are unfair to the different kinds of people around you? Do you identify more with a particular perspective in each of the above scenarios?

allowing ourselves to receive feedback that in turn influences our own identity. As shown in Figure 2.3, our understanding of ourselves influences the ways in which we present our self-concept to those around us. In turn, their reaction may impact the way that we conceptualize our own identity, which then continues the cyclical process of identity management.

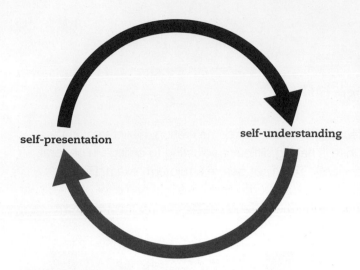

self-presentation   self-understanding

FIGURE 2.3
The Iterative Process of Identity Management

People are relatively unwilling to change their own beliefs about themselves, often in surprising ways. As a result, self-concepts are fairly stable. An individual who believes herself to be high achieving may continue to do so, despite overwhelming evidence to the contrary. As students proceed throughout their education and begin a college degree, they may sometimes find that the studying techniques that got them grades of A in high school are earning them Cs and Ds in college. Rather than changing study habits to meet the increased demands of a college workload, sometimes those students will blame classmates or study groups or even the quality of the faculty member's instruction. People's beliefs about themselves may cause them to react in unique ways as they attempt to resist information that conflicts with their current perceptions of the self.

Self-Fulfilling Prophecies

Self-Fulfilling Prophecy
A set of strongly held beliefs about one's self-concept that cause someone to interact in ways that make those beliefs come true.

Interestingly, the previously mentioned iterative process of identity management is closely related to a commonly discussed concept known as the **self-fulfilling prophecy**, in which an individual believes something about herself to such a degree that she unknowingly influences the situation until that belief becomes a reality.[15] For example, Kesha thought of herself as unattractive to the opposite sex, and as a result behaved quite awkwardly around men. Because of her awkwardness, she rarely received attention from any of the young men in her social circle *despite* having an appealing laugh and lots of friends. Although she was not unattractive, her belief that she was undesirable actually *made her seem undesirable* to the men around her, which in turn confirmed her belief. Even though Preston noticed Kesha across the room and wanted to get to know her better, his conversations with her quickly dissuaded him of such a notion.

BOX 2.4: Let's Get INTRApersonal

Self-Construal Scale[16]

W e each have our own way of viewing how we fit into our social world. As discussed in this chapter, often the culture or groups in which we find ourselves dramatically shape our self-construal, causing different perceptions of the importance of both group membership and one's own individuality. Do you know whether you tend to focus on your individual self or your social group memberships? When you work in groups, are you aiming for the success of the group as the whole or on being the best that you can be?

Scholars have found two different trends in groups and cultures around this issue, and you can use this self-assessment to gain insight into your own self-construal. This is a modified and shortened version of the Self-Construal Scale that was created by the original researcher (Theodore Singelis) in 1994 to help people understand what they think about their social relationships.

INSTRUCTIONS: Think carefully about your general feelings about the statements below, and then write the number that shows how much you agree or disagree with each one. It may seem like a couple of the questions are strange, but it will help you be able to calculate your own type of self-construal!

1	2	3	4	5
Strongly Disagree	Disagree	Undecided	Agree	Strongly Agree

_____ 1. Speaking up during a class is not a problem for me.

_____ 2. I would offer my seat in a bus to my professor.

_____ 3. I act the same way no matter who I am with.

_____ 4. Even when I strongly disagree with group members, I avoid arguing.

_____ 5. I enjoy being unique and different from others in many respects.

_____ 6. My happiness depends on the happiness of those around me.

_____ 7. I am comfortable with being singled out for praise or rewards.

_____ 8. I have respect for the authority figures with whom I interact.

_____ 9. I prefer to be direct and forthright when dealing with people I meet.

_____ 10. I often have the feeling that my relationships with others are more important than my own accomplishments.

Add up the total scores for the odd-numbered questions and the even-numbered questions separately. Is one higher than the other? A higher score on the odd-numbered questions means you are more likely to have an independent self-construal, which means that you may be more likely to think of yourself as an individual. A higher score on the even-numbered questions means that you are more likely to have an interdependent self-construal, which means that you derive much of your identity from your group memberships (for example, from your family or culture). The lowest score you can get on each section is a 5, and the highest score you can get is a 25.

What does this tell you about your own perspective on identity? Are you surprised by the results? How would you characterize your score? Remember, these are general tendencies. People vary their behavior depending on the specific situation.

SELF-MONITORING

Self-Monitoring
Paying attention to the set of auditory, visual, and social messages that one gives off in social interactions, as well as to the feedback and reactions of the intended audience.

Not only are people motivated to present themselves in a certain way, but also people are able to be self-aware of the ways in which they behave and communicate. When we engage in **self-monitoring**, we pay attention to the visual, auditory, and social messages that we send to the people around us. A high self-monitor is someone who pays close attention to the behaviors and reactions to the people around him. Phil, for example, carefully observes people's facial expressions as he tries to make a sale at the natural foods store. Whenever customers narrow their eyes or purse their lips, he realizes that they are unsure and works hard to make them more confident in him. Greg, however, is a low self-monitor who doesn't realize the extent to which his peers find him to be creepy. He fails to notice that his female friends flinch when he puts an arm around their shoulders, and as a result he doesn't modify his behavior and his classmates begin to like him less and less.

Interestingly, as people engage in this self-monitoring they may be influenced by their own perceptions of group membership(s). Someone who sees himself mostly as an individual may focus his self-monitoring on the messages that he personally sends. However, someone who thinks of herself more as a member of a group may be interested in the public messaging of her group (i.e., family, religious community, organization) and how they interact with others as a whole. Singelis found a way to determine how individuals see the self,[17] which may impact the messaging that each is motivated to monitor. As we see in Box 2.4, you likely have a tendency to see yourself either as a member of a group or as an individual. Using a modified version the Self-Construal Scale of Singelis,[18] each person is able to answer questions about how the happiness of others influences them or whether they think that relationships are more important than specific accomplishments. In so answering, by taking the self-assessment in Box 2.4 people are able to query not only beliefs about the people we meet but also our interactions with them.

SELF-PORTRAYAL AND SOCIAL MEDIA

One area in which people are very aware of the messages that they send about themselves is in the social media environment. Indeed, social media is an exercise in sending and receiving messages about the self. Although this book discusses the role and influence of social media technologies in every chapter, two key characteristics of self-presentation and social media are discussed here: (1) Social media gives users the opportunity to control the flow of information about themselves, and (2) social media often allows for immediate feedback.

Social Media and the Hyperpersonal Perspective

The use of social media may allow an individual to distort key elements of his interaction style, often in both desirable and undesirable ways. Indeed,

BOX 2.5: iPersonal

Identity, Mobile Health Apps, and Technology[19,20]

Advances in personal computing and mobile technology allow individuals to keep track of a variety of personal behaviors with relative ease. From scanning the bar code on a candy bar to find out the calories and fat content, to using GPS tracking to determine the exact length of a long-distance run, technology allows us to manage our health in ways previously unheard of.

Mobile health applications allow people to more closely monitor their physical well-being, but often these apps may link up to social media sites in a variety of expected and unexpected ways. For example, after eating a whole pizza herself, Gwen is shocked to see her calorie count has been publicly displayed to the members of her morning walking group. Craig, on the other hand, intentionally manages the settings on his phone so that everyone can see his long runs online without him having to brag about it.

Although these advances in health technology allow for individuals to manage weight, health, and a variety of beauty rituals, they may also unintentionally send a message about the user of the application that may not actually be intended.

Consider the following questions:

> Does this technology make me appear to care more about my self-presentation than I actually do?

> How might others react to my messages about my health-related behaviors?

> Does this application cause me to monitor my behaviors to an excessive degree?

> How does the use of technology for such personal matters influence my ability to retain a private life?

INSTRUCTIONS: Consider the impact of technology on the way that you present yourself to others. Does your technology usage present you as obsessed or relaxed about your health behaviors? Do you use social media in such a way that you don't present yourself as truly well-rounded? What might you do in order to maintain a healthy lifestyle yet not ostracize yourself from the friends and family who may not be quite so vigilant about their lifestyle? Carefully consider what steps you might take to improve your quality of life while also not seeming overbearing or aggressive as you message through technology.

people can try out new identities or can pretend to be something that they otherwise may not be. Interestingly, social media also gives people a venue to carefully monitor the messages that they are sending and often allows each individual to highlight positive messages about the self and limit or eliminate negative messages about the self. As such, interaction partners may develop a **hyperpersonal** perspective on the other person, as we find the information to be more socially desirable than we might otherwise experience in a face-to-face meeting or on a phone call.[21,22] Because we are only receiving limited

Hyperpersonal
The evaluation of an online interaction as more desirable than interactions with that same person through other channels, often because of the ability of both parties to limit access to undesirable information.

What Does Your Facebook Timeline Say about You? Why?[23]

Employers are increasingly using social media to learn about prospective employees and often have interns or dedicated employees who create profiles and use them to check out the profiles of applicants in an attempt to determine fit. Not thinking about getting a job anytime soon? Your online behaviors are often archived online, and some of that information may still be available to prospective employers, romantic partners, future roommates, or other people who may want to get a better idea of who you are. Even more important, the people who are already in your life may learn a lot about you based on what you post online. Consider the following scenarios about people's online selves:

> Dallas walked in on his roommate Eric (who doesn't drink) sleeping on the couch, posed him with many empty beer bottles, and took pictures; later that afternoon, Dallas posted these photos online, tagging Eric in each photo.

> Paula just had a rough breakup and is trying to get out there and meet new people. To try to catch the eye of a prospective partner, Paula posts selfies of herself wearing revealing outfits while having fun and being active. She also writes the occasional post about what she doesn't want in a relationship, and her friends notice that these posts seem sarcastic and even a little bitter.

> Brad is really conscientious about his career, and it isn't unusual for him to put in 60- to 70-hour workweeks. Because he works so much, it has become a running joke where he makes comments about "chilling and relaxing" on the job, and he often posts pictures of himself lounging at his desk or hanging out at the watercooler or taking advantage of the free coffee. His coworkers all get the humor, though, because these shots are often taken late at night after putting in a good 14 hours at work.

INSTRUCTIONS: Think carefully about each of the scenarios above. Have you seen these types of postings on other people's social media sites? If you didn't know the backstory about each of these individuals, what assumptions might you make about them? Do you think you would want to hire or date or befriend them? Why or why not? Take a minute and look over your own social media accounts. What might an outside observer think after viewing your recent usage? What assumptions would they make about your earlier posts? Maybe it's time to rethink your online persona!

information based on the desires of the person presenting herself online, we may not experience a full picture of our interaction partner, causing us to evaluate her in a more desirable way than we otherwise might.

Social Media and Immediate Feedback

Not only does social media allow us to test out ways of interacting and different points of view, but it also allows us to receive immediate feedback about the ways that we portray ourselves.[24] Because of this immediate feedback, we are able to change that portrayal relatively quickly and adapt our self-presentation until we are presenting a desired version of our self. Interestingly, our ultimate self-presentation does not always match our self-concept but, rather, is often seen as a version of ourselves that we would like to be. This **ideal self** is often a combination of social and cultural goals that we strive to fulfill.

Ideal Self
The combination of characteristics and identities that represent who an individual desires to become.

Chapter Summary

Identity is a very personal part of who we are, yet we are constantly trying to display our self-concept to the people with whom we interact. As we develop a sense of self from our group memberships and individual experiences, we also begin to see how we fit into our larger social world. Interestingly, we each create a variety of schemata to understand both ourselves and others, and these help frame how the world is viewed. From deciding what kinds of people fit together, to considering why people do a variety of everyday behaviors, we are constantly trying to make sense of the world around us. Every time we interact with someone, whether in the hyperpersonal world of social media or in face-to-face interaction in the classroom or at a coffee shop, people are constantly learning more about themselves and how they engage others in their lives.

First-Person Video   MindTap

An Awkward Blind Date

Apply what you've learned in this chapter by analyzing the "An Awkward Blind Date" video, using the accompanying questions as a guide. This video and these questions are available online with your MindTap Speech for *Interconnections: Interpersonal Communication Foundations and Contexts.*

Key Terms   MindTap

Actor–Observer Effect	**Biological Sex**	**Correspondence Bias**	Use flashcards to learn key concepts and take a quiz to test your knowledge.
Androgyny	**Blind Quadrant**	**External Attribution**	
Attribution	**Cognition**	**Femininity**	

Fundamental Attribution Error	Internal Attribution	Self-Esteem
Gender	Johari Window	Self-Fulfilling
Gender Expression	Looking-Glass Self	Prophecy
Hidden Quadrant	Masculinity	Self-Monitoring
Hyperpersonal	Open Quadrant	Social Identity Theory
Ideal Self	Religiosity	Transgender
Identity	Schemata	Transsexual
	Self-Concept	Unknown Quadrant

Discussion Questions

1. What do you consider to be the core part of your self-concept? Why do you think that this particular influence is the strongest?

2. Discuss a time when someone incorrectly assumed something about your identity. How did that make you feel? Did that assumption influence your future interactions with them?

3. What is the impact of your earliest experiences, perhaps with your family or a significant caregiver? How can you see that influence on your current experiences of self?

4. Think carefully about the ways you interact with the people around you. Would you say that you do a good job making attributions about their behavior and explaining yourself to them as well?

5. Consider your online presence. Do you portray yourself in a completely authentic way? If not, why might you be trying to send a different message? What do you wish was different about how others see you?

Making Connections

Think back to the first chapter and our definition of interpersonal communication. How does your unique self-identity influence your understanding of interpersonal relationships? What aspects of yourself are you most likely to put forward with new, unknown others?

Chapter Quiz

1. Which of the following common influences on identity is most likely to be related to the sex roles that you saw your family members play out when you were young?

    a. Gender
    b. Race
    c. Ethnicity
    d. Religion
    e. Group membership
    f. None of the above

2. Which of the following common influences on identity is most likely to be related to the culture of spirituality (or lack thereof) in your early social interactions?

    a. Gender
    b. Race
    c. Ethnicity
    d. Religion
    e. Group membership
    f. None of the above

3. Which of the following common influences on identity is most likely to be related to the color of your skin that others see when they meet you?

    a. Gender
    b. Race
    c. Ethnicity
    d. Religion
    e. Group membership
    f. None of the above

4. Godwin waved at his friend Derrick as he drove by, but his friend didn't wave back. If Godwin assumes that Derrick thinks too highly of himself, Godwin may incorrectly be making which of the following assumptions?

    a. Looking-glass self
    b. Social identity theories
    c. Hyperpersonal perspective
    d. Correspondence bias
    e. None of the above

5. Aidan and Shelby have a great relationship online, and chat at all hours of the evening. However, if Aidan is not quite as much fun in person, this could be due to which of the following?

    a. Looking-glass self
    b. Social identity theories
    c. Hyperpersonal perspective
    d. Correspondence bias
    e. None of the above

6. Richard is trying to figure out how to describe himself for a homework assignment from the first day of class, and he has found that he has mostly described himself according to his group memberships (e.g., AME Church member, brother in a specific black fraternity, and volunteer with Big Brothers). As such, we could say that Richard is relying on other people's perceptions of his group membership to define himself. This best represents which of the following?

    a. Looking-glass self
    b. Social identity theories
    c. Hyperpersonal perspective
    d. Correspondence bias
    e. None of the above

7. T/F If Sarah thinks she keeps on getting fired from jobs after a couple weeks because all of her bosses are incompetent or jealous of her, rather than focusing on her inability to get to work on time, she may be experiencing the actor–observer effect.

8. T/F If someone has high levels of both masculinity and femininity, that person can be described as androgynous.

9. T/F According to the perspective of the looking-glass self, if Jared notices that people react favorably to his "jock" persona that he tried out in college, he will likely use that feedback to continue to behave in that similar manner.

10. T/F According to perspectives on identity management, a self-fulfilling prophecy is when people pay particular attention to the visual, auditory, and social messages that we send to people around us.

Endnotes

1. For a brief overview see Bowman, J. M. (2009). Attachment theory. In S. W. Littlejohn & K. A. Foss (Eds.), *Encyclopedia of Communication Theory* (pp. 52–55). Thousand Oaks, CA: Sage.
2. Galvin, K. M., Bylund, C. L., & Brommel, B. J. *Family Communication: Cohesion and Change* (8th ed.). Boston, MA: Allyn and Bacon.
3. West, C., & Zimmerman, D. H. (1987). Doing gender. *Gender & society, 1*(2), 125–151.
4. Bem, S. L. (1974). The measurement of psychological androgyny. *Journal of Consulting and Clinical Psychology, 42*(2), 155–162. doi:10.1037/h0036215
5. For an introduction to the struggle of transgendered rights, see Currah, P. (2016). General editor's introduction. *Transgender Studies Quarterly, 3*(1–2), 1–4. doi:10.1215/23289252-3334115
6. Wetzstein, C. (2014, January 8). California transgender 'bathroom law' one step closer to ballot. *The Washington Times.* Retrieved from www.washingtontimes.com/news/2014/jan/8/california-transgender-bathroom-law-one-step-close
7. Turley, D. C. (2014, April 4). Gender-neutral bathroom campaign launches in Washington, DC. *Human Rights Campaign Blog.* Retrieved from www.hrc.org/m/gender-neutral-bathroom-campaign-launches-in-washington-dc
8. Leak, G. K., & Finken, L. L. (2011). The relationship between the constructs of religiousness and prejudice: A structural equation model analysis. *International Journal for the Psychology of Religion, 21*(1), 43–62. doi:10.1080/10508619.2011.532448
9. Tajfel, H. (2010). Social categorization, social identity and social comparison. In T. Postmes & N. R. Branscombe (Eds.), *Rediscovering Social Identity* (pp. 119–128). New York, NY: Psychology Press.
10. Cooley, C. H. (1902). *Human Nature and the Social Order.* New York, NY: Scribner.
11. Luft, J. (1970). *The Johari Window: A Graphic Model of Awareness in Relations.* Palo Alto, CA: National Press Books.
12. Gilbert, D. T., & Malone, P. S. (1995). The correspondence bias. *Psychological Bulletin, 117*(1), 21–38.
13. Ross, L. (1977). The intuitive psychologist and his shortcomings: Distortions in the attribution process.

In L. Berkowitz, *Advances in Experimental Social Psychology* (Vol. 10, pp. 173–220). New York, NY: Academic Press.
14. Sherrod, D. R., & Farber, J. (1975). The effect of previous actor/observer role experience on attribution of responsibility for failure. *Journal of Personality, 43*(2), 231–247. doi:10.1111/j.1467-6494.1975.tb00704.x
15. Merton, R. K. (1948). The self-fulfilling prophecy. *The Antioch Review, 8*(2), 193–210.
16. Singelis, T. M. (1994). The measurement of independent and interdependent self-construal. *Personality and Social Psychology Bulletin, 20*(5), 580–591.
17. Ibid.
18. Ibid.
19. Jussim, L., Harber, K. D., Crawford, J. T., Cain, T. R., & Cohen, F. (2005). Social reality makes the social mind: Self-fulfilling prophecy, stereotypes, bias, and accuracy. *Interaction Studies: Social Behaviour and Communication in Biological and Artificial Systems, 6*(1), 85–102. doi:10.1075/is.6.1.07jus
20. Vickey, T. A., Ginis, K., & Dabrowski, M. (2013). Twitter classification model: The ABC of two million fitness tweets. *Translational Behavioral Medicine, 3*(3), 304–311. doi:10.1007/s13142-013-0209-0
21. Walther, J. B. (1996). Computer-mediated communication: Impersonal, interpersonal, and hyperpersonal interaction. *Communication Research, 23*(1), 3–43.
22. For a review, see Walther, J. B., Van Der Heide, B., Ramirez, A., Burgoon, J. K., & Peña, J. (2015). Interpersonal and hyperpersonal dimensions of computer-mediated communication. In S. S. Sundar's (Ed.), *The Handbook of the Psychology of Communication Technology* (pp. 3–22). Hoboken, NJ: Wiley-Blackwell.
23. Jordán-Conde, Z., Mennecke, B., & Townsend, A. (2014). Late adolescent identity definition and intimate disclosure on Facebook. *Computers in Human Behavior, 33*, 356–366. doi:10.1016/j.chb.2013.07.015
24. Katz, E., Blumler, J. G., & Gurevitch, M. (1973). Uses and gratifications research. *Public Opinion Quarterly, 37*(4), 509–523. doi:10.1086/268109

Individual and Intercultural Motivations

Caiaimage/Tom Merton/OJO+/Getty Images

What draws people together?

How do individual and intercultural experiences shape interpersonal interactions?

MindTap®

Review the chapter's learning objectives and **start** with a quick warm-up activity.

Learning Objectives

After you finish reading this chapter, you will be able to:

Explain the goals of interpersonal communication.

Identify the three primary types of attraction.

Explain how group memberships influence attraction.

Analyze issues that emerge because of cultural differences.

Describe important characteristics that may impact communication across cultures.

MindTap®

Read, highlight, and take notes online.

Dariush first met Natalie in their university's residence halls. Although Dariush never expected to date someone quite like Natalie, something about her personality intrigued him. Even though he had always planned to become involved with someone who shared his same ethnic heritage and religious tradition, he found himself drawn to her as he interacted with her more and more. As their relationship grew and developed, they found more commonalities than differences, and after buying a house together after college, they decided to have a beachfront wedding ceremony that blended their Catholic and Zoroastrian faith traditions. Looking back on that first meeting, Dariush is surprised that he was so influenced by her Irish heritage; something that seems so minor now almost stopped him from getting to know Natalie on a deeper and more satisfying level.

INTERPERSONAL MOTIVATIONS

What draws people together? How do individual and intercultural experiences shape interpersonal interactions? In our everyday lives, we are constantly evaluating the people whom we meet and deciding whether they would make good friends, romantic partners, roommates, or coworkers. Sometimes, we like that someone simply seems to understand us. Other times, the mystery and intrigue of a different "kind" of person is what makes us want to spend more

Creativa Images/Shutterstock.com

Similarity
A resemblance to another person, or having a variety of things in common with that person.

Social Validation
An individual is likely to respond positively toward others who appear or behave similarly, because that similarity seems to affirm the choices and/or preferences of that individual.

time with them. Often, our everyday experiences as a member of a group influence who we approach or avoid as interpersonal relationships, causing us to interact with different people across a variety of cultures. Regardless of our individual and larger intercultural motivations, we choose to spend our time with certain people, and we determine that other people will not be a good "fit" with our personalities.

Forces of Attraction

Most people want to spend time with someone who seems to be able to understand them. In fact, **similarity** is a primary reason why many people may initially start friendships with each other.[1] Maybe you appreciate the fact that someone dresses like you or that she has the same kind of shoes. Maybe two people meet at church or a political rally and are happy to find that they share other life perspectives as well. It's even possible that fans of two separate sports teams are pleased to discover that they share a common dislike of yet another rival team. When you believe that you have some things in common with someone else on some general characteristic, it is easier to assume that you likely have many other shared similarities. This mental shortcut can cause us to infer that two people must have similar attitudes, values, and beliefs— even if that similarity only exists on a relatively shallow or broad level.

Some scholars have highlighted additional reasons that may explain why similarity often causes us to like someone. The **social validation** hypothesis argues that we may like people who are similar to us because they seem to affirm the choices that we have made, as well as our preferences.[2] For example, Adam is married and Connor has a serious girlfriend, but neither of their romantic partners likes action movies; Adam and Connor want to go see the newest blockbuster movie with each other (rather than their partners) because it makes them feel like they have similar good taste, and as they talk about the film they feel like they made the right

Pier Marco Tacca/Getty Images

BOX 3.1: Commendable Connections

Ethics *and* Social Validation

Kristin cares deeply about the environment, and desperately wants to do her part to leave a small ecological footprint on her surroundings. A fastidious recycler, Kristin even composts every biodegradable item that many others would easily toss into the garbage. While she is going to school, Kristin also works full time and commutes with the same people each morning on public transportation. After a few days on the same route to work, Kristin decides to start up a conversation with people on the bus to make new friends.

A few months later, Kristin is leading a discussion in class about environmental conservation, noting that public transportation is a great way to meet people who are different and to broaden her perspectives. After class, one of the students asks Kristin about the types of new friends that she has made. As Kristin describes her new friends, she realizes that they are all young, college-educated, eco-friendly men and women who are very similar to herself.

Later that evening, Kristin begins to feel like she's stuck in a rut. How did she end up with the same types of friends that she has always had? Starting tomorrow, she tells herself, she will try to expand her social group. Based on what we have learned from this chapter, though, we know that Kristin is not unique in her desire to make friends who are similar to herself. She doesn't need to spend time convincing these people about the environment's importance, because she has subconsciously sought out people who likely already agree. She can also easily discuss pop culture that interests her, because the similarity in education and age means that her peers are likely going to agree with her perspectives on these casual topics. Social validation explains that this type of shared communication is smoother, because we gravitate toward people who appear to share the same perspectives and beliefs—and even styles—as ourselves.

INSTRUCTIONS: If you were Kristin, would you feel guilty about having friends that are similar to yourself, or would you feel fortunate that you made these connections with like-minded people? Consider the role of friendships in your life. Is there a social obligation to try to develop relationships with people who are different from yourself? Have you made an extra effort to befriend someone who broadened your understanding of your social world? What advice would you give Kristin for her next week's commute?

choice in going to see the film together. Adam and Connor both reflect each other's preferences in something that may seem very simple, like taste in a movie. Imagine how much more significant it would be to have deeply held beliefs reflected!

Many people may be curious why an individual would want to be friends with someone who seems much the same as himself. After all, we often pursue friendships with people who can teach us things that we don't know, or individuals who have skills that we don't find within ourselves. Indeed, this sort of **complementarity** is another form of attraction[3] between people, where we may believe that a person's or a group's differences are positive and worth learning more about. Jerome, a deacon at his local Baptist church, really enjoys hanging out with his neighbor Moises, who is considering studying to become a rabbi

Complementarity
A difference in characteristic or interest from another person, often with one individual seen as having a strength where the other has a related weakness, or vice versa.

BOX 3.2: InterConnect
. . . .
Who Do You Want to Engage?

Do you find yourself interacting with people similar to yourself? Probably! Researchers have found that people typically tend to feel most comfortable with people who share their cultural experiences. There's even a term, **homophily**,[4] that describes our tendency to like people who have a lot in common with us. However, each of us wants to learn something new about ourselves and our world. According to scholars, self-expansion theory claims that we try to make new relationships with people who have different skills and/or characteristics that we don't possess.[5] For example,

> ❭ Glenn grew up in a rural area so he wants to spend time with Kristin to learn more about her cosmopolitan, outgoing nature.

> ❭ Brooke doesn't have a lot of experience with large families, but she admires Rosario's extended network of Mexican American cousins and enjoys spending time with them.

> ❭ Tyson wants to get to know Jennifer more because he's intrigued by her Jewish faith customs.

> ❭ Ben hasn't thought much about his own sense of heterosexual attraction, but he appreciates the feelings of community he has found within his campus's LGBTQ Pride organization.

INSTRUCTIONS: Think carefully about the people you know who are different from you. Jot down some names on a separate sheet of paper. What is *their* cultural background? Is there something about them that you would like to learn more about? What about your *own* culture? How has it made you who you are? What do you have to offer to someone different from yourself? What are the great things about your groups that you have benefited from, and in what areas might you want to experience some self-expansion of your own?

Homophily
The widespread bias that leads people to feel more comfortable around others who appear to share similar cultural experiences with themselves.

Proximity
A physical closeness to another person, whether geographically or in actual interaction.

because of the importance he places on his Jewish heritage; even though they are both strongly committed to different worldviews, each considers the other's strength of faith to be an important indicator of character and loyalty. And, by getting to know each other more completely, they each learn about a broader set of ethics, values, and traditions that they may otherwise never fully engage on their own.

Similarity or complementarity are not the only reasons that people might pursue friendships or other relationships. **Proximity** is also a strong motivator in interpersonal interactions.[6] Think about your friends from elementary school. Where did they spend most of their time? It's a safe bet that many of them lived quite close to you, or were in the same after-school programs, or even played on your childhood athletic teams. We don't always make friends with the people who are the most similar to us; sometimes, we are simply friends with someone because she is nearby. In fact, some of the people we spend the most time with are simply *available* to us. We may not have a great

BOX 3.3: iPersonal

Attraction and Technology

In the not too distant past, people had to enter each other's physical space in order to see whether they were physically attracted to one another. Whether checking someone out at a club or trying to make connections with others at the local grocery store, people used physical appearance and mannerisms to try to learn a lot about each other before attempting to interact directly with each other. In a modern, technology-rich environment, however, we can easily visit a social media website like Facebook to look at people in our extended social network, or we can rely on dating websites to meet unknown others to which we may not normally have access.

The increasing use of mobile technology has also allowed for people to use a wide variety of proximity-specific dating applications to try to meet a long-term romantic partner—or even a casual fling. Ben, a sophomore in college who is looking for short-term interactions, spends much of his free time on campus looking at the profiles of other students who use the same dating app on their smartphones. He checks out their photos, reads their brief descriptions of themselves, and tries to determine whether they should meet in person—given that the app says that they often are in the same building on campus. Although Ben has messaged quite a few of the nearby people to whom he was attracted, Ben has never actually gone so far as to meet up with one of these potential romantic encounters.

Peter, on the other hand, is looking for a "soul mate" and is using every technological advantage that he can gain. Having filled out a complete personality profile and getting matched with a wide variety of people, Peter's weeknights are regularly filled with these pseudo "blind dates" that he has met online. Far from being willing to leave love to chance, Peter is proactively seeking out a romantic fit. However, after a plethora of dates Peter feels no closer to a long-term commitment.

INSTRUCTIONS· Think carefully about the difference in approaches for both Ben and Peter. What types of attraction are each relying on? Is there similarity in their quest for romance or are the two fundamentally unique? Consider your romantic experiences and those of your friends. Is it true that there is no one true path to love?

deal in common with them, but they are convenient to spend time with and often don't require as much effort as other people. Indeed, as you navigate college you will likely find yourself more romantically attracted to those people with whom you frequently interact and less interested in people whom you rarely see; this **mere exposure effect** is seen with both friends and romantic partners over the course of our lives—and may even explain your *next* relationship![7]

Primary Components of Attraction

Saying that similarity, complementarity, and proximity are strong predictors of a burgeoning relationship is a very fair statement; however, we all realize that relationships are much more complicated than that. By 1974, McCroskey and

Mere Exposure Effect
An individual is more likely to be attracted to the people that he or she interacts with frequently, as compared to someone whom he or she rarely sees.

BOX 3.4: Let's Get INTRApersonal

Interpersonal Attractions Scale[8]

Have you ever stopped to think about why you are close to someone you care about? Often, we are attracted to people for a variety of reasons. Use this self-assessment to think about your relationship with someone you might like or your romantic partner. This survey is a modified and shortened version of a survey created by the original researchers (McCroskey & McCain) way back in 1974. It was used to look at how people evaluated others whom they did not know well.

INSTRUCTIONS: Think carefully about someone you think you might be attracted to. It may help you to write the person's name or initials at the top of the scale. Then, write the number that shows how much you agree or disagree with the statements below. At the end, you'll be able to calculate your current interpersonal attraction to this person!

1	2	3	4	5	6	7
Strongly Disagree	Moderately Disagree	Slightly Disagree	Neither Agree Nor Disagree	Slightly Agree	Moderately Agree	Strongly Agree

_____ 1. It would be easy to meet and talk with this person.

_____ 2. I find this person to be very physically attractive.

_____ 3. I have confidence in this person's ability to get a job done.

_____ 4. I think this person could be a friend of mine.

_____ 5. I'd like to have friendly chats with this person.

_____ 6. I think this person is quite good looking.

_____ 7. This person would probably be a good problem solver.

_____ 8. We will establish a personal relationship with each other.

_____ 9. This person could fit in well with my circle of friends.

_____ 10. This person looks very sexy.

Now, add up the total score. Is it high? Low? The highest score you can get is a 70, but it is very rare for people to score a perfect 70. What does this tell you about how attracted you are to this person? Did you notice that certain things seemed more important to you than others?

McCain had set out to try to determine the primary components of attraction using the Interpersonal Attractions Scale, a modified version of which can be found in Box 3.4.[8,9] Take a quick look at this modified and shortened version of their questions, keeping in mind someone you might like or a romantic partner as you take the self-assessment. How do their questions help you to consider the ways that you might find someone attractive? The full original questionnaire looks at enjoyment of interaction and physical appearance, in addition to other markers of attraction. Initially in their research using the Interpersonal Attractions Scale, they were interested in attraction within romantic relationships; these same principles of attraction likely hold true among family members, between colleagues at work, and with your friends and roommates. In Chapters 7 and 9, we are going to look at the steps of forming a relationship with one another and how to navigate the complex social processes associated with a variety of interaction partners. For now, however, let's focus on those things that drive us to seek out interactions with one another in the first place. Without these early components of attraction driving people toward one another throughout the history of humanity, our species may never have interacted enough for relationships to develop in the first place.

Social Attraction

The first of McCroskey and McCain's three primary components of attraction is **social attraction.** Not surprisingly, we are attracted to someone if we think that she would be fun to hang out with or that she would get along well with our friends. Whether she would be interested in the same activities as our friends, have interests that matched well with our social networks, or enjoy the same sense of humor, *social attraction* is based on the idea that there would be a smooth, seamless integration of that person into our peer groups that we would likely find personally satisfying. If Gabriel and his buddies enjoy playing poker, smoking cigars, and joking around after their weekly Monday evening classes, it would make sense for Gabriel to invite someone from one of his other morning classes who seems to have the same sense of humor and a similar skill level at playing cards. Marianne may think that Keith is cute, but if she thinks her two roommates will dislike his personality she may be hesitant to introduce the three of them to each other next weekend. Elfriede may simply like that she laughs a lot when she hangs out with Tiantian as they chat after their campus yoga class, and she looks forward to future interactions. Regardless of their many other motivations, each person is at least partially considering the level of social attraction that they have for the other people in their lives.

Social Attraction
The type of attraction that comes from the belief that a person would be fun to hang out with or would get along well with one's current friends.

Physical Attraction

In addition to social attraction, **physical attraction** is another motivator for interaction. If we like the way someone looks, we may want to hang out with them. Contrary to popular belief, not all *physical attraction* is based on a sexual interest in the other person. In fact, we are evaluating other people's looks constantly. When Tim—a semiprofessional bodybuilder and fitness model—goes to the gym, he may see another guy who has a similar build. Even though Tim is already socially connected outside of the gym—he has a serious girlfriend and a large social network—Tim thinks that the other guy at the gym could be a good workout buddy based solely on his physical appearance. Conversely, Stephanie works out at that same gym. When she first saw Tim, she knew she wanted to get to know him more because she found him physically fit and attractive. As she runs on the treadmill, she often watches him lift weights and imagines a romantic first date. Both of these cases demonstrate how we are always observing other people and making evaluations about whether we want future interactions with them, even before we even have spoken a single word to them.

Physical Attraction
The type of attraction that comes from a positive evaluation of the appearance of another individual, whether based on platonic or sexual interest.

boggy22/Getty Images

andresr/Getty Images

Task Attraction

Task Attraction
The type of attraction that comes from the belief that a person can assist in the completion of an otherwise difficult goal.

The last of McCroskey and McCain's three primary components of attraction is **task attraction**. This form of attraction can be the most difficult for people to wrap their minds around, as it seems very transactional or even may be characterized as shallow at first glance. However, often we are attracted to someone because he can help us to accomplish some goal that would be relatively difficult—or even impossible—without him. If Christina wants someone to run a 5K road race with her because she doesn't want to do it alone, she may work extra hard to make friends with a person who jogs regularly in her neighborhood. Erin may want to get romantically involved with a wine connoisseur because she is imagining the amazing tasting parties she can throw. And, WenTsing may want to be friends with a guy he knows at work, in part in order to get invited to the guy's annual Memorial Day weekend getaway at his cabin. Just because we have some form of task attraction to another person does not necessarily mean we are *only* forming a relationship to get something out of the interaction, however. Every friendship or romantic relationship likely involves some form of *task attraction*, but it is only one of many things influencing our desire to form a relationship with that person.

BEYOND INITIAL ATTRACTION

Chadwick and Pat met each other through mutual friends at a community event. Pat immediately noticed how strong Chadwick was as he carried lumber to help build a community garden in an inner-city neighborhood. After watching Chadwick talk with friends as they worked to build some planter boxes in their community, Pat realized that Chadwick might be just the kind of guy that Pat was looking for, and immediately struck up a conversation. Pat's physical attraction to Chadwick eventually led to a casual conversation during a break in the shade. So, what comes next? Our relationships with people don't just stop after initial attraction. After we realize that we might be attracted to people because of their physical, social, or task abilities, we may begin to pursue friendships, romantic relationships, or work partnerships based on the type of attraction that we perceive we have with these individuals. However, whether or not we stay friends or lovers or partners with these individuals depends quite a bit on whether we are getting what we need or want out of that relationship. That is, are our needs being met in a satisfying way? Do we see positive benefits for staying in these interpersonal relationships?

Hero Images Inc./Alamy Stock Photo

Scholars have tried to conceptualize the main reasons that individuals are drawn to live in community with one another. That is, what is it about being in a friendship or a romantic relationship or a part of a family that makes people satisfied? As early as 1958, Schutz[10] began to try to identify our fundamental reasons for getting into relationships, and scholars since then have been refining these lists and clarifying our needs and goals within relationships.

Interpersonal Goals

One of the most oft-used ways to conceptualize the primary motivations for getting into a relationship centers around three main goals that may influence our lives and drive our desire to connect.[11] It is believed that every relationship has *at least* one of these goals as a motivator, and each of these goals could potentially cause us to approach or avoid individuals that we come across throughout our daily interactions.

Goal 1: Self-Presentation

Omar is a new international transfer student who has started to hang out with a group of guys he met playing basketball on the outdoor courts at his community college. Last week, this group finally met up socially off campus for the first time, and Omar wanted to fit in with the guys. In an attempt to feel accepted, he made sure to put on a T-shirt for the local NBA team that all his friends seemed to talk about regularly. Once he arrived at his new friends' house, he immediately felt comfortable when he saw the posters on the walls and noticed the basketball hoop over the front door.

Omar successfully managed how he fit in by paying attention to his **self-presentation goals**, which are often thought of as both paying special attention to how other people view us and also working hard to present an image of ourselves that we want others to see.

Self-Presentation Goals
The desire to pay special attention to how other people view us and to work hard to present an image of ourselves that we want those people to see.

Bob Martin/Sports Illustrated/Getty Images

Interestingly, our self-presentation goals are not necessarily *always* associated with a desire to be well liked. For example, when Sandra began student teaching at a local middle school while she was finishing up her teaching credential, she was worried that students wouldn't take her seriously because she looked so young. Sandra put on severe clothing and toughened her speech, even going so far as to use difficult pop quizzes and harsh punishments in an attempt to make her students fear her. Although Sandra correctly realized that fear and respect were two totally different concepts, she decided to settle for whichever response her students were willing to give her, even if they didn't actually like her very much as a teacher. Her desire for a disciplined classroom environment outweighed her desire to have close relationships with her students.

Goal 2: Instrumental

Instrumental Goals
The desire to accomplish some task or get a benefit from another person.

Another type of goal that motivates people to relate—often without even realizing it—is an **instrumental goal**. Instrumental goals are often associated with a desire to accomplish some task or get some benefit from another person, and so it is easy to mistakenly assume that these types of goals are somehow manipulative. However, we are attracted to people because of what we can get *and* give in the relationship, and instrumental goals are a large part of this experience. For example, Amy and Nabeil have just begun dating. They head up to the mountains with her family for a long weekend. Amy's younger brother Bobby really seems to take a liking to Nabeil, particularly because Nabeil has promised Bobby that he will teach him to snowboard. As they spend an entire afternoon on the bunny slopes of the local snow-covered mountain, Nabeil and Bobby's friendship progresses, and Amy feels confirmed in her choice of a boyfriend. Later that evening, Amy wonders whether it is selfish to be happy that her new boyfriend has a skill that he can use to win over her family. She decides that it is probably not too selfish, as this is much more likely one of many characteristics that has drawn her to him.

In another example, Simone is an intern sound editor with a small independent film company. One of the benefits of having this internship is that

she often gets to go to local movie premieres and even meet some relatively well known Hollywood actors and actresses who travel to these events. When her classmate Kathy heard of this connection, she realized that Simone was even more interesting than she initially thought and ended up becoming her "plus-one" to many of these industry functions. As their relationship grows, Kathy and Simone discover that they have much more in common each moment that they spend together.

Goal 3: Relational

Finally, some people are simply drawn to connect with another person because of **relational goals**, which motivate us to pursue individuals because we think that the relationship we would have with them would be satisfying. For example,

Relational Goals
The desire to pursue individuals because of the belief that a relationship with them would be satisfying in some way.

- Tobias thinks that Michael would be a great person to bring on his family's summer vacation because Michael is interesting, fun, and likes to do the same sorts of things that Tobias does.

- Rhiannon asks Brandt to move in with her because she imagines a long future together filled with love and mutual respect.

- Perry simply wants to accompany Erin to her sorority formal because he knows that they laugh constantly and would likely be the life of the party if they went together.

All of these people believe that their lives would be enhanced somehow by the addition of the other person to both their social and individual experience.

GROUP MEMBERSHIP AND ATTRACTION

Goals inform and influence our interactions with others. Self-presentational, instrumental, and relational goals aren't limited only to *pairs* of people, however. These motivations for interacting with people or pursuing relationships with each other are just as relevant in larger contexts. Typically, we each want to find an entire group of people who have things in common with us, and sometimes we even enjoy the fact that we are members of these groups when others may not be. For example, Stacey has returned to college after spending time deployed overseas in the military. When classes started, Stacey noticed a tattoo on a male classmate that indicated his military affiliation. After class, Stacey chatted with him and discovered that there was an entire community on their college campus of people taking classes and hanging out who were also using the GI Bill to get a college degree. Finally, she felt like she had a group of people who understood some of the things that made her who she was. Stacey was lucky to have found an **in-group** on her campus, which is a group of people that she identifies with and shares things in common.[12]

On the other hand, Evan plays intramural water polo on his campus, and while he was able to get a group of men and women from his residence hall to form a team and get to know each other, they immediately became rivals with the team from a neighboring hall. As competition increased over the semester and tempers flared, Evan and his teammates began to see the other team as an **out-group**, or a set of people who were so different from themselves that they felt they could not relate. Although the creation of in-groups and out-groups typically makes you feel even closer to your own in-group members, it unfortunately also increases both conflict and negative

In-Group
Perceived members of an interconnected group who appear similar in specific ways that group members see as important criteria for inclusion.

Out-Group
People who are perceived as *not* members of an interconnected group because those individuals are different in ways that group members see as important criteria for exclusion.

Portland Press Herald/Getty Images

The University of Akron

evaluations of those people who are members of the out-group. Interestingly, this unfortunate side effect can happen even if there are no actual discernable differences between the members of the two groups, beyond their own group members' personal evaluations. In a famous research project, a bunch of young boys from similar neighborhoods were sent to summer camp and arbitrarily assigned to two different groups; over time, these two different groups developed their own identity (the Eagles and the Rattlers) as they created an in-group and an out-group. These two groups began to experience intergroup conflict, destroying each other's property on the camp's grounds and trying to inflict harm on one another, even though these children were otherwise much the same.[13,14]

Groupings are very important parts of our social experiences, and being part of a group may bring great personal satisfaction. Group membership is an important motivator in human relationships, and many people report that the inclusion created by the range of both communication and affection within a family or culture is often a significant contribution to their quality of life.[15] For example, think about how you characterize yourself as a type of person. You might think of your ethnic identity, or of your own family unit. Maybe your religious background (or lack thereof) strongly influences whom you identify with. It is possible that you are on a sports team or in a Greek-letter organization on your campus that holds great importance for you. Maybe you strongly identify with a particular community service organization or nonprofit, or your political leanings have become a core part of your identity. As we discussed in Chapter 2, each of these things helps us understand who we are. As such, we are often motivated to strongly affiliate with people who help us accomplish our goals within these relationships.

BOX 3.5: Communication Currents

Physical Attraction in Current Television

Pretty Little Liars, Season 4, Episode 9, "Into the Deep," http://bit.ly/2n7VJik

In the hit mystery-thriller *Pretty Little Liars,* four young women are left to pick up the pieces of a shattered relational group when one of their friends disappears. Based on a book series by Sara Shepherd, this show follows the lives and experiences of these women as they try to move on from what appears to be a mysterious and scandalous past that is barely alluded to throughout the series.

In this video clip, two characters Jake and Ezra are both giving interest and attention to one of the main characters, Aria. The difference in visual interest is apparent, and we see Aria taken aback by a view of the momentarily shirtless Jake. Clearly, her attraction is more than fleeting.

INSTRUCTIONS: Watch the video again, noting the differences in attraction expressed throughout the clip. How do different characters indicate to the audience that they find one another attractive? What is it about each character that seems appealing, given the brevity of the clip? If you are not familiar with the show, how might you describe the nature of the relationships among the characters?

COMMUNICATION CULTURES AND ATTRACTION

Relationships within large groups of people are complicated. Interpersonal communication becomes even more complicated when we think of the fact that we each start life as a member of a variety of different groups from our earliest moments—even the very second that we begin to communicate. It is from those groups that we learn who to approach and avoid, influencing our attraction to people across and within a variety of cultures. Our parents or caregivers teach us how to communicate very early in life,[16,17,18,19] and we interact based on their examples, their unique perspectives, and our own newly developing experiences. This process of **enculturation** causes us to act and relate in very specific ways:

Enculturation
The process of teaching someone how to think, behave, and interact using a system of both explicit and implicit rules and values.

- Maria was taught by her Russian parents to respect her elders and now always refers to people older than she is as "sir" or "ma'am" whenever they address her.

- Jim's mom and older siblings were shy, and so he observed them not speaking up in social situations; as such, Jim is regularly considered quiet when people first meet him even though he considers himself relatively outgoing.

These are just two examples of short-term **communication cultures**, when large groups of people come together who communicate similarly and have overlapping experiences of their world—and see themselves as distinct from others around them. Indeed, **culture** is defined by some scholars as "an accumulated pattern of values, beliefs, and behaviors shared by an identifiable group of people with a common history and verbal and nonverbal symbol system."[20]

The simple fact that every group has a unique set of communication patterns implies that each one of us necessarily has our own patterns as well. These unique individual patterns can often lead to communication **disfluencies**, or situations in which one person's understanding of a message he has sent differs in some way from the receiver's understanding of what that first person said. For example, in Eriko's culture, she was taught that deep conversations about a family member should only be conducted with that family member present. When her roommate Shondra began to talk about Shondra's twin sister's relationship with her new boyfriend, Eriko mistakenly assumed that Shondra was gossiping. In fact, Eriko assumed that Shondra disliked her own twin sister so much that they must be virtual strangers, because in Eriko's culture gossiping was reserved for disfavored people. However, Shondra cared so much for her own twin sister that she sought advice in the hope that she could help her sister get out of a destructive relationship. Eriko's pattern of communication was indeed very different than the one that Shondra was demonstrating. It may be easy for us to say that one roommate is more "correct" in the way that she communicates by sharing or withholding personal information, but this would simply demonstrate our *own* cultural communication patterns.

In addition to our background influences, we have also been influenced by the groupings of people with whom we come into contact. As such, the ways we interact with others is a direct result of our families and peers who teach us, correct us, and even form our self-images. If group membership influences our communication patterns so strongly, it may be useful to think about the ways that these large groups of people—cultures—differ.

Individualistic and Collectivistic Cultures

Growing up in Northern California, Mark was taught by his parents to work hard, achieve success, and "make it" on his own. In order to do this, Mark went to college far from home at a university in Texas, where he focused on his studies, rarely returning home to visit his family. He learned to rely on himself, and it was not surprising to anyone when he accepted a high-paying job in the midwestern

Communication Culture
A large group of people who communicate similarly and have overlapping experiences of their social world.

Culture
An accumulated pattern of values, beliefs, and behaviors shared by an identifiable group of people with a common history and verbal and nonverbal symbol system.

Disfluency
The disconnect between the intent of a message sender and the receiver's understanding of that message.

Individualism
A cultural emphasis on the solidarity or uniqueness of each individual within a system.

Collectivism
A cultural emphasis on the communal nature of groups within a social system.

region of the United States and moved out there alone in order to pursue his interests. Even though they don't spend much time with him, Mark's parents are proud of how he pursued his goals and became a "self-made" man. One of the most widely studied differences between types of cultures has to do with how individualistic or collectivistic those cultures are.[21] A culture characterized by **individualism**, like the United States or England, often emphasizes independence in individuals.

Collectivistic cultures, like Japan and India, focus much more on group membership, tending to emphasize obligations to group members and families far more than personal or individual success. Sanjay was raised by his grandmother in New Delhi and is finishing up college after taking a long break after his first year at university. He plans to accept a job at the New Delhi office of a large American firm. It took him a long time to graduate because his grandmother became ill the summer before he was supposed to begin his second year of college, and he returned home to take care of her and to manage the daily life of his younger siblings. Because of his collectivistic background, it was assumed by the entire family that Sanjay would return to his hometown for an extended time to take care of his siblings until his grandmother's health returned.

If Mark and Sanjay were to work on a project together through their corporate office, it wouldn't surprise us to learn that they have very different views of family and of their college experiences. In fact, whenever Mark describes the social aspects of his senior year of college—things like tailgates, internships, Greek Week, homecoming, or career fairs—Sanjay does not even recognize most of the references that Mark makes. In part, this is because they had very different motivations for how and when to pursue their degrees. As such, when they work collaboratively in their corporation, Mark and Sanjay simply avoid many personal discussions about their lives and focus mainly on getting the project done.

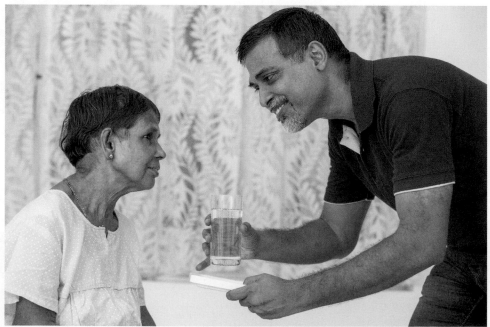

SoumenNath/Getty Images

BOX 3.6: Let's Get INTRApersonal

Culture and Self-Construal

What is your cultural background? Have you thought about how different sorts of experiences influence your attitudes toward others and yourself? Earlier in this chapter, we talked about the differences between individualism and collectivism. If you are curious whether you fit the norms for your culture, you can use this self-assessment to gain insight into your own cultural background. This survey was created by the original researcher (Singelis) in 1994.[22] It was used to look at how people saw themselves as members of a larger culture.

INSTRUCTIONS: Think carefully about the way you approach your world. Who are you? Then, write the number that shows how much you agree or disagree with the statements below. At the end, you'll be able to calculate your self-construal!

1	2	3	4	5	6	7
Strongly Disagree	Moderately Disagree	Slightly Disagree	Neither Agree Nor Disagree	Slightly Agree	Moderately Agree	Strongly Agree

_____ 1. I have respect for authority figures with whom I interact.

_____ 2. I'd rather say "No" directly than risk being misunderstood.

_____ 3. It is important for me to maintain harmony within my group.

_____ 4. Speaking up during a class is not a problem for me.

_____ 5. My happiness depends on the happiness of those around me.

_____ 6. Having a lively imagination is important to me.

_____ 7. I would offer my seat in a bus to my professor.

_____ 8. I am comfortable with being singled out for praise or rewards.

_____ 9. I respect people who are modest about themselves.

_____ 10. I am the same person at home that I am at school.

_____ 11. I will sacrifice my self-interest for the benefit of the group I am in.

_____ 12. Being able to take care of myself is a primary concern for me.

_____ 13. I often have the feeling that my relationships with others are more important than my own accomplishments.

_____ 14. I act the same way no matter who I am with.

_____ 15. I should take into consideration my parents' advice when making education/career plans.

_____ 16. I feel comfortable using someone's first name soon after I meet them, even when they are much older than I am.

_____ 17. It is important to me to respect decisions made by the group.

_____ 18. I prefer to be direct and forthright when dealing with people I've just met.

_____ 19. I will stay in a group if they need me, even when I'm not happy with the group.

_____ 20. I enjoy being unique and different from others in many respects.

_____ 21. If my brother or sister fails, I feel responsible.

_____ 22. My personal identity independent of others is very important to me.

_____ 23. Even when I strongly disagree with group members, I avoid an argument.

_____ 24. I value being in good health above everything.

(continued)

Now, add up the odd-numbered items separately, and then the even-numbered items. Which is higher? If you scored higher on the odd-numbered items, you are more collectivistic. However, if you scored higher on the even numbers, it is likely that you were raised in a more individualistic environment. Although scholars say that you may behave differently depending on the context, this survey allows you to see your general propensity toward independence versus interdependence.

It is easy for us to look at this one example and claim that Mark and Sanjay are simply "different." However, Mark and Sanjay don't just differ on one simple set of characteristics. In fact, many types of relational differences stem from how people personally experience their culture. Here we spend some time highlighting other differences that can occur when people categorize themselves into different cultures from one another.

Power-Distance in Culture

Power
The ability of a group or individual to direct the events or behaviors within a defined system.

The use of **power** is an important concept, as it influences how we act toward each other in a variety of ways. Although we are going to eventually talk about power within individual relationships more specifically in Chapter 7, it is important to note that cultures and societies differ in the way that they conceptualize power and where that power comes from. Some cultures seem to focus on power being something that you can eventually attain, almost like an object that seems just out of reach. Other cultures, however, think of power as something you are born with, like your hair color or a severe peanut allergy. The cultural view of a person's *origin* of power is one of the most fundamental differences in how people think of power.

Markus grew up in a wealthy suburb of Seattle. As the son of an executive member of a major U.S. corporation, he constantly heard his dad telling

Yadid Levy/robertharding/Alamy Stock Photo

stories of how he immigrated to the United States with little more than the clothes on his back. His entire life, Markus has been taught that he needs to work hard and develop himself as a person and especially that he needs to take advantage of opportunities that come his way. A little bit of sacrifice now may help him become a very successful, powerful person. While studying abroad in Brazil, however, Markus found out that his perspective on power was rather unique. His local roommate, Marcelo, was also from a similarly wealthy neighborhood, growing up in São Paulo, Brazil. Marcelo's parents encouraged him to take advantage of his background and to embrace opportunities, because they thought that he deserved to have power more than others. Marcelo was taught that social class was very important and that he was expected to "live up to" the standard of living that he was born into.

Although Markus and Marcelo have very similar socioeconomic backgrounds, they were both products of the power-distance that is reflected in their culture.[23] Markus grew up in an area influenced by the United States and Canada, two of the many countries with **low power-distance.** This means that Markus was most likely taught that all people are equal and deserve to have the same opportunities as each other. Admittedly, while some people grow up with more social or economic resources than other people—which inherently changes their personal experience—low power-distance cultures often claim that all people should be treated similarly and respected as individuals. Marcelo, on the other hand, grew up in a culture with **high power-distance**, much like many other countries in the equatorial regions of the world. High power-distance cultures often think that people are born with certain fundamental differences, and these differences influence how people are going to be able to attain different standards of living or positions of authority. A vestige of this high power-distance tradition is India's historical caste system in which certain people's family backgrounds cause them to be more or less likely to be able to pursue future careers and social standings.[24] Whether such cultural differences are implicit (thought about and experienced but rarely discussed) or explicit (part of a commonly held set of views that people may state verbally), high power-distance cultures tend to believe that a small concentrated group of people (e.g., royalty, politicians, high-ranking officials) naturally are endowed with more power than the average person. This clearly influences a wide range of communication behaviors within interpersonal relationships, including how parents and children interact,[25] who people are allowed to marry,[26] and how individuals relate to others in both school and the workplace.[27]

Low Power-Distance
A cultural belief that all people are equal and deserve to have the same opportunities as each other.

High Power-Distance
A cultural belief that people are born with fundamental differences that influence each person's access to opportunities.

Verbal Context and Culture

One final major difference between cultures has to do with how much they communicate with one another in a direct, verbal way. Have you ever been in a situation where you might have seen a couple "fight" about something without even saying a word? Leslie and Alex have been together

SIA KAMBOU/AFP/Getty Images

Iakov Filimonov/Shutterstock.com

High-Context Culture
A cultural manner of expression that encourages indirect expressions of emotion, opinion, and conflict through nonverbal means when interacting with a person of higher status.

Low-Context Culture
A cultural manner of expression that encourages direct expression of emotions and the open sharing of opinion regardless of status.

Ethnocentrism
A bias in favor of your own group or culture.

so long that they can express disagreement, have conflict, and even apologize to one another with only a glare, a raise of the eyebrows, or a nod of the head. If their friends or family members are around, these close relations can sometimes pick up on the fact that they are expressing disagreement, but to someone who doesn't know them well, it is barely perceivable.

Although this implicit interaction is common within specific close relationships, sometimes entire cultures may encourage communication in this indirect way.[28] **High-context cultures**, like those found in much of Asia and in tribal cultures around the world, are often accustomed to limiting the expression of disagreement, opinions, and different ideas to such indirect forms of verbal or nonverbal language. People often express these feelings off the record, and it is easy to appear noncombative in these situations. **Low-context cultures**, like those found throughout North America and northern Europe, encourage direct expression and sharing opinions. If conflict occurs in a low-context culture, it is much more acceptable for that conflict to occur openly and without fear of social sanctions or even repercussions from those people with higher power.

INTERCULTURAL COMPETENCE

One of the most destructive things that can negatively impact our willingness to engage other people as equals is **ethnocentrism**, which is seen as a bias in favor of your own group and your own culture; it is often described as being excessively focused on your own groupings.[29] People who are highly ethnocentric are often so focused on their own culture that they don't realize that there are multiple ways to accomplish the same goal.

Agustín was taught in his native Argentina that it is appropriate to greet male and female friends with a kiss on the cheek. After hanging out with a group of friends who are all originally from Mexico and the United States, he notices that they seem turned off by his familiar behaviors and may even think that he is a flirt or is "trying too hard" in the social situation; Agustín, on the other hand, thinks that his culture has figured out greetings in the most appropriate way and refuses to adapt. This kind of ethnocentric bias often causes people to think that their culture is the best or has the most correct way of approaching a problem. Even if they are offered an alternative perspective, they typically won't look beyond their own experiences to see different ways of doing things. In fact, the typical reaction from an ethnocentric individual is to assume that people from other cultures are incompetent and that they need to work on their communication patterns to become more able to navigate their world.

Fuse/Corbis/Getty Images

BOX 3.7: InterFace
. . . .

Intercultural Engagement with Diverse Others[30]

Have you ever looked down on someone because she didn't think like you do? If you are honest with yourself, you have to admit that this has happened once or twice. Many scholars think that we easily fall into a type of thinking that is characterized as "mine-is-better." One of the best ways to avoid this sort of bias is to simply be aware that you are beginning to start this pattern. Ruggiero (2004) offers two ways to notice that you are moving in this uncomfortable direction:

> **Feelings of "mine-is-better":** Sometimes, we feel happy when people do things the way that we do, and we experience a warm-and-fuzzy sensation that is pleasant or favorable. If someone thinks or acts differently than we do, we may feel disgust or anger or even want to attack their thinking immediately.

> **Thoughts of "mine-is-better":** Other times, we have an internal dialogue when faced with people who think like we do. If you ever find yourself congratulating your intelligence because a person or culture came to the same conclusion you did, you might need to be more critical of yourself. Also, immediately disregarding the thoughts/ideas of people who disagree with you can be a symptom of "mine-is-better."

Chapter Summary

Although the variety of influences on our interpersonal interactions may make factors influencing attraction seem random, there are actually very specific causes and impacts of attraction in our daily lives. A primary influence is the unique combination of similarity and complementarity, and it is easy to forget the complexity of these seemingly simple relational factors. In part, individuals are relying on these variables as they are constantly working to present themselves in a manner they believe is desirable, while they intentionally present themselves as more or less attractive depending on the context they are in and the goals they are trying to achieve. Additional details of attraction may prove very subtle and incredibly nuanced, such that what one person may find attractive is possibly unattractive or even repulsive to another. Regardless, attempts to understand our own attraction-related behaviors may give us insight into the ways we interact with the world around us.

Attraction is not only a dyadic experience. Indeed, we experience elements of attraction because of our cultural memberships or group interactions. As we gain a better understanding of the things that group members think are important through enculturation, we become even more skilled at managing our group and individual identities. This becomes particularly important with regard to our presentation of the self as independent or as a person with power or authority, as these characteristics are differentially favored from culture to culture. As we attempt to successfully interact in a diverse culture, we have to manage our natural tendencies to focus on ourselves and our memberships; perspective-taking and self-presentation exercises may help us achieve this most basic of goals.

MindTap°   First-Person Video

Chatty Tourists Abroad

Apply what you've learned in this chapter by analyzing the "Chatty Tourists Abroad" video, using the accompanying questions as a guide. This video and these questions are available online with your MindTap Speech for *Interconnections: Interpersonal Communication Foundations and Contexts.*

MindTap°   Key Terms

Use flashcards to learn key concepts and take a quiz to test your knowledge.

Collectivism	**Disfluency**	**Homophily**
Communication	**Enculturation**	**In-Group**
Culture	**Ethnocentrism**	**Individualism**
Complementarity	**High-Context Culture**	**Instrumental Goals**
Culture	**High Power-Distance**	**Low-Context Culture**

Low Power-Distance	Power	Similarity
Mere Exposure Effect	Proximity	Social Attraction
Out-Group	Relational Goals	Social Validation
Physical Attraction	Self-Presentation Goals	Task Attraction

Discussion Questions

1. Think about your first "crush" as a young person. What was it about that person that was most attractive? How have your standards for attraction changed or developed since that first romantic interest?

2. What type of culture exists on your campus? Are most people low or high context? Individualistic or collectivistic? Would you say that you personally fit into that campus cultural mold?

3. Think about your social media use. How do you present yourself in that mediated context? What things about yourself are you certain to include, and what characteristics are you most interested in *not* publicly displaying? Why?

4. Discuss a time when you have been a member of an out-group. What did that feel like? Compare that experience with a time that you were a member of the clear majority. How often do each of these experiences occur in your daily life?

5. Consider your current friendships. What do you get from each of those people? Were you strategic in choosing them as your close friends? If so, how?

Making Connections

In Chapter 2, we discussed our unique identity. As we broaden our discussion to the larger culture, how do you think your larger social groupings influence your motivation to engage others? Are you more a product of your self-identity or your culture? Is it possible to even disentangle the two?

Chapter Quiz

1. Which of the following goals of interpersonal relationships is focused on the ability of that relational partner to accomplish something that would be difficult alone?

    a. Instrumental   d. None of the above

    b. Relational   e. All of the above

    c. Self-presentation

2. Which of the following goals of interpersonal relationships is focused on the ability of that relationship to influence how other people view the partner or partners?

    a. Instrumental
    b. Relational
    c. Self-presentation
    d. None of the above
    e. All of the above

3. Which of the following types of attraction is mostly motivated by the idea that the other person would fit in with your group of friends?

    a. Physical
    b. Social
    c. Task
    d. None of the above
    e. All of the above

4. Which of the following intercultural communication terms deals with the belief that people innately deserve to be treated equally, regardless of social position?

    a. High context
    b. High power-distance
    c. Low power-distance
    d. Low context
    e. None of the above
    f. All of the above

5. Cheyenne is attracted to her next-door neighbor, in part because of all the interesting activities he does that Cheyenne herself would never have dreamed of doing. What is likely a factor in Cheyenne's attraction?

    a. Proximity
    b. Similarity
    c. Complementarity
    d. Both complementarity and proximity
    e. None of the above

6. T/F If you have a bias in which you favor your own culture over the experiences of other types of people, you can be described as ethnocentric.

7. T/F Individuals who belong to your close-knit group can be described as out-group members.

8. T/F Social validation may cause people to tend toward relationships with people who have beliefs similar to their own.

9. T/F Brenda told Manami to do the dishes while she was at the gym, but Manami misunderstood that it was a command and not a request if she happened to have time. When Brenda came home, the dirty dishes were still in the sink. This is an example of a communication disfluency.

10. T/F Bahram cares deeply about his family and has been raised to put his family before all of his own personal interests or goals. He likely has a collectivistic cultural background.

Endnotes

1. Montoya, R. M., & Horton, R. S. (2013). A meta-analytic investigation of processes underlying the similarity-attraction effect. *Journal of Social and Personal Relationships, 30*(1), 64–94. doi:10.1177/0265407512452989

2. For a review and critique of social validation, see Sunnafrank, M. (1984). A communication-based perspective on attitude similarity and interpersonal attraction in early acquaintance. *Communication Monographs, 51*(4), 372–380. doi:10.1080/03637758409390208

3. For a review, see Nairn, S. (2007). Complementarity, of relationship partners. In R. Baumeister & K. Vohs (Eds.), *Encyclopedia of Social Psychology* (p. 162). Thousand Oaks, CA: Sage. doi:10.4135/9781412956253.n95

4. McPherson, M., Smith-Lovin, L., & Cook, J. M. (2001). Birds of a feather: Homophily in social networks. *Annual Review of Sociology, 27*, 415–444. doi:10.1146/annurev.soc.27.1.415

5. Aron, A., & Aron, E. (1997). Self-expansion motivation and including other in the self. In S. Duck (Ed.), *Handbook of Personal Relationships: Theory, Research, and Interventions* (2nd ed., pp. 251–270). Hoboken, NJ: Wiley.

6. For a review, see Goodfriend, W. (2009). Proximity and attraction. In H. Reis & S. Sprecher (Eds.), *Encyclopedia of Human Relationships* (pp. 1298–1300). Thousand Oaks, CA: Sage. doi:10.4135/9781412958479.n420

7. Bornstein, R. F. (1989). Exposure and affect: Overview and meta-analysis of research, 1968–1987. *Psychological Bulletin, 106*, 265–289. doi:10.1037/0033-2909.106.2.265

8. McCroskey, J. C., & McCain, T. A. (1974). The measurement of interpersonal attraction. *Speech Monographs, 41*, 261–266. doi:10.1080/03637757409375845

9. For an example of current research engaging the framework, see Wotipka, C. D., & High, A. C. (2016). An idealized self or the real me? Predicting attraction to online dating profiles using selective self-presentation and warranting. *Communication Monographs, 83*(3), 281–302. doi:10.1080/03637751.2016.1198041

10. Schutz, W. C. (1958). *The Interpersonal Underworld.* Palo Alto, CA: Science and Behavior Books.

11. Canary, D. J., & Cody, M. J. (1994). *Interpersonal communication: A goals-based approach.* New York: St. Martin's Press.

12. Tajfel, H., Billig, M., Bundy, R. P., & Flament, C. (1971). Social categorization and intergroup behaviour. *European Journal of Social Psychology, 1*(2), 149–178. doi:10.1002/ejsp.2420010202

13. Sherif, M., Harvey, O. J., White, B. J., Hood, W., & Sherif, C. W. (1961). *Intergroup Conflict and Cooperation: The Robbers Cave Experiment* (pp. 155–184). Norman, OK: University Book Exchange.

14. For a neuroscience approach to similar phenomena, see Cárdenas, J. C., & Mantilla, C. (2015). Between-group competition, intra-group cooperation and relative performance. *Frontiers in Behavioral Neuroscience, 9*, 33. doi:10.3389/fnbeh.2015.00033

15. Barbato, C. A., Graham, E. E., & Perse, E. M. (2003). Communicating in the family: An examination of the relationship of family communication climate and interpersonal communication motives. *Journal of Family Communication, 3*(3), 123–148. doi:10.1207/S15327698JFC0303_01

16. Fernald, A. A. (1989). Intonation and communicative invent in mothers' speech to infants: Is the melody the message? *Child Development,60*, 1497–1510.

17. Fogel, A. E. (1987). Development of early expressive and communicative action: Reinterpreting the evidence from a dynamic systems perspective. *Developmental Psychology, 23*(6), 747–761.

18. Meltzoff, A. M. (1983). Newborn infants imitate adult facial gestures. *Child Development, 54*, 702–709.

19. Nagy, E. E. (2006). From imitation to conversation: The first dialogues with human neonates. *Infant and Child Development, 15*(3), 223–232.

20. Neuliep, J. W. (2012). *Intercultural Communication: A Contextual Approach* (5th ed.). Thousand Oaks, CA: Sage.

21. Gudykunst, W. B., Matsumoto, Y., Ting-Toomey, S., Nishida, T., Kim, K., & Heyman, S. (1996). The influence of cultural individualism-collectivism, self construals, and individual values on communication styles across cultures. *Human Communication Research, 22*(4), 510–543. doi:10.1111/j.1468-2958.1996.tb00377.x

22. Singelis, T. M. (1994). The measurement of independent and interdependent self-construal. *Personality and Social Psychology Bulletin, 20*(5), 580–591.

23. Hofstede, G. (2001). *Culture's Consequences: Comparing Values, Behaviors, Institutions, and Organizations across Nations* (2nd ed.). Thousand Oaks, CA: Sage.

24. Driver, E. D. (1962). Caste and occupational structure in central India, *Social Forces, 41*(1), 26–31.

25. Bayly, S. (1999). *Caste, Society, and Politics in India from the Eighteenth Century to the Modern Age.* Cambridge, UK: Cambridge University Press.

26. Shipman, A. C. S. (2012). Mate selection in modern India. *Dissertation Abstracts International Section A: Humanities and Social Sciences, 72*(9-A), 3355.

27. Richardson, R. M., & Smith, S. W. (2007). The influence of high/low-context culture and power distance on choice of communication media: Students' media choice to communicate with professors in Japan and America. *International Journal of Intercultural Relations, 71*(1), 479–501.

28. Chua, E. G., & Gudykunst, W. B. (1987). Conflict resolution in low- and high-context cultures. *Communication Research Reports, 4*, 32–37.

29. For a review, see Neuliep, J. W., & McCroskey, J. C. (1997). The development of a U.S. and generalized ethnocentrism scale. *Communication Research Reports, 14*(4), 385–398.

30. Ruggiero, V. R. (2004). *Beyond Feelings: A Guide to Critical Thinking* (7th ed.). Boston, MA: McGraw-Hill.

Verbal Messages

4

SebastianGauert/Getty Images

Even though she is no longer living at home, Michelle talks to her father, Sherrod, quite frequently, and they both characterize their relationship as rather close. However, despite their regular communication, Sherrod and his new wife, Libby, are unable to keep up with Michelle's taste in music, clothing, reading materials, and even romantic partners. Whenever a holiday comes around, Sherrod hints at things that he may want to get Michelle as a gift; often, Michelle's reply is that it sounds like an "interesting" option. Although he has never actually asked her about her word choice, Sherrod has come to realize that Michelle's description of specific books or certain types of clothes as "interesting" is really quite a condemnation of that selection. To Sherrod and Libby, any time Michelle says something is "interesting" they know to interpret that gift option as a nonstarter or a last resort. Indeed, around the house Sherrod and Libby have made it an inside joke, sarcastically using the term interesting to describe any unpleasant chores around the house that they are not looking forward to completing.

How do people assign meaning to words?

Why do people say one thing when they clearly mean another?

MindTap®

Review the chapter's learning objectives and **start** with a quick warm-up activity.

Learning Objectives

After you finish reading this chapter, you will be able to:

Distinguish between ethical and unethical verbal messages.

Give examples of the characteristics of language in relationship formation

Evaluate the components of quality messaging in verbal communication.

Explain key theories of verbal messages.

MindTap®

Read, highlight, and take notes online.

RHETORICAL FOUNDATIONS

How do people assign meaning to words? Why do people say one thing when they clearly mean another? It is often difficult for people to pin down exactly what another person means during a conversation, and this is often due to the complicated nature of the words we say and the meaning that we give to each of those words. Whether we are using words to define a relationship, communicate affection, explain a process, or even just order a complicated espresso drink from a local coffee shop, the words we use have a significant impact on the interaction between two people or among groups of people. Communicators must work hard to make sure that all parties can understand a message in order to create a shared understanding.

From the very beginnings of the communication discipline, scholars who focused on **rhetorical theory** looked at the words we use and how those words can best be articulated through the process of spoken or written communication. Ancient Greeks first characterized successful communication as a combination of three components of verbal communication, using the terms *logos*, *ethos*, and *pathos* to describe the influences of logical argument, speaker characteristics like credibility and charisma, and emotional engagement in a message.[1] For example, Jesse wanted to make one last-ditch effort to save his troubled marriage and knew plenty of logical arguments about the costs of divorce and the financial ramifications of splitting one household into two. However, Jesse also knew his audience (his wife, Lani) and correctly believed that she would be most responsive to *pathos;* as such, he gave a heartfelt description of the day that he first met Lani, with an emotional detailing of each moment he grew to love her more. Knowledge of the rhetorical impact of words may help individuals create an influential message for a variety of reasons. The most significant classical rhetoricians like Plato, Socrates, and Aristotle were able to describe ways to empower language to facilitate intellectual and/or moral growth.[2] Since those early days, both ancient and modern scholars have been able to articulate theoretical *and* practical uses for the application of rhetoric to facilitate shared understanding in our verbal messages.

CHARACTERISTICS OF LANGUAGE

In order to understand how to create a verbal message, we must first understand the primary structure of **verbal communication**. Verbal communication includes both intentional and unintentional messages that use **language**, which is an agreed-on system of **symbols** that allow humans to communicate. In verbal communication, these symbols often take the form of words, and are used to represent or stand for a wide variety of concrete things (e.g., squirrel, taqueria, cantaloupe) or even abstract ideas (e.g., love, hope, prosperity). Without language, almost no sounds or written words would be able to convey any messages beyond the most basic concepts. Indeed, language has many characteristics that make it able to convey meaning to a wide range of people who agree on the structure of sounds and symbols that are used.

Rhetorical Theory
The understanding of how humans use symbols to engage the communication process and influence an audience.

Logos
The use of logical argument in a message intended to influence an audience.

Ethos
The use of speaker characteristics like credibility and/or charisma in a message intended to influence an audience.

Pathos
The use of emotion and emotional engagement in a message intended to influence an audience.

Verbal Communication
Any communicative behavior that conveys an intentional or unintentional message using symbolic language.

Language
An agreed-on system of symbols that allow humans to communicate.

Symbols
Words or items that are used to represent or substitute for concrete things or abstract ideas.

Defamation
A statement that has a negative impact on an individual's reputation.

Slander
An impermanent statement of defamation that is spoken in an interpersonal or public context.

BOX 4.1: Commendable Connections

Ethics and Harmful Rhetoric[3]

When someone wants to persuade or influence another person, she constructs a message that relies on one or more of the foundational elements of rhetoric: *logos*, *ethos*, or *pathos*. However, it is sometimes tempting in the heat of the moment to fictionalize or exaggerate a statement in order to have greater impact on an audience's attitudes or behaviors.

Centre Daily Times/Getty Images

Have you ever been tempted to bend the truth a bit to get your way? If you are honest with yourself, you have to admit that this has likely happened in a variety of contexts. Perhaps you comment on a competitor's character or understate their performance or accomplishments in order to sway the audience's opinion and influence their perception of *pathos*.

However, if the statements that you make involve **defamation**—that is, those statements have a negative impact on an individual's reputation—there may be potential legal ramifications. Engaging in defamation can occur on a large public scale or even be as simple as the gossip that people casually engage in among friends. Two kinds of defamation occur in interpersonal interactions:

> **Slander:** An impermanent statement of defamation that is spoken in an interpersonal or public context. Bernadine is running for an Associated Students position on her college campus. While campaigning, Bernadine jealously says that her opponent Paola once tried to sway votes by promising a new bar in the center of campus. Bernadine is speaking in a slanderous manner if Paola has done nothing of the sort.

> **Libel:** A statement of defamation that is recorded in some written or otherwise permanent form. When Onar is competing for a promotion at work and posts hateful comments on Facebook about his colleague Douglas's personal hygiene habits even though they are not true, Onar has instead engaged in libelous speech.

INSTRUCTIONS: Take a personal inventory of your recent communication behaviors. Have you hurt someone in an attempt to get your way or to appear more desirable? What do you think about this kind of behavior? Does the fact that defamation may allow you to be the subject of a lawsuit make the behavior seem different? What would your response be if you were the target of one of these scenarios?

Language Is Symbolic

Think about the last thing that you ate, whether it was a garlic bagel this morning or a couple of street tacos from a food truck at lunch. Imagine that one of your friends was trying to make that same food item at home and called you on the phone to find out how to make it. Where would you begin? Each ingredient

Libel
A statement of defamation that is recorded in some written or otherwise permanent form.

Lana_M/Shutterstock.com

has a word that describes it, made up of a bunch of different letters. When you arrange those letters and say the word *garlic*, your friend likely knows the general characteristics of that ingredient, and you can use additional words to differentiate between a fresh clove of garlic, garlic salt, or the kind of toasted flaked garlic that often ends up on a fresh bagel. Imagine how difficult that bagel would be to describe if your friend had never heard of—or tasted—garlic in any form. In fact, every single thing that you can see or imagine—concepts as concrete as the book you are reading or as abstract and nuanced as the love you may feel for someone you care deeply about—has language that helps us understand or even share that meaning with another person.

Language Is Rule-Based

If you remember your early childhood school experiences, you probably remember classes that focused on grammar rules like punctuation and spelling. You likely diagrammed sentences until you got sick of them, and you took vocabulary tests to help you understand the meaning of the words that you encountered in books and in your daily life. In order to make language easier to understand, a system of rules has developed that allow for the use of language to be more standardized; that is, when both the sender and the receiver(s) understand the rules for communication they are more easily able to transmit an intended meaning. Gio's father was transferred to the United States from Peru when Gio was in the fifth grade. Because Gio had been learning the rules of the language in his English courses since kindergarten, he was able to slowly pick up the nuances of his new tongue rather quickly. Although he doesn't use English in his home, his schooling had taught him the basics of the language, so his transition to the United States was much easier than it was for his mother, who spoke only Spanish and French.

Language Can Change or Evolve

One difficulty that Gio encountered after moving to the United States, however, was understanding many of the variations in language that had evolved since his elementary school English textbook was written. Words and phrases are constantly being created or changing, depending on the habits and experiences of the people who speak that language. For example, consider terms for all the new technologies developed over the past years; while you may be adept at "tweeting" the location of an upcoming concert so that people can "google" the location and then use the "GPS" "app" on their "smartphone" to get there, during their own youth your parents and/or grandparents would have had no idea what was being discussed. Not only that, but words that already exist also develop new meanings depending on the context or the moment in time. Famously, words like *bad* or *sick* have changed their meaning from negative to positive, and words that used to be common parlance have become offensive or unusable as their layered meanings have become unpacked over the years.

Because language often has **dialects**—region-specific rules or words that don't exist in every community that speaks that language—the situation can get even more complicated. As regions and communities vary the rules and the words based on their dialect norms, a trip across country can feel like an immersive international experience. People in the northern United States may share more language similarities with Canadians than with people from Texas or Louisiana, and even those people from Texas may have difficulty understanding the Louisianans who are relatively nearby. English also has particular challenges in that it is constantly receiving new words from other languages or making some of those dialect rules more widespread.

Finally, individuals may even resort to the use of coded language like **idioms**, which are words or phrases that have special meaning within a culture or large group. Alexis returned to her residence hall after dashing through the rain; after having removed her wet clothes and changed into a dry outfit, she turned to her roommate and declared that it was "raining cats and dogs," knowing full well that her roommate would understand that it was raining hard outside, albeit only with drops of water. Each culture has its own set of idioms like "raining cats and dogs" (e.g., raining hard) or "chomping at the bit" (e.g., eager to start a new project) that may not make much sense if you don't have much verbal background in the culture or large group of individuals.

Sometimes a dyad or a small group of people may even create their own **personal idioms** or utilize **insider language** that is only understood within that small group. When Edgar tells his girlfriend Joy that he is going to "the library," Joy

Hill Street Studios/Blend Images/Getty Images

Dialect
Region-specific rules or words that are not necessarily shared by the larger language community.

Idioms
Words or phrases that have special meaning within a culture or large group.

Personal Idioms
Words or phrases that have a special meaning within a dyad or a small group of people.

Insider Language
See Personal Idioms

Andy Sacks/The Image Bank/Getty Images

BOX 4.2: **InterFace**

Verbal Engagement with Diverse Others

Derek doesn't feel comfortable using race-related terms so he just pretends like race doesn't exist. Years ago he correctly used the term African American to describe some peers, but now those same friends say they are black. His friend Emilio gets upset if he is called Hispanic or Mexican, but his teammate Carlos dislikes being called Latino or Chicano. Derek still doesn't know whether to use the term American Indian, Native American, or First Nations to describe his lab partner Abeytu. Yet his disengagement with race and race-based terminology only further upsets his peers.

When Luma's high school boyfriend came out as gay, Luma signed up for a course on Civil Rights and Sexuality at her university. Luma was shocked when her mom stormed out of the room after Luma said she was taking a class in Queer Studies. Luma's mom was upset by the use of the term *queer* and did not know that it was an accepted academic term; she remembered when "queer" was one of the more hateful names that were used to describe gay people.

Darshan unintentionally offends the women in his workplace because of the terms he uses with them. His peers think he is condescending when he calls them "honey," his boss assumes he is being sarcastic whenever he responds, "Yes, ma'am," and the owner of the company can't believe that Darshan can't remember that she is an unmarried lesbian who doesn't feel like she should be called "Mrs. Feeney" at all.

Although we may initially characterize people according to a wide variety of categories in order to make sense of the world around us, we need to remember that these first impressions rarely fit the life experiences of each person. So, what do you do when you interact with a wide variety of diverse others? Surprisingly, one of the best ways to engage one another is to simply ask what individuals prefer to be known as, or even to talk about what categories most fit them as people. Instead of offending people or avoiding topics completely, a respectful engagement may allow a greater understanding and may avoid confrontation or negative experiences.

INSTRUCTIONS: What are your responses to these scenarios? Do you find yourself reacting strongly to any particular characterization? With whom do you most identify? Consider the role of labels in your life. Are any of the terms you use to describe difference potentially off-putting? What advice would you give each of these people as they try to navigate their increasingly complex world?

Kemter/E+/Getty Images

knows to give him his space. Although other people nearby may think that Edgar is going to get some homework done, Joy knows that Edgar has used a code word and plans to grab a novel and spend some time in the bathroom. One common example of a personal idiom is a nickname or even a pet name used between romantic partners. These words may be crass or cute or demeaning or loving; regardless of the actual words used, the personal idioms have come to have a shared meaning within the relationship. April and Trent went to a comedy show on their first date and hated the misogynist comic. Now, April lovingly calls Trent "Honeybuns" around the house to remind him of their first date— their shared dislike of sexist terminology gives new meaning to an otherwise-demeaning phrase. Jun resorts to a more classic term "Snookums" to refer to his romantic partner Morgan, who in turn calls him "Mr. Snuggles." Jerome is built like a tank; his fraternity brothers have nicknamed him "Tiny" because they find humor in the contrast with his 270 pounds of solid muscle.

Language Varies by Culture or Context

Groups of people often change language to suit their own needs. In addition, the establishment of words or phrases that are understood by the in-group may allow members to easily distinguish members of their culture from among those who are potential outsiders. One way that these language communities may alter verbal content is by creating their own terminology for common human experiences.

Interestingly, some scholars have argued that although cultures use language to create meaning, they also see their social world based on the language that they use. Known as the **theory of linguistic relativity** or more commonly as the **Sapir-Whorf hypothesis**, this perspective claims that we cannot think about our world without language, so our understanding of our world is inherently linked to the language that we use.[4] As such, meaning is created by people and the language they use; cultures and subcultures with different languages or different patterns of language therefore *must* think about their world in different ways. Because they have a different set of words that they are using to contemplate and explain their world to themselves and other members of their culture, their social world is inherently different from other people with different language skills or vocabularies. Even though this hypothesis is still the subject of much debate, it highlights the relative importance that cultures must place on the use of and knowledge about their own language.

In one example of the creation of a separate language system, cultures or groups of people may use **euphemisms** to create meaning that may not be directly interpretable by someone outside of that group. Euphemisms are used to avoid difficult or inappropriate topics, and people may create generic or specific meanings through the use of words or phrases. For example, if a group of teens gossip about their peers and mentions that a couple is "doing it," they are using a euphemism that implies that the partners are having sex with one another; "hooking up" is less clear, with a wide range of erotic behavior possible but not necessarily implied. By using the phrases "doing it" or "hooking up," a conversational partner can hint at behavior by using words that likely have a shared meaning for other members of the group. In another example, a large extended family may want to be able to discuss the death of a loved one without having to bluntly discuss such a negative event; as such, they may resort to phrases like "passed on" or "went to a better place" or even "began looking down at us" in order to avoid the harsh reality of the loss.[5]

Some **subcultures** or communication contexts may assign new meaning to words or phrases, or even create completely new words. People

Theory of Linguistic Relativity
As we use language to describe and understand our social world, that social world is shaped by and interpreted through the verbal skills of the individual or culture.

Sapir-Whorf Hypothesis
See Theory of Linguistic Relativity.

Euphemisms
Words or phrases that ameliorate or soften the impact of otherwise blunt language or terminology.

Subculture
A portion of a larger culture that shares one or more characteristics that distinguish it from the larger group.

Jupiterimages/Stone/Getty Images

Slang
Informal words created by a subculture that distinguish users from a larger group.

Colloquialism
Informal words understood by individuals across broad communication cultures.

Jargon
Technical words and language used by professionals or members of an interest group.

use informal words known as **slang** (a type of **colloquialism**) or technical terms known as **jargon** to convey meaning to other members of a subculture, facilitating either informal interactions or easier communication by creating a shorthand that is understood by other members of that subculture. As a surfer in San Diego, Jad can throw around slang terms like *grom* to describe the young surfers who are making it hard for his "squad" of friends to surf, and can use jargon like "reef break" or "right-hander" to explain the beach conditions and the waves' direction that other surfers are likely to encounter. Other experienced surfers from Southern California are unlikely to even notice that he is using nonstandard English in his conversations. However, if Jad were to surf with English-speaking expatriates in Panama's Bocas del Toro, he may find that the locals there use some slightly different terminology or a mix of Spanish and English.

Although Jad is a member of a surf subculture, some of the regional influences may subtly shift the use of language and give nuanced meaning to both the slang and jargon. His larger knowledge base of surf terminology will likely mark him as an insider to the surfing culture, although minor discrepancies in language use may still indicate his tourist status.

Language Is Complex

If nothing else, our discussion of the verbal communication system has hinted at one key element of language: its complexity. There are formal

Nik Taylor Sport/Alamy Stock Photo

BOX 4.3: iPersonal
Jargon and Technology

Whenever the words *jargon* and *technology* are used together in a textbook, it's likely that the discussion will revolve around how technology is an example of an innovation that creates new jargon (i.e., the reappropriation of "mouse" or "web" or other such inanities.) However, technology not only creates jargon, but also allows users to navigate the complexities of the jargon that we encounter in an increasingly globalized society.

Recent technologies like compact tablet computers or even tiny smartphone components that can snap onto a watchband may break down the previous inaccessibility created by in-group jargon that typically marked members of certain subcultures. With the advent of user-updated online dictionaries (e.g., urbandictionary.com) or blogs and video content that make previously esoteric content accessible (e.g., youtube.com) an individual can easily access lists of context-specific jargon and their definitions without breaking conversational stride.

> Willow's grandmother was on the phone with her when Willow began discussing a funny Internet meme that she had been recently following. As Willow described the humorous gif images that users had uploaded, her grandmother looked up the word *meme* on her smartphone. Before Willow even finished her monologue, her grandmother was able to understand the meaning of the word and contribute to the conversation while avoiding embarrassment.

> Kyle's boss Mason phoned him and asked Kyle to fix the copier. As Kyle's phone lost service after confusing mumbles about "Xerox," "toner," and "hopper," he simply did a web search for the model number and saw both the manual for the machine as well as a user-uploaded video on how to solve the problem. By the time he arrived at the office, Kyle was able to clearly articulate the steps required, impressing Mason.

Because technology provides access to a large amount of information in a relatively quick time, people can easily use learned terminology to pose as members of a group to which they have not had previous access. Because one use of jargon was to distinguish members of the in-group and out-group, it will be interesting to see if shifting technologies cause a flattening of social barriers and also direct social change.

INSTRUCTIONS: What kinds of jargon are used in your interpersonal interactions? Think carefully about the ways that your use of terminology marks you as a member of a group, and how that same jargon distinguishes you from others. What is your reaction to individuals who do not have the same verbal fluency in those areas? How have you used technology to gain jargon-related understanding?

rules and informal rules, and each of these sets of rules can be influenced by the cultures, the subcultures, and even the smaller groups that use language. Words can be invented or redefined, and even the formal definitions (i.e., **denotative meanings** like those found in a dictionary) can have layers of variation where language communities have attached additional defining

Denotative Meaning
A formal definition for a word, like that found in a dictionary.

Connotative Meaning
A culture-specific set of understandings or interpretations associated with the formal definition for a word.

elements to a word (i.e., **connotative meanings** based on themes commonly associated with a denotative meaning). For example, consider the denotative meaning of the term *team*, which is technically a group of players in a competitive sport. For many athletes in professional or club sports, however, the connotative meaning of the word *team* describes a group of friends with a common goal who likely share a family atmosphere and commitment to one another. The word means more than what is implied by the dictionary definition, increasing the complexity of verbal information. Add to all this the idea that much of our verbal usage is contextual in nature, where conversants need to pay attention to the situation in which they find themselves in order to truly understand a response. If you have ever overheard children in a candy store, you can easily understand the words they use to select their treats without having any idea what they actually want to buy. "I want that kind there, and that one way over on the other side, right next to the kind of candy that you bought last week." Without the context given by observation and knowledge of their previous experience in the store, a casual listener would have no understanding of the selection of sweets. There is much more to the use of language than simply stringing letters together to make words to form a sentence.

Tania Kolinko/Shutterstock.com

MESSAGE CONSTRUCTION AND MANAGEMENT

Not only does much of language rely on rules in order to be widely understood, but also conversational interactions rely on a few basic expectations about how an individual will deliver those language-based messages. In 1975, Grice outlined the four key components of message construction, each of which helps to ensure a cooperative conversation where meaning gets shared and expressed in a culturally appropriate manner.[6] Although not every message necessarily shares each of these four features, Grice argues that people generally expect that interpersonal interactions will follow these general principles.

Messages Should Balance Quantity

The first principle of conversational interactions is the idea that contributions to a conversation should strike a balance between sharing enough information and sharing too much information. Although the amount of information that is necessary may vary from interaction to interaction and relationship to relationship, both participants are likely able to find a balance between too much and too little content. Yasamin came home very late

Monkey Business Images/Shutterstock.com

last night, and her partner Sean had been worried about her for hours. As Yasamin finally walked in the door, Sean breathlessly asked where Yasamin had been. When Yasamin responded, "I was out," as she walked into the bathroom, Sean was understandably upset. Yasamin did not find a healthy balance of the quantity of information and in doing so offended her partner. Jenna, on the other hand, experiences the opposite problem. When her daughter Mackenzie comes home from kindergarten, she seems set on giving a play-by-play real-time description of everything that happened during the previous half day of school. Mackenzie is not yet old enough to fully understand the norms of not oversharing information.

Balancing the amount of information is a difficult undertaking in any relationship. Talk too much, and you are seen as overly chatty; talk too little, and you can even be seen as moody or dull. As evidenced in their research on the amount of communication people convey, scholars McCroskey and Richmond[7] came up with a scale to measure the degree to which people talk too much, shown in Box 4.4. Looking at the scale items from this Talkaholic Scale, you can assess your own level of communication compulsion. Questions about irresistible urges to talk or self-awareness about the appropriate time for silence can help individuals know if they are a talkaholic; at the same time, you may want to self-assess your conversational style with the shortened and modified version of the scale found in Box 4.4.

Messages Should Possess Quality

Not only should messages share *enough* information, but also that information should be of sufficient quality. This principle has to do with trying to make sure that what is shared in an interpersonal message is true. That is,

BOX 4.4: Let's Get INTRApersonal
· ·
Compulsive Communication[8]

Do you know someone who can't seem to keep his mouth shut for a moment? Perhaps you are the kind of person who frequently wishes you could take back an entire conversation you just had? Even though verbal communication is one of the primary means to creating a close relationship with someone, that doesn't mean that we should overcommunicate with other people in an attempt to create stronger or more lasting relationships. If you think you might be someone who "overshares" regularly, you can use this self-assessment to gain insight into whether you are a talkaholic, or someone who compulsively and consistently communicates too much information. This is a modified and shortened version of the Talkaholic Scale that was created by the original researchers (McCroskey & Richmond) in 1993 to help identify characteristics of compulsive communicators.

INSTRUCTIONS: Think carefully about how you interact with your family, friends, roommates, or coworkers. Do you get feedback about your communication patterns? This scale may help you think about your own level of communication with those around you.

1	2	3	4	5	6	7
Strongly Disagree	Moderately Disagree	Slightly Disagree	Neither Agree Nor Disagree	Slightly Agree	Moderately Agree	Strongly Agree

_____ 1. I talk more than I should sometimes.

_____ 2. Sometimes I speak when I know it would be to my advantage to keep quiet.

_____ 3. I just can't stop talking too much.

_____ 4. I have an irresistible urge to converse.

_____ 5. Often I talk when I know I should remain silent.

_____ 6. In general, I speak more than I should.

_____ 7. Quite a few people have said I talk too much.

Now, add up the total score. Is it high? Low? The highest score you can get is a 49, but it is rare for someone to score that high. What does it tell you about how much you converse? Are you a talkaholic? What steps can you take to curb your compulsive communication tendencies?

don't say things that you believe to be false, but also don't say things that may not be true. Cymantha and her parents disagree over politics, and often family gatherings involve somewhat heated debates about government involvement in the lives of private citizens. Cymantha finds the conversations frustrating because her father often makes up facts about wiretapping and privacy issues, but her mother isn't much better because she's always citing statistics that she has heard from unreliable sources like her hairdresser or checkout-stand tabloids. Both of Cymantha's parents share messages of dubious quality.

Messages Should Relate Directly

Another principle has to do with a message and how it relates to the topic of discussion or other elements of the conversation at hand. If you are sharing information that is not relevant and thereby changing the topic or derailing discussion, you are violating this principle of cooperative conversation. Cedric and Amber may have figured out how to navigate their family life as siblings, but they each have their own way of getting out of trouble in uncooperative ways. When Cedric's parents confront him about campus parking

Simon Turner/Alamy Stock Photo

tickets that appear on his university tuition statement, he points to the rest of the bill and comments on the extraordinary costs of education and tries to change the subject. Amber, on the other hand, is failing her high school calculus class; when her mom tries to talk to her about strategies for success, Amber simply throws her hands up in the air and claims that she may have failed calculus but at least she hasn't gotten pregnant this semester like some of her other friends. Instead of constructively resolving the issues that Cedric and Amber's parents raised, they hoped that violating this principle could postpone difficult conversations.

Messages Should Retain Clarity

Finally, many argue that messages need to be presented in a manner that is clear and concise, with language that highlights important content and presents it in an orderly fashion. Even though it seems obvious for a communication course to focus on the manner in which a message is delivered, it is not as apparent that individuals actually expect others to present a message in a competent, straightforward manner. When Darius was unprepared for a recent presentation at his job, people walked away with comments about him "wasting their time" in the meeting. Even though Darius delivered all the necessary content, his manner of delivery caused people to feel like he had slighted them in some way.

VERBAL THEORIES

Not only are messages constructed in very specific ways, but also they serve to *function* in a wide variety of manners. This chapter also presents two foundational theories about important functions of verbal communication. Whether conveying information, creating relational closeness, or calming fears or nervousness about the unknown, verbal messages are able to uniquely impact interpersonal interactions in a direct and significant manner.

BOX 4.5: Communication Currents

Word Choice in Current Television

The Big Bang Theory, http://bit.ly/2n7LdHX

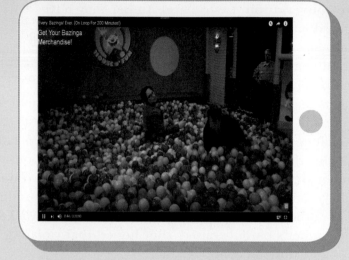

The most popular comedy on television for years, *The Big Bang Theory* glorifies and normalizes the lives of a handful of self-proclaimed "nerds." In this series, a group of socially awkward friends navigate their lives paying little to no attention to the social norms of mainstream America. As viewers watch the show, job-specific jargon is tossed around with relative ease, drawing on the career choices of engineers, physicists, and scientists who are characters in the television series. Sometimes credited for popularizing "geek culture," the series has become wildly successful.

In this video clip, we see a compilation of one character's use of a made-up word. As can be easily seen—regardless of familiarity with the program—the main character Sheldon's style and nuance shapes how the audience understands each situation in which Sheldon and his friends find themselves.

INSTRUCTIONS: Watch the video again, noting the different meaning in each scene for the word *bazinga*. In the clip, the nonsense word is clearly used to depict a variety of different attitudes and experiences associated with humorous play. How do you use a single word (like *love*, for example) to cover a multitude of experience? What are some ways that your word choice influences the ways that you successfully—or unsuccessfully—send messages to one another?

Self-Disclosure and Social Penetration Theory

Social Penetration Theory
Altman and Taylor's theory highlighting increasing relational depth as people move toward increasingly intimate conversational content.

Self-Disclosure
Revealing personal information about the self that cannot otherwise be discovered through observation or casual interaction.

In 1973, scholars Irwin Altman and Dalmas Taylor created **social penetration theory** to highlight stages of closeness that occur when people use verbal communication to share intimate or personal information about themselves,[9] as illustrated in Figure 4.1. This process of sharing personal information that partners could not otherwise know is known as **self-disclosure** and is a fundamental step in the creation of closeness among people. Self-disclosure can appear in many forms, like when Juan shares a wide range of topics about himself or when Ed talks deeply about a single negative experience he had as a child.[10,11,12] Altman and Taylor took that basic idea that conversation and self-disclosure can help strengthen or deepen relationships and highlighted four key stages—as well as a process of reversal—that these relationships necessarily progress through as relationships develop.

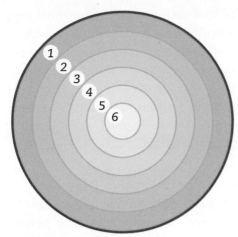

1: Biographical Data (Name, Age, Gender, etc.)
2: Preferences like Fashion, Food, and Music
3: Goals and Hopes for the Future
4: Closely-Held Beliefs and Religious Convictions
5: Deeply Personal Concerns, Fears, and Fantasies
6: Private Self-Concept

FIGURE 4.1
Social Penetration Theory and the "Relational Onion"

Orientation Stage

During the earliest moments in a relationship, people first get to know one another through brief talk about relatively trivial matters. When Kelsey and Margaret first found out that they would be paired as roommates in their freshman dorm, they eagerly set up a FaceTime chat so that they could get to know one another. That knowledge came slowly while they progressed through the **orientation stage**, as the first 15 minutes of their video conversation focused on topics like their names, ages, and comments about the weather in their respective

asiseeit/E+/Getty Images

towns. Halfway through the conversation, Kelsey realized that she regularly has this sort of conversation with random people she meets on the street or on the bus. If something didn't change, she feared she'd *never* get to know Margaret.

Exploratory-Affective Stage

Luckily, after the initial awkwardness of a first meeting, Kelsey and Margaret began to move into the **exploratory-affective stage** of social penetration, wherein both began to reveal more personal information about themselves, indicating the beginning of casual friendship. Self-disclosure occurred even though their conversation was not yet deep, instead focusing on their attitudes and opinions about topics that are widely known and discussed in public. From current events to their attitudes about the latest band, Kelsey and Margaret could easily have stayed in this stage of social penetration and had a fulfilling roommate relationship; most relationships don't progress beyond the exploratory-affective stage.

Affective Stage

Even though Kelsey and Margaret's initial FaceTime chat didn't get too personal, over the course of their first few months living as roommates

Orientation Stage
In this first stage of social penetration, conversations are brief and focus on trivial matters.

Exploratory-Affective Stage
In this second stage of social penetration, partners begin to reveal themselves as conversations move toward attitudes about matters of public interest.

Affective Stage
In this third stage of social penetration, relational partners begin to discuss personal issues or topics that they consider private, feeling sufficiently close to allow conflict to occur.

Stable Stage
In this final stage of social penetration, conversations are deep and personal, and partners have intimate knowledge of the thoughts and emotions of one another.

Depenetration
The process of withdrawing from the depth of a relationship by decreasing self-disclosure and revealing less personal information.

Uncertainty Reduction Theory
Berger and Calabrese's theory highlighting a desire to understand or predict attitudes and behaviors as a primary motivator in human communication.

self-disclosure increased as they began to discuss personal issues and topics that they considered private, slowly revealing more of their true selves. Deeply entrenched in the **affective stage**, these roommates became closer friends and accepted both conflict and criticism as acceptable parts of such a close roommate relationship. Even though Kelsey and Margaret were relatively recent roommates, they had reached enough depth in their relationship that they felt like they were going to be close friends throughout college.

Stable Stage

The final stage of social penetration theory is reserved for the closest of relational partners. Kelsey and Margaret lived together another full year before they eventually reached the **stable stage**, in which they self-disclosed often as they shared both intimate and incredibly personal information with one another. Kelsey could easily predict Margaret's moods from the moment she walked in the door to their shared off-campus apartment, and when Kelsey's boyfriend made a hurtful comment, Margaret immediately guessed how it made Kelsey feel. Regardless of relationship type, the stable stage is the deepest level of relationship closeness.

Depenetration

Just because a relationship has reached a specific stage, however, does not mean that the relationship must necessarily remain at that stage or progress toward greater depth or intimacy. Most relationships experience **depenetration** at some point, which is the slow withdrawal of personal information and self-disclosure from a relational partnership. Some relationships depenetrate because of a problem in the relationship, while others simply "fall apart" and the depenetration occurs naturally. After college, Kelsey and Margaret remained close. Kelsey's move across the country for a job, combined with

Margaret's marriage and desire to start a family, caused the partners to have less time to commit to one another. Although they stopped sharing some personal information or having deep conversations regularly, Kelsey and Margaret still make a point to keep in touch and would likely be characterized as being in the affective stage of social penetration.

Uncertainty Reduction Theory

One of the other seminal theories about the function of verbal communication was formulated by Charles Berger and his colleagues as early as the 1970s. **Uncertainty reduction theory** claims that we are motivated by a desire to make sense of our social environment, and as such we want to be able to explain, predict, and understand both the

Georgijevic/E+/Getty Images

attitudes and behaviors of the people with whom we interact.[13,14] When we cannot explain, predict, or understand these attitudes or behaviors, we are experiencing **uncertainty**, which is an uncomfortable state that we are motivated to relieve. Verbal communication is highlighted as one of the most fundamental ways to reduce uncertainty about another person. The process of question-and-answer as well as basic conversational interactions are likely to provide additional information about that person that will, in turn, reduce our uncertainty in that context or situation.

Uncertainty
An inability to understand or predict the attitudes and/or behaviors of an interaction partner.

Interestingly, the theory highlights three main situations when we are *most* motivated to reduce our uncertainty about our interaction partner:

- *We want to be able to predict and explain behaviors of people who are able to give us incentives or provide us with punishments of some kind.* When Kristoff started his new job, he spent hours chatting with his new coworkers to try to find out as much as he could about his boss. After doing his homework, he felt more comfortable interacting in his workplace environment.

- *We want to reduce uncertainty when we expect that we will have future interaction with that person.* Because we know we will interact again, we want to be able to easily navigate the experience of that interaction. Even though Sandra had a large social network and didn't feel like making new friends, she spent time talking to her next-door neighbor because she knew that they would likely see each other multiple times each week and wanted the interactions to go smoothly.

- *We are motivated to reduce uncertainty about the attitudes and behaviors of someone who is **deviant**, or who engages in behaviors that are considered beyond the range of what is normal in a culture or context.* Far from being turned off by her classmate's unusual clothing and off-putting attitude, Cassie found Kunai fascinating. Always in a studded jacket despite the summer warmth, Kunai's sleeve tattoos and large red Mohawk marked him as different from Cassie's typical experience in their small town. As such, Cassie admired his independent spirit and wanted to find out more about what made him tick.

Deviant
An individual who engages in behaviors considered beyond the range of what is normal in a culture or context.

Both social penetration theory and uncertainty reduction theory highlight the importance of verbal messaging in interpersonal relationships. Sometimes language serves to allow for self-disclosure and the relational closeness that typically follows, as people get to know one another more deeply and progress in their relationships. Other times, conversation simply enables people to understand the lives of those around them, easing fears of people who are different or powerful or are part of our daily routine. Regardless of the specific function, verbal communication is able to convey information easily and clearly to a receptive audience.

Dario Mitidieri/Contributor/Reportage Archive/Getty Images

BOX 4.6: InterConnect

Texting vs. Talking: What Is Your Preference?[15]

People may use a wide variety of communication technologies to enhance or replace the interactions that they have with other people. Over the past decade, the popularity of using text messaging has grown dramatically, causing a mixed response among both observers and academics. Admittedly, nothing can replace the quality of interaction in a face-to-face meeting. However, texting may allow for the quick dissemination of information, skipping the conversational pleasantries that slow down interpersonal communication.

> ❯ Janie wants to find out what she should bring home to her family for dinner but is in the middle of an important group meeting. She sends a quick text "Want 4 dinner?" to her entire family, knowing that quick responses like "Pizza" or "Mexican" will soon clutter her in-box.

> ❯ Madelyn needs to understand why she got a poor performance review at her part-time job. Although her boss prefers email and text to get things done, Madelyn asks for an appointment to discuss the information.

> ❯ Max has never been good at conflict. Lately his relationship with Marche has been difficult, and her recent voicemail was harsh and unfeeling. Not one to mince words, Max types a quick "It's over!" and then goes back to working on his bicycle.

> ❯ Darlene wants to know the address of the place she is supposed to meet her friend for dinner. Dialing the phone, Darlene doesn't realize that the quick question she asks is going to turn into a 15-minute conversation.

> ❯ Taraneh is playing a word game on her smartphone. Noticing a friend calling, she ignores the phone and types a message that she can't chat but can text because she's busy. Taraneh uses the time between texts to make moves in her game, hoping for a high score.

INSTRUCTIONS: Think carefully about each of the interactions above. Did each conversational partner make a right or wrong choice? Is there such a thing as right or wrong when it comes to selecting a channel for communication? How would you say that your relationships have developed with regard to texting or talking on the phone? Which of the interactions have more content, and why? Are you more your real self in one channel or the other?

Chapter Summary

Humans use language in a variety of messages, and the complicated way that we send and receive in these interpersonal relationships allows for the sharing of complicated ideas through verbal messages. Both culture and individual experience influence the ways that we assign meanings to words, as each person uses her own understanding of her world—as well as the influence of her social group—to create a shared meaning within a relationship. Scholars have been interested in verbal messages from the early days of rhetorical theory and have created a clear understanding of how language works. Language is symbolic, it is rule-based, and it is continually changing and evolving as both individuals and cultures shift in their interaction patterns.

Individuals gain a greater understanding of their social world depending on the language that they employ, as highlighted by the theory of linguistic relativity. In addition, those same individuals may *use* language to gain a greater understanding of one another and to create closeness, as discussed in social penetration theory. In fact, uncertainty reduction theory suggests that one of the primary motivations of human interaction is to gain understanding about one another and to reduce unknown information about one another. Just as we can use language and verbal messages to better understand the world around us, a broad understanding of the *theories* about language and verbal messages can help us to better navigate our interpersonal interactions with one another.

First-Person Video   MindTap®

Birthday Party Confusion

Apply what you've learned in this chapter by analyzing the "Birthday Party Confusion" video, using the accompanying questions as a guide. This video and these questions are available online with your MindTap Speech for *Interconnections: Interpersonal Communication Foundations and Contexts*.

Key Terms   MindTap®

Affective Stage	**Exploratory-Affective Stage**	**Personal Idioms**
Colloquialism	**Idioms**	**Rhetorical Theory**
Connotative Meaning	**Insider Language**	**Sapir-Whorf Hypothesis**
Defamation	**Jargon**	**Self-Disclosure**
Denotative Meaning	**Language**	**Slander**
Depenetration	**Libel**	**Slang**
Deviant	*Logos*	**Social Penetration Theory**
Dialect	**Orientation Stage**	**Stable Stage**
Ethos	*Pathos*	
Euphemisms		

Use flashcards to learn key concepts and take a quiz to test your knowledge.

Subculture	Theory of Linguistic	Uncertainty Reduction
Symbols	Relativity	Theory
	Uncertainty	Verbal Communication

Discussion Questions

1. Think about the people in your life who have the ability to reward or punish you. What steps have you taken—or do you plan to take—to reduce your uncertainties about them?

2. What would you claim as your "verbal subculture"? Are there specific words, phrases, or ways of speaking that mark you as different from other people? How has that influenced your ability to interact with others around you?

3. Think about your close relationships. Did they get deep relatively fast, or was the process slow and steady? Have you had any relationships that have lost their closeness and depth as time has passed? Why?

4. Discuss a time when you have felt completely lost in a conversation. What did that feel like? Compare that experience with a time when you were able to chat and joke and feel like a clear member of the in-group. Did you use slang or formal speech? How often do you feel that way?

5. Consider your current friendships. What stage of social penetration do you think you are in? What makes you think so? Do you want the relationships to become closer, get more distant, or stay relatively the same?

Making Connections

Sending and receiving messages is the primary social process. In Chapter 1, we talked about the basic ways that humans interact with one another. Consider your verbal behavior. How do you expect that people best understand you as an individual? How do people understand you as a member of a group?

Chapter Quiz

1. Which of the following stages of social penetration describes deep, personal conversations with the ability to predict partner's reactions?

   a. Stable
   b. Affective
   c. Exploratory-affective

   d. Orientation
   e. None of the above

2. Which of the following stages of social penetration describes initial interactions that are often characterized by shallow conversations?

    a. Stable
    b. Affective
    c. Exploratory-affective
    d. Orientation
    e. None of the above

3. While chatting after class where the instructor could overhear, Bryant loudly claimed that his roommate cheated on a recent test. In fact, Bryant's roommate did nothing of the sort. Which of the following describes Bryant's claim?

    a. Libel
    b. Euphemism
    c. Slander
    d. None of the above
    e. All of the above

4. Megan recently submitted a Yelp review for a local baked goods stand at the farmers' market, claiming to have found a couple hairs in a cupcake. In fact, Megan has never been to a farmers' market, and was simply hoping to steer traffic to her own bakery storefront. Which of the following describes Megan's review?

    a. Libel
    b. Euphemism
    c. Slander
    d. None of the above
    e. All of the above

5. Which of the following perspectives best highlights what motivates people to search out additional information from others who are relatively unknown?

    a. Social penetration
    b. Linguistic relativity
    c. Sapir-Whorf
    d. Uncertainty reduction
    e. All of the above
    f. None of the above

6. Which of the following perspectives best highlights the types of information that are shared between partners as they get increasingly close to one another?

    a. Social penetration
    b. Linguistic relativity
    c. Sapir-Whorf
    d. Uncertainty reduction
    e. All of the above
    f. None of the above

7. T/F Ciano is more likely to care about reducing uncertainty about his employer than about the person who sat next to him on a recent flight.

8. T/F Depenetration is the process through which people become less disclosive with one another.

9. T/F Using jargon is a successful messaging strategy because most everyone knows and understands those words.

10. T/F Focusing on content directly related to the discussion at hand is a way to ensure that conversations remain focused and relevant.

Endnotes

1. For an overview, see Foss, K. A. (2009). Rhetorical theory. In S. W. Littlejohn & K. A. Foss (Eds.), *Encyclopedia of Communication Theory* (pp. 853–857). Thousand Oaks, CA: Sage.

2. For an overview, see Prosser, M. H. (2009). Classical rhetorical theory. In S. W. Littlejohn & K. A. Foss (Eds.), *Encyclopedia of Communication Theory* (pp. 103–108). Thousand Oaks, CA: Sage.

3. Schmidt, L. D. (1962). Some legal considerations for counseling and clinical psychologists. *Journal of Counseling Psychology, 9*(1), 35–44. doi: 10.1037/h0041969

4. For a review, see Smith, M. V. (1996). Linguistic relativity: On hypotheses and confusions. *Communication and Cognition, 29*(1), 65–90.

5. For examples, see Rodenbach, R. A., Rodenbach, K. E., Tejani, M. A., & Epstein, R. M. (2016). Relationships between personal attitudes about death and communication with terminally ill patients: How oncology clinicians grapple with mortality. *Patient Education and Counseling, 99*(3), 356–363.

6. Grice, H. P. (1975). Logic and conversation. In P. Cole & J. L. Morgan (Eds.), *Syntax and Semantics 3: Speech Acts* (pp. 41–58). New York, NY: Academic Press.

7. McCroskey, J. C., & Richmond, V. P. (1993). Identifying compulsive communicators: The talkaholic scale. *Communication Research Reports, 10*(2), 107–114.

8. Ibid.

9. Altman, I., & Taylor, D. A. (1973). *Social Penetration: The Development of Interpersonal Relationships. Oxford,* England: Holt, Rinehart & Winston.

10. Gilbert, S. J. (1976). Self disclosure, intimacy, and communication in families. *The Family Coordinator, 25,* 221–230.

11. Wheeless, L. R., & Grotz, J. (1976). Conceptualization and measurement of reported self-disclosure. *Human Communication Research, 2,* 238–246.

12. Wheeless, L. R., & Grotz, J. (1977). The measurement of trust and its relationship to self-disclosure. *Human Communication Research, 3,* 250–257.

13. For an overview, see Knoblick, L. K. (2009). Uncertainty reduction theory. In S. W. Littlejohn & K. A. Foss (Eds.), *Encyclopedia of Communication Theory* (pp. 976–978). Thousand Oaks, CA: Sage.

14. Berger, C. R., & Calabrese, R. J. (1975). Some explorations in initial interaction and beyond: Toward a developmental theory of interpersonal communication. *Human Communication Research, 1,* 99–112.

15. Bowman, J. M., & Pace, R. (2015). Dual-tasking effects on Outcomes of mobile communication technology. *Communication Research Reports, 31*(2), 221–231. doi: 10.1080/08824096.2014907149

5

Listening

Asia Images Group Pte Ltd/Alamy Stock Photo

MindTap®

Review the chapter's learning objectives and **start** with a quick warm-up activity.

Learning Objectives

After you finish reading this chapter, you will be able to:

Outline the elements of effective listening.

Explain three types of listening.

Analyze message processing in interpersonal relationships.

Identify active and passive methods of hindering effective listening.

MindTap®

Read, highlight, and take notes online.

Mariella never thought that sharing a household with a romantic partner would be so difficult. Even though she loves Markus, Mariella doesn't feel like he is invested in their relationship. Although Mariella and Markus have a glass of wine and sit on the couch every evening to talk about their days at work, Markus can barely describe what Mariella does for a living, much less name her favorite coworkers or even her boss. For his part, Markus doesn't find a problem because he sees their nightly ritual as a time for Mariella to vent about her day and "get it out of her system" so that she can enjoy her life with him. Also, in his mind he feels justified because he spends more time talking to Mariella than do any of his coworkers with their partners. Markus truly sees each evening as a great sacrifice when he could instead be checking his investments or watching his favorite shows on Netflix. To him, giving at least an hour of his attention each night to hear Mariella discuss her day seems like a great show of respect and affection.

COMPARING HEARING AND LISTENING

Is there a difference between quantity and quality of attention to one's partner? What are the benefits of knowing how to listen within a relationship? A comprehensive discussion of the sending and receiving of interpersonal messages and the use of verbal language *must* include significant attention to the process of receiving

Source: YouTube/TED Talk

Hearing
The biological process of passively perceiving sounds in one's environment.

Listening
The process of actively receiving and attending to the potential meanings in messages.

those messages. Whether you are hearing a speaker at a seminar or political rally, watching a YouTube clip from a recent TED Talk, paying attention to a therapist or counselor in the office, or hearing an ad on your local radio station, effective communicators also practice the art of listening.

Conceptually distinct from passively **hearing** or perceiving sounds in our environment, **listening** is a process of actively receiving and attending to the potential meanings in messages. When a communicator moves from hearing to listening, she is actively and intentionally engaging in the shared process of communication. Many times, however, people are more focused on other distracting tasks and are not spending time actually listening to one another. Valentina and Cain have been married for years, but soccer season always

vectorfusionart/Shutterstock.com

seems to cause tension in their relationship. Each night, Valentina parks herself in front of the large flat-screen television in their den and spends hours watching the game. Whenever Cain comes in to ask a question about the next day's activities or to talk about what happened at work, Valentina nods and makes grunts like "mmhmm" and "yeah." However, the next day Valentina has no memory of the conversation; she even recently forgot to pick up their puppy from doggy day care one evening, a responsibility that they had discussed the night before. Although Cain knows that his wife is hearing the fact that he is talking to her, Valentina is clearly not listening to the substance of what he has to say.

LISTENING TO VERBAL MESSAGES AND MESSAGE PROCESSING

Beyond a simple awareness of noises—or of environmental features and their associated sounds—listening involves the intentional awareness and attention to messages that are delivered within a context. In a crowded corner of a trendy new restaurant, Charles and Jake can easily hear the private conversations of most everyone within 10 feet of their tiny table. Even though they could spend hours entertained by the relative strangers around them, Charles and Jake work hard to direct their attention solely toward one another. Beyond simply focusing on the sounds that the other is making, both Charles and Jake work to understand the messages that each intends to send through those sounds. With an understanding of the elements of effective listening, Charles and Jake are able to focus on their own interpersonal relationship despite the proximity and volume of the other relationships in their close personal space.

Types of Listening

Although all beneficial forms of listening are characterized by actively receiving and attending to messages sent from others, scholars John Stewart and Carole Huston were among the first to identify and use the metaphor of breathing as a representation of the exchange of ideas,[1] with the exhalation of breath representing the dissemination of a message and the inhalation of breath representing the process of listening—as well as focusing our attention on the essential nature of listening for human existence. Just like yogis can seek multiple forms of breathing throughout their practice of yoga, both Stewart and Huston describe three fundamental ways to inhale (i.e., actively listen) in one's daily life. If we summarize and simplify Stewart and Huston's three main forms of listening, we consider **dialogic listening** that focuses on constructing a shared meaning, **empathic listening** that focuses on constructing a shared experience, and **analytic listening** (i.e., **critical listening**) that focuses on deconstructing a message to its constitutive parts.

Dialogic Listening
The type of active listening in which both parties seek to co-construct shared meaning and understand each other's thoughts and feelings through conversation and dialogue.

Empathic Listening
The type of active listening that focuses on adopting the perspective of one's conversational partner and interpreting the world through that perspective.

Analytic Listening
The type of active listening in which one party seeks to analyze and/or critique the message and the implications of a communication interaction in order to determine the truth or veracity of the message.

Critical Listening
See Analytic Listening.

Mangostar/Shutterstock.com

Dialogic Listening

Dialogic listening is a form of listening wherein people are creating a shared meaning, such that they begin to construct a mental model of the thoughts and feelings of the other person(s) through conversation and dialogue. Both parties are engaged in sending and receiving messages with the purpose of creating greater understanding of one another. Much like a partnership on a classroom project or the collaboration that newlyweds have in making a home together, the final result of dialogic listening is typically more complex than could be created by one person alone. Indeed, the product of dialogic listening will often be a co-constructed understanding of one another that neither party could have expected on his own.

So how do people create shared meaning through dialogic listening? If you have ever worked on a class project with another person or in a small group, you are likely familiar with the way that you can brainstorm and discuss and analyze a project idea with great detail. By the end of a project meeting, the plan moving forward might look very different than any party expected when they came together to engage in conversation about their shared task. As people present their ideas and bring their attitudes, values, beliefs, knowledge, and experiences to the discussion, each person likely shapes the conversation so that each person has an expanded understanding of the topic at hand. This may allow for greater competency, creativity, or other unknown outcomes to develop across contexts.[2] Although each party may have been competent enough to write a paper or to prepare a presentation on an individual project, the experience of collaborating on a project allows people to construct a combined set of ideas that far exceeds those put forth by any one individual. As each person in a dialogic listening situation begins to add understanding or interpretation to a conversation, the other person (or persons) must respond in kind and adjust their understanding. Some scholars even consider dialogic listening to be akin to a collaborative art piece, in which each person's contribution to the process both inspires and constrains the subsequent actions of the other.[3,4]

Empathic Listening

Empathic listening is often described as the type of listening that focuses on adopting the perspective of one's conversational partner and interpreting the world through his perspective. Essentially, when you engage in empathic listening you are trying to see the world from another person's point of view and to better understand that person and his world as a result of that shared exchange. Although people may initially imagine that empathic listening is focused mostly on understanding their conversational partners, they are often surprised at the rich and varied insight that they themselves gain from

BOX 5.1: InterFace
. . . .
Respectfully Perceiving Diverse Others[5]

Jean-Claude is used to a traditional Parisian way of interacting with those around him. Because he is used to a lot of people filling a relatively compact city, he often finds himself feeling anonymous in public settings and rarely makes eye contact with people around him. Like most French people who live in densely populated areas, Jean-Claude does not attempt to interact with people he does not know while he is riding the crowded metro or shopping for groceries in the busy outdoor markets.

franckreporter/Getty Images

Because Chet came from a relatively small town in Texas, he is used to smiling at and acknowledging every person he sees. In his neighborhood, Chet would be considered rude (or an obvious outsider) if he were to ignore someone he passed in the street, and his parents would hear about the rudeness through the small town's extended social network and would then take corrective action. Driving into the nearby big city, Chet waves at nearly every vehicle that passes.

When Jean-Claude and Chet are paired up as roommates during their first year of college in the Texas state capital, each of them has difficulty understanding the other. But to make matters worse, they find it difficult to begin a conversation about the differences that confound their burgeoning relationship. "Why do you pretend to know everyone you meet?" is just as offensive a question to Chet as the one that is asked of Jean-Claude on a regular basis, "Do you really have to live up to the rude French stereotypes?", even though his demure countenance is actually a sign of respect for others' privacy.

Although people may want to address concerns they have about each other, sometimes the ways that we seek to reduce uncertainty about interaction partners reflect our own reservations or hesitations about the people we meet. Before reacting emotionally to what may seem like an insensitive question from someone who is very different from you, stop to ask yourself what she is really trying to discover through her query. You may find that people have similar motivations to relate with one another but are being shaped by the cultural backgrounds and experiences that are reflected in their questioning.

INSTRUCTIONS: How would you respond to either Chet's or Jean-Claude's question if it was asked of you? Do you find yourself interacting with people in an insensitive way, even when you are trying to behave in a friendly manner? What ways of behaving might people ask you about? Do you identify more with Chet or Jean-Claude, or do they both seem unusual to you?

looking at a problem or a concept from a completely different perspective. When staunchly conservative Michael wanted to better understand his roommate Craig's perspective on gay marriage, he chose to use empathic listening to consider the ideas and feelings of his gay friend. By trying to adopt Craig's perspective, he not only gained a greater understanding of why Craig might interpret marriage equality as an issue of social justice but also realized that Craig's personal struggle was similar to Michael's own understanding of racial

attator/Alamy Stock Photo

inequality that he felt he encountered every day as a Cuban American. Instead of simply understanding Craig's emotional and intellectual perspective, Michael was also able to see how Craig's stance on justice and equality was similar to his own, contextualizing his perspective in a whole new way.

Indeed, this sort of empathic listening that Michael and Craig encountered allows for individuals to engage in **perspective-taking**, which affords people insight into an issue or complex problem by looking at that issue from all sides. In complex negotiation systems, the facilitator of the discussion often needs to be able to understand the perspective of both parties, and to hear and describe the goals of the other.[6,7] For example, the official presiding over a mediated divorce would need to be able to translate the

Perspective-Taking
The attempt to look at a problem or situation from the point of view of the other person or persons who are involved in the same issue, regardless of one's level of agreement.

ASDF_MEDIA/Shutterstock.com

BOX 5.2: Commendable Connections
. . . .

Ethics and Empathic Listening[8]

Empathic listening is often described as trying to take the perspective of another person, using encouragement and displays of interest to get one's interpersonal partner to open up and share her thoughts fully. When considering all the behaviors that one might use in order to get someone to keep talking, it becomes apparent that the techniques used to engage in empathic listening look a lot like agreeing with something that is being said, from nodding and affirmative gestures to quick affirmations like "yes, go on" or "please continue."

However, sometimes we want to engage in empathic listening to more fully understand a conversational partner, but we find ourselves in sharp disagreement with the attitudes or behaviors that the person is describing. Particularly, someone may express a view that is insensitive to an individual or to a group of people, or somehow expresses a point of view that may be offensive to one or more people. In these kinds of situations, we may find ourselves caught between two polar ends of the spectrum of listening; on one hand, we want to show affirmation for the relational partner, while on the other hand we want to show disagreement or even contempt for some of the things that he is saying.

If someone is sharing information or attitudes that conflict with the deeply held values or beliefs of her partner, it may be in that partner's best interest to clarify that she wants to continue listening but that she doesn't like or agree with a statement. For example, one partner could interrupt "I don't share that point of view, but I'd like to hear more" or "I don't think I would use that term to describe (it, him/her, them), but maybe you can clarify as you continue." Even a confused or inquisitive face can help qualify the normal nonverbal behaviors like nodding that we engage in when trying to understand one another.

INSTRUCTIONS: Consider your recent conversations with close friends or a romantic partner. Have you ever felt that you needed to let them know that you didn't share a controversial attitude or belief? Did you let that person continue to talk without pointing out your discomfort, or did you express dissent in a positive way? How did each of you likely feel after such an encounter?

statements and sentiments of each party in a way that will both elicit a desired response and also remain faithful to the original intent of the message.

Analytic Listening

Analytic listening—sometimes referred to as "critical listening"—is a much more structured approach to paying attention to a message and processing elements of that message in an intentional way; in doing so, one or both parties seek to analyze and/or critique the message and the implications of a communication interaction in order to determine the truth or veracity of the message. For example, consider the messages sent when an individual

Kzenon/Shutterstock.com

is trying to purchase an expensive object of some sort, whether a car or a television or a piece of jewelry. The customer needs to take all the messages sent by the sales clerk (e.g., "It's the best one on the market!" or "You're really going to impress your date when you show him this!") and determine which ones are relevant to the desired goals and the situation at hand. Is the sales clerk stating opinion as fact? Is he representing the true state of being? Are the comments even relevant to the situation?

In order to cut through the irrelevant information and focus all your attention on a message, scholars suggest a few important steps in analytic listening:[9]

- **Prepare yourself for the receipt of a message.** Remove all distractions, ensure that you can hear the message being delivered, and make sure you are in the right state of mind to pay attention. Is there something that is causing you to respond more emotionally than you ought?

- **Organize the message upon receipt.** In whatever way possible, try to understand the basic structure of the message. Are there a few key concepts worth remembering or a flow to the message that will help you remember the main arguments? If you have something to write with, take notes on the main points so that you can evaluate them later.[10]

- **Consider the message as a whole.** At this point, it is helpful to take a moment to consider your own conclusions, based on the messages sent. What is the complete message that is being delivered to you, and how truthful or comprehensive of a picture does the message create? By looking at the intent of the message and the way that it was delivered, often individuals are able to see patterns that inform them about the worthiness of the message as a whole.

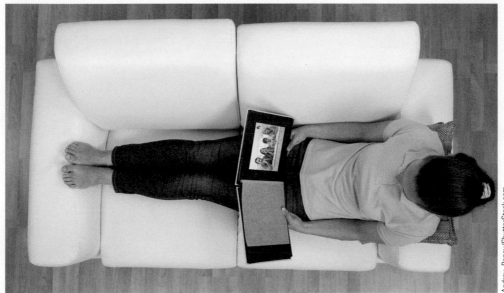

Andrey_Popov/ShutterStock.com

- **Determine a response to the message.** Finally, it becomes useful to consider what your actions should be upon receipt of the message. Is the sender expecting you to give a verbal response or to commit in any way? Are you being asked to make a change in attitudes or behavior or to simply listen to the message and show that you have understood? Once you realize what is being asked of you, it becomes much easier to act on a message that is received by determining whether that message deserves a response and—if so—what kind of message or action is justified.

In our previous example of a high-pressure sales situation in a jewelry store, the sales clerk may have made the comment that a certain piece of expensive jewelry "is the best one on the market." After listening to a variety of other descriptive characteristics, our customer Vanessa realizes that such a statement is irrelevant to her, particularly since she cannot afford such an investment anyway. After listening to the clerk describe the impact such a gift is likely to have on the recipient of the gift, Vanessa realizes that she just wants to let her mother know that she is thinking about her as she travels to visit colleges. Vanessa also considers her motives and realizes that she does not need to purchase an expensive piece of high-quality jewelry in order to express that sentiment. Indeed, Vanessa rethinks her whole strategy and instead decides to do a photo collage of pictures of her holding her mother's portrait in each location.

ELEMENTS OF EFFECTIVE LISTENING

Beyond simply hearing someone speaking and being able to acknowledge that sounds are reaching our ears and being transmitted to our brains, effective listening involves paying attention to these sounds and processing them to understand and engage the message that is being sent. In order to

fizkes/Shutterstock.com

be skilled at the process of listening, it is important that receivers engage the basic elements identified by a variety of scholars as necessary for effective listening in interpersonal interactions.[11],[12]

Reception

Reception
The most basic element of the listening process, in which sounds or sights can be seen or heard and are made available for cognition.

Noise
A physical or psychological barrier to the process of perceiving a communication event (from Chapter 1).

Hearing-Impaired
The inability of an individual to perceive some or all sounds across the spectrum of available sounds.

Attention
The second element of the listening process, in which a receiver devotes mental energy and awareness to the sounds or sights received from a sender.

Multitasking
Attempting to accomplish two or more distinct processes and/or interactions at the same time.

At the most basic level we find the element of **reception**. An individual must be able to receive a message before she can engage any of the other elements of effective listening. To receive a message, you must hear or see that message in the first place. As discussed in Chapter 1, this is often a complicated process. The **noise** that we have in our daily lives (e.g., physical noise like a gardener's leaf blower, or psychological noise like nervousness about an upcoming test) may cloud our ability to receive the most basic elements of a message. Additionally, other outside factors may weaken or even mute the sounds that we may otherwise hear, like if someone is temporarily wearing noise-canceling headphones or has been diagnosed as being **hearing-impaired**.

Attention

Not only does an individual need to be able to receive sounds in order to be an effective listener, but that individual must also pay **attention** to the sounds that he receives. Moving beyond simple hearing, listening is an active process. Without devoting both focus and attention to a message, a receiver is unable to engage a message beyond the most basic level of noting the presence of audible sound. One common reason for inattention includes the presence of other distracting items or tasks. Recent research shows that people are less likely to be able to **multitask** effectively than previously thought, with problems in both accomplishing a task and/or communicating effectively while trying to do more than one thing at once.[13]

BOX 5.3: Communication Currents

Engaged Perception in Current Television

The Ellen Show, "Do You Pass the Idiot Test?," http://bit.ly/2n7V2pw

North America's most beloved talk show host, Ellen DeGeneres, is famous for her rapport with the audience in her daytime program *The Ellen Show*. As a committed LGBT activist, Ellen has her finger on the pulse of both alternative and mainstream Hollywood. From hosting celebrities to dancing through the aisles to setting up hilarious games or activities with guests, Ellen is famous for her positivity and ability to bring joy into the lives of watchers.

As we watch the clip, Ellen asks a bunch of relatively obvious questions to her audience members with admittedly hilarious results. With these contestants being put on the spot, they are often too preoccupied to truly perceive the often obvious responses to the questions that they are asked.

INSTRUCTIONS: Watch the video again. After already knowing the answers to each question, are you surprised at how easy the responses "should" have been? Why do you think that these audience members didn't catch on to obvious cues in the questions? What do you think might have been distracting each of these individuals within the context?

Evaluation

Conversational partners not only hear and pay attention to information, but they must also critically engage that information in an element of effective listening known as **evaluation**. Far from being a passive process, listening requires that individuals think deeply about the information or interactions that they encounter in their daily lives, and then actively choose to categorize that information as true or false, helpful or unhelpful. Is the information that is presented to us going to be useful? Do we need to craft some sort of response or engage in some process as a result of hearing this information? Only through evaluating the material can we then move on to the next step in the process of active listening.

Evaluation
The third element of the listening process, this involves critically thinking about the various qualities of the messages that we have heard and making judgments about them.

Action

After having heard, paid attention to, and evaluated the qualities and characteristics of a message, we move toward determining whether we should take direct **action** with regard to a message or interaction. Whether an

Action
The fourth element of the listening process, this involves determining the type and scope of a response to a message.

BOX 5.4: Let's Get INTRApersonal

Listening Styles in Our Daily Lives[14]

People approach their daily interactions in a wide variety of ways. For some, interpersonal interactions are mostly about making relationships feel good to all parties. For others, getting a task or a job done is the primary goal. Have you considered how you tend to approach your interactions? When people are talking to you, do you have a specific goal in mind as you hear and listen to what they have to say?

Scholars have found four specific styles of listening, and you can use this self-assessment to gain insight into your own listening style(s). This is a modified and shortened version of the Listening Styles Profile that was created by the original researchers (Watson, Barker, & Weaver) in 1995 to help people understand how they listen in their interpersonal relationships.

INSTRUCTIONS: Think carefully about how you listen to your conversational partners in your daily life. Using the 5-point scale below, please indicate how often each of the following statements applies to you in your daily life.

1	2	3	4	5
Never	Infrequently	Sometimes	Frequently	Always

_____ 1. I become involved when listening to the problems of others.

_____ 2. When I listen to others, I quickly notice if they are pleased or disappointed.

_____ 3. I focus my attention on the other person's feelings when I am listening to them.

_____ 4. I am frustrated when others don't present their ideas in an orderly, efficient way.

_____ 5. I am impatient with people who ramble on during conversations.

_____ 6. I jump ahead and/or finish thoughts of speakers.

_____ 7. I like the challenge of listening to complex information.

_____ 8. I prefer to hear facts so I can personally evaluate them.

_____ 9. I ask questions to probe for additional information.

_____ 10. I interrupt others when I feel time pressure.

_____ 11. I begin a discussion by telling others how long I have to meet.

_____ 12. When hurried, I let the other person(s) know that I have a limited amount of time to listen.

Now, look at your answers. Separately add up your scores for items 1–3 (people-focused listening), items 4–6 (action-focused listening), items 7–9 (content-focused listening), and items 10–12 (time-focused listening). If you scored highest on items 1–3, you probably tend to focus on people's emotions and the ways that they are feeling as you are listening to them. If you scored highest on items 4–6, you more likely focus on outcomes and prefer communication to be clear and straightforward. If you scored highest on items 7–9, you probably pay careful attention to all information and want to know all available information before making a decision. Finally, if you scored highest on items 10–12 you likely prefer to handle your interactions quickly and efficiently, hoping that conversational partners would "get to the point."

Do you agree with the scoring list? How would you characterize yourself? Were you surprised by the results? Remember, these are general tendencies, but people can learn to listen in a variety of ways depending on their context.

informal or formal conversational response is necessary, or an email or phone call should be made, or a behavior needs to be performed as a result of the message that is sent—all of these are potential responses to an interaction deemed **actionable**. When Brett's best friend Georgina told him that Katya had a crush on him, Brett thought about what Georgina said before responding. After a few moments of surprise, Brett thanked Georgina for her honesty and then sent Katya a text message to ask if they could grab coffee sometime that week. Brett took direct action in two separate ways: He responded directly to the sender of the message (Georgina) and also used a communication medium to enact a relationship-starting behavior (with Katya). Not all messages necessarily require a response or an action, but in this case Katya was glad that Brett decided one was necessary.

nenetus/Shutterstock.com

Actionable
A message that can or should be responded to with an in-kind message or behavior.

Retention

Finally, effective listeners work on **retention** in order to remember or keep access to important information that is shared or discussed during an interpersonal interaction. Not all parts of a message must necessarily be remembered, but effective communicators often attempt to glean the key elements of an interaction. By repeating important elements of a message, taking notes, devoting energy toward a conversation, or even recording interactions (with permission, of course!), successful communicators retain the key parts of their interactions in order to be able to return to those topics or themes at future times. In the classroom, Derek works hard to listen effectively as his professor lectures. By taking notes, recording the classroom session, and even meeting immediately afterward to discuss key points with his professor, Derek ensures that his trips to office hours will be well informed and that he will be prepared come test-taking day.

Retention
The final element of the listening process, an effective listener typically attempts to actively remember information about the message that was sent.

Keisuke_N/Shutterstock.com

BOX 5.5: iPersonal

Stereotyping and Technology

Technology allows large amounts of information to be available with the swipe of a finger or the push of a button. However, such a large amount of information cannot be consumed completely, and people are often forced to engage in the quick categorization of information. When using any form of interpersonal communication or accessing any messages in a computer-mediated environment, it is easy to be distracted from truly listening to the content of those messages. The increase in access to data and information makes distracted processing a part of everyday life.

Often, people gloss over the substance of a message after a quick glance, just like you may make a quick assumption about a classmate or a potential love interest at a first glance. Does the person look like she will be fun to spend time with or a total drag? Just like that, we decide whether to pursue a relationship. Does an article/blog look credible because it uses the right font or formatting? Again, instantly we decide what is worth our attention and what is not, regardless of actual quality.

Not only that, but we are constantly assaulted with friend requests and opportunities for "connections" and even "winks" or "pokes" or even more inappropriately named requests for networking or companionship. In face-to-face contexts we may not be willing to dismiss someone's interest after only a second of consideration. Are we guilty of using knee-jerk reactions to define our social interactions?

Retailers and opinion leaders and celebrity bloggers are all well versed at getting people to see and pay attention to their messages. However, it is important to read and listen with an analytic perspective in order to make wise decisions about our resources and our time. For example,

> Is there something about the way this message looks or sounds that captured your attention?

> How are you reacting to this message and why?

> Is there substance to this message? If so, what is it?

> What are you being asked to do?

INSTRUCTIONS: Consider a recent message that you received through technology, whether it was a "push message" on your mobile device, a compelling YouTube clip, or an advertisement sent to your email. What was your immediate response? How did that message or visual image influence your emotions? Did you immediately make a decision about your next steps? Carefully consider what steps you might take to more critically engage your consumption of messages through technology.

HINDRANCES TO EFFECTIVE LISTENING

Not only should receivers work hard to listen well, but they should also try to avoid some common mistakes in everyday conversation. By actively avoiding some specific behaviors, interpersonal communication can be much more effective for all parties involved. In addition, it may prove helpful to consider your default listening style by taking the self-assessment in Box 5.4. Researchers Watson, Barker, and Weaver describe a few different listening styles that they identify using their Listening Styles Profile.[15] Looking at the shortened and modified version of their scale in Box 5.4, you can see that their items address concerns like frustration and impatience while listening, while also considering the behaviors and emotional connection that people often have while listening to someone else. As you use this excerpt from the Listening Styles Profile, you may be able to discover some of your own predilections that impact your ability to listen, influencing your experience as a listener. These styles may work in concert with—or in opposition to—additional active and passive hindrances to effective listening that we discuss next.

Active Hindrances to Effective Listening

Sometimes people engage in behaviors during a conversation that actively change the context and content of that conversation. These active hindrances to effective listening are often characterized by individuals taking control of an interaction and, in doing so, not paying attention to important information that could have emerged over the course of the conversation. One of the first active hindrances is **conversational narcissism**, in which a participant in an interpersonal interaction keeps changing the topic of conversation to focus attention on himself.[16] Cedric is relatively well-liked because of his amusing anecdotes, but he often leaves interactions feeling like he didn't really get to know his conversational partner. Cedric may not realize the extent to which he tries to change the topic of conversation toward his own experiences in order to set up his next funny story. Although he has crafted a number of entertaining stories, Cedric may not notice that the majority of his interactions follow much the same script.

Conversational Narcissism
Attempting to seek attention by shifting conversational topics to focus attention on the self.

Similar to conversational narcissism, **stage hogs** typically tend to have everyone's attention during an interaction. Unlike conversational narcissists, however, stage hogs may not focus on topics about themselves; stage hogs are happy to simply be the person speaking for the majority of time, talking about whatever the conversational topic may entail. Donald may not know much about a variety of topics, but he certainly has an opinion about each topic and is happy to share it, even if that opinion is newly formed and not well thought-out. If a stage hog loses control of the conversation at any point, she will often engage in **competitive interruption** in order to regain conversational control, interrupting interaction partners with the goal of once again leading or directing the conversation.[17,18]

Stage Hogs
Individuals whose goal is to be the primary or majority speaker in an interpersonal or small-group interaction.

Competitive Interruption
Active attempts to interrupt a conversational partner in order to gain control of the interaction.

In a more extreme listening behavior, sometimes an interpersonal partner seeks to attack or discredit a conversational partner. When an individual approaches an interaction with the goal of trying to find something to criticize or to attack a conversational partner, this form of **ambushing** often causes that listener to ignore or discredit other aspects of the speaker's content.[19] When Jake and Margaret went to their first session of marital counseling, Jake was so hurt by Margaret's infidelity that he only spoke out in order to discredit or embarrass her. The marriage counselor had to completely

Ambushing
An attempt to listen aggressively with the sole goal of finding an opportunity to attack a conversational partner.

BOX 5.6: InterConnect

Listening vs. Hearing: How Can You Remove Barriers?

I n our increasingly complex world, it is difficult to fully engage with every message that we receive in our daily lives. Indeed, if we truly listened to every message that we receive, we would likely have no time to engage in the most basic of daily activities like eating and sleeping. However, sometimes we don't actively engage in the listening process when we likely should, often for a variety of reasons. Consider the following scenarios where people are experiencing barriers to the listening process:

wavebreakmedia/Shutterstock.com

> Stanley loves playing backgammon. He keeps a travel board in his book bag, keeps a game with friends open on his computer desktop, and even plays regularly on a smartphone app with people all over the world. By pseudolistening while playing the game, he pretends to pay attention to his conversation partner by nodding and grunting when appropriate over dinner; however, his online backgammon game is causing him to miss out on the details of his close personal relationships.

> Sukhpreet is obsessed with television. She has a blog and a Facebook group devoted to the latest shows and is constantly getting people to talk about their favorite shows. However, she engages in selective listening and stops paying attention when the conversation moves away from television.

> Jason has had a long day at work. Having spent eight hours straight with his clients, Jason has no desire to engage in yet another interpersonal interaction. Upon arriving home, his neighbor tries to chat with him in the hallway. However, Jason barely goes through the motions because of information overload and the great number of conversations he has had throughout the day.

> Taisia and Janine have always been competitive at work. Even though they are assigned to the same project, they typically hope to find something wrong with a statement or idea that the other person makes in order to appear more important. By engaging in ambushing, Taisia and Janine are missing many good ideas and opportunities to find common ground.

INSTRUCTIONS: Think carefully about each of the scenarios above. In what way do these situations match your own personal experiences? Do you often struggle with giving your full and complete attention to individuals or groups that you have made a part of your life? What steps can you take to overcome some of these barriers to effective listening? Are you attending to the most important messages that you receive? Why or why not?

reframe the conversation and point out the disruptive nature of the comments before Jake was able to listen to Margaret's account of the last couple years of their marriage.

Passive Hindrances to Effective Listening

People don't always intend to ignore or avoid conversational content but may accidentally be unable to process the interaction to the fullest. These passive hindrances to effective listening are often characterized by a preoccupation or a laziness that can be overcome by being aware of some barriers in our everyday interactions.

When an individual has a lot on his mind but wants a conversational partner to think he is paying attention, he often engages in **pseudolistening**. By pretending to pay attention to a conversational partner, that individual is able to think about another topic while still making his partner feel affirmed—at least until that partner realizes that she wasn't receiving the full attention. Chip and Sammy like to talk about their day at school with their father when he returns home from work. As the years have gone by, however, both Chip and Sammy have realized that after a while their father's mind has wandered. Both Chip and Sammy like to then ask permission for things they know they may not otherwise be granted, often resulting in way too many sweets being consumed before dinner. Chip and Sammy both hope this trend continues until high school, when they plan to capitalize on the opportunity for later curfews and more permissiveness than their older siblings enjoyed.

Like pseudolistening, **selective listening** involves reduced attention from a conversational partner. Instead of ignoring all of the content, however, a selective listener focuses almost exclusively on information that she deems interesting or important. When an individual is faced with a situation where she is overwhelmed by the amount of interaction or content that she has experienced at one time, that **information overload** can cause her to engage in both pseudolistening and selective listening in an attempt to reduce conversational input. Unfortunately, much relational information and content is missed when listening is not given the full measure of attention that it deserves.

Pseudolistening
Pretending to pay attention to a conversational partner while actually giving most or all attention to something else entirely.

Selective Listening
Attending only to those parts of a message that are interesting or important to the receiver, ignoring other message content.

Information Overload
Having received a large amount of knowledge, experience, or interaction through face-to-face and mediated means, this situation occurs when a person can no longer take in additional information.

Chapter Summary

Listening is a far more complex process than many imagine. Moving beyond simply hearing or receiving sounds, a careful listener engages and reflects on the words used and the context in which a message is sent. The three different forms of listening (analytic, dialogic, and empathic) are each useful in a variety of situations, and a skilled communicator will be able to employ each type of listening depending on the needs of the context and the desires of the conversation partner. Additionally, good communicators are able to adapt their understanding based on the intent of the message sender, while also managing the competing demands of both internal and external distractions that may threaten to impede the listening process. Good communication involves the skilled sending and receiving of messages, and the communication process breaks down when one or more parties are unable to listen and understand elements of the message sent by an interpersonal partner.

MindTap°   First-Person Video

Mom and Dad Fighting

Apply what you've learned in this chapter by analyzing the "Mom and Dad Fighting" video, using the accompanying questions as a guide. This video and these questions are available online with your MindTap Speech for *Interconnections: Interpersonal Communication Foundations and Contexts.*

MindTap°   Key Terms

Use flashcards to learn key concepts and take a quiz to test your knowledge.

Action	**Critical Listening**	**Noise**
Actionable	**Dialogic Listening**	**Perspective-Taking**
Ambushing	**Empathic Listening**	**Pseudolistening**
Analytic Listening	**Evaluation**	**Reception**
Attention	**Hearing**	**Retention**
Competitive	**Hearing-Impaired**	**Selective Listening**
Interruption	**Information Overload**	**Stage Hogs**
Conversational	**Listening**	
Narcissism	**Multitasking**	

Discussion Questions

1. What is the most compelling part of a message to you? Is there something that is guaranteed to get a quick emotional reaction?

2. Have you ever felt like an interaction partner was only *hearing* what you were saying and not truly *listening*? How did that influence your future interactions?

3. Discuss a time when you have felt like someone truly tried to understand your perspective. How did that make you feel? Were you able to notice one or two things that made you feel "heard"?

4. Think about your close personal relationships. Would you say that you have good empathic interactions with each other?

5. Consider your current interactions with classmates or coworkers. What types of messages are shared between one another? Do you find yourself looking at the ways that you are all similar or noticing and celebrating the differences?

Making Connections

Verbal messages are useless without the attention of an audience. Consider your close interpersonal relationships. How do culture and identity influence your use of verbal messaging?

Chapter Quiz

1. Which of the following elements of effective listening is Tinto engaging after he thinks about a conversation he had with his boss and now formulates and delivers a well-reasoned response?

    a. Attention   d. Action

    b. Reception   e. Retention

    c. Evaluation   f. None of the above

2. Which of the following elements of effective listening is Shaylyn engaging when she puts down her textbook to devote mental energy to the conversation with her mother?

    a. Attention   d. Action

    b. Reception   e. Retention

    c. Evaluation   f. None of the above

3. Simone and Jessica are buying a car that they can share. After visiting used-auto lots, they quickly realize that salespeople are simply to try to get them to make a purchase based on emotion. Simone and Jessica are likely using which of the following types of listening?

    a. Dialogic listening   c. Analytic (critical) listening

    b. Empathic listening   d. None of the above

4. Brady wants to know why his boss behaved in such an abrupt manner last week, and so he and his boss had a long conversation about his boss's goals and motivations. After the interaction, Brady thinks he understands why his boss is stressed, because in his boss's mind Brady is underperforming. Brady has likely used which of the following types of listening?

    a. Dialogic listening   c. Analytic (critical) listening

    b. Empathic listening   d. None of the above

5. Before their conversation on Wednesday, Dario and Erin were unsure of how they wanted their relationship to look. After a long interactive conversation with one another, they feel that they have artfully constructed a shared understanding of their relationship status. In order to have reached such a mutually constructed understanding, both likely engaged in which form of listening?

    a. Dialogic listening   c. Analytic (critical) listening

    b. Empathic listening   d. None of the above

6. T/F When something is "actionable" it can usually be ignored in order to focus on more important parts of a message.

7. T/F When Sharon is perceiving sounds around her in a passive way, she is engaged in "listening."

8. T/F Jardin focuses solely on one thing at a time. In doing so, he is able to devote his attention to a single goal in a process known as multitasking.

9. T/F Pseudolistening is the process of pretending to pay attention by exhibiting such behaviors as nodding, smiling, and direct eye contact.

10. T/F If William is listening to Angelo with the sole intent of attacking something that he says or the way in which he delivers it, William is engaging in "ambushing."

Endnotes

1. Stewart, J., & Logan, C. E. (1998). Together: *Communicating Interpersonally*. Boston, MA: McGraw-Hill.

2. Fleming, S. (1997, February). Leadership for teacher empowerment: The relationship between the communication skills of principals, transformational leadership, and the empowerment of teachers. *Dissertation Abstracts International: Section A, 57*, 3336.

3. Stewart, J., Zediker, K. E., & Witteborn, S. (2012). Empathic and dialogic listening. In J. Stewart (Ed.), *Bridges Not Walls* (11th ed.). New York, NY: McGraw-Hill.

4. Stewart, J., & Logan, C. E. (1998). *Together: Communicating Interpersonally* (pp. 199–200). Boston, MA: McGraw-Hill.

5. Carroll, R. (1990). *Cultural Misunderstandings: The French-American Experience*. Chicago, IL: University of Chicago Press.

6. For a discussion of the impact of mediation, see Gold, L. (1982). The psychological context of the interdisciplinary co-mediation team model in marital dissolution. *Conciliation Courts Review, 20*(2), 45–53. doi:10.1111/j.174-1617.1982.tb00087.x

7. For an overview, see Roy, S., & Shaw, I. S. (Eds.). (2016). *Communicating Differences: Culture, Media, Peace and Conflict Negotiation*. New York, NY: Springer.

8. Rogers, C. (1980). *A Way of Being*. Boston, MA: Houghton Mifflin.

9. Stewart, J., & Logan, C. E. (1998). *Together: Communicating Interpersonally* (pp. 171–177). Boston, MA: McGraw-Hill.

10. Robin, A. L., Martello, J., Foxx, R. M., & Archable, C. (1977). Teaching note-taking skills to underachieving college students. *The Journal of Educational Research, 71*(2), 81–85.

11. Nichols, R. (1948). Factors in listening comprehension. *Quarterly Journal of Speech, 34*, 154–163.

12. For an overview of different approaches to listening, see Watson, K. W., Barker, L. L., & Weaver, J. B. (1995). The Listening Styles Profile (LSP-16): Development and validation of an instrument to assess four listening styles. *International Journal of Listening, 9*(1), 1–13. doi:10.1080/10904018.1995.10499138

13. Bowman, J. M., & Pace, R. C. (2014). Dual-tasking effects on outcomes of mobile communication technologies. *Communication Research Reports, 31*(2), 221–231. doi:10.1080/08824096.2014.907149

14. Watson, K. W., Barker, L. L., & Weaver, J. B. (1995). The Listening Styles Profile (LSP-16): Development and validation of an instrument to assess four listening styles. *International Journal of Listening, 9*(1), 1–13.

15. Ibid.

16. Vangelisti, A. L., Knapp, M. L., & Daly, J. A. (1990). Conversational narcissism. *Communication Monographs, 57*(4), 251–274. doi:10.1080/03637759009376202

17. Rogers, W. T., & Jones, S. S. (1975). Effects of dominance tendencies on floor holding and interruption behavior in dyadic interaction. *Human Communication Research, 1*(2), 113–122.

18. Lee, C. C., Lee, S., & Narayanan, S. S. (2008, September). An analysis of multimodal cues of interruption in dyadic spoken interactions. *INTERSPEECH*, 1678–1681.

19. Rothwell, J. D. (2012). *In Mixed Company: Communicating in Small Groups*. Boston, MA: Cengage Learning.

Monkey Business Images/Shutterstock.com

Shay is proud of her identity, self-described as a "queer woman of color," but she has discovered that other people often mislabel her by assigning meaning to behaviors that she does not intend as communicative. Because she can be reserved around people she does not know, Shay was dismayed to find that one of her group project members, Sid, had referred to her as "an angry black woman." When Shay asked Sid about it, he described a situation in class when the professor made an interesting comment about gay rights: when Shay crossed her arms and leaned back to think about the professor's intent, Sid assumed that Shay was openly expressing discontent and disagreement with the statement, which he considered rude. He also assumed that her blank facial expressions when she walked around campus were caused by feelings of superiority or aggression rather than the simple fact that Shay is painfully shy. After the conversation, Shay was glad to have cleared up the confusion but was upset by the fact that she was forced to have a conversation about these stereotypes yet again. It was frustrating having to fight against the misconceptions that other people had about her before they even took the time to get to know her.

What sorts of first impressions do you bring to a situation?

What assumptions do people automatically make about you before they even hear a word you have to say?

MindTap®

Review the chapter's learning objectives and **start** with a quick warm-up activity.

Learning Objectives

After you finish reading this chapter, you will be able to:

Define nonverbal communication.

Explain the characteristics that distinguish nonverbal and verbal messages.

Identify the common codes of nonverbal communication channels.

List some nonverbal challenges to common intercultural goals.

MindTap®

Read, highlight, and take notes online.

HuntstCck/Getty Images

NONVERBAL COMMUNICATION BASICS

What sorts of first impressions do you bring to a situation? What assumptions do people automatically make about you before they even hear a word you have to say? People create an understanding of other individuals based on characteristics like appearance, mannerisms, and the way that others carry themselves in public—often before they have even spoken a single word. Indeed, nonverbal communication is one of the most powerful ways that messages get sent from one person to another, despite the fact that many of those messages are not intentionally sent.

Nonverbal Communication
Any communicative characteristic or behavior that intentionally or unintentionally conveys a message without the use of verbal language.

Nonverbal communication is defined as any communicative characteristic or behavior that intentionally or unintentionally conveys a message without the use of verbal language (i.e., words). It is important to note that there are many things that people often incorrectly consider "nonverbal" when they are, in fact, special cases of verbal communication. For example, if Avalene were to use her right hand to "karate chop" her open horizontal left palm, wrapping that palm around the attacking hand, she has used American Sign Language (ASL), a verbal system of words that are acted out rather than spoken. If someone who "speaks" ASL observes Avalene making this motion, she will know that Avalene has signed the word *taco* and may be indicating a dinner preference. Because this language has been agreed on by a large group of people and the symbols have been assigned and made formal, ASL is *still* a verbal language even though it is not vocalized. However, if Avalene did not know the word for taco and mimed eating one to try to get someone to understand what she was talking about, this would be a nonverbal display. Scholars have often argued that our ability to create and share meaning through these nonverbal displays are a result of cultural experiences, inherited biological characteristics, and those personal experiences that are typical of most humans.[1]

NONVERBAL COMMUNICATION CHARACTERISTICS

In the preceding American Sign Language example, we were able to think of a few different ways to symbolize a simple delicious food item. What makes one gesture verbal while another is considered nonverbal, particularly since neither involves the use of sound? It may be helpful to consider some key characteristics of nonverbal communication to further enhance our understanding:

- **Nonverbal communication is everywhere**. In most every interpersonal interaction, nonverbal communication is present. From the smiles and eye contact in face-to-face interactions, to one's tone of voice on phone calls, to the use of emoticons in text messages or emails, most every interaction between humans involves some form of nonverbal expression.

- **Nonverbal communication is multichanneled.** We can send a wide range of nonverbal messages using a variety of **channels** at the same time, including the expressions on our face, the sound of our voices, the space we leave between ourselves and our conversational partners, our eye contact, the gestures we use to change our messages, and even the ways we choose to touch (or not touch) our interaction partners. This combination of audio, visual, and tactile messages allows us to convey rich layers of meaning with or without a verbal message.

- **Nonverbal communication channels are processed as a gestalt.** Even more importantly, we process each of these channels as a **gestalt**, which means that our mind puts the nonverbal elements of each channel together and then processes them all as a complete whole in an attempt to discover the underlying intent of the message. Most people even believe these nonverbal behaviors more than verbal messages, resulting in a natural bias to believe nonverbal body language more than a person's words.[2] Should the verbal message be discounted? Is it made stronger by the nonverbal messages? This can only be known by looking at all the components of the communication interaction.

NONVERBAL CODES

There are many different types of nonverbal communication displays, and each subset of nonverbal communication is typically referred to as a **nonverbal code**. Although we typically use many of these same codes at the same time, it is helpful to know the names of the seven most prominent codes separately to make it easy to refer to them throughout the chapter:

- **Appearance.** Understanding the importance placed on first impressions, this code is based mostly on the way that we interpret messages based on the look or shape of various aspects of our bodies and **physiognomy**, including characteristics like clothing, height, eye color, hair length, racial heritage, and level of attractiveness.

- **Kinesics.** Encompassing movements like smiles, waves, and pointing at something important, this code involves motion-based forms of communication like gestures or facial expressions. The name for the code is derived from the idea of "kinetic" motion.

- **Oculesics.** This code focuses on eye behavior like eye contact or gaze. The name is reminiscent of the word "ocular" that you may remember from a high school biology class during a discussion of the eyeball.

- **Proxemics.** Focusing on the complexities of people's use of their immediate environment, this code typically deals with personal space and

Channel
The mechanism through which a message is transmitted, whether using sight, sound, taste, touch, or smell (from Chapter 1).

Gestalt
A whole that is perceived as the combination of the sum of all parts.

Nonverbal Code
A category of communicative behaviors that have been grouped by nonverbal characteristics that they share.

Appearance
The communication code focused on nonverbal messages related to one's visual self-presentation.

Physiognomy
Facial features derived from one's sex and racial heritage (i.e., skin color, eye shape, hair texture, etc.)

Kinesics
The communication code focused on nonverbal messages related to motion-based forms of communication (i.e., gestures or facial expressions).

Oculesics
The communication code focused on nonverbal messages related to eye behavior (i.e., eye contact or gaze).

Andrey_Popov/Shutterstock.com

interpersonal distance, hence a name derived from "proximity" or the distance between two objects.

- **Haptics.** With a wide range of potential behaviors, this code is focused on different forms of touch or physical contact, whether an affectionate hug, a hand of assistance up a staircase, or a violent kick in the rear.

- **Vocalics.** When we change our voice in a wide variety of ways, we are using the vocal code of nonverbal communication. From loudness to tone to pitch to the length of our pauses, there are myriad combinations of ways that we can use our voices to change or enhance the verbal content.

- **Environmental features.** Finally, we may gather information or alter our communication style based on the context in which we find ourselves, including the objects that people place around them or the physical layout of a room.

Physical Appearance

One of the first things we notice about a new acquaintance is the way that he looks, often before that person has a chance to introduce himself. This early impression is often difficult to change once we have formed an understanding of the other person,[3] and these first impressions rarely offer a complete picture of any individual. What sorts of things are we relying on when we form an impression of another person?

Clothing and Artifacts

We use our clothing to send messages about ourselves, both intentionally and unintentionally. A T-shirt may have the name of our school or our favorite sports team, letting others know our preferences and group

Vocalics
The communication code focused on nonverbal messages related to vocal variation (i.e., loudness, tone, pitch, etc.).

Environmental Features
The communication code focused on nonverbal messages that people derive from the physical layout or objects within a particular setting.

membership. Wearing business attire during an interview may indicate a job candidate's preparation and
desire for employment. An individual who is dishev-
eled or is wearing wrinkled clothing may give another
person a clue that he has just woken up, even if it is
the middle of the day. A particular style or brand or
fit may indicate a regional, cultural, or socioeconomic
group affiliation.

Relatedly, **artifacts** are those items that we keep with
us (even though we may not wear them) that have communicative value much like clothing. A politician wanting to appear down-to-earth may choose to order a large
cup of coffee from Dunkin' Donuts rather than drink
her typical demitasse espresso from Starbucks. A new intern may borrow a roommate's leather briefcase to make
a strong first impression on a first morning at an investment capital firm. A child may stop using brightly colored
pencils with large sculpted erasers in an effort to show his older siblings that he
is "all grown up." Our clothes and our artifacts reveal a great deal about us, and
we often attempt to manipulate these revelations to appear more attractive and
competent, or to fit in in a desired way. However, these outside appearances
can be misinterpreted as well, sometimes even sending a message far different
than the one we intend. Some cultural norms may compel funeral attendees in
a particular region to wear all black, but a mourner from a different African culture may unintentionally offend other guests when she wears a bright color in a
personal celebration of the deceased's life.

JohnnyGreig/E+/Getty Images

Artifacts
Items or objects carried or
worn that have intentional or
unintentional communicative
value (e.g., a briefcase in a
professional environment).

Mesomorphs
A body shape characterized
by an athletic build, average
height, and a muscular,
V-shaped torso.

Endomorphs
A body shape characterized
by a rounded shape, shorter
height, and a large amount of
subcutaneous body fat.

Height and Body Shape

Interestingly, people may interpret our character or communication based
on some relatively unchangeable characteristics as well. Taller people are
often ascribed more traditionally masculine characteristics,[4] including stereotypes of assertiveness or leadership. In fact, height
is almost universally prized,[5] with social advantages
given to people solely because they look taller. The
picture is not quite as clear with body shape, however, as gender influences the culture's view of what
is considered more desirable. As seen in the middle
in Figure 6.1, **mesomorphs** are people characterized
by a V-shaped torso, an athletic build, and a moderate amount of body mass (mostly muscle). In North
America, this is often considered the most desired of
male body types, and there is much social pressure
for some men to work to create the illusion of a me-
somorphic body type.[6] As seen on the far right in
Figure 6.1, **endomorphs** are people characterized by
a rounder shape and a larger amount of subcutaneous body fat. Despite the fact that it is possible to be

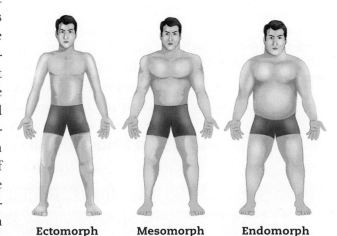

Ectomorph   Mesomorph   Endomorph

FIGURE 6.1
Representative Body Types

BOX 6.1: Communication Currents

Physical Norms in Current Television

Inside Amy Schumer, "Girl, You Don't Need Makeup," http://bit.ly/2n7PBXl

In the controversial Comedy Central television program *Inside Amy Schumer*, the host Amy satirizes and critiques popular culture, body image issues, and the female sex-negative culture that permeates the American television industrial complex. At first glance, much of her work is easy to dismiss as offensive, but a deeper look reveals a decidedly inclusive and egalitarian criticism of popular issues that are often not discussed.

As we watch this clip, Amy uses a "boy band" music video to satirize a falsely feminist perspective on self-presentation. By claiming that girls don't need makeup but being shocked by the results, the video cites the double standards that women often encounter with regard to physical appearance.

INSTRUCTIONS: Watch the video again. What might be initially offensive about the clip? Consider the message source, noting how the clip is challenging norms of physical attraction. What is the message for men in this clip? Is it different from the one for women? How might an understanding of the deeper message of this clip change your perceptions of physical norms?

Ectomorphs
A body shape characterized by a tall, slender shape with lean muscle mass.

quite healthy and fit with an endomorphic shape, cultural stereotypes of endomorphs often imply a slow, lazy, unhealthy set of habits being ascribed to people with this shape.[7] **Ectomorphs** fall on the other end of the spectrum, shown on the far left in Figure 6.1, often describing slender or lean individuals that have the least body mass of the three shapes. The recent North American trend of ectomorphic women serving as fashion models has standardized the ectomorph as "attractive" in our culture, leading many women to go to great lengths of diet/exercise/fashion to create the illusion of this body type, often in unhealthy ways.[8]

Gestures, Facial Expressions, and Eye Contact

Sometimes we can glance at someone and then quickly look away, satisfied that we have learned something important about him during that fleeting moment. Other times, we don't just look at that snapshot of someone's life and make assumptions or interpret messages. A longer

BOX 6.2: InterConnect
....
Body Image and Media Portrayals[9,10]

Every culture reflects a specific set of ideals, whether those ideals have to do with the best career choice, the perfect way to parent a child, or the most desirable location for a vacation. These ideals, in turn, influence what we study in college, whether we spank our children or use a time-out, and how we plan to travel or enjoy a "staycation" during the next long weekend. Cultures also reflect different perspectives on physical appearance, and these perspectives often inform our views on what is attractive among each sex and how we desire our own bodies to look.

Although some individuals may have heard about a great hidden vacation spot from their close group of friends or seen a brand-new parenting tactic at a local playground, many people across contexts watch the same images of physical appearance being championed across a wide range of media programming.

Paying too much attention to media portrayals of body type can often create a sense of dissatisfaction with one's own body type, negatively impacting one's own **body image**, and this sense of dissatisfaction is often pervasive regardless of ethnic groups. Even though there is a great range of body types and beautiful people around the world, media seems to pressure women to be thin and men to be muscular regardless of the type of media portrayed.

Although not every media consumer develops symptoms of extreme eating disorders like anorexia and bulimia, people who already have perceptions of body dissatisfaction seem to be the ones most likely to be impacted by media portrayals of idealized body types. The increased sexualization of these prevailing beauty ideals only serve to cause women and girls to internalize these cultural pressures.

INSTRUCTIONS: Think carefully about what you most want to look like. Feel free to write down the names of a couple famous people if that helps jog your memory. What makes you think that these people are the most attractive? What must they have to do to achieve this standard of beauty? Is it healthy or even possible for you to look like they do? Would changing your body type change your personality or surroundings in a significant way?

window of observation and interaction is necessary for us to believe we have the full picture. What are we observing as we spend this additional time? Often, we are looking at the movements of that person and trying to draw meaning from that movement.

Body Image
The perception that one has about the shape or attractiveness of one's own body, often in relation to a desired ideal.

altrendo images/Getty Images

Rayman/Photodisc/Getty Images

Kinesic Gestures

Over the course of human history, people have derived many different motions and gestures that communicate a message. Some of these gestures stand alone, such as when a referee in the United States holds both arms up in the air to signal a touchdown. Other gestures enhance the meaning of a message, like mimicking the arm movements of a runner when discussing a fast marathoner or holding a thumb and forefinger very close together when talking about the slim chances of getting something. Because there are so many different ways of using motion to send a message, scholars have come up with five main types of kinesic gestures:[11,12]

1. **Illustrators.** These gestures accompany verbal speech and help to illustrate the content of that message. If Alan gets back from a fly-fishing trip and tries to describe the size of a fish to his wife, Jen, he may place his hands a couple feet apart to indicate that it was rather large.

2. **Emblems.** These forms of gestures have a generally agreed-on meaning, but that meaning is not considered verbal. For example, if Stacey turns her head away from a potential suitor and holds her palm up in the guy's face, everyone in the close area knows that she has refused his advances quite clearly without saying a word.

3. **Adaptors.** These gestures communicate information, but often aren't intentionally displayed. Adaptors indicate a person's internal state and often relieve stress for the individual by releasing nervous energy associated with boredom, frustration, excitement, and/or stress. If you are in class right now, you may look around the room and notice quite a few people jiggling their legs up and down under the desk or playing with their hair.[I]

4. **Regulators.** These kinesic gestures simply aid in the regulation of turn-taking among conversational participants. If Stefan finished describing his idea and turned to another member of the group and directed an open palm to her, Stefan is likely indicating that he has finished talking and would now like to hear what she has to say.

5. **Displays of emotion.** These kinesic gestures are sometimes called **affect displays** and describe the facial expressions associated with the emotional experience of the sender. If Hee-Sun bites her lip and widens her eyes as she describes an upcoming half marathon that she plans to run, she has unintentionally let everyone know that she is nervous about next week's race. These displays of emotion are described in greater detail next.

Illustrators
A set of kinesic movements that accompany speech and illustrate message content.

Emblems
A set of kinesic movements that have an agreed-on meaning within a culture.

Adaptors
A set of kinesic movements that indicate a person's internal state by releasing energy, often unintentionally encoded.

Regulators
A set of kinesic movements that aid in the regulation of conversational turn-taking.

Affect Displays
A set of kinesic movements displayed in the face that indicate the sender's emotional experience (i.e., facial expressions).

[I]This is likely due to the excitement associated with this topic.

Facial Expressions

Although we may be relatively limited in the broader categories of basic emotions (with scholars largely only agreeing on seven "pure" human emotions—fear, happiness, anger, sadness, disgust, contempt, and surprise[13]), the potential implications of humans trying to **encode** and **decode** those facial expressions may seem limitless. Add to that complexity the fact that we can both intentionally form facial expressions and unintentionally leak our true emotions through momentary **microexpressions**, and the picture is even further complicated.[14] With approximately 20 muscles in the human face related specifically to emotional expression,[15] the possibilities for sending messages by moving one's facial features are unfathomable. Consider just the mouth alone: If Xochitl wants to convey a deep appreciation for a gift she received from Kory and Bryan, how should she smile? Should her teeth show as she smiles, or should she keep her lips closed? What is the difference between an open mouth smile and one where she just turns up one corner of her mouth? And, to compound matters even further, consider that Xochitl rarely smiles, so any facial expression of warmth may be deeply rewarding to both Kory and Bryan. Add in the mouth movements for anger, disgust, or any other emotion, and it becomes increasingly clear just how complex interpreting facial expressions can be.[16]

Eye Contact and Oculesics

We don't only use our hands when we want to increase meaning for a conversational partner. Many times, our eyes can send messages of interest, admonition, anger, or a wide range of other messages. Monica often talks about the time she first got her fiancée's attention across a crowded room with an intentionally flirtatious period of prolonged eye contact. Tyrone describes how his mother could get him to behave as a child with a single specific look and that to this day he knows he's in trouble if that look ever appears and lasts too long. Emma knows when Mary is listening because Mary keeps eye

Encode
To create a verbal or nonverbal message that represents the sender's idea (i.e., through language/expression/gesture; from Chapter 1).

Decode
To interpret a sender's idea based on a verbal or nonverbal message (from Chapter 1).

Microexpression
The unintentional brief "flash" of a person's emotional experience through facial expressions.

Daxiao Productions/Shutterstock.com

BOX 6.3: iPersonal

Emotion and Technology[17]

Whenever we talk with our close friends or family members, we are able to change or alter our messages by using our facial expressions. By using direct eye contact to convey deep sadness about a loss, or by winking after a sarcastic remark, a conversational partner is able to understand our intent and our attitude as we interact in a face-to-face setting. When we are on the phone, we can at least use our voice to convey similar messages, although we must be careful to send the message clearly since our facial expressions cannot aid our message construction.

In a culture where we often use tweets and text messages to handle much of our interpersonal communication, some may claim that we have lost our ability to express complex emotions. Yet people familiar with these mediated forms of communication seem to experience just as rich interactions as those people that do not rely on such channels. Despite the limitations of a text-based form of communication, people have found ways to share their emotional state through technology.

True Images/Alamy Stock Photo

Do you use **emoticons** or **emojis** in your emails and texts? If so, that smiley face that you put at the end of your message is considered by many to be a nonverbal expression of emotion. By "smiling" at the end of a statement, you are able to convey goodwill and a positive sentiment with just a couple keystrokes. Similarly, you may use a frowny face or a variety of other combinations of symbols and letters to indicate things like laughter, sadness, sarcasm, anger, or a wide variety of other emotional expressions.

As with other forms of nonverbal communication, however, it is important to be intentional and careful in your use of these emotional expressions. If you use too many smiley faces in a professional context you may not be taken seriously, and if you use a winky face with a relatively new contact she may not know whether you are trying to indicate sarcasm or romantic interest. As with all communicative expression, there is great opportunity for misinterpretation of messages.

INSTRUCTIONS: Think carefully about what abbreviations and/or emoticons you use. Make a list of all the possible interpretations of those nonverbal messages, and keep that list by your computer. Be sure to look that list over the next time you use an emoticon, and think of all the possible interpretations of that message. Does the recipient know you well enough to be able to reliably interpret what you intend to convey?

contact as they chat, and William knows his manager doesn't like his idea when his eyes seem to "glaze over" with disinterest. When Alex plays basketball, he tries to "stare down" members of the other team to get them to feel threatened by his skill. Although we can use oculesics like eye contact in many ways,

gaze seems to be most associated with either threat or affection,[18] so it seems clear that there are great opportunities for miscommunication as well. If Helen was singing karaoke and Sienna made prolonged eye contact with her, Helen may feel like she should stop singing when Sienna was actually trying to show support. Bill may remain quiet while traveling on an airplane because the person seated next to him glared menacingly when he sat down, but really that person was hoping to start up a conversation and was looking for an opportunity to introduce himself.

Touch, Space, and Expectations

It is always uncomfortable when someone stands too close. Yet if you are having a conversation with someone from across the room, he often seems uninvolved or emotionally inaccessible. When we like or admire a person, we are often more willing to let her shake our hands warmly or put an arm around our shoulder. However, if we find someone annoying or creepy or repulsive, we are often unwilling to touch that person at all. What is the appropriate distance to stand from an unknown other, and how do we know when we are supposed to touch that person or when that touch will be seen as offensive? Although there is no "correct" answer to these questions, there are some norms and guidelines for our use of both **haptics** and **proxemics** in interpersonal interactions.

Proxemics

Personal space is a general term used to describe the portable egg-shaped distance around our body that we consider ourselves "owning," as seen in Figure 6.2, but our use of proxemic space is much more complex than just that. To be sure, rather than just one region of personal space, scholars have identified four specific zones wherein specific culturally based rules and norms govern each.[19] The following four zones include an approximate numerical range of distance as measured in North America; that distance can vary according to the cultural norms of each location elsewhere around the world.

1. **Intimate distance (0–18 inches).** This range of distance for North Americans includes actual contact to very close interpersonal distances, and as such few people are allowed in one's intimate zones. Typically, it is reserved for romantic partners or very close family members or exceptional friends. In this distance, you are aware of a person using all of your senses: you can hear his whispers and the sounds he creates by small movements, feel his body heat, smell his cologne and hygiene, see him in great detail, and easily touch him if you so desire. Because of this strong ability to influence behaviors, people are incredibly protective of the region of their intimate distance.

2. **Personal-casual distance (18 inches–4 feet).** This range for North Americans includes interaction partners with whom you have had previous interactions. The closer side of the personal-casual distance is typically reserved for closer friends and family and is where private interactions occur. The further region of the zone is where casual acquaintances typically tend to interact, and the increased distance causes interactions to be slightly more public in nature.

Emoticon
A "nonverbal" symbol used in text-based channels to represent emotions or facial expressions (i.e., an emotion icon) or alter the meaning of a message (e.g., using ;) to indicate a wink).

Emoji
A small graphic image used in text-based channels to nonverbally alter the meaning of a message (e.g., using ☺ to indicate happiness).

Gaze
An intentional form of eye contact that is steady and unbroken.

Haptics
The communication code focused on nonverbal messages related to touch or other forms of physical contact.

Proxemics
The communication code focused on nonverbal messages related to personal space and interpersonal distance.

Intimate Distance
A range of distance from one's body, typically 0 to 18 inches, that is reserved for very close interaction partners (i.e., family and romantic partners).

Personal-Casual Distance
A range of distance from one's body, typically 18 to 48 inches, that is reserved for friends and acquaintances.

FIGURE 6.2
The Shape of Personal Space

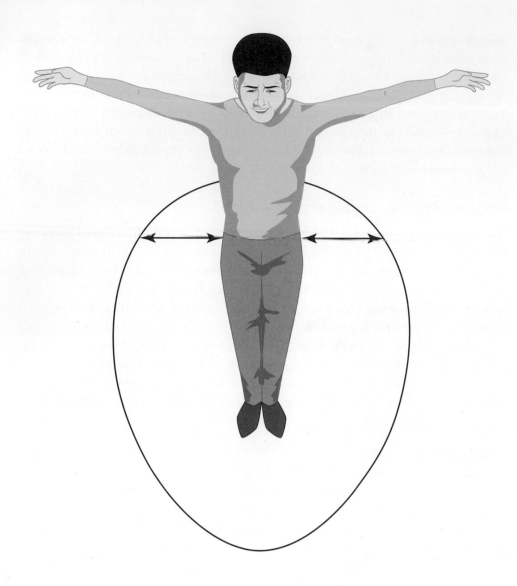

Social-Consultative Distance
A range of distance from one's body, typically 4 to 8 feet, that is where most interaction with unknown others occurs.

3. **Social-consultative distance (4–8 feet).** This distance is typically where North American business transactions occur (from corporate mergers to buying coffee from a barista) or social encounters between unknown others. Although the interaction in this zone may be quite enjoyable, it is often not personal or unique in nature. Because you typically can't reach out and touch a person that is four or more feet away, the association with these nonintimate relationships is believed to be the origin of the phrase "keeping someone at arm's length."

Public Distance
A range of distance from one's body, typically beyond 8 feet, wherein personal interaction is not necessary and unknown others are given access.

4. **Public distance (8 or more feet).** The public distance is where individuals allow most unknown others free passage. If someone is going to interact with another person in her public distance, often that interaction is somewhat more formal, and can even be open for observation or comment from other noninteractants. People in each other's public distances are typically not focusing solely on that other person, so conversational involvement and engagement are often reduced as other stimulants in the environment can distract participants.

Burlingham/ShutterStock.com

Haptics

The use of touch is also quite easy to misconstrue. Like eye contact, haptic touch is a primary means of communicating both affection and threat.[20] If Jake and his girlfriend, Shondra, are socializing with her coworkers for the first time, when she places her hand on his forearm, she might be trying to tell him something. Jake must immediately try to determine whether Shondra is trying to warn him that he'll be in trouble if he continues telling the joke he has started or whether Shondra is instead letting him know how happy she is that he is making such an effort to be relatable. In fact, there are so many different types of touch that scholars have focused their efforts on describing five main broad categories of touching behaviors:[21]

Sarah Edwards/WENN Ltd/Alamy Stock Photo

1. **Functional/professional.** These types of touch are the least intimate, characterized by one-sided touches needed to perform some task. For example, when Cheyenne is touched while receiving a manicure or when Stan gets a haircut from his barber, they have both experienced functional/professional forms of touch.

2. **Social/polite.** The most rule-governed of the forms of touches, social/polite touch is often characterized by implicit rules within a culture. For example, Bryn almost instinctively knows how long to shake hands during a job interview, and the touch is done out of a sense of obligation and ritual.

3. **Friendship/warmth.** People who know each other relatively well often engage in this type of touch. Typically occurring in public settings, these forms of touch convey

BOX 6.4: Let's Get INTRApersonal

The Touch Avoidance Measure[22, 23]

D o you think of yourself as "touchy-feely"? Do you have a hard time expressing affection to the people around you? Although we may never completely understand our motivations or experiences, sometimes it is helpful to think about the situations in which you do or don't feel comfortable with touch, or perhaps the characteristics of kinds of people you are willing to touch or let yourself be touched by. In 1978 scholars were curious whether people had patterns associated with their touch behavior. Use this self-assessment to start thinking about how you use touch in your daily life. This survey is a modified and shortened version of a survey created by the original researchers (Andersen & Leibowitz, 1978) to look at individual touch behavior.

INSTRUCTIONS: Think carefully about your general feelings about touching and being touched. Then write the number that shows how much you agree or disagree with the statements below. It may seem repetitive, but stick with it! At the end, you'll be able to calculate your own willingness to engage in interpersonal touch!

1	2	3	4	5
Strongly Disagree	Disagree	Undecided	Agree	Strongly Agree

_____ 1. A hug from a same-sex friend is a true sign of friendship.

_____ 2. Opposite-sex friends enjoy it when I touch them.

_____ 3. I often put my arm around friends of the same sex.

_____ 4. I find it easy to be touched by a member of the other sex.

_____ 5. People shouldn't be so uptight about touching people of the same sex.

_____ 6. I like it when members of the opposite sex touch me.

_____ 7. I wish I were free to show emotions by touching members of the same sex.

_____ 8. I am comfortable kissing relatives of the opposite sex.

Add up the total score. Is it high? Low? The lowest score you can get is an 8, and the highest score you can get is a 40. Lower scores mean that you are more likely to avoid engaging in touch, while higher scores mean you are relatively comfortable with touch.

Now, add up the total score for the odd-numbered questions and the even-numbered questions separately. Is one higher than the other? A lower score on the odd-numbered questions means you are more likely to avoid touch from members of the same sex. A lower score on the even-numbered questions means you are more likely to avoid touch from members of the opposite sex. The lowest score you can get is a 4, and the highest score you can get is a 20.

What does this tell you about your own touch behaviors? Are you surprised by the results?

caring or interest. A high five between friends on the playing field or a pat on the back during a funeral are good examples of friendship/warmth touches.

4. **Love/intimacy.** This type of touch is highly regulated, as it must be received from a close relational partner for it to be perceived positively. No matter how well intentioned Greg may be, if he uses love/intimacy with a nonintimate he is most likely going to be unwelcome in future interactions and may make both parties feel uncomfortable.

5. **Sexual arousal.** This type of touch is reserved for the most intimate interactions and is often perceived as quite intense. For an example of this type of touch, it may be best if you consult another type of publication.

As can be seen in the preceding sections, the functions of both touch and interpersonal distance have been carefully categorized by scholars. Still, the practical question of *using* both touch and interpersonal distance remains. As we can see in Box 6.4, scholar Peter Andersen (2005)[24] conceptualized a way to determine our own unique perspective on touch, with questions focusing on our attitudes toward touch and whether we enjoy being touched. Look at the questions in Box 6.4 to consider how your culture and personal experience has influenced your attitudes toward touch. Are you touch-avoidant? Depending on your experience, you may feel that certain touch behaviors are normal, while others may seem taboo. How do we know what behaviors are acceptable and what behaviors are frowned on in our culture? Fortunately, there is a general understanding of the impact of these nonverbal behaviors that has been outlined in expectancy violation theory that may shed some light on this concern.

Expectancy Violation Theory

In early research on nonverbal codes, scholars realized that there was no clear, easy set of rules that seemed to govern any individual person's reaction to the use of touch or space. Even more significantly, often that person's reaction to touch or space changed depending on the person with whom she was interacting. In formulating **expectancy violation theory**,[25] Burgoon was able to highlight some key characteristics of interaction partners that appear to govern interactions between known and unknown others.

We all know—generally—what we must do to be considered "normal" within our own culture. Although the specifics may remain less clear, certain things seem obvious. Even young children know not to karate chop people in the throat when they first meet them, and it is unwise to celebrate a year of working together by throwing one's coffee all over the other's new outfit. If it is commonly assumed that there are normative rules that we must follow to be considered competent communicators, then it would seem that any

Expectancy Violation Theory
Burgoon's theory that unexpected behaviors cause us to evaluate and assign valence to the nature of our relationship with interaction partners.

©Sebastian Gauert /Shutterstock.com

Jul ▪ Velychko/ShutterStock.com

Valence
The degree of positivity or negativity that we assign to a particular person or relationship.

deviation from that set of "appropriate" behaviors would be viewed rather negatively, causing recipients to view the other more negatively.

However, it seems that this is not always the case because there are a few characteristics that must be taken into account. If we have a certain view of another person—either a positive or negative **valence**—and he does something that is considered relatively nonnormative, we then begin to think about the nature of our relationship and change our perceptions accordingly. If Chara has positive feelings for—perhaps even a crush on—Jim, if he does something out of character that Chara is likely to enjoy (like giving Chara a huge hug the next time that he sees her at a local campus coffee shop), then Chara may grow to like Jim even more. However, if Chara really dislikes Benjamin *and he does the exact same thing*, Chara will likely find herself even more repulsed by Benjamin and think of him as a "creeper."

As such, expectancy violation theory proposes that we should behave as expected *unless* we know that we are liked or viewed positively by the recipient of that behavior. If the behavior is likely to be viewed positively as well, then engaging in that behavior (e.g., physical contact, close interpersonal distance, extended eye contact, a large smile) is likely to have a positive impact on that person's evaluation of us. (Please be aware, however, that if you don't know what the other person thinks about you, it is a huge gamble!)

Vocal Characteristics and Communication Accommodation

When we think about using our voices, it is easy to assume that we vocalize messages in whatever way feels natural, and that the voice is simply a method of delivering a verbal message. Surprisingly, it is our nonverbal vocal characteristics that may most influence how a message is received. Consider sarcasm, for example: when people use the phrase "I hate you!" they could be actually expressing a very positive emotion; Sarah screamed, "I hate you so much!" after walking in on an elaborate surprise party in her honor, but the tone of voice made it clear that she was ecstatic to be the guest of honor and was incredibly thankful for her friends' efforts. We can use our voice to change a message's meaning, or we can even use our voices to put someone at ease or to indicate deep affection.

Paralanguage
Nonverbal behaviors that modify or intensify the meaning of a verbal message.

Because our nonverbal vocal characteristics so often modify a verbal message, vocalics are often considered a **paralanguage** because they occur "alongside language" and modify or intensify the meaning of the verbal message. If someone describing his upcoming college graduation said "Yeah, I suppose you could say I'm somewhat excited...," it could be taken in very different ways. Clearly, if it was spoken loudly, quickly, and with warm tones, we would

BOX 6.5: InterFace

Nonverbal Engagement with Diverse Others[26, 27, 28]

We can't always clearly define love, but we know it when we feel it. Similarly, we don't always know the right distance to keep apart from another person as we interact, but we are certainly aware of when it feels right or when it feels wrong. Fascinatingly, that distance may change depending on our own experiences and the culture in which we find ourselves. Our ethnic heritage, our regional differences, our religious background, and a wide variety of other factors may influence how close we are willing to interact with one another.

Within the United States, we find that people are more willing to stand closer or even touch as we move further south and further west. Someone from, say, San Diego, is much more likely to be comfortable with close interactions than, say, someone from Boston. However, we can't make a comfortable bet that everyone in San Diego is touchy-feely or that New Englanders will automatically shun contact. Indeed, a wide variety of other characteristics may influence our willingness to interact closely.

ERIC LAFFORGUE/Corbis Documentary/Getty Images

People of Latin, Mediterranean, or Middle Eastern ancestry typically are more likely to interact closely, while those of Northern European, Asian, or Indian descent tend to prefer more personal space. Indeed, there is a wide variety of difference in interaction just based on one's cultural background even within a specific region or life stage. In the United States, children of African ancestry tend to interact more closely than children of Northern European ancestry, a pattern that reverses as they move to adulthood.

What else may influence our personal interaction distance? If your religious background discourages close contact with members of the opposite sex, then you are unlikely to interact in such a manner. If your parents or caregiver encouraged deference to your elders, then you may afford older people a larger bubble of personal space than you may with your peers. If you tend to come from a culture that gives great respect to people of authority, then you may be less likely to directly approach a faculty member when you see her on campus.

As we learned with expectancy violation theory in this chapter, the safest bet is to behave in a way that most people would find acceptable. If you find yourself in a situation where you are very dissimilar to most others, watch the people around you and how closely they interact with one another. Become a student of observation, even taking notes if that is helpful. Then, try to mimic the most common nonverbal distances in a safe, respectful manner. You may be surprised at how quickly you "fit in."

be inclined to think that the speaker was attempting to indicate a great level of excitement despite his muted choice of words. However, the same phrase could be spoken hesitantly and relatively quietly to indicate a thoughtful contemplation and perhaps an apprehension about what is coming after college.

BOX 6.6: **Commendable Connections**

Ethics and Communication Accommodation[29]

Emily is a transplant to the Northeast from her native Tennessee and she is attempting to get on her boss's good side because she wants increased hourly wages for herself and all of her coworkers who are struggling to live off of their meager income. She knows her employer has a strong connection to his own southern heritage, so Emily accentuates her slight drawl and makes minor adjustments to her clothing style to reflect her southern roots. Noticing that her boss also speaks relatively slowly and quietly, she has even begun to do the same in order to seem more similar to him. Her coworkers have begun to notice her efforts and are amazed at the transformation in her workplace demeanor. Emily plans to ask her boss about a raise for everyone next week.

How much is too much change? There is a fine line between making small adjustments in your communication pattern and trying to become a different person. As we interact with people around us, we know that small accommodations to the speech patterns and behaviors of the other are likely to get them to pay attention to us and to increase the effectiveness of our messages. However, many people feel uncomfortable with the idea that you can become a different person when you interact with different types of people. At what point does this accommodation become manipulation?

One helpful consideration around the issue of the ethics of accommodation has to do with the intent of the message sender. If a message is sent in the best interest of the other person, is it acceptable to try to be as persuasive as possible? If a persuasive attempt will allow the message sender to accomplish some social good—or to gain personally—does that eventual outcome excuse that person's unnatural behavior?

INSTRUCTIONS: If you were her coworker, what advice would you give Emily? Do you think her behavior is justified? All of us have at some time made adjustments in our communication style—whether small or large—depending on the situation that we may find ourselves. Consider a time when you may have done something like Emily is doing as she communicates with her boss. What changes did you make in your communication style? Did you make the right choice in accommodating your behaviors?

Vocal Characteristics

Vocalics are common, and people are typically quite comfortable with varying these nonverbal communication behaviors as they deliver a message. Scholars[30,31] have identified a wide range of vocal behaviors, and we highlight the most commonly discussed vocal characteristics here:

Rate
The vocalic designation for the speed at which a person speaks.

1. **Rate.** The speed at which a person speaks, ranging from very slow to very fast. As discussed in the following, cultural norms of speech rate may vary depending on region or location.

Rhythm
The vocalic designation for the cadence or musicality of one's voice.

2. **Rhythm.** The cadence of one's speech, sometimes thought of as the musicality of voice.

Win McNamee/Getty Images

3. **Pitch.** The high or low sound of one's voice, often associated with gender roles; men are more likely to speak with a deep masculine voice after puberty, while women often affect a high feminine voice.

4. **Loudness.** Ranging from a barely audible whisper to a shout, people can change the loudness of their speech with relative ease. Interestingly, loudness is often context specific. A whisper during a church service may seem louder than a shout across the room at a lively concert.

5. **Accent.** A wide range of factors influence the different ways that the same words may be spoken. Sherri lived in Texas for a few years, so she may add a hint of an "r" to the word *wash*, leading to confusion when she asks someone where she can "warsh" her hands.

6. **Vocal fillers (sometimes called vocal segregates and vocalized pauses).** When people are speaking but need time to find a word or think about what they want to say next, they often vocalize, using sounds like "um," "uh," "ah," and "er." These vocal fillers allow the speaker to hold her place in the conversation while considering her next thought.

Communication Accommodation Theory

Scholars have discovered that people often intentionally alter their use of vocalics, whether consciously or subconsciously. In order to better facilitate the flow of conversation, people will often match their use of vocalics to the people around them through a process known as **speech convergence**, particularly if both parties have positive regard for one another or if the parties have high reward value(s). (Alternately, parties with negative regard for one another can conversely engage in the process known as **speech divergence.) Communication accommodation theory**[32] proposes that these minor shifts allow conversational partners to develop a

Pitch
The vocalic designation for the high or low sound of one's voice.

Loudness
The vocalic designation for the ease/ability of one's voice to be heard at increasing distance.

Accent
A catchall vocalic designation for a wide variety of linguistic factors that influence a pattern of ways that words may be spoken.

Vocal Fillers
The vocalic designation for sounds used to fill pauses or empty spaces by a speaker (i.e., vocal segregates or vocalized pauses).

Vocal Segregates
See Vocal Fillers.

Vocalized Pauses
See Vocal Fillers.

Speech Convergence
The conscious or subconscious alteration of vocal characteristics to make speech more similar to that of desirable conversational partners.

Speech Divergence
The conscious or subconscious alteration of vocal characteristics to make speech less similar to undesirable conversational partners.

Communication Accommodation Theory
Giles's theory that people alter their use of vocalics in specific communication contexts, becoming more similar in their use of vocalics with desirable conversational partners (i.e., speech convergence) and less similar with undesirable conversational partners (i.e., speech divergence).

WAYHOME studio/Shutterstock.com

feeling of closeness with one another, as well as a sense of identification that they belong to the same group.[33]

Chester and Billy Ray are two very different people from opposite ends of the country, and they have been paired with one another as college roommates. Initially, Chester may notice that Billy Ray talks quite slowly, even though Billy Ray may consider that rate of conversation to be normal. Billy Ray, however, believes that Chester talks too fast and is difficult to understand as a result. However, over time as they get closer and closer, they may find that it is much easier to interact; although they assume that they have developed a skill set associated with simply understanding each other better, speech convergence implies that they may have actually ended up speaking at a very similar rate when they are together. Have you noticed this similar pattern for rate, loudness, speed, or accent in any of your own personal experiences? Regardless of the different groups or cultures of which we consider ourselves a part, we may be surprised to find that we have been strongly influenced to use vocalics in a specific way and that we may change those vocalics when we encounter the vocal characteristics of dissimilar others.

INTERCULTURAL CHALLENGES AND NONVERBAL COMMUNICATION

One difficult situation arises when we don't actually know how we are supposed to behave in a specific situation. Sure, it is easy to look at the patterns and behaviors of those around us and make inferences, but real-time encoding of nonverbal communication is somewhat more complicated when we are interacting with someone from a different culture or group membership.

Although we may construct a message that seems very clearly to mean something relatively obvious, we have to remember that we are encoding that message based on our experience within *our* culture. The recipient of that message may be decoding that same message in a very different way depending on *his* own cultural experience.[34] The difficulty of these two frames of reference is particularly highlighted when considering nonverbal communication, which is often learned through one's own cultural experience.

For example, the same gesture may have wildly different meanings across a variety of cultures. In North America, people use the "OK" hand sign to indicate a neutral or positive emotion; that same gesture in South America has an incredibly negative connotation, and the misunderstanding created by that cultural difference has been well documented.[35] If you have ever gone to shake someone's hand and she has refused, claiming she "doesn't shake hands," then you have likely felt some sense of disconnect. Why might someone not shake hands with a relatively unknown other? Culture may dictate that physical touch is reserved for close friends or business associates. Perhaps religion dictates that people of opposite sexes should not touch. Maybe the person is simply ill and so we are reading too much into it!

Glowimages/Glowimages/Getty Images

Cultural attitudes about some nonverbal codes may also reflect the values that people place on interactions or even a state of being. If we are able to notice the items or behaviors to which people give attention, then we may gain insight into some underlying cultural attitudes about an important characteristic of that culture. For example, North Americans are well documented in their general concern for their own body smell, managing or covering "offensive" odors to a much greater extent than most other cultures.[36] This may reflect broader attitudes toward a North American understanding of personal space and use of touch[37]; after all, if you aren't near it you can't smell it! Such an attitude toward natural body odors becomes entrenched in one culture yet is unnoticed or irrelevant in another culture, reflecting the outcome of different cultural sensitivities and attitudes that influence how we communicate with one another. Regardless, using nonverbal communication with people of different cultures can lead to increased understanding, even though decoding intercultural messages may prove quite complicated.

BOX 6.7: **InterConnect**

Self-Presentation and Putting Your Best Foot Forward

All this talk about nonverbal communication can make us feel a little concerned. After all, the multichanneled nature of nonverbal communication may be overwhelming. Are there any tips for how to appear to be a more competent communicator?

Luckily, we can use theory from this chapter to inform our own decisions. If you know someone likes you and you want them to like you more, expectancy violation theory helps you understand that you can feel free to do unexpected things—within reason—as long as those behaviors are likely to be viewed positively by the other person. If we don't know whether the person likes us—or we are aware that he doesn't like us—we should try to follow the norms and expectations of our culture.

If we are interacting with someone from a different culture who communicates very differently than we do, one way to put that person at ease and to facilitate an easier flow of conversation may be to subtly shift our vocal characteristics to be slightly more similar than different.

Some people may be tempted to think that this sort of conversational adaptation is a form of manipulation. However, it is important to note that all competent communicators adapt to their communication environment and audience. These theories help us to do the same with our nonverbal communication codes and channels.

Let's spend a little time reflecting on our communication patterns. Feel free to journal or jot down some notes on a separate piece of paper. How do you present yourself? What do people likely think when they first see you from afar? When they first interact with you?

What is your "best foot forward"? Based on your understanding of your culture and the people you surround yourself with, what do you think are the rules and expectations that they bring to each communication interaction?

Chapter Summary

Although people often use language to communicate important messages to each other, much of our communication is influenced by our nonverbal communication behaviors. Without relying on verbal language, nonverbal communication can alter or intensify a message, or can serve as the entire message in and of itself. In movies, when one person winks at another the audience knows exactly what message was intended to be sent, whether the winker was trying to indicate sarcasm or romantic interest. However, have you ever been winked at in a public setting and wondered if the person is flirting, joking, or just trying to get something out of her contact lens? As we learned in this chapter, nonverbal communication is much more complicated to interpret than a simple Hollywood-style wink. In all contexts, in all situations, nonverbal communication is being used. We are encoding and decoding messages—both intentional and unintentional—from a variety of communication channels within each and every interaction. Instead of relying on just one of those communication channels, we process all of them at once as a whole as we make judgment calls as to which channel is more or less important. Think of how complicated this experience must be, as we process our interaction partner's facial expressions, use of personal space, eye contact, movements and touch, and various vocal characteristics as we try to infer meaning.

Luckily, two key theories give us insight into how we can successfully manage our own nonverbal communication. Burgoon's expectancy violation theory helped us to see how unexpected behaviors cause people to evaluate the nature of the relationship based on valence, so unless we know that the other person evaluates us positively and won't dislike the unexpected behavior we should probably try to follow social norms. Giles's communication accommodation theory demonstrated that subtle shifts in nonverbal communication style can help others see us as more similar or more different, influencing their perception of the interaction and participants. Our interpersonal relationships are formed and shaped by more than just the words we use. Indeed, nonverbal communication may be the most fundamental method of human communication within our close relationships.

First-Person Video   MindTap®

Friends of the Roommate Meet

Apply what you've learned in this chapter by analyzing the "Friends of the Roommate Meet" video, using the accompanying questions as a guide. This video and these questions available online with your MindTap Speech for *Interconnections: Interpersonal Communication Foundations and Contexts.*

Key Terms   MindTap®

Accent	**Ectomorphs**	**Gestalt**
Adaptors	**Emblems**	**Haptics**
Affect Displays	**Emoji**	**Illustrators**
Appearance	**Emoticon**	**Intimate Distance**
Artifacts	**Encode**	**Kinesics**
Body Image	**Endomorphs**	**Loudness**
Channel	**Environmental**	**Mesomorphs**
Communication	**Features**	**Microexpression**
Accommodation	**Expectancy Violation**	**Nonverbal Code**
Theory	**Theory**	**Nonverbal**
Decode	**Gaze**	**Communication**

Use flashcards to learn key concepts and take a quiz to test your knowledge.

Oculesics
Paralanguage
Personal-Casual
    Distance
Physiognomy
Pitch
Proxemics

Public Distance
Rate
Regulators
Rhythm
Social-Consultative
    Distance
Speech Convergence

Speech Divergence
Valence
Vocal Fillers
Vocal Segregates
Vocalics
Vocalized Pauses

Discussion Questions

1. Think of a time when you got in trouble as a child. How did you know that you were going to be punished? What was it about your caregiver's, coach's, or teacher's body language that clued you in?

2. Which of the nonverbal codes do you most rely on to send a message? Do you use touch or facial expressions, perhaps gestures to accompany a speech? Do different codes matter more or less depending on the context?

3. Do you text message or use a mobile chat to communicate with your friends? If so, think about (or even look at) the emoticons and/or abbreviations that you use. When do you find yourself wanting to use them? Why?

4. How do you think you appear to others as a first impression? What do you do in order to try to appear that way? Is there anything you wish you could change about the first impression that you make?

5. Think about someone famous that you admire and perhaps want to be more like. Are there any mannerisms or patterns of speech that you have picked up from them? Would your friends or family say that you have things in common with that famous person?

Making Connections

Nonverbal messages influence our daily lives, and we ascribe positive and negative evaluations to the interactions we have with people around us. Consider expectancy violation theory from this chapter. How do our individual identities (discussed in Chapter 2) influence our evaluation of the people around us? How does our culture (from Chapter 3) influence our understanding of what is normative or expected?

Chapter Quiz

1. Which of the following channels of communication can be used to communicate nonverbally?

   a. Sight
   b. Sound
   c. Taste

   d. Touch
   e. None of the above
   f. All of the above

2. Which of the following nonverbal codes deals with personal space?

    a. Kinesics   d. Appearance

    b. Proxemics   e. Oculesics

    c. Haptics   f. Vocalics

3. Which of the following nonverbal codes deals with the use of touch?

    a. Kinesics   d. Appearance

    b. Proxemics   e. Oculesics

    c. Haptics   f. Vocalics

4. When we carry something with us that sends a message to others, which of the following terms describes that object?

    a. Communicand   d. Relic

    b. Artifact   e. Tome

    c. Gaze   f. None of the above

5. Varnce is lifting weights regularly and taking extra protein to try to get a muscular physique. Which of the following body types does Varnce likely want to emulate?

    a. Ectomorph   d. Endomorph

    b. Mesomorph   e. All of the above

    c. Kinemorph   f. None of the above

6. Which of the following types of kinesic would Chester use to describe the size of the giant rabbit he saw in his family's yard?

    a. Affect display   d. Ideograph

    b. Illustrator   e. Adaptor

    c. Baton   f. None of the above

7. T/F Nonverbal communication includes only those communication characteristics that accompany verbal language.

8. T/F If Chase knows that Steffie likes him, and he knows that Steffie enjoys flowers, Chase may unexpectedly give Steffie flowers. Burgoon's expectancy violation theory predicts that Steffie will probably like Chase even more.

9. T/F We are processing nonverbal communication as a gestalt when we separately look at each communication channel on its own.

10. T/F Even when people come from different cultures, they correctly decode nonverbal cues as the message encoder intended.

Endnotes

1. Ekman, P., & Friesen, W. V. (1969). The repertoire of nonverbal behavior: Categories, origins, usage, and coding. *Semiotica, 1*, 49–98.

2. Afifi, W. (2007). Nonverbal communication. In B. B. Whaley & W. Samter (Eds.), *Explaining Communication: Contemporary Theories and Exemplars,* (p. 39). London: Routledge.

3. Ambady, N., & Skowronski, J. J. (2008). *First Impressions.* New York, NY: Guilford.

4. Judge, T. A., & Cable, D. M. (2004). The effects of physical height on workplace success and income: Preliminary test of a theoretical model. *Journal of Applied Psychology, 89,* 428–441.

5. For a review, see Knapp, M. L., & Hall, J. A. (2010). *Nonverbal Communication in Human Interaction*. Boston, MA: Cengage Learning.

6. Michaels, M. S., Parent, M. C., & Moradi, B. (2013). Does exposure to muscularity-idealizing images have self-objectification consequences for heterosexual and sexual minority men? *Psychology of Men & Masculinity, 14*(2), 175–183.

7. For an overview of both past and recent literature, see Politano, G. M., & Politano, P. M. (2011). The obesity epidemic and current perceptions of somatotypes by children. *North American Journal of Psychology, 13*(3), 349–358.

8. Strife, S. R., & Rickard, K. (2011). The conceptualization of anorexia: The pro-ana perspective. *Affilia: Journal of Women & Social Work, 26*(2), 213–217.

9. Ferguson, C. J. (2013). In the eye of the beholder: Thin-ideal media affects some, but not most, viewers in a meta-analytic review of body dissatisfaction in women and men. *Psychology of Popular Media Culture, 2*(1), 20–37.

10. Vandenbosch, L., & Eggermont, S. (2012). Understanding sexual objectification: A comprehensive approach toward media exposure and girls' internalization of beauty ideals, self-objectification, and body surveillance. *Journal of Communication, 62*(5), 869–887.

11. For a review of a portion of the functional approach, see Andersen, P. A. (1999). *Nonverbal Communication: Forms and Functions*. Mountain View, CA: Mayfield.

12. For a review of the full functional approach, see Burgoon, J. K., Buller, D. B., & Woodall, W. G. (1996). *Nonverbal Communication: The Unspoken Dialogue*. New York, NY: McGraw-Hill.

13. Ekman, P. (2003). *Emotions Revealed: Recognizing Faces and Feelings to Improve Communication and Emotional Life*. New York, NY: Times Books.

14. For an overview, see Ekman, P. (2009). Lie catching and microexpressions. In C. Martin (Ed.), *The Philosophy of Deception* (pp. 118–133). London: Oxford University Press.

15. Waller, B. M., Vick, S., Parr, L. A., Bard, K. A., Pasqualini, M. C. S., Gothard, K. M., & Fuglevand, A. J. (2006). Intramuscular electrical stimulation of facial muscles in humans and chimpanzees: Duchenne revisited and extended. *Emotion, 6*(3), 367–382.

16. Interestingly, facial hair can also impact the evaluation of a communicator. For additional discussion of this further nuance, see Dixson, B. J. W., & Rantala, M. J. (2016). The role of facial and body hair distribution in women's judgments of men's sexual attractiveness. *Archives of Sexual Behavior, 45*(4), 877–889. doi:10.1007/s10508-015-0588-z

17. Lo, S. (2008). The nonverbal communication functions of emoticons in computer-mediated communication. *CyberPsychology & Behavior, 11*, 595–597. doi:10.1089/cpb.2007.0132

18. For an overview, see Argyle, M., & Cook, M. (1976). *Gaze and Mutual Gaze*. Cambridge, UK: Cambridge University Press.

19. Hall, E. T. (1959). *The Silent Language*. Garden City, NY: Doubleday.

20. Argyle, M., & Cook, M. (1976). *Gaze and Mutual Gaze*. Cambridge, UK: Cambridge University Press.

21. Heslin, R. (1974, May). *Steps toward a Taxonomy of Touching*. Paper presented at the annual convention of the Midwestern Psychological Association, Chicago.

22. Andersen, P. A. (2005). The touch avoidance measure. In V. Manusov (Ed.), *The Sourcebook of Nonverbal Measures: Going beyond Words* (pp. 57–65). Mahwah, NJ: Lawrence Erlbaum.

23. Andersen, P. A., & Leibowitz, K. (1978). The development and nature of the construct touch avoidance. *Environmental Psychology and Nonverbal Behavior, 3*, 89–106.

24. Andersen, P. A. (2005). The touch avoidance measure. In V. Manusov (Ed.), *The Sourcebook of Nonverbal Measures: Going beyond Words* (pp. 57–65). Mahwah, NJ: Lawrence Erlbaum.

25. Burgoon, J. K. (1978). A communication model of personal space violations: Explication and an initial test. *Human Communication Research, 4*, 129–142.

26. Halberstadt, A. G. (1985). Race, socioeconomic status and nonverbal behavior. In A. W. Siegman & S. Feldstein (Eds.), *Multichannel Integrations of Nonverbal Behavior*. Hillsdale, NJ: Lawrence Erlbaum.

27. Burgoon, J. K., Buller, D. B., Woodall, W. G. (1996). *Nonverbal Communication: The Unspoken Dialogue* (p. 99). New York, NY: McGraw-Hill.

28. Watson, O. M. (1970). *Proxemic Behavior: A Cross-Cultural Study*. The Hague, Netherlands: Mouton.

29. Giles, H. (1973). Accent mobility: A model and some data. *Anthropological Linguistics, 15*, 87–105.

30. Trager, G. L. (1958). Paralanguage: A first approximation. *Studies in Linguistics, 13*, 1–12.

31. McCroskey, J. C. (2001). *An Introduction to Rhetorical Communication* (8th ed.). Englewood Cliffs, NJ: Prentice Hall.

32. Giles, H. (1973). Accent mobility: A model and some data. *Anthropological Linguistics, 15*, 87–105.

33. For an example using body posturing, see Bahns, A. J., Crandall, C. S., Gillath, O., & Wilmer, J. B. (2016). Nonverbal communication of similarity via the torso: It's in the bag. *Journal of Nonverbal Behavior, 40*(2), 151–170. doi:10.1007/s10919-016-0227-y

34. Klopf, D. W., & Park, M. S. (1982). *Cross-Cultural Communication: An Introduction to the Fundamentals*. Seoul, Korea: Han Shin.

35. Richmond, V. P. & McCroskey, J. C. (2004). *Nonverbal Behavior in Interpersonal Relations* (5th ed.). Boston, MA: Allyn & Bacon.

36. Ibid.

37. Remland, M. S., Jones, T. S., & Brinkman, H. (1995). Interpersonal distance, body orientation, and touch: Effects of culture, gender, and age. *The Journal of Social Psychology, 135*(3), 281–297.

What helps people maintain a relationship?

Why do people have trouble with interpersonal change?

MindTap®

Review the chapter's learning objectives and **start** with a quick warm-up activity.

Learning Objectives

After you finish reading this chapter, you will be able to:

Describe relationship-maintaining behaviors.

Define relational turning points.

Identify three patterns of conflict that drive interactions in relationships.

MindTap®

Read, highlight, and take notes online.

Sylvia and Gavin have been romantic partners for years. After a casual encounter at a pub in their 20s that led to a surprise pregnancy decades ago, both Sylvia and Gavin are now accustomed to their family being the most significant part of their shared relationship. However, the last of their children left for college this year, and Gavin worries about what their future relationship together will look like. He and Sylvia have always been equal partners in creating their family, with shared roles and responsibilities that structure their lives. Gavin goes to the assembly plant and makes dinner for everyone when he comes home. Sylvia does the laundry and plants vegetables whenever she has a moment free after working her swing shift as a nurse at the hospital. They don't typically have time to pursue their own interests, but a life spent juggling children has ensured that most of their activities revolved around their children's schedules, anyway. Just this morning, however, Sylvia came home and asked Gavin if he wanted to order pizza and play cards after work tonight instead of making dinner. Gavin agreed, but privately he was reticent; this isn't part of their tried-and-true routine.

RELATIONAL MAINTENANCE

What helps people maintain a relationship? Why do people have trouble with interpersonal change? As relationships continue over long periods, most people are subject to a wide range of influences and factors that may cause their relationships to evolve in some significant way. From romantic partners experiencing a difficulty like the loss of a job or a betrayal, to best friends who have known each other since elementary school and now attend college in different cities or states, all relationships are subject to a wide range of factors that may cause shifts—positive or negative—in the way that those relationships are experienced. As a result, most relationships engage in some form of **relational maintenance**, wherein partners try to keep a relationship in a desired condition. Relational maintenance typically involves keeping a relationship at the current level, meaning that partners work toward *not allowing* that relationship to decline but also *not forcing* that relationship to necessarily be strengthened on a variety of characteristics, either. In our earlier example, Gavin and Sylvia are comfortable with their relationship, and Gavin hopes to maintain the closeness and intimacy with Sylvia despite their changing relational circumstances.

Relational Maintenance
Working to keep a relationship in a specific desired state or condition.

Relationship-Maintaining Behaviors

When people like Gavin and Sylvia work to keep a relationship at a desired level, we may describe them as using **relationship-maintaining behaviors**.[1,2,3] These behaviors may include a variety of relationship-focused things like those seen in Table 7.1, including regular communication and accomplishing tasks that are important to the partner. Scholar Laura Stafford came up with a way to measure these kinds of relationship-maintaining behaviors,[4] a modified version of which appears in Box 7.2. Take a look at the assessment. Each question has a different focus, whether querying behaviors like holding conversations or sharing experiences. How do the items in Box 7.2 expand your own understanding of relationship-maintaining behaviors? The variety of behaviors that help maintain a relationship are as diverse as the individuals in each relationship. Suzanne and Hiland have a weekly date night, in which they relinquish their daughter, Betty, to a babysitter and take a bottle of wine to their apartment building's rooftop to watch the sun set over the city. Dylan knows that Isaac has a long day each Tuesday, taking two classes after putting in a full work shift, and so Dylan tries to clean up the apartment and get some of their laundry done after his own job before Isaac comes home. Marianne and Elliot have been married for

Relationship-Maintaining Behaviors
Communication or action enacted with an intent of maintaining or increasing the strength of an interpersonal relationship.

ekgarin/Shutterstock.com

TABLE 7.1 Selected Relationship-Maintaining Behaviors[5,6,7]

Spending time with shared friends	Talking about the relationship together	Sharing tasks or work with one another
Helping equally with tasks that need to be done	Attempting to make interactions enjoyable	Showing love for one another
Sharing thoughts and feelings with each other	Showing patience and forgiveness	Talking about the future of the relationship
Avoiding direct criticism of one another	Highlighting commitment to one another	Behaving with courtesy toward one another
Sharing what each partner wants from the relationship	Acting cheerful and positive together	Including friends and family in activities together

almost 30 years, and use their shared morning commute to hash out the plans for the week so that their discussion during evening commutes can simply be relationship focused. Like those in these examples, scholars have come up with a wide range of relationship-maintaining behaviors, each of which is able to be categorized into one of seven specific types.

Positivity

The first category of relationship-maintaining behaviors, **positivity**, involves relational partners being cheerful and optimistic with one another. Although this category does not imply that members ought to avoid talking about deep, serious issues, it does note the importance of being generally pleasant for one's partner to be around. When Leonora comes home from class, she is often exhausted and stressed about everything that is due over the next few weeks. However, each day after locking up her bicycle, Leonora pauses for a few minutes to calm herself down and to release all the stresses that have happened earlier in the day. By the time she walks in the front door to greet her large extended family, Leonora is able to appear optimistic and engaged with each member she greets. Positivity is a significant component of enjoyable relationships; whether through smiling or expressing affection or avoiding constant criticism, positivity is an essential part of maintaining a close relationship.

Positivity
Relationship-maintaining behaviors wherein partners affirm one another and mutually express positive emotions.

Understanding

The second category of relationship-maintaining behaviors, **understanding**, involves relational partners who accept one another for who they are and attempt to engage in perspective taking to know where they are coming from. Although Francois doesn't know what it is like to be a surgeon in a busy hospital, he does understand that careers can be stressful and tries to apply that knowledge to what his partner must feel like after a day working

Understanding
Relationship-maintaining behaviors wherein partners provide acceptance and engage in perspective taking with one another.

at the hospital. Georgina and Walt don't have similar family backgrounds, but they realize that their attitudes toward celebrating the holiday season are influenced by their individual history and are glad that they can understand where each other is coming from. Dave and Jeremy are two roommates who met through their local program for recovering alcoholics; because of this shared experience, they are able to support one another in overcoming addiction by avoiding situations and behaviors that may be triggers.

Self-Disclosure

Self-Disclosure
Relationship-maintaining behaviors wherein partners reveal personal information about the self that cannot otherwise be discovered through observation or casual interaction (from Chapter 4).

The third category of relationship-maintaining behaviors, **self-disclosure**, involves relational partners who share deeply personal information with one another that may otherwise be unknown. As discussed in Chapter 4, self-disclosure allows partners to gain both a greater depth *and* breadth of knowledge about one another, increasing perceptions of relational closeness and providing an opportunity to create trust or a sense of security. When Mara and Alanna talk with one another about their past relationships, they may discuss painful information that they wouldn't share with anybody who wasn't important to them. Chester and Melissa gossip about their coworkers, privately indicating attitudes and opinions that could easily get them fired if they were more widely known. Hope and August make sure to spend the half hour after they put the kids to bed chatting; before doing the dishes or getting ready for bed, each grabs a cocktail and retires to the den to debrief the other about the day. These partners are able to remain close because they

Nico Kai/The Image Bank/Getty Images

talk about those things that are significant in their daily lives, gaining greater knowledge about one another and being able to react accordingly.

Relationship Talks

The fourth category of relationship-maintaining behaviors, **relationship talks**, involves relational partners having conversations *about their relationships.* Besides simply interacting, these talks focus on the status of the relationship and give partners the chance to make sure that they have a similar investment in one another. Jared and Peggy are just starting out in their dating partnership, so when Peggy begins to apply to out-of-state graduate schools, they sit down to have a conversation about what her acceptance might mean to their pairing. Faith and Kelly are thinking about buying a house together and so discuss whether marriage or children are in their plans. When Pax asks Jody to move in with him, Pax makes it clear that he sees it as a way to get to know each other more but does not necessarily imply a permanent future together. By conversing about the current status of their relationships and what they may look like in the future, these pairs are helping to mutually gauge their shared interests and overlapping plans.

Relationship Talks
Relationship-maintaining behaviors wherein partners discuss the current state of their partnership and any plans or ideas about the future of their relationship together.

Assurances

The fifth category of relationship-maintaining behaviors, **assurances**, involves relational partners providing evidence of their commitment to one another. Whether that commitment is demonstrated through nonverbal expressions of committal or through direct verbal statements that indicate faithfulness to one another or a comment on the relationship status, assurances help to reaffirm the nature of the shared relationship. When Carl and Alisha were dealing with some relationship issues, Carl realized that Alisha needed a demonstration of his commitment to her; when Carl suggested wearing matching outfits to an upcoming costume party, Alisha knew that Carl was not trying to use these social situations to find a new partner. River and Anthony were experiencing a wide range of emotions when River's father got transferred to a new military base; as Anthony gave his final good-bye, he told River that they'd always be best friends despite the distance between them. Shelly and Oswald have decided to attend Shelly's high school reunion together despite the presence

Assurances
Relationship-maintaining behaviors wherein partners use either verbal or nonverbal messaging to express their commitment to one another.

ableimages/Alamy Stock Photo

BOX 7.1: iPersonal

Assurances, Calendaring, and Technology

In an increasingly technology-rich society, there are a variety of technological advances that make the very fabric of relationships look different. With the widespread diffusion of technologies like smartphones and tablet computing, people have access to a wide range of reminders and points of accessibility for the Internet that allow them to maintain their relationships in unique and interesting ways, often providing assurances to a wide variety of relational partners.

Consider the following examples of people using technology to keep their relationship in a desired state. What are your reactions to each?

> Enrique and Michelle have been married for 10 years, and today is a significant date for him to remember. Having forgotten their anniversary years before and having dealt with the repercussions, Enrique pulls out his smartphone while Michelle is getting in the shower so that he can enroll in an annual floral-delivery system, ensuring that he never misses an anniversary date again. Five minutes and one large credit card bill later, Enrique has flowers arranged to be delivered on this date for the next 10 years.

> Cartwright and Ender have been friends for years. Having had lives that drifted apart because of school and work commitments, Ender has set up calendar reminders on his email server that encourage him to send a "spontaneous note or phone call" every three weeks. Since the reminders were set up, Cartwright has responded quite positively to Ender's interactions and feels much closer than he did before.

> Brock uses Facebook to find the birthdays of his clients and coworkers. Once he has a list, he uses an online application to have a card personalized, printed, "hand-signed," and mailed for him for a small fee each year. Clients particularly are impressed by his "remembrance" of their special days.

Because technology provides so many opportunities to increase interaction with one another, standards of communication and closeness may vary widely among the different relationships in a person's daily experience. As technology continues to shape and be shaped by interpersonal interactions, the very nature of relational maintenance may shift in both subtle and obvious ways.

INSTRUCTIONS: What kinds of technology are used in your interpersonal relationships? Think carefully about the above ways of using technology to impact the feelings of closeness in interpersonal relationships. What is your reaction to each of these forms of relational maintenance? Do any of them go too far in an attempt to help people keep their interpersonal relationships in a desired state?

of many of her ex-boyfriends; from the moment they walked in the door, Shelly put her hand in Oswald's to remind him that she had picked a future with *him* and all the other people they'd meet that evening were part of her history. From the little gestures to the large conversations, assurances allow partners to express their relational fidelity to one another.

Tasking

The sixth category of relationship-maintaining behaviors, **tasking**, involves relational partners sharing tasks with one other to facilitate a friendship, family relationship, romantic relationship, or work partnership. By contributing to the success of the relationship through the accomplishment of shared efforts, tasking ensures that partners share tasks equally or contribute similar effort to the partnership. Katya has a demanding high-paying job that often requires her to work long hours, so her partner Eduardo takes care of the primary parenting of their four-year-old child, Starr. Friends and roommates Eli and Isaac have figured out a perfect balance for their evening routine; because Eli loves to cook but hates doing dishes or cleaning the kitchen, each takes on part of the responsibility for dinner time and allows the other to use the time to read and study for classes.

Tasking
Relationship-maintaining behaviors wherein partners balance the work within the relationship by each accomplishing mutually beneficial tasks.

Networks

The seventh category of relationship-maintaining behaviors, **networks**, involves relational partners sharing their extended social groupings of friends and family with one another. The resulting network of individuals helps to maintain the strength and stability of the social bonding by allowing for overlapping support systems and shared relationships. When Emily invited Keith to spend a holiday at a cabin she visits each year, he knew that she was increasing their relationship quality because her family and old friends would all be there for the long weekend. Fletcher invited his boss Marty to his family's Thanksgiving, knowing that it would increase Marty's understanding and empathy with Fletcher. Sun and Mari held a small cocktail reception to celebrate their engagement, hoping to create one big social group out of their two separate lives. By overlapping or extending networks of people, each of these individuals is more easily able to maintain a satisfying and beneficial relationship.

Networks
Relationship-maintaining behaviors wherein partners intentionally overlap friend and family relationships.

Geber86/E+/Getty Images

BOX 7.2: Let's Get INTRApersonal

Relational Maintenance Behaviors Scale[8]

Are you curious about the behaviors of your close relationship partner? Do you wonder whether and in what way he or she is working to keep your relationship intact? Or, are you interested in looking at your relationship from his or her perspective, trying to find out areas for improvement? In 2011 researcher Laura Stafford looked at much of the research on relational maintenance, identifying a set of questions that help to characterize behaviors that people use to keep their relationship in a desired state. Even though the questions were developed to focus on married couples, we present a shortened and modified version of that scale in the hopes that it may be applied to other close relationships.

INSTRUCTIONS: Think carefully about how your relationship partner interacts with you. Does she or he exhibit a wide range of relationship-focused behaviors? Use the following numbers to indicate your agreement with each statement. This scale may also help you think about the effort that you put forth in this relationship.

1	2	3	4	5	6	7
Strongly Disagree	Moderately Disagree	Slightly Disagree	Neither Agree Nor Disagree	Slightly Agree	Moderately Agree	Strongly Agree

_____ 1. My partner acts positively with me.

_____ 2. My partner apologizes when he/she is wrong.

_____ 3. My partner is open about his/her feelings.

_____ 4. My partner discusses our relationship quality.

_____ 5. My partner talks about our plans for the future.

_____ 6. My partner helps with tasks that need to be done.

_____ 7. My partner spends time with our families.

_____ 8. My partner is upbeat when we are together.

_____ 9. My partner does not judge me.

_____ 10. My partner encourages me to share my thoughts with him/her.

_____ 11. My partner talks about our relationship.

_____ 12. My partner shows me how much I mean to him/her.

_____ 13. My partner shares in the joint responsibilities that face us.

_____ 14. My partner includes our friends in our activities.

Now, add up the scores for each category:

_____ Positivity is the score on number 1 plus the score on number 8.

_____ Understanding is the score on number 2 plus the score on number 9.

_____ Self-disclosure is the score on number 3 plus the score on number 10.

_____ Relationship talks is the score on number 4 plus the score on number 11.

_____ Assurances is the score on number 5 plus the score on number 12.

_____ Tasking is the score on number 6 plus the score on number 13.

_____ Networks is the score on number 7 plus the score on number 14.

Which category scores highest? Lowest? Considering our earlier discussion about these categories, what does this tell you about areas of both strength and weakness in your current relationship? Are you motivated to make a change? If so, what steps do you think you should take?

Voluntary and Involuntary Relationships

Maintaining a changing relationship may look different in each interpersonal pairing depending on characteristics of that relationship. Two new friends who are just getting to know one another may find it relatively simple to keep the relationship at its depth but may also not be too upset if that relationship were to end. Long-term romantic partners or married couples, however, may find that their relationship is much more complicated; the depth and enmeshment of their partnership may motivate greater effort to maintaining both civility and fidelity during conflict.

Certain types of relationships are inherently different from one another and place additional strains on the maintenance of that relationship. For example, siblings may find themselves forced to overcome conflict encounters that they might otherwise ignore if the other person was simply a classmate or friend. One reason for such a difference is because of the involuntary nature of the relationship. **Involuntary relationships** are characterized by the fact that they are not selected by one's own volition but are rather created regardless of the desire of one or both partners.[9] A common example of involuntary relationships include family relationships, where blood ties often create feelings of obligation or commitment regardless of one's actual attitude or behavior toward that person.[10] Faith and Emma are twins who could hardly be more different from one another; sharing a room growing up meant that the organized Emma was constantly annoyed by Faith's messy and disorganized clutter.

Had they been college roommates, Faith and Emma likely would have asked for a room change at the end of the first semester. However, being twin sisters means that both Faith and Emma are involuntarily attached and will remain in relationship with one another for the long haul. Involuntary relationship structures may actually prove beneficial for the development of people, however, possibly teaching them both coping skills and adaptability that may serve them in other life contexts.[11]

Involuntary Relationships
Partnerships characterized by situation or obligation rather than self-selection and one's own volition.

Mark Goebel Photo Gallery/Archive Photos/Getty Images

Voluntary Relationships
Partnerships characterized by self-selection and one's own volition rather than by forces outside the relationship pairing.

By contrast, **voluntary relationships** are characterized by the fact that individuals self-select their participation in the partnership, choosing to be in relationships like friendships or romantic partnerships. Because these people opt in to the relationship, they can similarly opt out of the relationship, and the resulting levels of commitment may be expected to vary widely depending on the situation or context.

Interestingly, the level of degree to which a relationship is perceived as voluntary or involuntary may shift or alter over time. For example, if Mary is committed to her faith tradition and marries her fiancée, Samuel, in a full Catholic Mass, she may believe that her relationship has been made permanent by the wedding vows and is no longer a voluntary relationship. By choosing to define marriage in a specific way according to her religious perspective, Mary now sees her partnership with Samuel as involuntary despite the fact that it was viewed as completely self-selected only months ago.

Alternatively, Bartholomew suffered trauma associated with abuse by members of his family growing up. Having become legally emancipated from his parents at age 16, Bartholomew has no legal obligation or ties to his blood relatives and may decide to ignore his own perceptions of involuntary ties to his former family. Even if he chose *not* to take legal action, Bartholomew may have elected not to engage with his family of origin. The definitions, contexts, and manners of engaging in relational interactions are much more complicated than a simple label, so similarly the characterizations of voluntary and involuntary relationships are necessarily subject to an understanding of the specific relationship under scrutiny.

Relational Dialectics

Regardless of the labels that we use to define or categorize or even distinguish relationships from one another, all relationships share a variety of struggles

that are considered relatively common. Far from indicating a decline or loss of relationship, certain struggles may serve as a relational "motor"; that is, the tension created by certain relational strains may cause people to interact and engage with one another in a variety of ways, adding energy and movement to a relationship that would otherwise be quite stagnant.[12] Known as **relational dialectics** or **dialectic tensions**, these opposing forces cause people to communicate with one another as they find a balance between otherwise polarizing relational goals.[13,14,15,16]

Connection and Autonomy

The first tension that must be navigated within a close relationship often has to do with the struggle between **connection** and **autonomy**. This struggle typically has to do with how independent each relational partner feels from one another and can be seen as a continuum from connection at one end of the spectrum, characterized by extreme closeness, to autonomy at the other end of the spectrum, characterized by complete separation from one another (as in Figure 7.1). All close relationships are confronted with this tension, as people desire to be seen as independent, making their own choices in life; at the same time, partners typically want or need to involve the other in decision making and time spent together in order to truly have a partnership. In long-distance relationships, this dialectic tension is obvious to partners.[17] As friends, families, and couples navigate the tricky balance between connection and autonomy, they often experience moments of tension when there is a disconnect between relational partners. When Ainsworth and Jaimee go to a social function together, they typically arrive and make their greetings as a couple. Ainsworth is relatively shy in social situations, and so he wants to stay near Jaimee in order to feel comfortable navigating most social situations.

Jaimee, however, is a bit more independent and feels smothered when Ainsworth "awkwardly" sticks by her side during conversations the whole evening. After excusing herself to pretend to go to the bathroom just so she can get some space, Jaimee decides to confront Ainsworth on the ride home about whether they really need to spend every moment together at future events. Even though Jaimee and Ainsworth have decided to be in a romantic relationship with one another, the extent to which they behave as a couple will cause them to need to work out the details of their relationship.

Openness and Closedness

Not only do relational partners need to decide how much time they want to share with each other, but also they must decide how much *information* they want to share with one another. As shown in Figure 7.2, this dialectic tension involves one end of the spectrum with complete information sharing and self-disclosure among partners, known

Relational Dialectics
The opposing forces or tensions of relationships wherein partners struggle to find a balance between competing relational goals.

Dialectic Tensions
See Relational Dialectics.

Connection
Interdependence associated with a desire to be seen as part of a dyad within a relationship.

Autonomy
Independence associated with a desire to be seen as an individual within a relationship.

Connection   **Autonomy**

phil holmes/Alamy Stock Vector

FIGURE 7.1
The Connection–Autonomy Tension

Openness   **Closedness**

phil holmes/Alamy Stock Vector

FIGURE 7.2
The Openness–Closedness Tension

Openness
The sharing of both broad and deep ranges of information with a romantic partner associated with a desire to be seen as fully known.

Closedness
The withholding of private information from a romantic partner associated with a desire to be seen as mysterious or more interesting.

Predictability
The enactment of regular patterns of behavior associated with a desire to be seen as having routines within a relationship.

Novelty
The enactment of various and/ or new behaviors associated with a desire to be seen as spontaneous within a relationship.

Image Source/DigitalVision/Getty Images

as **openness**, and the other end of the continuum with complete privacy and relatively little shared information between relational partners, known as **closedness**. Although it is nearly impossible for relational partners to share every little piece of information about themselves—or, for that matter, to conceal every little piece of information—people often struggle with where to locate a relationship between these two opposite sides.[18] On one hand, people believe that open and honest disclosure of information may be helpful within a relationship and allow for complete understanding of one another, but in reality there is simply too much possible information for something like this to occur. On the other hand, some may argue that the management of personal information allows a person to present his or her best self to a partner and avoid potential conflict around unimportant topics.

Connor's coworker Erica has made her interest in him known to colleagues around the office, but Connor has worked hard to make it clear that he is committed to his girlfriend Annika and would like such conversations to cease. Despite his mature handling of the situation, he has not told Annika about Erica's interest for fear that Annika might overreact or become jealous. Admittedly, Connor also enjoys the fact that he has once again been an object of desire but would be horrified if anyone found out that he experiences such a base emotion. In an otherwise disclosive relationship, Connor has chosen to conceal information that he feels would be relatively unhelpful to their shared goals.

Predictability and Novelty

The third major dialectic tension found within most close relationships has to do with the degree of routine that is a part of the shared experiences of the couple. Known as **predictability**, relational partners often develop patterns of behavior wherein they feel comfortable in being able to foreknow the reactions and experiences of the other person. Giuseppe has already made restaurant reservations for the anniversary of his business launch, as he and his partner Brent always return annually to the restaurant where they first laid out their business plan together.

Sometimes, however, partners get sick of the "same old thing" and express a desire to experience **novelty** by introducing spontaneity into the relationship. For this year's Valentine's Day, Jared has bought a humorously risqué fireman outfit to wear when he meets his wife at the door after work, a practice unheard of in their vanilla relationship together. Even though he knows he'll feel awkward wearing it at first, the look of surprise on her face will be worth the embarrassment. Jared's wife had just said that they needed to get out of a rut and be more spontaneous. As shown in Figure 7.3, these two poles of predictability and novelty are often at separate ends of the continuum, but a healthy balance is found somewhere in the middle, with relationships having both routine and excitement as normal parts of daily life.

BOX 7.3: Let's Get INTRApersonal

Comfort with Uncertainty[19,20,21]

D o you get nervous or anxious when you don't have a plan for every situation? Perhaps you are more comfortable just "going with the flow" and seeing what happens in new situations? Regardless of your general tendencies, uncertainty causes some general discomfort for everyone, but some cultures or individuals are particularly prone to feeling uncomfortable when they don't fully understand the encounters or experiences in their daily lives. Scholars have created scales that look at a cultural approach to uncertainty, an organizational approach to uncertainty, and even an individual approach to uncertainty in order to help us understand our own adjustment to novel experiences. In order to better discuss your own perspective, you can take this self-assessment to gain insight into your own comfort with uncertainty. This is an original scale, loosely based on Hwang's (2005) modification of Dorfman and Howell's (1988) and Hofstede's (1980) scales, with this version created to identify avoiders of uncertainty during their college years.

INSTRUCTIONS: Think carefully about how you go through your daily life as a college student. How do you feel about unfamiliar or novel situations? Indicate your agreement with the following statements to better understand your own level of comfort with uncertainty

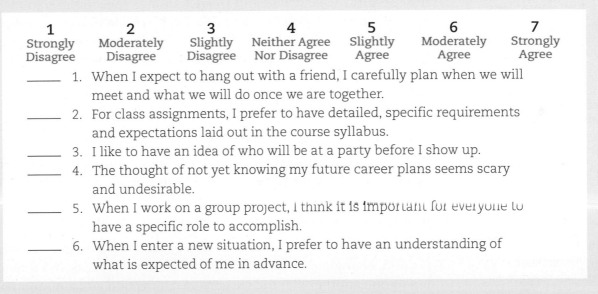

1	2	3	4	5	6	7
Strongly Disagree	Moderately Disagree	Slightly Disagree	Neither Agree Nor Disagree	Slightly Agree	Moderately Agree	Strongly Agree

_____ 1. When I expect to hang out with a friend, I carefully plan when we will meet and what we will do once we are together.

_____ 2. For class assignments, I prefer to have detailed, specific requirements and expectations laid out in the course syllabus.

_____ 3. I like to have an idea of who will be at a party before I show up.

_____ 4. The thought of not yet knowing my future career plans seems scary and undesirable.

_____ 5. When I work on a group project, I think it is important for everyone to have a specific role to accomplish.

_____ 6. When I enter a new situation, I prefer to have an understanding of what is expected of me in advance.

Now, add up the total score. Is it high? Low? The highest score you can get is a 42, but it is unusual for someone to score that high. If you have a relatively low score you are comfortable with the novel or unfamiliar situations you may encounter in daily life. If you have a high score, you may work to reduce your uncertainty in these situations in order to feel more at ease. What does it tell you about yourself? How might this influence your daily life?

Managing Relational Dialectics

Not only do relational dialectics add energy and movement to a relationship as partners interact with one another; they also offer relational partners the opportunity to address one another and determine the best strategy for

Predictability   **Novelty**

phil holmes/Alamy Stock Vector

FIGURE 7.3
The Predictability-Novelty Tension

Selection
Choosing one pole of a relational dialectic at the expense of the other.

Separation
Relegating one pole of a relational dialectic to certain contexts/periods and the other extreme to yet other contexts/periods.

Neutralization
Compromising between the two poles of a relational dialectic so that each one is satisfied to some degree.

Reframing
Changing the conversation about relational dialectics in order to remove any seeming tension between the two poles.

managing the stress and change that often occurs around these dialectic tensions. Scholars have identified four primary ways that couples engage these dialectics in their relationships in order to reduce the stress associated with the tension.[22,23]

- Couples choosing the strategy of **selection** opt to pick one end of the dialectic tension at the expense of the other end, prioritizing one pole over the other. Kenny and Erica live every day of their relationship like it's a first date, choosing to always engage in spontaneous and unplanned activities like amusement parks and music festivals, ignoring their desires for a stable continuity.

- Relational partners that select **separation** as a maintenance strategy often decide either to alternate between both ends of the relational dialectics or to segment their life into different contexts in which each polar end may be prioritized. Chad and Derrick discuss their past relationships in great detail but don't talk about Chad's childhood history of verbal abuse or Derrick's struggle with his father's alcoholism. By separating topics or contexts, Chad and Derrick's relationship is characterized as both incredibly disclosive and also quite secretive depending on the topic.

- Couples who decide to opt for **neutralization** of the tension are characterized by compromise. Rather than selecting one pole or the other, relational partners decide to find a solution that incorporates both ends of the dialectic. Mark and Jaiden often fought about how much time they should spend together, but they finally decided on a schedule that gave Jaiden the free time to see her friends but also gave Mark enough opportunity to get his relational needs met through quality time.

- Finally, some couples choose to engage in a **reframing** of the dialectic tension, changing the narrative so that no tension exists. By communicating to one another that the tensions of connection and autonomy are two sides of the same coin, Hansheng and Lily have convinced themselves that time spent together *and* time spent alone are both steps toward a deeper relationship.

Because of the importance that individuals place on these tensions, people have to use communication and interaction to navigate the complexities of their close relationships. With changing goals and competing desires that fluctuate throughout the course of a relationship, relational dialectics ensure that friends, family members, romantic partners, and others in relationships are constantly engaging one another to arrive at a greater understanding of their shared lives. As these tensions compete with one another, the nature of a relationship can shift and change in both obvious and subtle ways.

BOX 7.4: InterConnect

What Do You Do to Keep Your Relationship Exciting? Stable?[24]

Marty and Tamara have been together for 15 years. Having met in their senior year of high school during a campus visit at their local university, they were inseparable throughout college. Close friends of the couple even began calling them "Martamara," a combination of both names. Watching them attend other's formals for their Greek-letter organizations and meet at the campus gymnasium each morning to do cardio together, no one was surprised that Marty and Tamara quickly moved in together after graduation.

Fast-forward a few years, and Marty is worried about how to keep their relationship exciting. Because Tamara has no interest in marriage and Marty doesn't want children, Marty fears that the couple has hit a stagnant point in their relationship. Because of this, Marty plans to sit down tonight and spend some time looking online for exciting activities to spice up their partnership. If he can't come up with *something* that will meet his needs, he figures he can at least contact a local shelter to adopt a dog or cat and mix things up at home.

After growing up in a transient home on the verge of bankruptcy, Tamara enjoys the stability that she has in her relationship with Marty. Far from wanting excitement, Tamara is thankful for the calm and consistency that Marty brings to her life. Knowing that nothing has changed over the past couple years brings comfort to her, and as she leaves work early to do the grocery shopping for the week she stays consistent with that part of her normal Tuesday routine. She doesn't need a shopping list, as she simply buys the same memorized products that she has purchased every other week.

INSTRUCTIONS: Think carefully about each of the perspectives described above. How do you think Marty and Tamara are doing as a couple? Do you believe the feelings of one of them is more valid than the feelings of the other? If so, which one? Although many people are searching for excitement in their relationships, just as many people are hoping for stability with their romantic partners. What do you think is the best advice for Marty to keep his relationship interesting? How would you counsel Tamara when Marty expresses a desire for excitement? How would you encourage the couple to deal with the disagreement that is sure to arise?

CHARTING A RELATIONSHIP

As relationships develop and evolve over time, it becomes useful to be able to describe those relationships and the changes that each undergoes. After all, even though Chet and Marie have been lovingly married for 65 years, they were once two awkward teenagers going on a double date with friends, certain that they were going to have an awful evening. Clearly something changed between that initial dislike to their first kiss, and their first day as a married couple shares little in common with the recent holiday celebration with their children, grandchildren, and a great-grandchild in attendance. In order to more completely understand individual relationships and their shifts over time, scholars have developed a unique way to approach the analysis and categorization of these relational states.

Relational Turning Points

Turning Points Analysis
The method of charting variation in relational commitment as associated with significant events or experiences.

Relational Turning Points
The events or experiences that facilitate moments of change within relationships.

One way to understand and describe a relationship as it changes over time is to do a **turning points analysis**, where scholars look at the variation in relational commitment by charting specific **relational turning points** associated with two interaction partners. Almost exclusively used to describe romantic relationships, the turning points approach to pairs of people looks at the significant events or experiences that facilitate change within their relationship.[25,26] By examining the memorable or salient moments that occur over the course of the relationship, partners can see how individual events impacted the relationship or signaled changing levels of commitment with one another. When Tariq invited Parisa home to meet his family, Tariq was both reflecting his devotion to her as well as intensifying his level of connection with her. Many months later, when Parisa thought she had caught Tariq cheating on her and it turned out that he was being secretive about the purchase of an engagement ring, the experience caused both partners to once again evaluate their level of commitment to one another. As shown in Figure 7.4, a variety of relational experiences can cause both increases and decreases in commitment over the course of even the most stable romantic relationships.

The specific types of turning points may be a varied and flexible list, but some are relatively common within romantic relationships, as shown in Figure 7.5. Whether describing when a relationship becomes exclusive, or when a couple moves in together or gets engaged, or when the partners have their first fight, these events may signal moments of change within the relationship. Relational turning points come in many forms, however, and they are each defined within the context of the specific relationship. That is, what may be a turning point for one couple may be a relatively mundane event in the life of another partnership. When Ann and Breanna were first dating, Breanna was starting a new job at a high-powered law firm. Ann suddenly noticed that Breanna consistently ignored her ringing mobile phone when she and Ann were spending time together, and to Ann this signaled that she was more important to Breanna than her job, a status that Ann never felt in previous relationships. Even more than the first kiss or the first time they said, "I love you," Ann points to this event as the moment that cemented their relationship and fostered her commitment to Breanna.

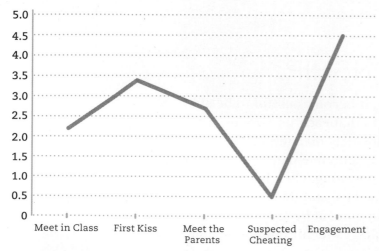

FIGURE 7.4

Parisa and Tariq's Relational Turning Points

Long-Distance Relationships

One specific turning point that scholars often discuss is the onset of long-distance relationships. Scholars note that these relationships are not limited to romantic relationships,[27] but rather, they include any

FIGURE 7.5
Some of Baxter and Bullis's Turning Point Types[28]

relationships that experience geographic separation between partners. This **long-distance** or **distal relationship** is one in which one or both parties perceive the other as living a significant distance away from them, as compared to a **geographically close** or **proximal relationship**, where partners live relatively nearby. Lisa and Jason are fraternal twins who have been forced to carry on a long-distance family relationship when they each accepted highly desirable jobs on opposite coasts after their college graduation, but family holidays together and the frequency of flights between their cities made the separation acceptable. On the other hand, boyfriends Jake and Adam live in a major urban area and don't own cars; when Adam moved across the city to attend graduate school on a different subway line than the one that Jake frequented, he complained to his friends about the difficulties he confronted in his "long-distance" dating relationship. Whether the geographic separation is enforced by a major boundary like an international border crossing or something as simple as the difficulties of a rush hour commute, different people assign varied meaning and importance to their experience of geographic separation.

Long-Distance Relationship
A relationship having a separation of psychologically significant physical space.

Distal Relationship
See Long-Distance Relationship.

Geographically Close Relationship
A relationship with no significant perceived physical separation.

Proximal Relationship
See Geographically Close Relationship.

BOX 7.5: InterFace

Relational Change with Diverse Others

Kelly grew up in the heart of a large urban area and attended an award-winning high school that attracted students of all backgrounds. As the only white female among her close friends, Kelly became used to the slang and speech patterns of a wide variety of cultures and ethnic groups and fluently switched among them with her friends. After deciding to join a university campus organization that was similarly multicultural, Kelly was surprised to find that members were offended by her casual appropriation of terminology and style, assuming that her ability to drop into different language patterns was a caricature of their culture. Ashamed and confused, Kelly stopped attending the weekly meetings.

Ty's grandfather suffered severe post-traumatic stress from his time in the Korean War and spoke of his experience with great disdain at family gatherings. After Ty's professor assigned Ty to a group project with three other people, Ty enjoyed working closely with the other group members until he made an insensitive joke about *kimchee*, a Korean cultural delicacy. One of the group members, Michelle, commented that she was half Korean and resented his remark. Ty didn't back down, and their relationship suffered, but at his family's holiday gathering Ty spoke up that perhaps not all of his grandfather's stereotypes were fair.

Hero Images/Hero Images/Getty Images

Kendra and Rashaan had a rough first month as roommates. Because she didn't know anyone in her transfer student dorm, Rashaan had hoped to become close with her new roommate until she found out that Kendra was bisexual. Having grown up in a conservative home and attending a small private high school, Rashaan had never met anyone who didn't claim a heterosexual background. Fearful that other students would think *she* was gay if they became friends, Rashaan took a few weeks before she really felt comfortable beginning to get to know Kendra.

Researchers have found that people approach intercultural interactions from different places based on their range of experiences.[29] Depending on whether we have had many encounters with people who seem different than ourselves or who belong to different groupings, we may make sense of our interactions in different ways. A person who has had a lot of experience with diverse others may start off their relationships with relatively few assumptions or stereotypes about other cultures. For a person who has had relatively few intercultural interactions, it may take time for relationships to move from initial encounters toward depth and friendship. As discussed in Chapter 4, one of the classic ways to move toward more comfortable interactions with one another is to first share information about your own self.

INSTRUCTIONS: How do you feel when you read these stories? Are any of these individuals caught in a situation in which you have recently found yourself? Consider the ways in which competent communicators should engage with people around them. How would you suggest that the various people in these stories should respond? Why do you think each person/group in these stories feels the way that they do?

Distal College Relationships

Although they may happen at a wide variety of life stages, during the college years long-distance romantic relationships are relatively common. Even though lingering high school relationships may cause freshmen to have an even higher proportion of distal relationships among college students,[30] almost one out of every three college-aged relationships are long distance.[31] Although these distal college relationships often share many characteristics with those that are more geographically close, romantic partners do report greater uncertainty about their long-distance relationships and may have lower levels of overall relational satisfaction, depending on the frequency of visits or their beliefs about the future together.[32,33,34] Interestingly, researchers have found that college-aged women may adjust better to the separation associated with long-distance relationships than do college-aged men.[35] Regardless of gender, however, some scholars have noted that certain characteristics are better predictors of long-term stability in long-distance relationships, including things like higher self-esteem, greater optimism, and lower amounts of anxiety or depression associated with the relationship.[36] Contrary to popular belief, researchers have consistently found that long-distance relationships are no more likely to terminate than are other relationships,[37] perhaps due to the similar communication behaviors associated with emotional intimacy in both distal and proximal romantic relationships.[38] Engaging in these consistent relationship-focused behaviors is an essential practice of a healthy romantic relationship regardless of the geographic distance between partners.

Centrifugal Perspective
In order for a close relationship to continue, effort, energy, and other resources must be put into the maintenance of the partnership's desired state.

Centripetal Perspective
People naturally tend toward one another, and the maintenance of a close relationship can be relatively effortless.

RELATIONSHIP-FOCUSED BEHAVIORS

When relational partners are focused on maintaining a close relationship, most scholars agree that work must be done. Most scholars take a **centrifugal perspective** of relational maintenance, which implies that relationships take time, effort, energy, expense, and other relational costs in order to keep that relationship in repair. (The less commonly held counterpoint is called the **centripetal perspective**, where a minority of scholars suggest that perhaps relationships may last quite easily until something drives them apart.) Some efforts toward maintaining a relationship are relatively simple like acknowledging birthdays or anniversaries. Other efforts seem relatively obvious and straightforward based on our previous discussions, such as communication strategies like regular interaction and engaging in self-disclosure. Still, some efforts are important but relatively difficult to engage fully, such as setting aside focused quality time for a relational partner, or engaging in conflict in a healthy way. And, in romantic relationships, physical intimacy

becomes an additional layer of relationship maintenance behaviors that is essential to long-term success.

Conflict and Relational Change

People who interact with one another necessarily find themselves in disagreement at times. When Lincoln asks his daughters Mari and Lorena where they want to go out to dinner, Mari screams, "Pizza!" and Lorena counters with a loud "Tacos!" Lucky for their family harmony, the eclectic diner down the street can easily accommodate some mediocre version of each of those items.

However, most disagreements or competing goals are not so easily resolved, such as when Lincoln and his ex-wife, Camila, found they had completely different understandings of marital faithfulness. Instead of approaching the topic with maturity and reason, both partners were unable to engage in **conflict** in a healthy way. Conflict is the active process of attempting to resolve a situation where two or more people perceive that they have competing or incompatible goals. Mari and Lorena's goals were compatible because they found a restaurant that served both dishes; Camila and Lincoln found that one partner's goal of an open relationship was in direct contradiction to the other's desire for sexual exclusivity. The manner in which conflict is handled within a relationship—as well as the nature of the specific needs/goals/desires that are in opposition—can have significant impact on whether that conflict is resolved in a relationship-focused manner or whether that conflict causes harm to one or both interaction partners; the process of conflict can prove either beneficial or detrimental to a relationship.[39] To that end, conflict that is harmful to relationships is discussed in greater depth in Chapter 8.

Conflict Patterns

One of the strongest indicators of whether conflict is going to prove beneficial or detrimental to a relationship may be related to the style of conflict

Conflict
The active process of navigating disagreement over access to resources, people, or opportunities in which one or more parties perceive incompatible goals.

Tiko Aramyan/Shutterstock.com

that is used by interaction partners once they realize that they have oppositional goals. Most broadly, conflict can be discussed and categorized by the degree to which partners engage in **cooperation** and in **directness**,[40] where cooperation involves the mutual consideration of the goals of both interaction partners, and where directness involves a willingness to engage the process of conflict and to communicate openly about that conflict. The most productive forms of conflict within relationships may be characterized as having both direct communication and a willingness to cooperate to reach a mutually beneficial goal. However, not every form of conflict can be said to have both characteristics. Scholars have identified five main patterns of conflict, characterized by the degree of concern that partners display for both themselves and for their relational partner:[41,42,43]

- **Competing.** The first conflict pattern is one in which an individual has a high concern for self but a low concern for his interaction partner. As such, he typically wants to "win" at the conflict episode, often willing to do most anything to achieve that goal. Because tangible outcomes may prove easier to quantify than relational characteristics, individuals with a competitive pattern may be more willing to hurt a relationship to gain more observable outcomes. When Ashika and Ben first realized that they had different plans for where to go during spring break, the couple decided to talk through their options. However, when Ben spent much of the time extolling the virtues of his tropical beachfront choice and bashing Ashika's favorite mountain lake she remembered from her childhood, he didn't realize that he was creating a rift in their relationship even though they ended up with a glorious suntan.

- **Collaborating.** The second conflict pattern is one in which an individual has a high concern for self and also a high concern for her interaction partner. As such, she often puts great energy into finding out the underlying needs or desires within the relationship to see if there is a mutually beneficial solution that will make each partner happy. Katelyn and

Cooperation
The dimension of conflict styles that involves the mutual consideration of the goals of both interaction partners.

Directness
The dimension of conflict styles that involves the willingness to engage the process of conflict and to communicate openly about that conflict.

Competing
With a high concern for self and a low concern for others, this conflict style focuses on "winning" the conflict encounter at the expense of the interaction partner.

Collaborating
With a high concern for self and a high concern for others, this conflict style focuses on reaching a mutually beneficial solution with an interaction partner.

Burlingham/Shutterstock.com

Bristol have decided to buy their first home, and Katelyn has always wanted to experience life in a city. Bristol grew up wanting a dog because her siblings had severe allergies, but she can't imagine a dog stuck indoors in a high-rise. After discussing ideas with each other, they were able to have their realtor locate them a downtown condominium with a private fenced balcony near a large public park.

Avoiding

With a low concern for self and a low concern for others, this conflict style focuses on ignoring the competing goals that led to relational conflict between interaction partners.

- **Avoiding.** The third conflict pattern is one in which an individual has a low concern for self and a low concern for his interaction partner. As such, individuals who follow this pattern often ignore problems and avoid conflict in the hopes that the competing goals will somehow resolve themselves. Samuel and Takeko rarely discuss her alcohol consumption. Because Samuel grew up as the child of an alcoholic, he was very clear in not wanting to date someone who drank. Now that they are married, Takeko often drinks in the morning after Samuel leaves for work, hoping to sober up by the time he returns from home so he doesn't find out.

Accommodating

With a low concern for self and a high concern for others, this conflict style focuses on giving in to all or most demands of the interaction partner.

- **Accommodating.** The fourth conflict pattern is one in which an individual has a low concern for self but a high concern for his interaction partner. As such, he often actively attempts to solve relationship problems but often gives in to the goals or demands of the other. Frank and Sebastian have been dating exclusively for almost a decade since they met at an out-of-state conference. Now that gay marriage has been legalized in their home states, Frank is needling Sebastian in the hopes of getting a proposal. Even though Sebastian finds the idea of a formal commitment terrifying and had hoped to never marry, he finally proposed to Frank rather than face the prospect of possibly losing his affection.

Compromising

With a moderate concern for both self and others, this conflict style focuses on each interaction partner giving up some aspect of her competing goals in exchange for other(s).

- **Compromising.** The fifth conflict pattern is one in which an individual has a moderate concern for both self and her interaction partner. As such, each partner often gives up some goals in whole or part in order to retain the ability to pursue other goals in whole or part. Ashten was surprised when her boyfriend, Dan, decided to attend a low-ranked graduate school just so they could live in the same city. However, in doing so he claimed he had demonstrated his commitment and subsequently made her promise to wait an extra couple years to get engaged, despite her desire to begin planning a quicker shared future.

As you can see from the five patterns of conflict, people vary widely in their concern for both themselves and their relational partner. Although many may agree that having a healthy concern for both the self and the other are important, collaboration may not be an essential component of conflict management in every situation. Bobbie-Jo and Garret are remodeling their downstairs bathroom, and it has come time to pick out a small window covering for the tiny space. Although Garret likes the ease of blinds, he never uses that bathroom, and Bobbie-Jo much prefers some reasonably priced curtains.

BOX 7.6: Communication Currents

Conflict Patterns in Current Television

The Walking Dead, Season 5, Episode 16, "Conquer," http://bit.ly/2n7QK14

I n the award-winning television show *The Walking Dead,* a group of individuals come together after surviving a nationwide apocalyptic plague that turns normal citizens into flesh-eating zombies. In the show, the main character Rick Grimes leads a ragtag band of misfits as they struggle to survive and thrive despite the crumbling remains of American society. In a dystopia now characterized by survival and the requisite selfishness that lies at the core of the human experience, Rick and his new "family" have struggled to create rules and norms that fit their survival needs.

As we watch this video clip, Rick and his family have found sanctuary at a walled-in neighborhood that seems to have withstood the onslaught of zombies. As part of their agreement to be allowed to settle in this area, each member of Rick's group has agreed to the set social rules that help to enforce the peace. As a result, members of this small "society" seem not to understand the outside world and the horrors of existence. As can be seen in the video, Rick's host Deanna (the older woman) and Rick's friend Maggie (the younger woman) are discussing a recent conflict event in which Rick waved a gun in an attempt to maintain order.

INSTRUCTIONS: Watch the video again, paying careful attention to the conflict between the two characters in the scene. How does each character handle the situation? What pattern of conflict do you see emerging? Consider how you would feel if you were in a similar argument. How would you suggest that each woman should respond in order to calm the tension in the situation? Do you think that the tension is warranted in this scene?

Instead of wasting the time and effort on coming to a collaborative decision, Garrick accommodates Bobbie-Jo's desire for curtains because he honestly doesn't care; Garrick would much rather use his energy to argue for a larger television in the den.

Regardless of the manner through which people tend to handle conflict, it is an important process in all relationships. However, not every moment of disagreement is worth engaging in the process; sometimes, choosing to avoid communication on an unimportant topic can be an equally effective strategy.[44] However, sometimes choosing to give in to the demands of others can influence both parties' perceptions of power within the relationship.[45]

Power in Conflict Encounters

When relational partners engage in conflict, it is essential to note that these partners are also using that conflict process as an opportunity to explore and/or demonstrate their **power** within the relationship. Power is viewed as an individual's ability to influence other people or events,[46] and that ability to influence may come in a variety of forms. Regardless of the way that power looks within a partnership, it is important to note that relational power does not exist without at least two people involved in the allocation of that power. One person does not have power over another unless that other person is willing to give up power within the dyad. Neville and Sumiko have been best friends since the first day they moved into the dorms across the hall from one another. Because Neville believes that Sumiko is smarter at all things related to school, he allows her to make plans and set schedules when studying for their shared classes. Recently, Neville had plans to go see a basketball game on campus but canceled those plans when Sumiko told Neville that he couldn't go out the night before a large midterm examination. By allowing her to so strongly influence both events and experiences in his own life, Neville has given Sumiko great relational power.

When looking at relationships, scholars have identified many different types of interpersonal power based on a variety of characteristics.[47] Each of the following is a way in which individuals may choose to wield or accede power:

- **Status.** Some individuals have interpersonal power because of the social groups to which they belong. When Mike and Tabby started dating

Power
The ability of a group or individual to direct the people, events, or behaviors within a defined system.

Status
Interpersonal power derived from one's membership in a social group.

Folio Images/Alamy Stock Photo

in high school, their pairing seemed perfectly matched as the lacrosse team captain and as a member of the dance team. However, when Tabby continued to dance in college and Mike decided to focus on his studies, Tabby found herself having greater social status when they attended parties and functions as a couple, which ultimately influenced her power within their shared relationship.

- **Position power.** Also known as **structural power**, some people gain interpersonal power from holding a particular role or title that has certain expectations, giving that person power. Because Heath met his fiancée Valentina through the yoga class that she taught each weekend, they initially had a lot of life goals in common. However, whenever they meet other yogis in the area, Heath is clearly seen by these new acquaintances as "Valentina's sidekick" while she is the one that gets all the attention. Valentina's position in the yoga community gives her a relative power over Heath, which he begrudgingly accepts as inevitable.

Position Power
Interpersonal power derived from one's role or title and the associated expectations.

Structural Power
See Position Power.

- **Personality dominance.** Not to be confused with "social dominance,"[48] personality dominance refers to an individual's predisposition or yearning toward seeking out or displaying power over other individuals through influence or control, regardless of either person's position within a social hierarchy.[49] For whatever reason, Logan feels the need to display power; a bully as a youth, Logan now inexplicably withholds access to important county documents despite his position as an information officer for the county seat of government. As someone with personality dominance as a character trait, Logan has a desire to demonstrate power to those with whom he interacts.

Personality Dominance
Interpersonal power displayed as a consequence of a person's individual yearning or predisposition toward demonstrating influence or control over others, regardless of position.

Wavebreak Media ltd/Alamy Stock Photo

Competence
Interpersonal power that comes from possessing skills that lead to decision making, task accomplishment, topical discussions, or other desired outcomes.

Experienced Power
Interpersonal power that is derived from an individual's perception or feeling about his or her own influence over people or events.

Perceived Power
Interpersonal power that comes from other people believing that a person has influence over people or events.

- **Competence.** Some individuals uniquely possess a skill or set of skills that allows them to navigate social situations and contribute to social interaction functions like decision making, task accomplishment, or topical discussions. With these unique skills or ranges of expertise, such individuals necessarily have power when in that situation. When Daniel picked up Gentry to go to a drive-in movie together, Daniel's automobile troubles could have caused major problems if Gentry hadn't worked as a mechanic after school before attending college; as such, Gentry was able to take charge of the situation and facilitate a temporary fix that would last the whole evening.

- **Experienced power.** When someone believes that she has power, she may actually create her own sense of interpersonal power and thus behave in powerful ways based on those self-perceptions or feelings of power. Even though Troy was a relatively incompetent manager of people, he truly believed that he had a knack for working with others. Because of this, he acted decisively and swiftly and displayed influence over events in his workplace.

- **Perceived power.** Outside observers sometimes give interpersonal power to other people depending on the manner in which they perceive those people as powerful. Because Ximena was so physically attractive, other volunteers who also labored at the shelter assumed she must have competence in a wide variety of other areas as well. When decisions or situations arose that needed attention, she was often the *de facto* leader despite her relatively new status at the organization.

Conflict is both an inevitable and a necessary part of navigating close relationships. Whenever people relate to one another in significant ways, they likely find that some of their individual goals are not perfectly aligned with one another, often leading to an opportunity for communication to navigate this relational hurdle. As people experience interpersonal conflict—and the resultant influence of power—within their relationships, the most successful communicators learn to adapt their communication patterns accordingly. Regardless of the degree of power that someone brings to a situation or the manner in which his partner may approach conflict, there is always a choice about how to engage in the most relationship-focused forms of conflict-related maintenance behaviors. Not all conflict is constructive to relationships, however, and we discuss conflict that is harmful or transgressive within a relationship in Chapter 8.

Physical Intimacy

A discussion of maintaining close relationships would not be complete without a frank discussion of physical intimacy and its role in relationships. From early family relationships, where a parent may use touch to console or provide care for a young child, to the high fives and "good game" experienced while playing as a member of a team, people can easily become used to physical touch as a powerful expression of affection or inclusion, signaling a close

personal relationship. Grandparents Stacey and Jon have had a fulfilling, long-term relationship with one another and are now approaching their 30th wedding anniversary. Despite their advancing years and declining energy, Jon has booked a weekend retreat at the resort where they had their honeymoon and hopes to re-create the setting of their first sexual encounter so many years ago. When people like Stacey and Jon become engaged in long-term romantic relationships with one another, the role of physical intimacy becomes a particularly important topic in terms of relationship-focused maintenance behaviors.

Short-Term Sexual Behaviors

It is important to distinguish between physical intimacy in these long-term romantic relationships and other forms of sexual encounters, however. Scholars often make a distinction between what is called **short-term sex** and **long-term sex**. Although long-term sex involves people in relationships over a perceived significant period, short-term sex occurs when a couple has sex without having an emotionally close relationship.[50] These short-term sexual encounters are also called **casual sex** and encompass **hookups**, **friends-with-benefits**, or **booty-call** relationships. Hookups occur among people who have little or no sexual commitment and are nominally acquainted, while friends-with-benefits are friends who have no commitment yet engage in sexual behaviors with one another.[51,52] Although many people may use the term, a specific definition of a booty-call is hard to pin down; booty-call relationships may span a variety of relationship interactions but typically involve an on-demand short-term sexual partner with no commitments that

Short-Term Sex
Sexual encounters between two people who do not have an emotionally close relationship.

Long-Term Sex
Sexual intimacy between people in relationships over a perceived significant period.

Casual Sex
See Short-Term Sex.

Hookups
Brief sexual encounters between nominally acquainted people (strangers or casual acquaintances) who have little or no sexual commitment to one another, typically not lasting longer than one night.

Friends-with-Benefits
Sexual encounters between friends who have little or no sexual commitment to one another.

Booty-Call
Sexual encounters between on-demand short-term sexual partners with no commitments to one another, which may recur over a long time.

may or may not reoccur over a long time. Men are more likely than are women to pursue these casual sexual relationships regardless of relationship type, but both men and women prefer unattached sexual partners over those already in relationships.[53] These short-term sexual interactions serve very different functions from those provided by a long-term sexual relationship, and as such partners may look for a variety of different types of characteristics in sexual partners depending on their goals. Research has shown that heterosexual, gay, and lesbian partners want different things from long-term sexual partners (e.g., intellectual, emotional, and relational characteristics) than from short-term partners (e.g., physical characteristics).[54] Regardless of desire and need, sex in short-term relationships looks very different from the maintenance behaviors associated with sexual intimacy in long-term relationships.

Long-Term Sexual Behaviors

Sexual behavior in long-term relationships induces a variety of positive interpersonal functions that were discussed in previous chapters. From feelings of closeness to increased relational satisfaction, sexual behavior among long-term romantic partners is a relationship-focused behavior that can bring pleasure and a positive experience to both partners. Indeed, sexual satisfaction is closely related to each relationship context, with established relationships reporting greater satisfaction than casual relationships.[55] In long-term relationships, sexual behaviors increase perceptions of love and intimacy—and contrary to some cultural perceptions—long-term partners generally experience a greater frequency of sexual encounters than do single individuals, with cohabiting opposite-sex partners and same-sex male partners reporting more frequent sex than married opposite-sex partners.[56]

Despite the importance of sexual engagement and the increased frequency of sex within long-term relationships, sexual behaviors typically begin to occur less often across the life span. Some scholars claim that the desire to engage in sexual activity is closely related to hormones that regulate mating, and partnered men may experience the gradual lessening of testosterone production as they remain in long-term relationships, particularly if they spend much time around women and children.[57] Indeed, regardless of relationship context sexual interaction among partners lessens in frequency—and sexual disinterest increases—over the course of the long-term relationship as partners age.[58] All is not lost, however; because of widespread differences in both preferences and desires for sexual behavior, conversations about both sexual needs and desires allow for the maintenance of greater sexual satisfaction over time in long-term romantic partners.[62] Although it will require confronting personal anxiety and perhaps even feelings of jealousy, it is important to discuss expectations,

BOX 7.7: Commendable Connections

Ethics and Sexual Encounters[59,60,61]

Although there is some slight variation in the exact numbers, scholars have found that over three-quarters of college students are likely to have hooked up with someone in the last year, with hookups defined as brief sexual encounters between nominally acquainted people (strangers or casual acquaintances) who have little or no sexual commitment to one another, typically not lasting longer than one night.[59,60] Although a hookup may not necessarily include intercourse, it often results in sexual satisfaction for one or both partners.

The debate about hookups occurs in both formal and informal settings, with a range of attitudes and perspectives that may focus on frequency, safety, morality, and/or the impacts of such short-term relationships, just to name a few. However, regardless of one's attitudes, the prevalence of these sexual encounters makes it important to have a discussion of the ethics involved in sexual activity with short-term and long-term sexual partners.

In his book, scholar Paul Abramson offers many ethical principles for sexual activity, many focusing on the communication patterns that emerge around sexual encounters.[61] One ethical principle, is to "speak up/speak out" with a focus on both self-reflection and open communication about sexual behaviors:

> **Inner monologue:** It is essential for individuals to do a self-inventory of their *own* goals, desires, and needs before engaging in sexual activity with another person. Reflection and thought *before* one finds oneself in the midst of a sexual encounter can allow clarity and composure during an admittedly distracting experience.

> **Partner dialogue:** After knowing one's own boundaries and desires, it is up to *both* partners to openly communicate about sexual activity that is about to occur. Beyond simply gaining consent (an *essential* first step), dialogue ensures that sexual encounters are not filled with regret for one or both partners.

INSTRUCTIONS: Take a personal inventory of your recent communication behaviors. Have you openly discussed your feelings about sexual involvement with your family, friends, or romantic partners? How do those conversations look different depending on who you are talking to? *Should* those conversations vary based on the audience? Have you ever engaged in unwanted sexual activity, or encouraged someone else to engage in said behavior? What might ethical communication look like between two people who are interested in brief or long-term sexual encounters?

needs, and desires with partners, as differing expectations for sexual behavior likely lead to relationships falling out of maintenance.[63]

Chapter Summary

Relationships are complicated social phenomena, and people must put in effort in order to keep a relationship healthy or to move that relationship toward a greater level of closeness. Scholars agree that—without work—relational partners tend toward growing apart from one another. Interestingly, one of the major areas that require work is in finding balance in interpersonal relationships. From openness to closedness, connection to autonomy, and predictability to novelty, people are constantly negotiating with one another how their relationship will respond to changing relational dialectics. These tensions and others often shift as relationships move through time, with key markers in the relationship described as relational turning points. Many of these key experiences—like a first kiss or a couple moving across the country for graduate school—can have an influence on the trajectory of most any interpersonal interaction.

All relationships experience moments of change or tension. Indeed, all types of relationships negotiate conflict and balance power as part of regular maintenance. However, there are clear ways that people can ensure that conflict episodes or demonstrations of power are more beneficial than detrimental for relationships. Relationship-focused behaviors include a variety of communication behaviors that enhance a partnership in both verbal and nonverbal ways, focusing on the language and physical expressions that enhance one's understanding of a relational partner.

MindTap®

First-Person Video

Long-Distance Partners Skype

Apply what you've learned in this chapter by analyzing the "Long-Distance Partners Skype" video, using the accompanying questions as a guide. This video and these questions are available online with your MindTap Speech for *Interconnections: Interpersonal Communication Foundations and Contexts*.

MindTap®

Key Terms

Use flashcards to learn key concepts and take a quiz to test your knowledge.

Accommodating	Centripetal Perspective	Connection
Assurances		Cooperation
Autonomy	Closedness	Dialectic Tensions
Avoiding	Collaborating	Directness
Booty-Call	Competence	Distal Relationship
Casual Sex	Competing	Experienced Power
Centrifugal Perspective	Compromising	Friends-with-Benefits
	Conflict	

Geographically Close
   Relationship
Hookups
Involuntary
   Relationships
Long-Distance
   Relationship
Long-Term Sex
Networks
Neutralization
Novelty
Openness
Perceived Power
Personality Dominance

Position Power
Positivity
Power
Predictability
Proximal Relationship
Reframing
Relational Dialectics
Relational Maintenance
Relational Turning
   Points
Relationship-
   Maintaining
   Behaviors
Relationship Talks

Selection
Self-Disclosure
Separation
Short-Term Sex
Status
Structural Power
Tasking
Turning Points Analysis
Understanding
Voluntary
   Relationships

Discussion Questions

1. Think about your closest relationship, whether with a friend, family member, or romantic partner. What sorts of relationship-maintaining behaviors do you engage in with that person?

2. Often relationships end because one or both parties have competing views of certain relational dialectics. Consider a friendship or romantic partnership in your life that has ended or faded. Do any of the dialectic tensions describe a problem that you were having with your partner? How might you handle these tensions in the future?

3. Think carefully about each of the dialectic tensions. Which one of the tensions do you most struggle with? What does this tell you about yourself as a relational person? Do you seek out certain types of people as a result? Why?

4. Discuss a time when you have experienced conflict in a close relationship. What did that feel like? Compare your conflict pattern in that relationship with one in another situation. Do you have a consistent pattern? Are you pleased with how you handle interpersonal conflict?

5. Consider the role of physical intimacy in your life. Are there certain elements of physical touch you are comfortable with? Are there other elements of intimacy that you prefer to avoid? Make a communication plan for how to discuss both of these topics with your current and/or future romantic partners.

Making Connections

Relational maintenance is generally thought of as a lot of work. In particular, that closeness is often maintained through conversation and affection. How might the verbal messages from Chapter 4 and the nonverbal messages from Chapter 6 cocreate meaning within a long-term relationship?

Chapter Quiz

1. Which of the following types of relationship-maintaining behaviors describes verbal and nonverbal expressions of commitment or faithfulness?

   a. Assurances
   b. Tasking
   c. Networks
   d. Self-disclosure
   e. Relationship talks
   f. Understanding

2. Which of the following types of relationship-maintaining behaviors describes mutual effort toward the work associated with a partnership?

   a. Assurances
   b. Tasking
   c. Networks
   d. Self-disclosure
   e. Relationship talks
   f. Understanding

3. Bryana and Suravi are experiencing conflict in their roommate relationship. If Suravi wants to win at all costs, which of the following patterns of conflict is she most likely displaying?

   a. Collaborating
   b. Avoiding
   c. Competing
   d. Accommodating
   e. Compromising
   f. None of the above

4. Bryana and Suravi are experiencing conflict in their roommate relationship. If Bryana instead would prefer to pretend like nothing is wrong in the hopes that the issues resolve themselves, which of the following patterns of conflict is she most likely displaying?

   a. Collaborating
   b. Avoiding
   c. Competing
   d. Accommodating
   e. Compromising
   f. None of the above

5. Which of the following patterns of conflict show a high concern for self?

   a. Collaborating and compromising
   b. Avoiding and accommodating
   c. Competing and collaborating
   d. Accommodating and collaborating
   e. Only compromising
   f. None of the above

6. T/F Relational maintenance is a term used to describe a situation in which people enact behaviors to cause a close partnership to diminish in closeness.

7. T/F Sarah always tries to practice empathy and then show an appropriate level of forgiveness with her romantic partner. This is an example of a relationship-maintaining behavior.

8. T/F A proximal relationship is one which takes place over a long distance, with partners rarely seeing one another.

9. T/F Predictability is one end of a continuum of relational dialectics, with the other end being closeness.

10. T/F All relationships experience significant moments called turning points, and these turning points are the same for every relationship.

Endnotes

1. For an overview, see Stafford, L. (2011). Measuring relationship maintenance behaviors: Critique and development of the revised relationship maintenance behavior scale. *Journal of Social and Personal Relationships, 28*(2), 278–303. doi:10.1177/0265407510378125

2. Stafford, L., & Canary, D. J. (1991). Maintenance strategies and romantic relationship type, gender, and relational characteristics. *Journal of Social and Personal Relationships, 8*, 217–242.

3. Stafford, L., Dainton, M., & Haas, S. M. (2000). Measuring routine and strategic relational maintenance: Scale revision, sex versus gender roles, and the prediction of relational characteristics. *Communication Monographs, 67*, 306–323.

4. Stafford, L. (2011). Measuring relationship maintenance behaviors: Critique and development of the revised relationship maintenance behavior scale. *Journal of Social and Personal Relationships, 28*, 278–303. doi:10.1177/0265407510378125

5. For an overview, see Stafford, L. (2011). Measuring relationship maintenance behaviors: Critique and development of the revised relationship maintenance behavior scale. *Journal of Social and Personal Relationships, 28*(2), 278–303. doi:10.1177/0265407510378125

6. Stafford, L., & Canary, D. J. (1991). Maintenance strategies and romantic relationship type, gender, and relational characteristics. *Journal of Social and Personal Relationships, 8*, 217–242.

7. Stafford, L., Dainton, M., & Haas, S. M. (2000). Measuring routine and strategic relational maintenance: Scale revision, sex versus gender roles, and the prediction of relational characteristics. *Communication Monographs, 67*, 306–323.

8. Stafford, L. (2011). Measuring relationship maintenance behaviors: Critique and development of the revised relationship maintenance behavior scale. *Journal of Social and Personal Relationships, 28*, 278–303. doi:10.1177/0265407510378125

9. For an overview, see Fitzpatrick, M. A., & Badzinski, D. M. (1994). All in the family: Interpersonal communication in kin relationships. In M. L. Knapp & G. R. Miller (Eds.), *Handbook of Interpersonal Communication* (2nd ed., pp. 726–771). Thousand Oaks, CA: Sage.

10. For an overview, see Schrodt, P., & Phillips, K. E. (2016). Self-disclosure and relational uncertainty as mediators of family communication patterns and relational outcomes in sibling relationships. *Communication Monographs, 83*(4), 1–19.

11. For an overview on related research, see Floyd, K. (1995). Gender and closeness among friends and siblings. *The Journal of Psychology, 129*(2), 193–202. doi:10.1080/00223980.1995.9914958

12. Baxter, L. A. (2006). Relational dialectics theory: Multivocal dialogues of family communication. In D. O. Braithwaite & L. A. Baxter (Eds.), *Engaging Theories in Family Communication: Multiple Perspectives* (pp. 130–145). Thousand Oaks, CA: Sage.

13. Baxter, L. A. (1990). Dialectical contradictions in relationship development. *Journal of Social and Personal Relationships, 7*, 69–88.

14. Baxter, L. A., & Montgomery, B. M. (1996). *Relating: Dialogues and Dialectics*. New York, NY: Guilford Press.

15. Baxter, L. A. (2006). Relational dialectics theory: Multivocal dialogues of family communication. In D. O. Braithwaite &

L. A. Baxter (Eds.), *Engaging Theories in Family Communication: Multiple Perspectives* (pp. 130–145). Thousand Oaks, CA: Sage.

16. Baxter, L. A. (2009). Relational dialectics. In S. W. Littlejohn & K. A. Foss (Eds.), *Encyclopedia of Communication Theory* (pp. 837–840). Thousand Oaks, CA: Sage.

17. Sahlstein, E. M. (2004). Relating at a distance: Negotiating being together and being apart in long-distance relationships. *Journal of Social and Personal Relationships, 21*(5), 689–710. doi:10.1177/0265407504046115

18. As exemplar, see Romo, L. K., Dinsmore, D. R., & Watterson, T. C. (2016). "Coming out" as an alcoholic: How former problem drinkers negotiate disclosure of their nondrinking identity. *Health Communication, 31*(3), 336–345.

19. Hwang, Y. (2005). Investigating enterprise systems adoption: Uncertainty avoidance, intrinsic motivation, and the technology acceptance model. *European Journal of Information Systems, 14*, 150–161.

20. Dorfman, P. W., & Howell, J. P. (1988). Dimensions of national culture and effective leadership patterns: Hofstede revisited. *Advances in Interna-tional Comparative Management, 3*, 127–150.

21. Hofstede, G. (1980). *Culture's Consequences: International Differences in Work-Related Values*. Beverly Hills, CA: Sage.

22. Baxter, L. A., & Montgomery, B. M. (1998). Dialogism and relational dialectics. In B. M. Montgomery & L. A. Baxter (Eds.), *Dialectical Approaches to Studying Personal Relationships* (pp. 155–184). Mahwah, NJ: Lawrence Erlbaum.

23. For an overview and application, see O'Hara, L. L. (2016). Discursive struggles in "diabetes management": A case study using Baxter's relational dialectics 2.0. *Western Journal of Communication*, doi:10.1080/10570314.2016.1241425.

24. Bowman, J. M., & Pace, R. (2014). Dual-tasking effects on outcomes of mobile communication technologies. *Communication Research Reports, 31*(2), 221–231.

25. Baxter, L. A., & Bullis, C. (1986). Turning points in developing romantic relationships. *Human Communication Research, 12*(4), 469–493.

26. Dailey, R. M., LeFebvre, L., Crook, B., & Brody, N. (2016). Relational uncertainty and communication in on-again/off-again romantic relationships: Assessing changes and patterns across recalled turning points. *Western Journal of Communication, 80*(3), 239–263.

27. Stafford, L. (2005). *Maintaining Long-Distance and Cross-Residential Relationships*. Mahwah, NJ: Lawrence Erlbaum.

28. Baxter, L. A., & Bullis, C. (1986). Turning points in developing romantic relationships. *Human Communication Research, 12*(4), 469–493.

29. Halualani, R. T., Chitgopekar, A., Morrison, J. H. T. A., & Dodge, P. S. (2004). Who's interacting? And what are they talking about—Intercultural contact and interaction among multicultural university students. *International Journal of Intercultural Relations, 28*(5), 353–372.

30. Aylor, B. A. (2003). Maintaining long-distance relationships. In D. J. Canary & M. Dainton (Eds.), *Maintaining relationships through communication: Relational, contextual, and cultural variations* (pp. 127–139). Mahwah, NJ: Lawrence Erlbaum.

31. Stafford, L., & Reske, J. R. (1990). Idealization and communication in long-distance premarital relationships. *Family Relations, 39,* 274–279.

32. Sahlstein, E. M. (2006). Making plans: Praxis strategies for negotiating uncertainty-certainty in long-distance relationships. *Western Journal of Communication, 70*(2), 147–165. doi:10.1080/10570310600710042

33. Van Horn, K. R., Arnone, A., Nesbitt, K., Desilets, L., Sears, T., Giffin, M., & Brudi, R. (1997). Physical distance and interpersonal characteristics in college students' romantic relationships. *Personal Relationships, 4,* 25–34.

34. Maguire, K. C. (2007). "Will it ever end?": A (re)examination of uncertainty in college student long-distance dating relationships. *Communication Quarterly, 55*(4), 415–432. doi:10.1080/01463370701658002

35. Helgeson, V. S. (1991). Long-distance romantic relationships: Sex differences in adjustment and breakup. *Personality and Social Psychology Bulletin, 20*(3), 254–265. doi:10.1177/0146167294203003

36. Cameron, J. J., & Ross, M. (2007). In times of uncertainty: Predicting the survival of long-distance relationships. *The Journal of Social Psychology, 147*(6), 581–606.

37. For a review of these studies, see Van Horn, K. R., Arnone, A., Nesbitt, K., Desilets, L., Sears, T., Giffin, M., & Brudi, R. (1997). Physical distance and interpersonal characteristics in college students' romantic relationships. *Personal Relationships, 4,* 25–34.

38. Sigman, S. (1991). Handling the discontinuous aspects of continuing social relationships: Towards research of the persistence of social forms. *Communication Theory, 1*(2), 106–127.

39. For a brief discussion of both possibilities, see Gottman, J. M., Coan, J., Carrere, S., & Swanson, C. (1998). Predicting marital happiness and stability from newlywed interactions. *Journal of Marriage and the Family, 60,* 5–22.

40. Sillars, A. L., Canary, D. J., & Tafoya, M. (2004). Communication, conflict, and the quality of family relationships. In A. L. Vangelisti (Ed.), *Handbook of Family Interaction* (pp. 413–446). Mahwah, NJ: Lawrence Erlbaum.

41. Blake, R. R., & Mouton, J. S. (1964). *The Managerial Grid.* Houston, TX: Gulf.

42. Kilmann, R. H., & Thomas, K. W. (1977). Developing a forced-choice measure of conflict-handling behavior: The "mode" instrument. *Educational and Psychological Measurement, 37,* 309–325.

43. Shell, G. R. (2001). Bargaining styles and negotiation: The Thomas-Kilmann Conflict Mode Instrument in negotiation training. *Negotiation Journal, 17*(2), 155–174.

44. For a discussion, see La Valley, A. G., & Guerrero, L. K. (2012). Perceptions of conflict behavior and relational satisfaction in adult parent-child relationships: A dyadic analysis from an attachment perspective. *Communication Research, 39*(1), 48–78. doi:10.1177/0093650210391655

45. Hocker, J. L., & Wilmot, W. W. (1998). *Interpersonal Conflict* (5th ed.). Dubuque, IA: Brown & Benchmark.

46. Donahue, W. A., & Kolt, R. (1992). *Managing Interpersonal Conflict.* Newbury Park, CA: Sage.

47. Mast, M. S. (2010). Interpersonal behavior and social perception in a hierarchy: The interpersonal power and behaviour model. *European Review of Social Psychology, 21,* 1–33. doi:10.1080/10463283.2010.486942

48. Sidanius, J., & Pratto, F. (2001). *Social Dominance: An Intergroup Theory of Social Hierarchy and Oppression.* Cambridge, UK: Cambridge University Press.

49. Ellyson, S. L., & Dovidio, J. F. (1985). Power, dominance, and nonverbal behavior: Basic concepts and issues. In S. L. Ellyson & J. F. Dovidio (Eds.), *Power, Dominance, and Nonverbal Behavior* (pp. 1–27). New York, NY: Springer.

50. Guerrero, L. K., Andersen, P. A., & Afifi, W. A. (2011). *Close Encounters: Communication in Relationships* (3rd ed.). Thousand Oaks, CA: Sage.

51. Jonason, P. K. (2013). Four functions for four relationships: Consensus definitions of university students. *Archives of Sexual Behavior, 42,* 1407–1414. doi:10.1007/s10508-013-0189-7

52. For an overview of hookup culture, see Aubrey, J. S., & Smith, S. E. (2016). The impact of exposure to sexually oriented media on the endorsement of hookup culture: A panel study of first-year college students. *Mass Communication and Society, 19*(1), 74–101.

53. Shackelford, T. K., Goetz, A. T., LaMunyon, C. W., Quintus, B. J., & Weeks-Shackelford, V. A. (2004). Sex differences in sexual psychology produce sex-similar preferences for a short-term mate. *Archives of Sexual Behavior, 33*(4), 405–412.

54. Regan, P. C., Medina, R., & Joshi, A. (2001). Partner preference among homosexual men and women: What is desirable in a sex partner is not necessarily desirable in a romantic partner. *Social Behavior and Personality, 29*(7), 625–633. doi:10.2224/sbp.2001.29.7.625

55. Berscheid, E., & Regan, P. (2005). Mate selection. *The Psychology of Interpersonal Relationships.* Upper Saddle River, NJ: Pearson Education.

56. Ibid.

57. Van Anders, S. M., & Watson, N. V. (2006). Relationship status and testosterone in North American heterosexual and non-heterosexual men and women: Cross-sectional and longitudinal data. *Psychoneuroendocrinology, 31,* 715–723.

58. Berscheid, E., & Regan, P. (2005). Mate selection. *The Psychology of Interpersonal Relationships.* Upper Saddle River, NJ: Pearson Education.

59. Paul, E. L., McManus, B., & Hayes, A. (2000). "Hookups": Characteristics and correlates of college students' spontaneous and anonymous sexual experiences. *Journal of Sex Research, 37,* 76–88.

60. Abramson, P. R. (2010). *Sex Appeal: Six Ethical Principles for the 21st Century.* New York, NY: Oxford University Press.

61. For a review of college students' perceptions, see Barriger, M., & Velez-Blasini, C. J. (2013). Descriptive and injunctive social norm overestimation in hooking up and their role as predictors of hook-up activity in a college student sample. *Journal of Sex Research, 50*(1), 84–94.

62. MacNeil, S., & Byers, E. S. (2009). Role of sexual self-disclosure in the sexual satisfaction of long-term heterosexual couples. *Journal of Sex Research, 46*(1), 13–14.

63. For a review, see Hull, T. H. (2008). Sexual pleasure and well-being. *International Journal of Sexual Health, 20*(102), 133–145. doi:10.1080/19317610802157234

Radius Images/Alamy Stock Photo

What types of things may lead to hurt feelings?

At what point does something become a "legitimate" problem between two people?

MindTap®

Review the chapter's learning objectives and **start** with a quick warm-up activity.

Learning Objectives

After you finish reading this chapter, you will be able to:

Identify examples of relational transgressions.

List some common aggressive behaviors across cultures.

Identify unhealthy conflict behaviors that lead to relational ruin.

Compare the types of deception and how they differ from one another.

MindTap®

Read, highlight, and take notes online.

Quince and Barret met through an online roommate-matching service in their local area. Quince had screened quite a few potential roommates, but Barret seemed like the most logical choice. Similar interests, a nearby hometown, and a very active lifestyle made Quince feel comfortable at their first meeting. After a few months, though, Barret started to get on Quince's nerves. Every day, Quince found dishes in the sink, which didn't seem to fit Barret's self-characterization as "clean." Barret's long-term romantic partner came over often, and they occasionally sat on the couch watching horror movies late into the night, which annoyed Quince. The final straw for Quince was when he came home to find that Barret had borrowed his last box of pasta to make dinner. After asking Barret to move out, Quince realized he would need to explain his reasoning. A couple days later, as he was helping Barret carry boxes to his car, Quince finally described the things that had made this particular roommate situation uncomfortable for him.

RELATIONAL TRANSGRESSIONS

What types of things may lead to hurt feelings? At what point does something become a "legitimate" problem between two people? Every day, we encounter difficulties in our relationships. Sometimes, these relational difficulties may be

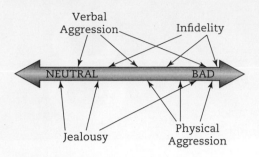

FIGURE 8.1
Continuum of Relational Behaviors

as simple as a feeling of frustration with a relational partner. Other times, that partner may lie or cheat or even physically harm the other. Such a wide range of difficult situations does not lend itself to easy categorization. Although some people may be tempted to locate these transgressions on a continuum of behavior like that seen in Figure 8.1, in truth there is no easy system for determining that one behavior is worse than another behavior. The location on the continuum of each of these types of relational difficulties—and additional others—depends on the individual experiences of each partner, as well as their combined relationship.

In truth, a frank discussion of relational difficulties may be surprising. Unavoidably, every individual creates minor problems for those around her as each intentionally or unintentionally causes pain or annoyance with a variety of people. Many of those problems are easily handled and don't lead to confrontation at all. When Aparna goes through the drive-through to get a burger and accidentally gets onion on her sandwich despite a request to the contrary, she simply removes it from the top and thinks nothing more of it. Star unknowingly drops a candy bar wrapper in Bill's office when she pulls her phone out of her purse, and Bill later picks it up without harboring any ill will. But when Jaden tracks mud through the kitchen for the third time this week, his mother gets angry and yells at him for being inconsiderate. Jaden's mom feels that she cannot handle this type of disrespect any more.

What makes Jaden's behavior different from that of Star or Ellen? After all, each instance resulted in a minor amount of work being done that otherwise wouldn't have been necessary. The answer may surprise you. Jaden's behavior is a problem *because* his mom *felt* that it was problematic. Any type of behavior may be considered a **transgression** between two people if at least one of them feels that a relational rule has been violated. **Relational rules** can be implicit or explicit. **Implicit rules** are those that two partners may never have discussed but were just assumed to be rules within the relationship; **explicit rules**, however, are clearly stated and discussed by relational partners.[1] In the example that opened this chapter, if Barret grew up in a household where dishes were rinsed and stored in the sink until the end of the week when they were washed or placed in a dishwasher, he may have assumed that his placing of dirty dishes in the sink was an acceptable or even a considerate roommate behavior. Quince, however, clearly believed that Barret was breaking some relationship rules. Obviously, Barret was unintentionally hurting the relationship by not cleaning up after himself, but even more so, Quince felt that Barret was deceptive in describing himself as "clean" on the roommate-matching website.

Relational transgressions come in many forms, and partners' reactions to those relational transgressions can vary greatly depending on the situation as well as the relationship itself. Over the course of this chapter, we'll consider a variety of things that may be considered relational transgressions, including various forms of aggression and conflict, deception, envy and jealousy, and various forms of infidelity or cheating.

Transgression
Any behavior or experience where one relational partner feels that the other partner has violated a relational rule.

Relational Rule
A norm or standard for interpersonal behavior that is assumed to be agreed on within a specific relationship.

Implicit Rules
Relational rules that are implied rather than directly stated.

Explicit Rules
Relational rules that are clearly stated by one or more parties within a relationship.

AGGRESSION

Melanie wasn't too excited to play on her boyfriend Cad's adult kickball team, but the opportunity to socialize with a group of other active people in a competitive setting made her give in to his urgings. When the team went out to grab a celebratory drink after the game, Cad decided to make a toast in honor of the team's narrow margin of victory. However, Melanie's smile faded as the speech began with "Despite my own girlfriend's complete lack of coordination on the kickball field . . ." Melanie quickly looked away, trying to hide the tears that had become much more common each time that Cad began to drink. She found it hard to articulate her dissatisfaction with his sense of humor, however, because he was always so quick to apologize the next morning.

Stefan went to the grocery store to grab some snacks for an upcoming study session. While there, he noticed a particularly disruptive child trying to grab all the potato chip bags off the shelf and throw them into his mother's shopping cart. When she got off her cell phone and noticed what happened, the boy's mother simply walked up, looked him in the eye, and then backhanded his face, and pointed to the shelves. As Stefan watched the boy silently return all the bags to the shelf, he couldn't help but feel that he had witnessed something serious even though he himself had been spanked as a child.

Aggression comes in many forms, each of which may have quite negative impacts on the quality of an interaction. Often when people talk about aggression they are thinking of **physical aggression**, or violent acts like hitting, kicking, biting, using weapons, or any other act that intentionally causes physical harm to a person. However, **communicative aggression** is much more common and includes any act that intentionally causes psychological harm to a person; this type of aggression includes name-calling, yelling, threatening

Physical Aggression
Violence that uses real or perceived force to intentionally cause physical harm to a person.

Communicative Aggression
Violence that uses implicit or explicit messages to intentionally cause psychological harm to a person.

George Rudy/Shutterstock.com

others and bullying, or even using speech to turn someone's social network against them. Although there are many laws to deal with physical aggression like fighting, violence, or physical abuse, often forms of communicative aggression get thought of as some type of "protected speech" or simply as the "expressing of an opinion." Regardless of the current state of our ever-changing legal definitions, it is important to understand that aggression can be experienced with similar impact regardless of whether that aggression is physical or experienced through communication.[2]

Verbal Aggression
Screaming at another person or using an offensive tone of voice during an interaction.

Humiliation
Degrading or mocking another person or revealing information about that person that they would prefer to remain private.

Isolation
Trying to break apart or restrict the social connections of another person.

Types of Communicative Aggression

Because of the wide variety of behaviors that can be considered communicative aggression, communication scholars Rene Daily, Carmen Lee, and Brian Spitzberg have tried to break down communicative aggression into its constitutive parts, and in doing so have come up with 11 different ways that people act aggressively while using communication:[3]

- **Verbal aggression** includes screaming at another person or using an offensive tone of voice during an interaction.

- **Humiliation** includes degrading or mocking another person or revealing information about that person that they would prefer to remain private.

- **Isolation** includes trying to break apart or restrict the social connections of another person, even going so far as to turn his or her social network against him or her.

BOX 8.1: InterFace
. . . .
Confrontation with Diverse Others[4]

It is easy to have a lapse in communication quality because each person has a different frame of reference for understanding a situation or a point of view. When people have a relatively similar cultural background, both parties can draw on their shared experiences to explain what is meant and to generate a more complete understanding. For example, Sandra wants to get a new puppy and is looking at a Froston as a possible breed. Sandra's friend Marta has never heard of this kind of dog before, but Sandra quickly explains that her desired puppy is a cross between a French Bulldog and a Boston Terrier. Her other friend Alex worked as a groomer at a local pet store and has a lot of experience with both breeds; he can imagine what the dog would look like. On the other hand, Marta's mother is allergic to pets, so Marta can't even begin to imagine what kind of dog Sandra plans to get. A shared set of experiences or knowledge leads Alex and Sandra to communicate more easily about pets than can Marta and Sandra.

JStaley401/Shutterstock.com

What about a situation where the stakes are higher? If conflict is occurring in the workplace or during a class group project, it makes sense that people who understand each other would naturally communicate more easily, unintentionally alienating other members who don't understand the references. Jian wants to discuss two possible products thoroughly before making a purchasing decision for her company, and as she often discusses ideas with her other Asian friends she plays the devil's advocate in these meetings to point out the pros and cons of each product even though she has a clear personal preference. Miguel shares that same preference and doesn't understand why they have to waste so much time coming to a decision that they already agree on. Instead of each person trying to see the benefits of the other's decision-making style, the meeting quickly devolves into harsh overgeneralizations with sotto voce comments about "indecisive Asians" and "impulsive Latinos." In truth, both Jian's and Miguel's unique perspectives on the decision-making process have merit.

Kathryn Sorrels (2013) recommended taking into consideration six strategies for addressing conflict between cultures.

1. Use *inquiry* to attempt to see the situation from another person's perspective.

2. Understand that each person has a wide variety of *frames* like ethnicity, religion, and sexual orientation that influence how she sees her world.

3. Realize that our *positioning* in relation to others influences how much power we feel we can bring to a conflict situation.

(Continued)

4. Engage in *dialogue* with others to understand and affirm the differences that make others uniquely different from yourself.

5. *Reflect* on your own interactions and the challenges and successes that arose.

6. Engage others around you through direct social *action*. Be the change!

INSTRUCTIONS: Think about a specific situation where you have disagreed with someone who is dissimilar from yourself. Would understanding his own personal perspective have lessened the conflict? Could you have talked it out? How did your own personal experience cause you to misunderstand the other perspective? What can you do next time to avoid this sort of conflict?

Withdrawal
Intentionally neglecting a relationship or ignoring the other person.

Name-Calling
Using any negative names or offensive profanity.

Dominance
Controlling behavior intended to influence decisions or behavior.

Freedom Restriction
Monitoring another person and/or denying him or her the everyday autonomy afforded to other people.

Insecurity Induction
Threatening a person's sense of well-being, whether through deception, acting secretive, or implying potential infidelity or an impending breakup.

- **Withdrawal** includes intentional neglect of a relationship or ignoring the other person.

- **Name-calling** includes the use of any negative names or offensive profanity.

- **Dominance** includes using controlling behavior intended to influence decisions or behavior.

- **Freedom restriction** includes the monitoring of another person and/or the denial of everyday autonomy afforded to other people.

- **Insecurity induction** includes implicit or explicit threats to a person's sense of well-being, whether through deception, acting secretive, or implying potential infidelity or an impending breakup.

- Additional forms of communicative aggression can include an attempt to engage in *degrading dominance* of a relational partner, excessive or unwanted *risk taking,* or even *threatening valued resources* of that interaction partner's experience.

Although these wide-ranging behaviors may seem to fall on a continuum of severity, each individual's experience of the behavior may determine his own personal reaction to this kind of interpersonal interaction. Is one better or worse than another? This is not an easy question. As with any transgression, each of us has a different response to—and experience of—physical or communicative aggression in our own lives.

UNHEALTHY CONFLICT

Conflict
The active process of navigating disagreement over access to resources, people, or opportunities in which one or more parties perceive incompatible goals (from Chapter 7).

As discussed in Chapter 7, constructive forms of **conflict** can be quite beneficial within a relationship. In fact, scholars have rarely found that healthy relationships can even exist without relational partners who engage in—and resolve—regular conflict.[5] However, it is also important to note that some conflict interactions can be perceived by one or both relational partners as a transgression, particularly if a conflict-free relationship seems

BOX 8.2: iPersonal

Bullying and Technology[6]

Every movie about children seems to have a bully in it. Whether that person is stealing kids' milk money, pulling on someone's pigtails, or trying to meet up for a fight under the bleachers, bullying is a common theme in popular culture and has been experienced to some degree by almost everyone at some point in their lives. With the increasing access to Internet communication over the past 20 years, new mediated forms of bullying have become common, such that this so-called **cyberbullying** has become a relatively well-know phenomenon. Constant degrading text messages, Facebook pages dedicated to making fun of peers, online forums for anonymous gossip, or even hastily sent emails that are too harshly worded all can create uncomfortable or hurtful situations that may continue to impact people over a long period of time.

Interestingly, scholars have found that our increased access to technology has not given the "typical" bully an additional venue to wreak havoc in the lives of his victims. Instead, different types of people are more likely to cyberbully than pick a fight in person or harass face-to-face, with females much more likely to cyberbully than to harass someone in person. Also, men and women are more likely to bully to a much greater degree when they are using technology than they would if they could directly see the victim's negative reaction to their behavior.

However, victims aren't the only people who are hurt by the effects of bullying. Indeed, scholars have found that observers of the behavior have a negative reaction, as well as the bullies themselves. The outlook for the futures of people who bully others is not a bright one if their overall behavior doesn't change; there is greater likelihood of difficulties in school, substance abuse, depression, and even thoughts of suicide. Stopping bullying, whether it occurs face-to-face or in an online environment, has become a major goal of many educators, parents, and politicians. Greater attention to your own experience may help you to be able to assist in these efforts to help both the victims and perpetrators of bullying.

INSTRUCTIONS: Think carefully about your experience with bullying in an online environment. Have you ever been tempted to engage in bullying yourself? What made you engage that person, or decide against that course of action? Now think about a time when someone has acted aggressively toward you through email, texting, or in a social media environment. Do you think that the interaction would have gone differently if that person were able to see your reaction directly? Next time you are tempted to strike out against someone, imagine that she is right there with you and see if that changes the way you behave.

---

to be a particularly important implicit or explicit rule in the dyad. So, what makes conflict seem like a transgression within the relationship? If one or both partners are uncomfortable with conflict, this can cause problems. But, even more important, how relational partners react to one another during a conflict (whether a friend, coworker, family member, or romantic partner) can have a serious impact on whether each person perceives that conflict as transgressive or healthy. Ellen has moved back home with her family to save money as she finishes her final year of college. Having been treated as an

Cyberbullying
Using computer-mediated forms of communicative aggression to harass or threaten someone intentionally.

adult by her peers as well as the campus faculty and staff, she finds it difficult to handle that her stepmother Paige still sees her as the little baby girl that she has known for almost two decades. As Paige's unasked-for advice about life, attempts to help Ellen with homework, and constant requests for help around the house begin to eat away at Ellen's sense of independence, Paige notices that the constant conflict with Ellen has led to a stage where her stepdaughter has begun acting like Paige isn't even there. Instead of addressing the difficulties around the house and moving toward a constructive resolution, Ellen's withdrawal from interaction only makes her stepmom want to try to parent Ellen more. Eventually, *not* addressing the issue may lead to Ellen moving back out. Both Ellen and Paige have allowed themselves to be trapped in an unhealthy pattern of conflict.

Ellen's unwillingness to move toward a constructive resolution could—in part—stem from having a low tolerance for disagreement, a characteristic that many people have to varying degrees. In Box 8.3, you can take a modified version of a scale that measures your own willingness to engage in disagreement with relational partners. How would you answer the modified version of Teven, Richmond, and McCroskey's survey[7] in Box 8.3? Considering that the survey includes questions about general feelings towards conflict or about leaving a conversation rather than disagreeing with another person, how do you think Ellen would score? How does her probable score relate to your own answers on the scale?

The Four Horsemen of the Apocalypse

If *some* conflict can be healthy and lead to a better relationship, how do we distinguish that type of conflict from unhealthy, relationship-hurting conflict?

JGI/Jamie Grill/Blend Images/Getty Images

BOX 8.3: Let's Get INTRApersonal

Tolerance for Disagreement Scale[8]

How do you feel when people disagree with those things that you believe to be true? Do you enjoy having your thoughts and ideas challenged, or does this type of conflict create feelings of discomfort as you interact with others? Typically, each person has a different willingness to engage in arguments with those around them. If you haven't thought about your own tolerance for disagreement (TFD), you can use this self-assessment to think about your own attitudes toward conflict. This survey is a modified version of a survey created by the original researchers (Teven, Richmond, & McCroskey) in 1998 to look at how people felt about disagreement in their own interpersonal interactions.

INSTRUCTIONS: Think carefully about your feelings and attitudes about conflict. Then, write the number that shows how much you agree or disagree with the statements below. At the end, you'll be able to calculate your current tolerance for disagreement in interpersonal interactions!

1	2	3	4	5
Strongly Disagree	Disagree	Neither Agree Nor Disagree	Agree	Strongly Agree

_____ 1. I don't like to be in situations where people are in disagreement.

_____ 2. It is more fun to be involved in a discussion where there is a lot of disagreement.

_____ 3. I prefer being in groups where everyone's beliefs are the same as mine.

_____ 4. I enjoy talking to people with points of view different than mine.

_____ 5. I prefer to change the topic of discussion when disagreement occurs.

_____ 6. Disagreements are generally helpful.

_____ 7. I would prefer to work independently rather than to work with other people and have disagreements.

_____ 8. I tend to create disagreements in conversations because it serves a useful purpose.

_____ 9. I would prefer joining a group where no disagreements occur.

_____ 10. I enjoy arguing with other people about things on which we disagree.

_____ 11. I don't like to disagree with other people.

_____ 12. I enjoy disagreeing with others.

_____ 13. Given a choice, I would leave a conversation rather than continue a disagreement.

_____ 14. Disagreement stimulates a conversation and causes me to communicate more.

_____ 15. I avoid talking with people who I think will disagree with me.

Now, add up the total score for the even numbers and for the odd numbers and use the following formula to find a total score:

48 points   +   _____   −   _____   =   _____

Even Score   Odd Score   Your TFD Score

(Continued)

The authors of the scale claim that a score over 46 indicates a high tolerance for disagreement, while a score under 32 indicates a low tolerance for disagreement. Do you have a high or low tolerance, or (like most people) do you fall somewhere in between? What does this tell you about how you handle conflict with the people around you? Were you surprised by your score?

Is there a way for us to know the difference between the two? Researcher John Gottman has done research on romantic partners to determine the subtle distinctions between healthy and unhealthy conflict.[9] Although his research focuses on romantic interactions, it is widely discussed that these same four general types of behavior signal unhealthy interactions in most any form of interpersonal communication. And, as evidenced by Gottman's somewhat theatrical description of these behaviors as the Four Horsemen of the Apocalypse, these conflict styles can serve as indicators of the potential dramatic ending of a relationship and should be seen as an early-warning system for relational destruction:

Criticism
An expression of disapproval or a critique of another person.

- **The First Horseman: Criticism.** The first signal that there is unhealthy conflict in a relationship may be an expression of disapproval or a critique of another person. Some forms of criticism can be healthy, such as when a person articulates a problem that they have with another person's behaviors in an attempt to find resolution. However, when that criticism focuses more on who that person *is* (i.e., their character or their personality[10]) rather than on his specific changeable *behaviors*, this is often an indicator of a bigger problem. If Edmon has concerns about Hector's cleanliness around the house, he may choose to say, "Geez, Hector, you are such a lazy, dirty slob," rather than simply asking him to wash his dishes regularly and not leave laundry all over the bathroom floor.

Contempt
An obvious expression of disdain or the articulation of a belief that the other person is worthless.

- **The Second Horseman: Contempt.** The second signal of unhealthy conflict within a relationship may include an obvious expression of disdain or even the belief that the other person is worthless. This expression of contempt may include making fun of the other person verbally or nonverbally, or simply expressing that the other person is not worth the time or effort that she may otherwise deserve. Hidcote and Ronaldo have had an unfortunate relationship as coworkers after a misunderstanding during a postwork happy hour. Now that Ronaldo has been promoted and is Hidcote's boss, Ronaldo often finds himself having to make presentations that Hidcote attends. Hidcote is quick to show his displeasure with most anything Ronaldo suggests, often with a snort of laughter, a furrowed brow, or an audible sigh whenever Ronaldo pauses in conversation.

Defensiveness
Warding off the complaints or criticisms of another without accepting responsibility for any of the expressed concerns.

- **The Third Horseman: Defensiveness.** The third signal of destructive conflict that may lead to the ending of a relationship includes a pattern of warding off the complaints of the other while refusing to accept responsibility for concerns expressed by a relational partner.

Hoxton/Justin Pumfrey/Hoxton/Getty Images

Hermione may have a genuine concern about being stood up by Kat for their Friday night plans, but Kat's unwillingness to admit that she should have managed her schedule better—or at least let Hermione know of a change in plans—causes an escalation of the tension in their relationship.

- **The Fourth Horseman: Stonewalling.** The final signal of problematic conflict is the complete abandonment of interaction with a relational partner. By refusing to engage with the other person, conflict resolution is almost completely beyond hope. Unfortunately, this is usually the indication of the beginning of the end of the relationship, as one or both partners is so emotionally discouraged that they cannot find the strength or emotional energy to work on any form of relational repair. Chyna and Ben are at their wit's end. Other than the most basic forms of communication about who gets the car on Tuesday evening and whether the electricity bill has been paid, these long-term romantic partners are behaving more like uninvolved roommates who share a single bed. Although Chyna and Ben each separately tell their friends that they wish things could be back to "normal," Ben has felt so discouraged by Chyna's constant degrading comments that he cannot even look her in the eye without feeling bad about himself. Chyna wants to apologize for her behavior, but without Ben being willing to engage she feels like there is no point in attempting to move forward.

Stonewalling
Ceasing all significant interaction with a relational partner.

Conflict Management Styles

Five main types of conflict management have been identified across a variety of relationships and contexts.[11,12] The conflict management styles are as diverse as the individuals that employ them, each focusing on different levels of assertiveness and cooperation to manage conflict:

Accommodating
Being cooperative yet unassertive with one's relationship partner, often ignoring one's own needs in order to satisfy the needs, goals, or desires of the relationship partner.

Avoiding
Being uncooperative yet unassertive with one's relationship partner, often ignoring the conflict.

Collaborating
Being cooperative yet assertive, acknowledging the conflict and working together to resolve it in a way that satisfies both partners.

Competing
Being uncooperative yet assertive, with a focus on "winning" the conflict.

Compromising
Being cooperative yet assertive, with each partner giving up part of his or her own goals to arrive at a conclusion.

- **Accommodating** styles of conflict management focus on being cooperative yet unassertive with one's relationship partner, often ignoring one's own needs in order to satisfy the needs, goals, or desires of the relationship partner.

- **Avoiding** conflict management styles focus on ignoring the conflict, a tactic that is both uncooperative and yet unassertive with one's partner.

- **Collaborating** with one's partner is both cooperative and assertive, acknowledging the conflict and working together to resolve the conflict in a way that satisfies both partners.

- **Competing** conflict management styles focus on "winning" the conflict, where both partners are uncooperative and assertive in their desire to come out on top.

- **Compromising** is a conflict management strategy that is both cooperative and assertive, but each partner gives up part of his or her own goals in arriving at a conclusion to the conflict episode.

Although it would seem likely that an assertive, cooperative solution to conflict is the "best" strategy to satisfy both parties, it's actually much more complicated than that. Some topics that become sources of conflict are not equally important to all parties, so one partner may be willing to accommodate on certain topics in order to save time, energy, or social esteem. Spencer has done a lot of research on cable packages for his new apartment, presenting a couple of different options to his roommates that each are missing some channels but give access to other channels. Because the cost difference among all packages is minimal, his roommate Brian is willing to accommodate to the needs of the other roommates. Thomas, however, is willing to compete with his roommates to ensure that the pay-per-view station is part of their cable package because of his love of European soccer matches that are otherwise unavailable in his area. Brian has told Spencer that he'll go along with whatever the group decides, but Thomas has informed Spencer that he will only contribute toward the cost of cable if his favorite channel is included. Spencer can hardly wait to hear the input from his other roommates.

DECEPTION

Stavos decided to go back to college after a few years in the military. He married his high school sweetheart at 18, had two children relatively quickly, and is now pursuing his bachelor's degree in his late 20s. A dedicated student, Stavos studies quite a bit and gets decent grades. Although his wife is supportive and he loves his children wholeheartedly, he occasionally misses the comradery of his former military community. With the opening of a new bar in town, the Library Pub, he thinks he has found the perfect solution. Once or twice each month he tells his wife and kids that he is going to meet up with some guys at the Library, allowing them to think he is studying in the book repository on campus when in fact he's having a night drinking beer and sharing old stories about his days in the military. Although he has a strong aversion to lying, Stavos feels comfortable allowing his wife and kids to misunderstand the situation.

Is Stavos in a gray area of truthfulness, or is his behavior relatively straightforward in its dishonesty? To know, we must first define **deception**, which is often conceptualized as a deliberate attempt to cause a receiver to believe something that the communicator considers false.[13] Notice the importance of intention: If you don't mean to deceive someone because *you think you are telling the truth* but you are incorrect, you are not being deceptive. Similarly, if you say something sarcastic and reasonably expect that your audience will understand your sarcasm, then you are not being deceptive in your statement or behavior *even if that statement is false.* According to the preceding definition, Stavos may not have necessarily told an outright lie, but his behavior definitely was constructed in a way to deceive his wife and children. If deception encompasses much more than lying, it becomes useful to understand why people sometimes consider deception to be a relational transgression and to outline the four main types of deception that occur in interpersonal relationships.

Deception
The deliberate attempt to cause a receiver to believe something that the communicator considers false.

Transgressions Associated with Deception

As mentioned before, any communicative act that violates a relational rule may be seen as a transgression. Highlighted in Figure 8.2, deception is common, yet people believe honesty is an important part of a relationship and expect truthfulness from a friend, family member, coworker, or romantic partner.[14] In an overview of his work, leading deception scholar Steven McCornack claims that deception is "uncooperative, unethical, impractical, and destructive" because of how it violates the assumption of truthfulness among conversational partners.[15] Indeed, it does seem like engaging in deception is not playing by the rules of normal interaction. However, can someone deceive a relational partner for all the *right* reasons? As a young child, Jeremy was told that he could be whomever he wanted to be when he grew up. Although Jeremy may never quite achieve his childhood goal of becoming a superhero, he still thinks that most anything is possible, and he recently helped chair a successful social justice festival on his campus that many others said couldn't be done. Laura is a realtor with a wide range of community connections; when planning her partner's surprise birthday party she asked much of her entire small town to join in on the deception so as not to accidentally let Simon find out about the upcoming festivities. Seth and Mariella have decided to get a divorce; given their daughter's upcoming

FIGURE 8.2
Frequency of Deception Detection in Close Relationships

filadendron/E+/Getty Images

college graduation, they decide to wait until a couple days after the commencement ceremonies to tell her the bad news. Each of these situations is clearly deceptive. However, each of these situations may or may not seem like an acceptable pattern of behavior, depending on your attitudes, experiences, and behaviors. Was Jeremy's mother wrong to encourage him toward greatness? Should Laura have ruined the surprise by being completely honest with Simon? Do Seth and Mariella have an obligation to let their daughter know the news immediately? The answer may prove different for every person in every context and every situation.

BOX 8.4: **Commendable Connections**

Ethics and Deception

Roshni and Bill had been casually interacting before and after their workouts at the track for a couple weeks when they ran into each other at a mutual friend's party. After hitting it off, they began dating each other exclusively. As their mutual attraction to one another deepened, Roshni wanted to move toward a more physical relationship. Knowing the stereotypes about men, Roshni assumed that Bill was onboard with escalating their physical contact beyond the recent hand-holding and chaste end-of-date kisses.

Wanting to lighten the mood and start a conversation about sex, Roshni made a poorly worded joke about romance that unintentionally (and incorrectly) implied that she was a virgin. Bill then breathed an audible sigh of relief, explaining that his conservative values and religious background had led him to choose to wait until marriage to have sex, and that he was glad to have someone who understood his perspective because this conversation had been difficult for him in the past. Not wanting to break the intimacy of the moment, Roshni chose not to correct Bill's misunderstanding.

Fast-forward quite a few months, and Roshni now pretends that she doesn't believe in having premarital sex. Although she loves Bill and is willing to abstain, she feels increasingly guilty about deceiving Bill; not only that, but Roshni constantly worries about Bill dramatically discovering her deception, through some clichéd locker-room scene found in every typical high school movie. To say that Roshni is uncomfortable with how things have unfolded is a bit of an understatement.

INSTRUCTIONS: Think carefully about what you would do in the situation if you were Roshni. Do you think Roshni had a lapse in judgment? If so, when did Roshni make her first ethical mistake? Although pretending to not believe in premarital sex is clearly deceptive, do you think that Roshni was wrong to not correct Bill's initial misunderstanding about Roshni's joke?

Does Bill have a right to know about Roshni's sexual past? Does Bill have a right to know about Roshni's deceptive interaction with him? What would you imagine Bill would say if he found out the truth now, or in six months, or on their wedding night? Should Roshni ever tell Bill the truth about this early deception in their relationship?

Types of Deception

Not every form of deception looks alike. Indeed, people may deceive each other in a wide variety of ways, even with the best of intentions. Regardless of the reason for deception, scholars have found four primary forms of deception[16,17] that typically occur in interpersonal relationships:

- **Falsification.** When people think of deception, they usually think of falsification, or fabricating information and behaving as though it is true. Most "lies" fall under this category, such as when Stanley told his teacher that his dog ate his homework when, in reality, Stanley spent most of the evening playing video games.

- **Omission.** If someone leaves something out of a story that *should* be in the story, then an omission of key information has occurred. When Kelly tells her roommate Malia that she was studying at a coffee shop all evening, Malia's reaction may have been much different if Kelly admitted that she was studying with Malia's ex-boyfriend.

- **Exaggeration.** Taking facts or ideas that are essentially true but then fudging the specific details is a type of deception called exaggeration. After fishing, Alan may imply that he caught a trout a few feet long when, in fact, photographic evidence suggests that he had hooked little more than a guppy.

- **Equivocation.** If someone attempts to change the topic, give a misleading response, or avoid answering a question without appearing to have done so, this is known as equivocation. Sherri doesn't want to hurt her friend's feelings, but when Efren asks whether she likes his horrible new hairstyle Sherri gives him a huge smile and says, "Oh, I see you got a haircut! Who does your hair?" By dodging the actual question but allowing Efren to feel positive about himself, Sherri did not technically "lie" but instead equivocated in her response.

Falsification
A type of deception involving the fabrication of information and presenting it as truth.

Omission
A type of deception involving leaving something out of a testimony or story that should be conveyed.

Exaggeration
A type of deception involving taking facts or ideas that are essentially true but then changing the specific details.

Equivocation
A type of deception that involves changing a topic or avoiding questions without appearing to have done so.

Radius Images/Radius Images/Getty Images

Motivation for Deception

Clearly, our motivation for deception is widespread. From wanting to protect the other person to hoping to save ourselves from pain or punishment, there are a wide variety of reasons to deceive. In the late 1980s, Sandra Metts began to disentangle the different motivations for people who engage in deceptive interactions. Most obviously, people who deceive do so for a **self-focused motive**,[18] which means that they want to avoid a wide variety of personal consequences or discomfort by deceiving another person. Whether these deceptive acts are significant or relatively trivial, the person most benefiting from the deception is the person who is engaging in that deception. When Zina goes to a coffee shop, she gives the name "Michelle" to the barista in order to avoid the inevitable jokes about Xena the Warrior Princess from the 1990s' television series. Brock, on the other hand, allows others to believe that he played college football because he doesn't want them to know that his time on the football field was as a male cheerleader. Kenny and Bristol each separately lie about their shared romantic relationship as they pursue one-night stands during their bachelor and bachelorette parties. From the relatively innocuous to the potentially disastrous, each of these deceptive acts supports the deceiver's image, contributes to the deceiver's sense of well-being, or even protects the deceiver from harm or other ill effects.

Not all motivations for deception are quite so selfish, however. Metts also highlighted a **partner-focused motive**,[19,20] which involves deceiving a relational partner to maintain or enhance *his* self-esteem, to keep him from personal harm, or to protect him from a wide variety of potentially harmful outcomes. As they head out the door to attend a cousin's wedding, Natasha asks her sister Talicia if her dress is a bit too low-cut for a family function; Talicia tells her that she looks perfect for the occasion despite a secret agreement with Natasha's self-assessment, knowing that Natasha didn't bring another outfit to the event and can't do anything about it anyway. Tad and Nate are both hoping to join a Greek-letter organization, and during Rush, Nate accidentally leans up against the fraternity's founding photo, knocking it off the wall; Tad convinces Nate that they should look at a different house for some made-up reason instead of letting Nate know that he has committed an unforgivable offense and would never be invited to join.

Jake calls his friend Taryn to see if she and her husband want to come to a barbecue, but Taryn explains that her husband Bill dislikes spending time with Jake's annoying new boyfriend, Rick; when Jake describes the phone call to Rick, however, he simply says that Taryn and Bill are going to be out of town for the long weekend and cannot hang out. Although there may be minor benefits to the deceiver in each of these situations, the main beneficiary of the deceptive interaction is the person being deceived.

Self-Focused Motive
The act of a speaker engaging in deception with the goal of a tangible or intangible benefit to that speaker.

Partner-Focused Motive
The act of a speaker engaging in deception with the goal of a tangible or intangible benefit to the audience.

Glowimages/Glowimages/Getty Images

BOX 8.5: Communication Currents

Dealing with Deception in Current Television

Game of Thrones, **Season 4, Episode 6, "Laws of Gods and Men,"** http://bit.ly/2n7RoMc

I n the wildly popular television show *Game of Thrones*, we meet a group of individuals engaged in a long-term struggle for power, wealth, or esteem. All of these individuals are trying to better themselves or their culture as they navigate a fictional violent world throughout this HBO fantasy drama. Although few characters survive very long, the families of Lannister, Stark, and Targaryen struggle to regain control of the Iron Throne, the symbolic center of power and authority in the fantastical world of the Seven Kingdoms of Westeros.

As we watch this video clip, Tyrion dramatically confronts his father, Tywin, while on trial for a murder that he did not commit. His father knows that Tyrion is innocent yet participates in the deceptive trial in order to finally rid himself of his son, with whom he has always had a strained relationship. Tyrion calls out his sister, Cersei, who is participating in the trial as the accuser; Cersei claims that her brother Tyrion has murdered her eldest son, the former king.

INSTRUCTIONS: Watch the video again, paying careful attention to the discussion between the two main characters in the scene. For what motives does Tyrion claim that the deception is being carried out? Consider how you would feel if you were the victim of an unfounded accusation. How would you respond in such a situation? Do you think that the gravity of this accusation should result in a stronger response?

Finally, Metts discussed a somewhat confusing type of motivation known as a **relationship-focused motive**.[21] Essentially, a relationship-focused motive is one in which the goal for the deception is the preservation of a relational state like a marriage or a pair of best friends. Rather than benefiting one partner or the other, this kind of deception primarily is focused on keeping a relationship at a desired level and limiting any experiences that may hurt the relationship. Interestingly, even when the primary motivation is relationship focused, often a combination of partner-focused or self-focused motives is also present to some degree. If knowledge of Carly's fleeting romance with a coworker is likely to break up her marriage, she may deceive her partner to keep that relationship together; in doing so, she is also protecting her partner's feelings and avoiding the damage to her public image of being outed as a cheater.

Relationship-Focused Motive
The act of a speaker engaging in deception with the goal of either mutual benefit or the preservation of the connection between the speaker and the audience.

Detecting Deception

With deception being a relatively common feature of human interaction, whether on a large or a small scale, you may desire help in figuring out if you are being deceived by the people in your lives. Despite the popularity of television shows that purport to be able to train you to be better lie detectors, and regardless of dramatic movies that feature people with this purported ability to know if someone is lying, deception detection is not an ability that can be taught with great success. In fact, there are no perfect indicators of deception,[22] and the behaviors that people often believe may be indicative of deception are actually often the exact opposite.[23]

For example, Kilian knows that Bryce has always naively believed that no one can comfortably look someone in the eye when he tells a lie; because of this knowledge, Kilian can purposefully look Bryce directly in the eye when he claims to have won a serve during their weekly racquetball game and Bryce will believe it, even though Kilian is completely trying to throw the game in his own favor.

What should you do in this situation, then? Should people just go throughout their lives being deceived without knowing any better? Interestingly, some people may argue that being deceived by a relational partner and not being suspicious may actually be beneficial in close relationships. Although clearly deception may cause trust to diminish and can lead to open conflict, deception can also help people to successfully navigate a relationship during difficult moments that could lead to conflict.[24] When Bill stops to eat fast food on the way home from work so that he can seem to maintain a healthy diet while at home, not telling his partner about his "cheating" also ensures that he will not have to engage in a disagreement about the merits of a healthy lifestyle (assuming that he doesn't spill bacon grease on his necktie). In this case, ignorance of Bill's willing omission of relevant information *may actually be* bliss. Other partner-focused forms of deception may continue perceptions of satisfaction within relationships by making that person have more confidence or a better self-concept.[25]

Interestingly, one of the few reliable ways to detect deception is to already be quite familiar with someone and to know that person's behaviors and mannerisms. When that relationship is already established, it is easier to notice deviations from their normal communication patterns, which may indicate stress associated with deceptive acts. Regardless of whether you think that a "typical liar" looks someone in the eye, you may be able to tell that your friend Daler is being deceptive if he has noticeably more or

Tim Boyle/Getty Images News/Getty Images

Chuleeporn/ShutterStock.com

less eye contact than he usually does.[26] *The most reliable way to detect deception is to observe patterns and behaviors that fall outside the range of someone's normal behaviors.*

INFIDELITY

Jake's Intro to American Film class screens movies and hosts discussions at a local cinema complex near campus. Normally Jake gets his girlfriend, Shayne, to come to the screenings and they turn it into a weekly date night, but she had to work late last Saturday evening. Instead, Jake was sitting with his study group watching the film, and at a particularly emotional part of the film, Jake accidentally reached over and grabbed his classmate Lisa's hand. Once he realized what he had done, Jake could have let go and acted authentically embarrassed. However, Lisa didn't seem to mind what had happened, and Jake had to admit to himself that he had found her attractive; as such, Jake held on to Lisa's hand for another five minutes before a sense of guilt settled over him. Had this happened to a character on screen in one of the movies he watched, he would have despised the character's lack of faithfulness; now that something like this had happened to him, Jake wasn't sure what to do—if anything—about this seemingly minor physical encounter. He doesn't really think holding hands is that big of a deal in the big scheme of things, but he is certain that he would be upset if Shayne held another guy's hand at the movies for five minutes.

Betrayal
A perceived relational state when one or both partners are unsupportive or even work against the goals or desires of the other partner.

Infidelity
A situation in which one or both partners are unfaithful to the other in a close romantic relationship.

Sexual Infidelity
Erotic or sexual activity with someone other than your romantic partner.

Emotional Infidelity
Forming a romantic attachment with someone other than your romantic partner.

Types of Infidelity

In scripted dramas like the ones in Jake's film class, an explosive plot twist often results from a particular category of transgressions within close romantic relationships: a type of **betrayal** known as **infidelity**. Infidelity is a situation in which one or both partners are unfaithful to the other in a close romantic relationship, and it comes in two main forms. Each individual betrayal situation may include one or both forms of infidelity. **Sexual infidelity** is the easiest to describe, as the boundaries for this type of behavior are often clearly defined within a relationship. Sexual infidelity includes any type of erotic or sexual activity with someone other than your romantic partner. Notice the wide range of behaviors that may constitute sexual infidelity! A couple doesn't have to have traditional penetrative sex to commit this form of betrayal; a partner sharing a romantic kiss with someone else can be considered an act of sexual infidelity under this definition.

Emotional infidelity is much more difficult to define, as the criterion for emotional infidelity is that it involves forming a notable romantic

attachment to an individual other than your partner. Sandra found herself falling into the same
old cliché. Her secretary, Alexis, was fun and
engaging, and they hit it off as coworkers. One
day Alexis's banter became a bit more personal,
joking about "experimenting" in college with
other women. Although Sandra is in a committed relationship and has had a loving domestic
partner for years, Alexis is intriguing and attractive and new. Although Sandra would never
have a physical affair with anyone, she finds
herself texting Alexis at all hours and thinking
about her far more often than she feels is right.

How strong does a romantic attachment need to be to count as infidelity?
Each situation varies, and there is no one satisfying point at which emotional infidelity can be clearly labeled. This is why many people counsel
their friends and loved ones to flee from any type of attraction to someone other than their romantic partner. As attachments develop and grow,
suddenly people may find themselves in over their heads and part of yet
another relationship statistic.

Responses to Infidelity

Interestingly, couples react very differently to experiences of infidelity within
a relationship. Whether conflict occurs, a breakup ensues, or the couple
begins a process of reconciliation, none can argue against the idea that
infidelity serves as a large relational turning point within a relationship. The
impact of infidelity is hard to ignore.

Research has highlighted differences between how men and women
respond to the two main types of infidelity. After an initial reaction of
disbelief, there are sex differences in how individuals respond to their partner's infidelity. Men are much more likely to get upset over sexual infidelity
than emotional infidelity, while women get more upset over emotional infidelity than over sexual infidelity. Many different explanations abound, including an evolutionary perspective highlighting men's desire to establish
and guarantee an unchallenged paternity within his romantic partnership,
as well as women's desire to maintain their sole status as relational partner in
order to provide unchallenged access to both the protection and resources
their partner may provide.[27] Some scholars take a different approach, arguing that different types of infidelity may indicate to each sex a more sweeping
betrayal of a romantic partner, with men assuming that women practicing
sexual infidelity must also be emotionally attached and women assuming that
men who are emotionally unfaithful must necessarily be having sexual relations outside their partnership.[28,29] Regardless of sex, however, either sexual
or emotional infidelity almost always has negative consequences within a
romantic relationship.

BOX 8.6: InterConnect

. . . .

Is It Worth It? An Analysis of Your Attitudes toward Betrayal

Betrayal in a relationship is often painful for everyone involved, but can have a surprisingly long-term impact on people's attitudes toward the person actually doing the betraying. Pick had been in a relationship with Laura for a long time, and he had kissed another woman early on in the relationship before he felt he had fully committed to Laura. Being completely open and honest with Laura, Pick had a conversation about faithfulness and sobriety, setting some boundaries and engaging their shared social network to help make sure that he doesn't make any of these mistakes again.

After years of faithfulness through times good and bad, Pick and Laura have moved in together, and their lives have become relationally enmeshed to the point where they even got a dog to practice coparenting. Just last week, however, Pick was traveling for work when his new coworker got him drunk, and they hooked up in a conference hotel room. Now, Laura has found out about his behavior from mutual acquaintances, and Pick finds himself alone, with all of their mutual friends taking her side against him and leaving Pick no one to offer him emotional support.

Pick is now struggling with depression and finds it difficult to maintain his self-esteem. Former friends have told him "once a cheater, always a cheater" and have written him off completely. Laura moved out with the dog and hasn't answered his text messages and phone calls, nor has she responded to the flowers he has sent to her office. As his social isolation continues, he readily admits that his one night of passion was not worth the loss of a partner who he loved so deeply. His work has begun to suffer, as clients claim he doesn't seem engaged and his mind is apparently on something else. Pick would agree completely.

INSTRUCTIONS: What are your thoughts on this situation? Think carefully about Pick's behavior and the attitudes expressed by Pick and Laura's social network. Did Pick deserve that second chance? What about a third chance? What would you do if you were Pick's friend? Is his social isolation a fitting punishment for his sexual infidelity? Although the behaviors associated with betrayal are often short-lived, the consequences linger. Does Pick's story influence your own desire to remain faithful in current or future relationships?

JEALOUSY AND ENVY

The last two forms of relational transgressions that we discuss in this chapter are closely related and often confused. These two transgressions involve a desire for resources or for a relationship and often come into play when it is difficult for someone to gain access to those resources or that relationship. Cel is in a long-term relationship with her partner, Stan, and they have enjoyed a relatively stable relationship. However, Cel has noticed that Stan's boss has a lot of influence over the choices that he makes, including mundane things like encouraging him to wear certain ties to important meetings. Although Stan would argue that there is no threat to their relationship, Cel begins to dwell on her decreasing influence and to express nervousness that she may lose Stan to his boss or to another woman. In this situation, Cel is experiencing **jealousy**, which is a desire to protect a relationship (or a resource) from some outside party. Notice how different this is than our typical, day-to-day use of the word! To take it out of the relational realm for a second, if you already have a pint of ice cream in your fridge and you want to make sure that you get to eat it when you get home, that protective feeling you have for your own stuff is rightly termed jealousy. If, however, you wanted to have some of the snacks that your friends are eating, you are experiencing **envy**, which is a desire to have the relationship, the characteristics, or the access to resources of those individuals who you observe—or at least that you have the desire for them *not* to have it![30] When Wilhelmina asked Brent to her sorority formal, Kim was devastated. She had planned to ask Brent and was now envious of Wilhelmina. When Wilhelmina found out that Kim desperately wanted to take Brent, Wilhelmina jealously guarded Brent from Kim's influence. (Admittedly, this is not the typical use of the terminology!)

What is the personal impact of experiencing jealousy within a relationship? Although you may see jealousy depicted in television and film as a necessary part of a healthy relationship, in actuality jealousy does have some negative impact on relationships. Scholars have found a wide range of responses to the feeling of jealousy, but there are only two constructive responses to jealousy that can actually strengthen the relationship. Healthy, open communication about jealous feelings can allow partners to manage jealousy; similarly, if the jealous partner engages in positive behaviors to try to improve the relationship or to make herself a better relational partner, this can also cause a positive relational response.[31] If jealousy is not managed directly with the relationship partner, however, it may lead to negative emotions or experiences that can lead to the decline of the relationship.

Jealousy
A desire to protect a relationship or a resource from an outside party.

Envy
A desire to have the relationship, the characteristics, or the access to resources of an outside party.

Jacob Lund/ShutterStock.com

Chapter Summary

Although the subtleties of transgressions are often relationship-specific, a wide variety of behaviors may be considered transgressive if one or both partners believe that behavior violates a relational rule. More common forms of transgressions include aggression, deception, infidelity, and expressions of jealousy or envy. Interestingly, transgressions can be committed for multiple reasons and aren't always motivated by selfishness despite the preponderance of media portrayals to the contrary. Individuals may engage in behaviors like deception in order to protect the experience of their relational partners, adding complexity to the otherwise straightforward definition of behaviors commonly known as transgressions.

Although a partner's response to a potentially transgressive behavior necessarily defines that behavior as a transgression, these responses also provide additional insight into the relationship itself. Our discussion of the Four Horsemen of the Apocalypse allows us to understand the types of responses that relational partners may display to one another, while also offering a clear set of warning signs that may indicate a relationship on the decline if an intervention of some sort is not implemented. Regardless of the transgression type and the potential for relational impact, each dyad or group navigates the experience of a relational transgression in a variety of ways. What may be potentially disastrous to some people may be relatively unimportant to others; both individual and cultural backgrounds contribute to the experience of relationship transgressions and their influence on the involved relationships.

MindTap®

First-Person Video

The Couple with the Ailing Parent

Apply what you've learned in this chapter by analyzing the "The Couple with the Ailing Parent" video, using the accompanying questions as a guide. This video and these questions are available online with your MindTap Speech for *Interconnections: Interpersonal Communication Foundations and Contexts.*

MindTap®

Key Terms

Use flashcards to learn key concepts and take a quiz to test your knowledge.

Accommodating	Conflict	Envy
Avoiding	Contempt	Equivocation
Betrayal	Criticism	Exaggeration
Collaborating	Cyberbullying	Explicit Rules
Communicative Aggression	Deception	Falsification
	Defensiveness	Freedom Restriction
Competing	Dominance	Humiliation
Compromising	Emotional Infidelity	Implicit Rules

Infidelity	**Partner-Focused**	**Self-Focused Motive**
Insecurity Induction	**Motive**	**Sexual Infidelity**
Isolation	**Physical Aggression**	**Stonewalling**
Jealousy	**Relational Rule**	**Transgression**
Name-Calling	**Relationship-Focused**	**Verbal Aggression**
Omission	**Motive**	**Withdrawal**

Discussion Questions

1. Think about a time when you felt betrayed by a friend or a romantic partner. What type of transgression occurred? Was it intentional? Did you ever create a situation where she or he felt betrayed by you?

2. What is your online behavior like? Does your social media usage reflect the "real" you or are you deceptive in your profile or postings? What do you think the impact might be of everyone trying to present their online selves in the best possible light? Does this create unrealistic expectations?

3. Think about a time that a relationship soured. In what ways did you notice the Four Horsemen of the Apocalypse? Be specific in describing an interaction that occurred.

4. What is your attitude toward infidelity? Do you think that emotional or sexual infidelity is "worse," or do you feel equally about each? How do you think your sex influences your attitudes toward infidelity?

5. Consider your current friendships. What are some rules that you have in that relationship about how friends should behave? Have you and your friend(s) discussed these rules, or are they simply implied?

Making Connections

Some relational difficulties are easy to point to, such as when a person clearly lied about a verifiable fact or raised her voice in an inappropriate situation. Other times, it may seem that a difficulty emerged simply because a relational partner "felt" or "seemed" a certain way. How does our understanding of the self from Chapter 2 relate to our perceptions of relational difficulties? Do people need "proof" to be able to claim that they have been victimized?

Chapter Quiz

1. Which of the following behaviors in a relationship can be considered a relational transgression?

   a. Deception
   b. Unhealthy conflict
   c. Infidelity
   d. Aggression
   e. None of the above
   f. All of the above

2. Which of the following types of aggression is not considered physical aggression?

   a. Hitting   d. Biting
   b. Yelling   e. Using weapons
   c. Kicking   f. All of the above

3. Jaden doesn't want to lose his buddy Karl, even though he feels them drifting apart. If he intentionally tries to break up Karl's other relationships, which of the following forms of communicative aggression is he using?

   a. Withdrawal   d. Dominance
   b. Name-calling   e. Freedom restriction
   c. Isolation   f. Humiliation

4. Karl finds out about Jaden's behavior and tries to embarrass him in front of the entire friendship group by revealing Jaden's elementary school secret. Clearly, Jaden and Karl have issues. Which of the following forms of communicative aggression is he using?

   a. Withdrawal   d. Dominance
   b. Name-calling   e. Freedom restriction
   c. Isolation   f. Humiliation

5. Which of the following best exemplifies Gottman's description of an unhealthy relationship where one partner is expressing disapproval of the other?

   a. Criticism   d. Stonewalling
   b. Defensiveness   e. None of the above
   c. Contempt

6. T/F In order to be considered a transgression, one or both romantic partners must have violated an explicit rule.

7. T/F Not all forms of conflict are necessarily bad for a relationship.

8. T/F After losing all hope of working on her relationship, Trina simply refuses to engage. Her complete lack of communication with her partner is known as stonewalling.

9. T/F Brick has updated his Tinder profile to highlight that he started a successful business and saw profits increase fourfold in most recent year-to-year comparisons. In truth, he was talking about his elementary school lemonade stand. Brick has engaged in the type of deception known as equivocation.

10. T/F At the zoo, Cedric throws a pretzel at a zebra and scares it off. When his mom asks him if he had anything to do with the animal's discomfort, Cedric distracts his mom by pretending to fall and then crying. Cedric has engaged in the type of deception known as equivocation.

Endnotes

1. As exemplar, see Eden, J., & Veksler, A. E. (2016). Relational maintenance in the Digital Age: Implicit rules and multiple modalities. *Communication Quarterly, 64*(2), 119–144.

2. For an overview of bullying, see Holt, M. K., Green, J. G., Tsay-Vogel, M., Davidson, J., & Brown, C. (2016). Multidisciplinary approaches to research on bullying in adolescence. *Adolescent Research Review, 2(1),* 1–10.

3. Dailey, R. M., Lee, C. M., & Spitzberg, B. H. (2007). Communicative aggression: Toward a more interactional view of psychological abuse. In B. H. Spitzberg & W. R. Cupach (Eds.), *The Dark Side of Interpersonal Communication* (2nd ed., pp. 297–326). Mahwah, NJ: Lawrence Erlbaum.

4. Sorrels, K. *Intercultural Communication: Globalization and Social Justice* (pp. 220–222). Thousand Oaks, CA: Sage.

5. Cramer, D. (2002). Linking conflict management behaviours and relational satisfaction: The intervening role of conflict outcome satisfaction. *Journal of Social and Personal Relationships, 19,* 431–438.

6. For a review of these findings, see Kowalski, R. M. (2007). Teasing and bullying. In B. H. Spitzberg & W. R. Cupach (Eds.), *The Dark Side of Interpersonal Communication* (2nd ed., pp. 169–197). Mahwah, NJ: Lawrence Erlbaum.

7. Teven, J. J., Richmond, V. P., & McCroskey, J. C. (1998). Measuring tolerance for disagreement. *Communication Research Reports,* 15, 209–217.

8. Ibid.

9. Gottman, J. M. (1993). A theory of marital dissolution and stability. *Journal of Family Psychology, 7,* 57–75.

10. Floyd, K. (2009). *Interpersonal Communication: The Whole Story* (p. 396). Boston, MA: McGraw-Hill.

11. For the original instrument, see Thomas K. W., & Kilmann, R. H. (1974). *Thomas–Kilmann Conflict MODE Instrument.* Tuxedo, NY: Xicom.

12. For an update and overview, see Thomas, K. W. (1992). Conflict and conflict management: Reflections and update. *Journal of Organizational Behavior, 13,* 265–274. doi:10.1002/job.4030130307

13. Dunbar, N. (2009). Deception detection. In S. W. Littlejohn & K. A. Foss (Eds.), *Encyclopedia of Communication Theory* (pp. 291–292). Thousand Oaks, CA: Sage.

14. Levine, T. R., Park, H. S., & McCornack, S. A. (1999). Accuracy in detecting truths and lies: Documenting the "veracity effect." *Communication Monographs, 66,* 125–144.

15. McCornack, S. (2013). *Reflect & Relate: An Introduction to Interpersonal Communication* (p. 201). Boston, MA: Bedford St. Martin's.

16. Buller, D. B., Burgoon, J. K., White, C. H., Ebesu, A. S. (1994). Interpersonal deception: VII. Behavioral profiles of falsification, equivocation, and concealment. *Journal of Language and Social Psychology, 13*(4), 366–395.

17. For cross-disciplinary titles, see Peterson, C. (1996). Deception in intimate relationships. *International Journal of Psychology, 31*(6), 279–288.

18. Metts, S. (1989). An exploratory investigation of deception in close relationships. *Journal of Social and Personal Relationships, 6*(2), 159–179.

19. Ibid.

20. For different terminology, see DePaulo, B. M., & Kashy, D. A. (1998). Everyday lies in close and casual relationships. *Journal of Personality and Social Psychology, 74*(1), 63–79.

21. Metts, S. (1989). An exploratory investigation of deception in close relationships. *Journal of Social and Personal Relationships, 6*(2), 159–179.

22. Levine, T. R., Kim, R. K., & Blair, J. P. (2010). Inaccuracy at detecting true and false confessions and denials: An initial test of a projected motive model of veracity judgments. *Human Communication Research, 36,* 82–102.

23. For a brief overview of judgment accuracy, see Burgoon, J. K. (2009). Interpersonal deception theory. In S. W. Littlejohn & K. A. Foss (Eds.), *Encyclopedia of Communication Theory* (pp. 551–553). Thousand Oaks, CA: Sage.

24. For a review of the relational benefits of deception, see Guerrero, L. K., Andersen, P. A., & Afifi, W. A. (2014). *Close Encounters: Communication in Relationships* (4th ed., pp. 332–333). Thousand Oaks, CA: Sage.

25. Cole, T. (2001). Lying to the one you love: The use of deception in romantic relationships. *Journal of Social and Personal Relationships, 18,* 107–129.

26. Greene, J. O., O'Hair, H. D., Cody, M. J., & Yen, C. (1985). Planning and control of behavior during deception. *Human Communication Research, 11*(3), 335–364.

27. Tafoya, M. A., & Spitzberg, B. H. (2007). The dark side of infidelity: Its nature, prevalence, and communicative functions. In B. H. Spitzberg & W. R. Cupach (Eds.), *The Dark Side of Interpersonal Communication* (2nd ed., pp. 201–242). Mahwah, NJ: Lawrence Erlbaum.

28. For a critique and a brief review of both perspectives (and additional models), see DeSteno, D. A., & Salovey, P. (1996). Genes, jealousy, and the replication of misspecified models. *Psychological Science 7*(6), 376–377.

29. For an overview of infidelity in same-sex couples, see Compton, B. L., & Bowman, J. M. (2016). Perceived cross-orientation infidelity: Heterosexual perceptions of same-sex cheating in exclusive relationships. *Journal of Homosexuality,* doi. 10.1080/00918369.2016.1244447

30. Guerrero, L. K., & Andersen, P. A. (2000). Emotion in close relationships. In C. Hendricks & S. S. Hendrick (Eds.), *Close Relationships: A Sourcebook* (pp. 171–183). Thousand Oaks, CA: Sage.

31. Guerrero, L. K., Hannawa, A. F., & Babin, B. A. (2011). The communicative responses to jealousy scale: Revision, empirical validation, and associations with relational satisfaction. *Communication Methods and Measures, 5,* 223–249.

Romantic Relationships

David Levingstone/DigitalVision/Getty Images

Warren never expected to have a long-term relationship. After a variety of awkward prom dates and some fumbling first encounters with women, he finally allowed himself to openly embrace his long-held suspicion that he was gay—despite his conservative upbringing and an unsupportive family. Because of his misunderstandings of what he perceived to be "gay culture," Warren had already resigned himself to a lifetime of casual relationships and one-night stands. However, sometime during the end of his second year of college, Warren met Tomás, and they began to date exclusively. Although Warren had no preconceptions that Tomás was "the one," he was pleasantly surprised to find that he enjoyed having a monogamous, exclusive relationship. In fact, Warren was surprised to find just how closely his relationship patterns mirrored those of his other friends, as well as those romances he had seen on television or in film. In talking with his other gay, straight, and lesbian friends, Warren realized that many of their relationships followed similar patterns. Even though his sexual orientation brought some unique challenges to his love life, Warren was pleasantly surprised to realize that he and Tomás weren't as "unusual" as his family sometimes made him feel.

9

How do romantic relationships change over time?

Is there a difference between types of relationships?

MindTap®

Review the chapter's learning objectives and **start** with a quick warm-up activity.

Learning Objectives

After you finish reading this chapter, you will be able to:

Name behaviors that are exhibited during romantic relationship formation and dissolution.

List the components of Sternberg's model of love.

Identify common attachment-related relational behaviors.

MindTap®

Read, highlight, and take notes online.

ROMANTIC RELATIONSHIPS

How do romantic relationships change over time? Is there a difference between types of relationships? Whether you are getting ready for your first date or have been married for 35 years, there are many things that can help us better understand the complex nature of romantic relationships. These types of relationships can span a continuum of relational behaviors—from a furtive hookup after a concert to a public vow of commitment—yet each romantic relationship addresses the presence (or absence) of relational factors like love, sex, commitment, and the increasing intimacy associated with romance.

Romantic relationships come in many different forms and vary along a variety of dimensions. In this chapter, we explore these relationships and how they develop over time. Let's start with a commonly discussed difference in relationships: the distinction between casual and committed romantic relationships. This distinction is not necessarily a definitive one, as some relationships that start as **casual** may eventually evolve into **committed relationships**.[1,2] Indeed, it is not common for a relationship to start out committed unless some external factor (arranged marriage, religious tradition, conservatism, etc.) imposes a level of **commitment** on the couple. Marianne recently found this out about her own parents. When she asked them about how they got together, she discovered that Marianne's father had just broken up with his high school girlfriend and Marianne's mother had wanted a fling because she was bored. Twenty-four years later, Marianne's parents find themselves more attached to one another than ever before. So, what then *is* commitment? Although we discuss commitment in greater depth later in the chapter, an easy way to think about commitment is as an attachment to another person that motivates the continuation of a relationship. Casual relationships, on the other hand, typically are seen as "open" and do not involve a sense of obligation or responsibility for the other person.[3] Regardless of type, these relationships may still go through parallel processes early in their history.

Relationship Stages

As noted in the introduction to this chapter, diverse people with a wide range of interpersonal experiences may still experience similarities during the initial stages of their romantic relationships. Interestingly, relationships often develop in similar manners as people come together. For example, Ben and Ashley are strengthening their attraction to one another by deepening their conversation each time they run into each other at the gym. Lisa and Caelin both live in small rural towns, yet they have been developing a better understanding of one another despite the long distance through a constant stream of text messages that get more and more personal. From the very beginnings to the final moments, romantic relationships are constantly shifting as partners experience relational change.

In his flagship book on the nature of social intercourse, author Mark Knapp notes that there is a range of ideas about the ways that people come together—and move apart—from one another in their interpersonal relationships, and he proposes a set of prototypes of "how people seem to move in and out and around these stages"[4] (see Figure 9.1). His use of such variable terminology is

---

Casual Relationship
The relationship type where partners have no definitive obligation toward one another and are often free to date others.

Committed Relationship
The relationship type where couples have a clearly defined obligation toward one another and are monogamous.

Commitment
An attachment decision that motivates the continuation of a relationship with another person over time.

noteworthy in that it acknowledges the ebbs and flows of human interaction. Brad and Melissa have been dating for 6 years, and Brad seems no closer to a formal commitment than he did back in college. Craig and Ken have been partners for 14 years and now own a house together in rural Florida. Chet and Amy are pregnant after a whirlwind romance. Winnie and Suyin are parenting Suyin's son from her first marriage but are finding the experience much more challenging than they had expected. Garret just had a tough breakup and wonders whether he wants to even try to get back on the dating market again. All of these people are moving through various stages of relationships as they get closer or more distant from one another. Although relationships may continue to vary and change, we become increasingly aware that romance is a process and that each relationship looks distinct from one another.

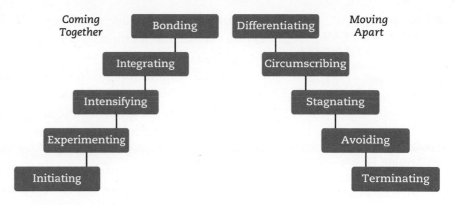

FIGURE 9.1
Knapp's Stage Theories of Relational Development and Relational De-Escalation

Knapp's Stages of Coming Together

As people get closer to one another, scholars have studied five distinct stages in their **relational development**.[5,6] Each stage is unique because of the characteristics that each relational partner typically displays, both toward one another and toward those observers outside the relationship. The time that it takes any one couple to move from each stage to the next, however, is highly variable and is often relationship-specific. One pairing may take months to get from the first

Relational Development
The process of two people increasing in intimacy and perceptions of closeness with one another.

vgajic/iStock/Getty Images

Initiating
The first stage of coming together, this part of relational development is characterized by the brief interaction and evaluation of one's relational partner.

Social Information Processing Theory
Joseph Walther's theory that computer-mediated communication can share the same characteristics and depth as face-to-face communication, given enough time.

stage to the second, while another couple may progress through multiple stages in one evening. Regardless, it becomes useful to describe and name each stage.

INITIATING   The first stage in relational development is called **initiating**, and it typically involves those behaviors that people exhibit when they meet one another for the first time. Whether we meet someone in class or in a bar, or even in an online or professional context, we may consider the potential for a relationship with them. From the observations that we can make at first glance about someone to any background knowledge that we may have heard about them to the way that the interaction feels, the first stage often involves evaluating whether that person is a desirable interaction partner and whether she is available to engage at that particular moment. Depending on the evaluation of those characteristics, we typically decide whether or not to engage the other person in an initial encounter.

BOX 9.1: iPersonal

Dating, Hookups, Information Processing, and Technology[7,8,9,10,11,12,13,14,15,16]

Using technology to find romance online is not a new concept. From the very early days of the Internet, people have been using verbal language and text-based symbols to express a variety of thoughts, ideas, emotions, and social information. Now that mobile technologies allow location-specific Internet networking to occur, a wide variety of applications has transformed the online social environment.

Social information processing theory (SIPT) deals with how people form relationships online. Indeed, communication scholar Joseph Walther used SIPT to describe that any form of communication between people can be used to establish social relationships with one another. Just as we use nonverbal cues to interpret people's true meanings in what they say, we can use an individual's manner of computer-mediated communication to form impressions about him, easily deciding whether we are likely to have a sociable experience over time.

Interestingly, recent mobile applications allow for people to pursue friendship, casual relationships, or even quick sexual interactions with just an initial "swipe" of the finger. For example, Tinder or Grindr allow for people who are relatively nearby one another to evaluate a single photograph of that person and decide whether they want future interaction; if both parties find each other mutually attractive, a connection is made for flirting, texting, conversation, dating, or even sexual activity.

Because technology gives the opportunity to reach and engage large numbers of relatively unknown strangers with ease, it has dramatically changed the way that relationships are pursued. Whether one wants a long-term relationship promised by one of the many "pro-monogamy" dating websites or a quick anonymous hookup, options are readily available to the technology savvy.

INSTRUCTIONS: Consider the role of the Internet or mobile devices in forming relationships with people, both nearby and long-distance. Have you ever used technology to meet another person? If so, how did that relationship differ from your face-to-face relationships that you formed, if at all? Do you think there are any differences between people that may influence their use of technology?

During the initiating stage, one or both interaction partners typically try to present themselves in the most positive manner. Communication scholars note that different types of people often try to highlight different characteristics of themselves during these intitial interaction phases, whether they want to appear playful or sexy or even polite.[17,18] Because her last boyfriend found her career goals somewhat intimidating, Stacy now works hard to present herself as goofy and fun when she first meets Irwin at a speed dating event. Irwin, however, tries to present himself as strong and sexual by wearing a tight V-neck shirt and rolling up the sleeves. Within moments, both Irwin and Stacy have made *some* sort of impression on each other, for better or for worse. Although the initiating stage may last for a very short time, the effect of those impressions may have a dramatic impact on whether the relationship moves toward the next stage of relational development.

West Rock/The Image Bank/Getty Images

EXPERIMENTING The second stage of coming together typically occurs in relatively rapid succession after the first one, and this **experimenting** stage is characterized by "small talk" to find similarities or shared experiences. Demographic information like hometown or major in college is often shared during this stage, and people seek to find **commonalities** that they can use to characterize each other according to known categories to increase understanding, even if they are in an online or social media environment.[19,20] It may be helpful to think of the experimenting stage as the "cocktail hour" of interpersonal interactions, as people use casual conversation to gain a casual and informal understanding of one another.

Conversations about shared experiences not only bring people closer together, but they also allow each partner to develop a fuller picture of one another.[21] Partners still engage in impression management at this point, only sharing information that they imagine the other person will consider positive. When Mark and Monica met during their chemistry laboratory on campus, they chatted about their residence halls, the high schools they attended, and where they worked over the summer. After initially finding relatively little in common, they finally realized that they had attended the same summer camp years before, immediately sharing a bond and affinity beyond that which they had felt at first glance. After finding these shared experiences and commonalities, Mark and Monica are ready to progress toward the third stage of relational development—should they both want the process to continue.

INTENSIFYING The third stage of coming together is known as **intensifying** and is characterized by a shared understanding of increasing closeness with a relational partner. At this point, both parties are aware of the relationship development process that is occurring, and increasing emotional and physical intimacy behaviors emerge as partners begin to tentatively attempt more and more intense demonstrations of intimacy. Jeff brushes

Experimenting
The second stage of coming together, this part of relational development is characterized by small talk and other attempts to discover relevant information about one's relational partner.

Commonalities
Information that people identify as held in common, whether attitudes, values, beliefs, experiences, or demographic characteristics, often resulting in perceptions of similarity.

Intensifying
The third stage of coming together, this part of relational development is characterized by increased emotional and physical intimacy with one's relational partner.

National Geographic Creative/Alamy

Sandra's hand at the movie theater, in an attempt to see if she seems open to holding hands with him. Derrick begins to open up with his partner about his fears about finding a job after graduation, but starts the conversation light and casual to see if such deep topics will have a relatively positive reception.

As we discussed in Chapter 4, these types of self-disclosure are an indicator of intimacy and closeness.[22] In Knapp's stages of coming together, true self-disclosure also begins to occur during the intensifying stage, and people begin to behave as though they are close friends in their conversations.[23] Partners may share deep information that they normally wouldn't talk about with strangers, they may refer to one another using the terms "*we*" or "*us*" indicating the nature of the partnership,[24] or they may find that they don't need to explain themselves to one another because they already have a history of experiences on which to draw. While watching a teen comedy, Mac and Loisy began to talk about the difficulties of middle school, and Mac explained how difficult it was that people called him a "sissy" for playing the bagpipes; in doing so, Mac cemented their closeness by opening up to her. Sarah and Michael have an easy time talking about where to have her birthday party next weekend, even though an outsider might be clueless; they already have shared understanding about the topic as Michael brainstorms, "Hey, I know we didn't like that one place on Maple Street, but I really think your brothers would want to go to that restaurant where you liked that pasta salad!" As the closeness between a couple intensifies, they see much greater shared verbal and nonverbal understanding between one another, often with less explanation required to create that understanding. As the relationship progresses even further, we move on toward the fourth stage of coming together.

racorn/Shutterstock.com

INTEGRATING When a relationship reaches the **integrating** stage, typically both relationship partners now speak or behave in such a way that they demonstrate their shared identity with one another. Attitudes, values, and behaviors are seen as shared, and outside parties often describe the partners as a pair rather than as two separate individuals.[25] When Jenn showed up to a retirement party alone, immediately all of her work colleagues inquired about her husband, Matt, because they were surprised to see her without him. Tyler and Fernando went to a basketball game on campus, and they wore matching jerseys of their favorite player. Since Tadame and Darnell had been dating since high school, Tadame still wears Darnell's class ring on a chain around her neck every day. When Lisa and Martha are shopping for skinny jeans together, they immediately lock eyes when "their song" starts playing on the hipster boutique's vinyl speaker system. Each of these couples has a way of demonstrating their togetherness to one another.

Not only does the couple typically seem like a unified front to their now-integrated social circles, but the couple also demonstrates their "oneness" to one another. The two relational partners may develop a set of opinions and interests that they share *as a couple* and may begin to dress or speak or act similarly, a direct application of communication accommodation theory from Chapter 6.[26] In addition, the variety of sexual behaviors that some pairs

Integrating
The fourth stage of coming together, this part of relational development is characterized by both verbal and nonverbal demonstrations of the closeness shared with one's relational partner.

Josh Liba/Moment/Getty Image

exhibit at this stage may also serve as yet another physical reminder of the metaphor of "two becoming one."[27]

Finally, the couple can sometimes even find something (or someone) external to the relationship that demonstrates the nature of their integration, whether it is as frivolous as a love for going on wine-tasting trips together, or as complex as having pets or children in common. During this integrating stage, the relationship itself becomes almost as significant a player as each individual partner. The dialectic tensions of connection/autonomy[28] that we discussed in Chapter 7 become particularly highlighted during this stage, as the relational partners struggle to maintain both their independence and their interdependence as a couple.

Bonding
The fifth stage of coming together, this part of relational development is characterized by both verbal and nonverbal demonstrations of the closeness shared with one's relational partner.

BONDING The final stage of coming together, **bonding**, highlights the formalization of the relationship between partners through a traditional announcement, ritual, or other public means of highlighting the establishment of the relationship. As the couple participates in some civic or social or religious ritual, they proclaim the existence of their union to the world around them. From an engagement or a wedding service to a commitment ceremony between long-term partners to the exchange of artifacts that symbolizes a union between individuals or families, this kind of bonding ritual allows for a couple to be formally recognized in some capacity by the people and institutions

that most matter to the couple.[29,30] This formal recognition both enables and constrains the couple as they work to act out their new social or cultural role among peers and with one another. This ritualized type of formal bonding is often viewed as the highest level of coming together, although couples can obviously gain increased understanding and experience with one another after having bonded; such a ceremony is often more akin to the "beginning" of the rest of one's life, rather than serving as an ultimate goal in and of itself.

Knapp's Stages of Moving Apart

Relationships are fluid and dynamic, and can look very different from one moment to the next. Indeed, as a variety of life events happen, people may increase in closeness with one another, as when either tragedy or joy causes relationship partners to turn toward one another for support and encouragement. Just as scholar Mark Knapp clearly outlined the five stages of relational development with one another as he highlighted the process of coming together, so has he also outlined their direct opposite: the stages of moving apart.[31] In these five stages, we see **relational de-escalation** as two people move further apart from one another.

It is essential to note up front that the process is not determinant; just as every couple who initiates a relationship *does not necessarily* end up with a formal bonding like marriage, similarly couples who engage in some of the stages of moving apart *do not necessarily* terminate the relationship or move completely apart from one another. Instead, couples often move in and around and among the stages, and each life event or relational turning point[32] is an opportunity for the couple to reevaluate their relational standing with one another.

DIFFERENTIATING Just like the stages of coming together signaled incremental increases in perceptions of closeness with one another, the stages of moving apart highlight a loss in perceptions of closeness or intimacy. The first step of **differentiating** involves the creation or highlighting of differences between relational partners, and attention is often focused on the related decrease in intimacy resulting from that distinctness or separation. Commonalities that were previously celebrated among relational partners are now rendered null, as each person attempts to establish or highlight elements of her own personality that are distinct from her partner. Partners may even stop using plural pronouns like "*we*" or "*us*" that they began using earlier in the relationship.[33] Although Jim and Lena used to celebrate their shared love for Indian food as they began to spend time with one another, Jim is now quick to point out that he prefers the cuisine from Northern India, while his estranged wife prefers the South Indian style of cooking.

Not only do people tend to highlight the types of behaviors that make each partner distinct from one another, but also each partner may talk in great depth as he or she points out differences in attitudes, values, beliefs, behaviors, and experiences. Indeed, most emphases in conversations with one another or with close friends highlight those unshared interests or activities that now exist within the relationship. As a result of this increasing separation, one or both relationship partners may move away from the use of words like "*we*" or "*us*" and instead focus on individual experience and ownership.

Relational De-Escalation
The process of decreasing perceptions of closeness, intimacy, and interaction as one moves apart from one's relational partner.

Differentiating
The first stage of moving apart, this part of relational de-escalation is characterized by the development or accentuation of differences between one and one's relational partner.

marin_bulat/Shutterstock.com

When Jacquie and Mark began to experience struggle in their partnership, they stopped using the phrase "our home" to describe where they lived and instead referred to "the apartment," "my car," and "your tools" to describe the different aspects of their common living arrangement.

One of the most obvious forms of differentiation may be a couple's use of conflict to establish separateness from one another. As discussed in Chapter 8, conflict can have a variety of relational benefits or can be quite detrimental to the relationship. Regardless of whether the couple enters a constructive or destructive pattern of communicating conflict with one another, that conflict is often seen as a potential harbinger of moving apart if maintenance behaviors are not swiftly employed to assuage the impact of that conflict on the relationship. However, not all couples use conflict or fighting to engage in differentiation, so it cannot be seen as the sole indicator of a relationship in decline.

CIRCUMSCRIBING Even more obvious than outright conflict and fighting, the **circumscribing** stage becomes one marker of the increasing distance among relational partners, where a decrease in self-disclosure serves as evidence of decreased intimacy. Certain conversational topics become off-limits, and people may be likely to keep discussions at a shallow level. Using our knowledge of social penetration theory from Chapter 4,[34] we can point toward relational depenetration as an indicator of this stage of coming apart. Outside observers may not always be able to notice a couple in the circumscribing stage, however, as relational partners are often good at reverting back to previous levels of breadth and depth when they feel it is important to "perform" their relationship for the benefit of those around them. Carole and Jean have not had a good conversation in weeks. Although they have discussed shopping lists, plans for hosting their daughter's slumber party, and getting the oil changed in Carole's car, nothing about their relationship has been discussed during conversation since Jean found out that Carole cheated during a work-related business trip. However, when they attend the local Neighborhood Watch meeting, Carole and Jean fall right back into their old roles of joking, laughing, and being the social center of the gathering; immediately on returning home, each engage in solitary activities in different parts of the house.

STAGNATING Taking restricted communication to an even deeper level, **stagnating** occurs when partners have little to no interaction with one another and sometimes even behave as strangers toward one another. Perhaps in part because they have grown angry or tired of one another, one or both partners believe that the other has nothing new or noteworthy to contribute to the relationship, and much communication ceases.[35] If partners *do* interact with one another, it is often limited to task-related information with almost no relational content; partners in this stage typically derive relational satisfaction from positive interactions with a wide range of people external to the

Circumscribing
The second stage of moving apart, this part of relational de-escalation is characterized by lessened intimacy and the restriction of self-disclosure shared with one's relational partner.

Stagnating
The third stage of moving apart, this part of relational de-escalation is characterized by relational inactivity and little to no communication with one's relational partner.

Noel Hendrickson/Photodisc/Getty Images

relationship, whether through career, volunteering, hobbies, or social networks developed apart from the romantic partner. Even though both partners may spend time regularly with one another, the intimacy of the relationship is restricted or eliminated because of the lack of interaction. Myles and Laura have been together for many months now, and to be honest neither is able to recount to their friends what they first saw in each other. Still, Myles likes being able to say that he has a girlfriend, and Laura would rather have someone than be alone, even if she isn't excited about spending time together. On weekends, they come together to each do their independent activities around one another, with each playing on his or her iPad and reading over meals. Myles has no idea what is going on in Laura's life, and Laura hasn't felt comfortable sharing personal information about her mom's recent health issues. In general, they feel more like new roommates than romantic partners.

AVOIDING When partners spend time together without interacting, the natural next step in moving apart is to finally stop spending time together, known as **avoiding**. Because of the restriction or elimination of intimacy among partners, and the awkward experience of spending time with someone who is treated—or treats the other—as a stranger, many relational partners take the next step and avoid spending time with one another. Should it be necessary for partners to actually see one another, the time spent together may be intentionally limited by one or both parties. Kerry, for example, needed to get her boyfriend's portion of the rent check to pay the landlord but didn't want to have to discuss their failing relationship; when she dropped by the library to grab the check from him, she intentionally left the car in plain view, still running with the radio on, in order to make it clear that she didn't intend to stay long. Although Chad and Brandon both work at the same corporation, they avoid one another as much as possible and don't acknowledge each other when

Avoiding
The fourth stage of moving apart, this part of relational de-escalation is characterized by the complete cessation of all interaction with one's relational partner.

they accidentally share the same physical space; clearly, their relationship needs serious work or else they may eventually move toward the final stage of moving apart.

TERMINATING As we look at the stages of relationships moving apart and their associated behaviors, it seems natural that the final step in de-escalation is **terminating** the relationship. Although the life span of a relationship varies widely, if a relationship is not maintained as discussed in Chapter 7, or if the relationship is actively threatened, the ending of the relationship may seem inevitable. For relationships that only moved through the initiating stage of relational development, the termination of the relationship is relatively unnoticeable as one or both partners go their

Terminating
The fifth stage of moving apart, this part of relational de-escalation is the formal ending of the relationship with one's former relational partner.

BOX 9.2: Commendable Connections

Ethics and Moving On[36,37]

Songs and poetry and films all portray the difficulties of breaking up with a romantic partner. Indeed, regardless of whether the person is the "dumper" or the "dumped," there is likely to be a wide range of emotions ranging from anger to fear to pain to relief—sometimes, even a desire for revenge. However, these feelings of distress or anger may result from—and be related to—a wide variety of ethical considerations.

Researchers have found that university students are likely to experience "breakup distress," which includes a lack of sleep, a preoccupation with the partner, and a wide variety of emotional and performance issues. Those people who experienced insecurity during the breakup—or who were controlled or manipulated during the breakup itself—are much more likely to experience these detrimental behaviors.

People are also much more likely to engage in retributive sexual behavior (i.e., "revenge sex") as a way to try to get over a former romantic partner. Partners may assume that sexual activity will "get their ex out of their system" or will anger their former partner once he learns of the sexual activity. The longer that the relationship lasted (or the greater the commitment), the more likely that sexual behaviors are used to cope with the termination of a close relationship.

Marcos Mesa Sam Wordley/Shutterstock.com

INSTRUCTIONS: Consider your emotional and physical behaviors during a breakup. Do you use ethical communication to avoid causing breakup distress in your romantic partner? Do you engage in retributive physical romantic activity, and if so does that activity serve to benefit a sexual partner? That is, are you simply "using" someone because of your own emotional needs? Take a personal inventory of your breakup behaviors. What would your response be if you were the target of one of these revenge-themed scenarios?

separate ways. For casual dating partners, the termination carries much emotional weight, but the repercussions are likely less noticeable to both the former members of the relationship and their larger social circle.[38] As people progress further along the stages of relational development, however, there are many more patterns of intimacy and communication that need to be adapted to the new relational state—or lack thereof. Roommates Brian and Derrick each found themselves attracted to Samantha, but Brian's initial flirting was poorly received. Derrick got a first date with Samantha, and it wasn't until they had been talking on the phone for weeks that they decided that they were truly incompatible. Regardless of relational length, both Derrick and Brian find themselves in a similar situation: no relationship, no interaction, and no communication with Samantha. Regardless of the quality and type of relationship that one has, the outcome of the terminating stage is typically the end of all relational opportunity with that individual.

Jon Feingersh/Blend Images/Alamy Stock Photo

LOVE AND OTHER MATTERS

One cannot go anywhere without hearing the word "*love*" being thrown around in a casual manner. Whether it is Brad discussing his love for the onion rings down at the local pub or Sarah trying to decide if she and Quentin love one another since they are sleeping together, the word "*love*" carries great weight and cultural cache within most any culture but it is often overused. Think about all the different things that you have described with love in just the past week alone! However, we notice that even though people may be able to describe the subtle difference between **liking** and **loving**,[39] it is a cultural norm to use the word "*love*" because it shows a depth of emotion. Much like when we sarcastically use the phrase "I'm going to kill him/her" when we really mean that we are going to have a stern talk with a friend of ours who is in trouble, we often use the word "*love*" to exaggerate how much we "like" something. It is important to note that we don't necessarily love every single thing for which we feel positive emotion, yet generating a definition of love is not a simple task. Instead, we can describe what love is by demonstrating the characteristics that love has.

Liking
A positive attitude toward a person, object, or idea.

Loving
A strong attitude toward another person composed of multiple components of interpersonal attraction.

Love is demonstrated in many different forms. As we see in selections from the Relational Closeness Inventory[40] as shown in Box 9.3, a survey created to measure closeness among romantic couples, scholars Berscheid, Snyder, and Omoto defined the closeness that comes from—or leads to—feelings of love in a variety of ways. From considering whether you and your partner do everyday tasks like laundry together, or influence each other's current and future plans, or simply spend time together doing fun things, the different ways to measure relational closeness highlighted in Box 9.3 help us see how truly diverse different aspects of love can be. In order to address the complexity of the concept of love, one inventory looks at the different aspects of love in three different parts.

BOX 9.3: Let's Get INTRApersonal

Relational Closeness Inventory[41]

Do you often think about how close you and your romantic partner *really* are? Perhaps you spend a lot of time trying to define your relationship based on your interactions and behaviors? Even though there is no fair measurement that works for every single relationship, sometimes it is helpful to answer some questions about your experiences with your romantic partner to reflect on how you spend time together; you can use this self-assessment to gain insight into your relationship behaviors. This is a modified and much-shortened version of the Relationship Closeness Inventory that was created by the original researchers (Berscheid, Snyder, & Omoto) in 1989 to help people process their interpersonal relationships.

INSTRUCTIONS: Think carefully about how you interact with your partner.

1. DURING THE PAST WEEK, what is the average amount of time, per day, that you spent *alone with your partner*? ___hour(s) ___minutes

INSTRUCTIONS: For each of the activities listed, please check all of those that you have engaged in *alone with your partner in the past week*.

_____ did laundry

_____ prepared a meal

_____ watched TV

_____ attended a non-class lecture or presentation

_____ went to a grocery store

_____ went for a walk/drive

_____ discussed things of a personal nature

_____ planned a party/social event

_____ went on a trip (e.g., vacation or weekend)

_____ cleaned house/apartment

_____ went to church/religious function

_____ worked on homework

_____ engaged in sexual relations

_____ talked on the phone

_____ went to a movie

_____ ate a meal

_____ participated in a sporting activity

_____ outdoor recreation (e.g., sailing)

INSTRUCTIONS: Using the 7-point scale below, please indicate the extent to which you agree or disagree by writing the appropriate number in the space corresponding to each item.

1	2	3	4	5	6	7
Strongly Disagree	Moderately Disagree	Slightly Disagree	Neither Agree Nor Disagree	Slightly Agree	Moderately Agree	Strongly Agree

_____ My partner will influence my future financial security.

_____ My partner does *not* influence everyday things in my life.

_____ My partner influences important things in my life.

_____ My partner influences which parties and other social events I attend.

_____ My partner influences the extent to which I accept responsibilities in our relationship.

_____ My partner *does not* influence how much time I spend doing household work.

_____ My partner does *not* influence how I choose to spend my money.

_____ My partner influences the way I feel about myself.

_____ My partner *does not* influence my moods.

_____ My partner influences the basic values that I hold.

Now, look at your answers. What kinds of things characterize your relationship with your partner? Do they have influence on your life? Do you spend time together? Do you engage in diverse activities together? Each person and each relationship may look very different depending on when this survey is taken and with whom you are partnered.

Triangular Theory of Love

Love is demonstrated in many different forms. One of the easiest ways to think of the complexities of love is to break it down into three basic components and consider how "much" of each a typical relationship has. Just like you can make a cookie with much flour, moderate sugar, and some butter, you can make a croissant out of much butter, moderate flour, and some sugar; even though the essential components are similar, the outcomes look very different depending on the manner in which those components were combined. Sternberg's **triangular theory of love**[42] describes the three components of love as passion, intimacy, and commitment (see Figure 9.2).

Dennis Gottlieb/Getty Images

Triangular Theory of Love
Sternberg's theory that love is composed of three primary components—passion, intimacy, and commitment— each of which may be expressed to varying degrees within a relationship.

Passion

When we are passionate about something, we experience strong emotions or motivations when we think about or have contact with the object of our passion. Whether we are motivated to work toward social justice or we feel

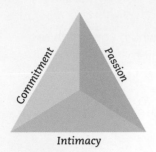

FIGURE 9.2
Sternberg's Triangular Theory

Passion
The sense of excitement or arousal that drives people to take action.

Intimacy
The sense of closeness, liking, and emotional connection to another person.

a strong compulsion to spend time with our romantic partner, **passion** is a sense of excitement that drives us to take action. As the first of three components of love, passion is the driving force that encourages people to affiliate with one another. Because passion is often experienced as waves of excitement, intensity, or arousal, passion can drive people to make impulsive decisions but likely wanes in strength at another point in the relationship. People often describe passion as causing intensely high "highs" and decidedly low "lows" of emotion.

Intimacy

As we have discussed throughout this text, **intimacy** is the feeling of closeness and positive feeling that emerges from a variety of behaviors, from self-disclosive conversation to a caring hug at the end of a rough day. The triangular theory of love highlights intimacy as one of the components of love, because relationships cannot last or be sustained without this type of emotional connection between two people. Whether intimacy is developed quickly within a relationship or takes a long time to flourish and grow, it is a fundamental part of interpersonal closeness and the warmth associated with love.

Commitment

Finally, as we have discussed earlier in the chapter, commitment is a choice that people make within their interpersonal relationships, and that commitment is demonstrated by both the decision to love one's partner and to work to maintain that decision over time. As a result, commitment is believed to be the strongest predictor of relational longevity over time.[43] Making the choice to maintain a relationship over time does not guarantee the quality of a relationship, but it does increase the likelihood that the relationship will last.

Sternberg's triangular theory points out that each of these three components is an indicator of love but that each component can be expressed to a *great* degree, to a *moderate* degree, or *not expressed at all*; the degree and duration of expression may depend on the individuals in the relationship, the timing of the relationship, or a variety of other situational and contextual differences. Regardless, each component influences the lived experience of the relational partners. Tommy met Nadine as she attended his community college during her study abroad experience. Because the relationship was built mainly on physical passion, their infatuation was characterized by an idealized version of each other, ignoring the fact that they didn't speak the same language and would have to be apart at the end of the semester. On the other side of the country, Preet and Chance were introduced after their marriage had been arranged; now, the slow and subtle courting process and their strong religious convictions ensure that they have an intimate, committed relationship based on an initial friendship that developed over time. Each relationship varies in the levels of passion, intimacy, and commitment over time, and so love may look different as those components shift in emphasis throughout the relationship.

Peter Bernik/Shutterstock.com

BOX 9.4: Communication Currents

Portrayals of Love in Current Television

***Downton Abbey*, Season 5 Trailer, "Sex and Love" http://bit.ly/2n7TP1I**

In the period drama *Downton Abbey*, a household of British aristocracy and their employees come to terms with cultural shifts throughout the post-Edwardian era. While each character struggles with the shifts in economy, politics, and social structure, the series begins to highlight the love life of Lady Mary Crawley, a young socialite who comes of age in an era torn between the traditions of old and the changing sexual and relational norms of her culture.

As we watch the clips and cast interviews, multiple comments are made about the main character's romantic relationships. This video highlights the struggles of a bygone era, while also reminding us of the influence of culture and background on relationship experiences. Although the period attitudes toward romance may seem old-fashioned, future generations may view our cultural attitudes in a similar light someday.

INSTRUCTIONS: Watch the video again, paying careful attention to the ways that Mary is portrayed as fitting into the norm while also struggling against it. Why do you imagine that Mary struggles in her romantic behavior? Consider how you respond to the norms and influences that you experience in your daily life. How do they impact your relational expectations and ways of demonstrating affection?

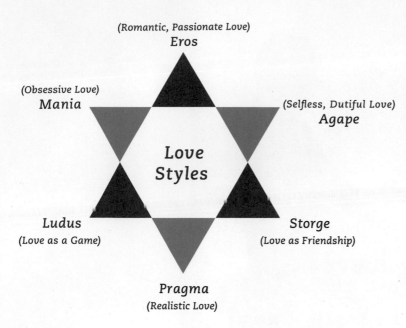

FIGURE 9.3 Lee's Love Styles

Love Styles

Now that there is a clear explanation of the primary components of love, it may be helpful to consider the ways that people actually express those components of passion, intimacy, and commitment. Scholars believe that we express love with one another based on both our cultural background and our individual experiences. These come together to inform and influence our expressions of love, such that each person has a definite manner of expressing love to—and interacting with—a romantic partner, known as a **love style**. In the 1970s, John Lee came up with a typology of the different preconceptions that people bring to a relationship, finding three primary love styles and three secondary love styles[44,45,46] (see Figure 9.3), each of which influences our approach to experiencing and demonstrating affection toward one another.

Primary Love Styles

The first three love styles are primary love styles and have little to no overlap with one another, each influencing our approach to affection in relationships.

- **Storge** is a love style characterized by friendship, often with a focus on both intimacy and commitment. Storgic lovers tend to focus on a long-term relationship and avoid passion.[47]

- **Eros** is a love style characterized by passion, often with a focus on both attraction and sexual interest. Erotic lovers tend to focus on finding someone who wants them and on finding what they themselves consider beautiful.[48]

- **Ludus** is a love style characterized by viewing love as a game, often with a focus on both casual interaction and fun. Ludic lovers tend to focus on the hunt for a partner and are rarely monogamous or serious in a relationship.[49]

Secondary Love Styles

The next three love styles are secondary love styles, and each of the three is typically seen as the combination of two separate primary love styles as displayed in a relationship.

- **Agape** is a love style characterized by nurturance, often with a focus on demonstrating care and compassion. This love style is a blend of the storge and eros types of love. Agapic lovers tend to focus on reason and duty without expecting much from the relational partner.[50]

Love Style
An individual- and culture-specific way of approaching and experiencing love with one's romantic partner.

Storge
The love style most characterized by friendship, intimacy, and commitment.

Eros
The love style most characterized by passion, attraction, and sexual interest.

Ludus
The love style most characterized by playfulness and a lack of commitment.

Agape
The love style most characterized by nurturance and care.

BOX 9.5: InterFace

Relational Initiation with Diverse Others

Kimpton's parents emphasized a traditional relationship style. As such, he always focused on demonstrating chivalry and respect for women, but he always believed that as a man it was his duty to make the first "move" when it came to dating and relationships.

Makaio grew up in a culturally rich area of a large urban center, so her exposure to relationship types was wide and varied. Although she has a definite preference for one gender, she refers to herself as "soul-sexual" and is willing to start a romantic relationship with any man or woman who she finds emotionally compelling.

Breyn's parents were open about discussing sex and relationships, but her boyfriend Chris comes from a religious background where those sorts of discussions are taboo. Since Breyn and Chris haven't talked about whether they will engage in sexual activity with one another if they date each other exclusively, Breyn is uncomfortable as she tries to decide whether she and Chris have a chance together.

nd3000/Shutterstock.com

Badi is attractive and outgoing but expects to have an arranged marriage set up by both partners' families. As such, any relationships that Badi starts while in college are destined for friendship or casual interaction. The possibility of "love at first sight" is not even an option worth discussing.

Although people are typically motivated to have close, intimate relationships with a variety of people around them, not everyone approaches the people in their lives from the same perspective. So, how do you deal with such a wide range of relationship types and individuals? Rather than using a one-size-fits-all approach to interacting with the people that you find compelling in your life, often simple conversations about backgrounds and expectations can easily assuage any fears or hang-ups in relational style.

INSTRUCTIONS: What are your responses to these scenarios? Do you find yourself shocked or amazed at one or more of the perspectives that these people have shared? With whom do you most identify? Consider your own relationship styles and the past experiences that you have had with romantic interactions. How would you approach or interact with each of these diverse individuals?

- **Pragma** is a love style characterized by practicality, often with a focus on both logic and relational problem solving. This love style is a blend of the storge and ludus types of love. Pragmatic lovers tend to focus on making sure that the demographic characteristics of both partners blend well with one another and make sense.[51]

Pragma
The love style most characterized by practicality, logic, and relational problem solving.

Mania
The love style most characterized by control and a demand for loyalty.

- **Mania** is a love style characterized by territoriality, often with a focus on both loyalty and control. This love style is a blend of the eros and ludus types of love. Manic lovers tend to focus on jealously protecting the relationship from outside intrusion.[52]

There are both positive and negative factors to each of the love styles, and a person can change his love style as he gains additional experience and cultural information about relationships. Each of these six love styles is seen as a tendency or a predilection, but by no means does one's love style have to remain unchanged. In fact, some scholars argue that a more robust predictor of our relationship types actually started in our earliest interactions as a small child.

ATTACHMENT

Attachment Theory
Bowlby's theory that early interpersonal experiences as a child influence the pattern of relying on relational partners for interdependence, security, and affection.

Secure
The style of attachment that is characterized by high self-worth and an ability to rely on others for relational needs.

Scholars found that our experiences as an infant—from the moment we first interacted with a caregiver like a parent or guardian—were closely related to the ways that we interact with relational partners later in life. In a concept known as **attachment theory**, Bowlby[53,54,55,56] and colleagues believed that we first developed our sense of self-worth as well as our understanding of whether we can depend on others based on how much attention we received when we expressed needs for nourishment or care as an infant. Scholars have extended this research line to include those experiences and interactions that we have up throughout our childhood and even into our adolescent and young adult experiences.

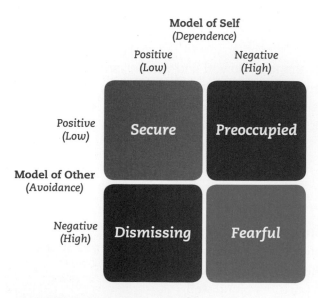

FIGURE 9.4
Four Quadrants of Attachment Theory

The Four Attachment Styles

Based on those experiences, the argument is that we may have either a positive or a negative sense of our own self-worth, as well as a positive or negative view of whether others can meet our relational needs. The four possible combinations of these two factors (see Figure 9.4) create the four main attachment styles described by researchers over the past 50 years.

Secure Attachments

For people who have a high sense of self-worth as well as a belief that others can meet their relational needs, the **secure** style of attachment is often characterized as the "most desirable" pattern because of the trust and positive attitudes associated with such a relationship. Franklin enjoys a close relationship with his fiancée and trusts her completely when he travels for business; whenever relationship issues arise between the two of

ptadeb/Shutterstock.com

them, he always gives her the benefit of the doubt because he believes they wouldn't intentionally hurt one another.

Dismissive Attachment

People who still have a high sense of self-worth but do not feel the need to rely on a partner to meet their needs are known as having a **dismissive** attachment style, and these people often downplay the importance of close relationships in their everyday lives. Melinda enjoys her career and her pets and has no desire to find a romantic partner; because she has a positive view of herself, she doesn't feel the need to form close connections with the people around her.

Preoccupied Attachment

Although they believe that people can meet one another's relational needs, the low self-esteem of the **preoccupied** individual (also known as the **anxious-ambivalent** individual) often ensures that she feels unworthy of other people's love. Because they fear abandonment, these people often exhibit a greater amount of relational monitoring and a high desire for interdependence. Irene knows that her boyfriend is going to a bachelor party this weekend without the intention to cheat, but her fear that she doesn't deserve him makes her worry the entire weekend that he may find someone better while traveling.

Fearful-Avoidant Attachment

Finally, there is a group of people who neither believe that they nor other people are able to have satisfying relationships; these

Dismissive
The style of attachment that is characterized by high self-worth but no desire to turn to others to provide a sense of intimacy.

Preoccupied
The style of attachment that is characterized by low self-worth and a belief that others are able to fulfill their relational needs but will likely not.

Anxious-Ambivalent
See Preoccupied.

Majesticca/Shutterstock.com

Fearful-Avoidant
The style of attachment that is characterized by low self-worth and a belief that relational partners are unable to meet relational needs.

fearful-avoidant individuals will reject or disbelieve any attempts at intimacy or closeness, even though they may desire such relationships in their personal lives. Darren doesn't believe that anyone can love him like he wants to be loved, so instead he eschews all relational attempts and defines himself as a "lone wolf."

BOX 9.6: InterConnect

What Attracted You to Your Dating Partner?

People find one another to be "datable" for a variety of reasons. Interestingly, for some it is often the smallest thing that may lead to a lifelong romance, or a simple summer fling. Others may perform an intellectual calculus of sorts, as they use complex criteria to determine whether someone is worth their time.

Regardless of background and culture and a variety of other individual differences, each relationship likely looks dramatically different than other relationships in one's social circle, although there may be elements of that relationship style that reflect our own behaviors.

Alistair Berg/Getty Images

> ❯ Sylvana first noticed Rick's body as they worked out at the same gym. Although she never considered herself a "physical" dater, she definitely made sure to catch his attention after her workout.

> ❯ Caelin took her niece to the local park and saw Chad volunteering by coaching a group of elementary school children. Given her desire for an altruistic spouse, Caelin decided that Chad fit her criteria.

> ❯ Monica and Garrick met during their chemistry lab. Because they both share the same major, Garrick and Monica studied together most every night for the next three years and are still together to this day.

> ❯ Asim is still trying to get the attention of the attractive new assistant in the office down the hall from his place of employment. Both of them seem to have similar taste in clothing and apparel, wearing an obscure brand of shoes that few others have ever discovered.

INSTRUCTIONS: Think carefully about each of the descriptions above. Are Sylvana, Caelin, Monica, or Asim similar to one another? Do you think that their motivations are very different? Each of us finds something worthwhile about the people we date. What has attracted you to your "crushes" in the past? How would you describe your relationship type? Have you ever dated anyone who seemed very different from your "usual"? Did it work out?

Chapter Summary

Both casual and committed relationships tend to move in similar ways as people get closer to one another. Although relationships are constantly shifting between getting closer together and moving further apart, there are common characteristics of different stages of relational development that can help us gain insight into the behaviors of romantic partners. From the first moment that a couple locks eyes, to the different paths of a long-term commitment or a casual fling, people get to know one another in often very similar manners. Not only that, but breakups and the termination of those relationships often occur in structured, predictable patterns.

Many committed romantic relationships are based on love and closeness, and the triangular theory of love helps us to understand the three-pronged ways that people balance their passion, intimacy, and commitment to one another. Love also manifests itself in a variety of styles, and people may find themselves either very similar or very different from one another in their expression of love. Although attachment theory implies that our approaches to love are relatively stable, each relationship looks unique as two partners come together and communicate as members of a romantic relationship.

First-Person Video

MindTap®

Selfies to Remember

Apply what you've learned in this chapter by analyzing the "Selfies to Remember" video, using the accompanying questions as a guide. The video and questions are available online in your MindTap Speech for *Interconnections: Interpersonal Communication Foundations and Contexts.*

Key Terms

MindTap®

Agape	**Experimenting**	**Relational**
Anxious-Ambivalent	**Fearful-Avoidant**	**De-escalation**
Attachment Theory	**Initiating**	**Relational**
Avoiding	**Integrating**	**Development**
Bonding	**Intensifying**	**Secure**
Casual Relationship	**Intimacy**	**Social Information**
Circumscribing	**Liking**	**Processing Theory**
Commitment	**Love Style**	**Stagnating**
Committed	**Loving**	**Storge**
Relationship	**Ludus**	**Terminating**
Commonalities	**Mania**	**Triangular Theory of**
Differentiating	**Passion**	**Love**
Dismissive	**Pragma**	
Eros	**Preoccupied**	

Use flashcards to learn key concepts and take a quiz to test your knowledge.

Discussion Questions

1. Think about the people in your life who have been in long-term relationships, whether parents or coaches or teachers or friends. How do they express their love to one another?

2. What are your thoughts on attachment theory? Do you believe that early experiences can have such a significant influence on later life?

3. Think about your close relationships. How do you express love and affection toward the people you care about?

4. Discuss a time when you were attracted to someone different from you. What was that like? Did your interaction seem easy or difficult? Did a relationship develop?

5. Out of all of the love styles, which do you think your culture encourages? Are there specific examples of messages that confirm your thoughts, whether through media or cultural sayings?

Making Connections

Romantic relationships share a unique set of characteristics that make them different from family or workplace relationships. How might relational maintenance (Chapter 7) look different for a romantic relationship as compared to a variety of other relationship types?

Chapter Quiz

1. Which of the following stages of coming together describes the beginning of self-disclosure and relational intimacy?

    a. Experimenting   d. Integrating
    b. Initiating   e. Intensifying
    c. Bonding   f. None of the above

2. Which of the following stages of coming together describes a public commitment toward one another expressed through ritual?

    a. Experimenting   d. Integrating
    b. Initiating   e. Intensifying
    c. Bonding   f. None of the above

3. Which of the following stages of coming together describes a movement from inclusive language (we/us) to exclusive language (you/me)?

    a. Experimenting   d. Integrating
    b. Initiating   e. Intensifying
    c. Bonding   f. None of the above

4. Which of the following attachment styles best describes someone who feels that both he and his partner are able to fulfill each other's needs?

    a. Secure   d. Dismissive

    b. Preoccupied   e. Anxious-ambivalent

    c. Fearful-avoidant   f. None of the above

5. Which of the following attachment styles best describes someone who has high self-esteem but feels that any partner is unable to fulfill her needs?

    a. Secure   d. Dismissive

    b. Preoccupied   e. Anxious-ambivalent

    c. Fearful-avoidant   f. None of the above

6. T/F Guo-Ming is ready to break up with a romantic partner and works hard to not run into her at work. Guo-Ming is likely in the *avoiding* stage of relational de-escalation.

7. T/F Zane finally had the breakup conversation with his romantic partner, and they no longer see one another. Zane is likely in the *circumscribing* stage of relational de-escalation.

8. T/F According to Sternberg, the three basic components of love are passion, intimacy, and commitment.

9. T/F Commitment is a feeling that is not based on a choice but, rather, an emotional state.

10. T/F If Cathy has a *fearful-avoidant* attachment style, she is unlikely to trust that her partner Lisa will be supportive.

Endnotes

1. Schindler, I., Fagundes, C. P., & Murdock, K. W. (2010). Predictors of romantic relationship formation: Attachment style, prior relationships, and dating goals. *Personal Relationships, 17,* 97–105.

2. For a discussion, see Nieder, T., & Seiffge-Krenke, I. (2001). Coping with stress in different phases of romantic development. *Journal of Adolescence, 24*(3), 297–311.

3. Katz, J., & Schneider, M. E. (2013). Casual hook up sex during the first year of college: Prospective associations with attitudes about sex and love relationships. *Archives of Sexual Behavior, 42*(8), 1451–1462.

4. Knapp, M. L. (1978). *Social Intercourse: From Greeting to Goodbye* (p. vii). Boston, MA: Allyn & Bacon.

5. Knapp, M. L. (1984). *Interpersonal Communication and Human Relationships.* Newton, MA: Allyn & Bacon.

6. Knapp, M. L. (1978). *Social Intercourse: From Greeting to Goodbye.* Boston, MA: Allyn & Bacon.

7. Walther, J. B. (2008). Social information processing theory. In L. A. Baxter & D. O. Braithwewaite (Eds.), *Engaging Theories in Interpersonal Communication: Multiple Perspectives* (pp. 391–404). Thousand Oaks, CA: Sage.

8. McWilliams, S., & Barrett, A. E. (2014). Online dating in middle and later life: Gendered expectations and experiences. *Journal of Family Issues, 35*(3), 411–436.

9. Holloway, I. W., Rice, E., Gibbs, J., Winetrobe, H., Dunlap, S., & Rhoades, H. (2013). Acceptability of smartphone application-based hiv prevention among young men who have sex with men. *AIDS and Behavior, 18,* 285–296.

10. Summers, N. (2013). Dating app Tinder catches fire. *Business Week.* Retrieved from http://www.businessweek.com/articles/2013-09-05/dating-app-tinder-catches-fire

11. Toma, C. L., & Hancock, J. T. (2012). What lies beneath: The linguistic traces of deception in online dating profiles. *Journal of Communication, 62*(1), 78–97.

12. Witt, E. (2014). Love me Tinder. *GQ.* Retrieved from http://www.gq.com/life/relationships/201402/tinder-online-dating-sex-app

13. Cali, B. E., Coleman, J. M., & Campbell, C. (2013). Stranger danger? Women's self-protection intent and the continuing stigma of online dating. *Cyberpsychology, Behavior, and Social Networking, 16*(2), 853–857.

14. Vernon, P. (2010). Grindr: A new sexual revolution? *The Guardian.* Retrieved from http://www.theguardian.com/media/2010/jul/04/grindr-the-new-sexual-revolution

15. Guadagno, R. E., Okdie, B. M., & Kruse, S. A. (2012). Dating deception: Gender, online dating, and exaggerated self-presentation. *Computers in Human Behavior, 28*(2), 642–647.

16. Goedel, W. C., Krebs, P., Greene, R. E., & Duncan, D. T. (2016). Associations between perceived weight status, body dissatisfaction, and self-objectification on sexual sensation seeking and sexual risk behaviors among men who have sex with men using Grindr. Advanced online publication. *Behavioral Medicine.* doi: 10.1080/08964289.2015.1121130

17. Hall, J. A., Carter, S., Cody, M. J., & Albright, J. M. (2010). Individual differences in the communication of romantic interest: Development of the flirting styles inventory. *Communication Quarterly, 58*(4), 365–393.

18. Hall, J. (2013). *The Five Flirting Styles: Use the Science of Flirting to Attract the Love You Really Want.* Buffalo, NY: Harlequin.

19. Angelique, M., Celine, J., & Gueguen, N. (2013). Similarity facilitates relationships on social networks: A field experiment on Facebook. *Psychological Reports, 113*(1), 217–220.

20. Morry, M. M., Kito, M., & Ortiz, L. (2011). The attraction-similarity model and dating couples: Projection, perceived similarity, and psychological benefits. *Personal Relationships, 18*(1), 125–143.

21. Tidwell, N. D., Eastwick, P. W., & Finkel, E. J. (2013). Perceived, not actual, similarity predicts initial attraction in a live romantic context: Evidence from the speed-dating paradigm. *Personal Relationships, 20*(2), 199–215.

22. Altman, I., & Taylor, D. A. (1973). *Social Penetration: The Development of Interpersonal Relationships.* Oxford, England: Holt, Rinehart, & Winston.

23. Knapp, M. L. (1978). *Social Intercourse: From Greeting to Goodbye* (p. vii). Boston, MA: Allyn & Bacon.

24. For a review, see Fitzsimons, G. M., & Kay, A. C. (2004). Language and interpersonal cognition: Causal effects of variations in pronoun usage on perceptions of closeness. *Personality and Social Psychology Bulletin, 30*(5), 547–557.

25. Knapp, M. L. (1978). *Social Intercourse: From Greeting to Goodbye* (p. vii). Boston, MA: Allyn & Bacon.

26. Giles, H. (1973). Accent mobility: A model and some data. *Anthropological Linguistics, 15,* 87–105.

27. Colson, M., Lemaire, A., Pinton, P., Hamidi, K., & Klein, P. (2006). Sexual behaviors and mental perception, satisfaction and expectations of sex life in men and women in France. *Journal of Sexual Medicine, 3,* 121–131.

28. Baxter, L. A., & Montgomery, B. M. (1996). *Relating: Dialogues and Dialectics.* New York, NY: Guilford Press.

29. McQueeney, K. B. (2003). The new religious rite: A symbolic interactionist case study of lesbian commitment rituals. *Journal of Lesbian Studies, 7*(2), 49–70.

30. Riggle, E. D., Rothblum, E. D., Rostosky, S. S., Clark, J. B., & Balsam, K. F. (2016). "The secret of our success": Long-term same-sex couples' perceptions of their relationship longevity. *Journal of GLBT Family Studies, 12*(4), 319–334.

31. Knapp, M. L. (1978). *Social Intercourse: From Greeting to Goodbye* (p. vii). Boston, MA: Allyn & Bacon.

32. Baxter, L. A., & Bullis, C. (1986). Turning points in developing romantic relationships. *Human Communication Research, 12*(4), 469–493.

33. Blackburn, K., Brody, N., & LeFebvre, L. (2014). The I's, we's, and she/he's of breakups: Public and private pronoun usage in relationship dissolution accounts. *Journal of Language and Social Psychology, 33*(2), 202–213.

34. Altman, I., & Taylor, D. A. (1973). *Social Penetration: The Development of Interpersonal Relationships.* Oxford, England: Holt, Rinehart & Winston.

35. Samouilidas, L. (1975). Marital relationships: Frustration and fulfillment. *The American Journal of Psychoanalysis, 35*(4), 365–375.

36. Pelaez, M., Field, T., Diego, M., Deeds, O., & Delgado, J. (2011). Insecurity, control, and disinterest behaviors are related to breakup distress in university students. *College Student Journal, 45*(2), 333–340.

37. Barber, L. L., & Cooper, M. L. (2014). Rebound sex: Sexual motives and behaviors following a relationship breakup. *Archives of Sexual Behavior, 43,* 251–265.

38. Knapp, M. L. (1984). *Interpersonal Communication and Human Relationships.* Newton, MA: Allyn & Bacon.

39. Rubin, Z. (1970). Measurement of romantic love. *Journal of Personality and Social Psychology, 16*(2), 265–273.

40. Ibid.

41. Berscheid, E., Snyder, M., & Omoto, A. M. (1989). The Relationship Closeness Inventory: Assessing the closeness of interpersonal relationships. *Journal of Personality and Social Psychology, 57*(5), 792–807.

42. Sternberg, R. J. (1986). A triangular theory of love. *Psychological Review, 93*(2), 119–135.

43. Hendrick, S. S., Hendrick, C., & Adler, N. L. (1988). Romantic relationships: Love, satisfaction, and staying together. *Journal of Personality and Social Psychology, 54*(6), 980–988.

44. Lee, J. A. (1988). Love styles. In R. J. Sternberg & M. L. Barnes (Eds.), *The Psychology of Love* (pp. 38–67). New Haven, CT: Yale University Press.

45. Lee, J. A. (1973). *Colours of Love: An Exploration of the Ways of Loving.* Ontario, Canada: New Press.

46. Lee, J. A. (1977). A typology of styles of loving. *Personality and Social Psychology Bulletin, 3,* 173–182.

47. Ibid.

48. Ibid.

49. Ibid.

50. Ibid.

51. Ibid.

52. Ibid.

53. Bowlby, J. (1982). *Attachment and Loss: Vol. 1. Attachment.* New York, NY: Basic Books. (Original work published 1969)

54. Collins, N. L., & Feeney, B. C. (2004). An attachment theory perspective on closeness and intimacy. In D. J. Mashek & A. Aron (Eds.), *Handbook of Closeness and Intimacy* (pp. 163–187). Mahwah, NJ: Lawrence Erlbaum.

55. Feeney, J. A., Noller, P., & Roberts, N. (2000). Attachment and close relationships. In C. Hendrick & S. S. Hendrick (Eds.), *Close Relationships: A Sourcebook* (pp. 185–201). Thousand Oaks, CA: Sage.

56. Pietromonaco, P. R., & Beck, L. A. (2015). Attachment processes in adult romantic relationships. In M. Mikulincer, P. R. Shaver, J. A. Simpson, & J. F. Dovidio (Eds.), *APA Handbook of Personality and Social Psychology, Vol. 3. Interpersonal Relations* (pp. 33–64). Washington, DC: American Psychological Association. doi:10.1037/14344-002

Families

10

Portra Images/DigitalVision/Getty Images

What makes someone "family"?

Why do people have such different understandings about how families should look and interact?

MindTap®

Review the chapter's learning objectives and **start** with a quick warm-up activity.

Learning Objectives

After you finish reading this chapter, you will be able to:

Describe multiple perspectives on defining "family."

Identify and compare different family structures.

Recognize behaviors that influence a family system.

MindTap®

Read, highlight, and take notes online.

For her first-year journalism class, Aineki was asked to interview her peers and write a story about something that each one of them shared in common. After considering a variety of topics, Aineki realized that everyone she knew came from somewhere, and so decided to choose "family" as the topic of her main story. After conducting only a few interviews, however, Aineki was frustrated because there seemed to be no overlap between stories. Her roommate Eva felt lost in a large family with four siblings, both parents, and her grandmother all under one roof. Aineki herself is close to her mother, a single parent who had only one child. Johnson, Aineki's lab partner from chemistry class, was raised by his father and stepmom after his own biological mother died during her military service, but Johnson has never thought of his biological siblings differently than his older half brother. Her next-door neighbor Sun-Yi was raised by a stay-at-home dad, and Sun-Yi's roommate Merissa was the first at her high school to have two loving adoptive fathers. Aineki almost gave up hope on using "family" as a topic for her paper on similarity, until she noticed that the basic family wants, needs, and goals can be congruent regardless of the way that the household may appear to outsiders.

OUR FIRST RELATIONSHIPS

What makes someone "family"? Why do people have such different understandings about how families should look and interact? Even though everyone has some experience of family, not all experiences are similar, nor are they all positive. But for the most part, the relationships we have in our families are among the first relationships that we experience, and we are often influenced by those family relationships throughout the course of our everyday lives. Whether a parent encouraged you to reach your fullest potential or a sibling bullied you into submission, the impact of family on our early development is hard to ignore. Our reactions to both positive and negative family experiences shape the course of our lives and teach us how we want to behave as family to future generations.

DEFINING THE FAMILY

Families are as diverse as the individuals within those families, and so an understanding of family must be broad enough to include all these possible definitions. Floyd, Mikkelson, and Judd (2006)[1] have argued that there are three main "lenses" through which each family can be viewed, and a person's individual definition of a family will necessarily be influenced by one or more of these three components. If you look at family through a **role lens**, you are likely to see families as groups of people where members behave like a family and who feel like they are family to one another through love, support, and attachment. Barry is an only child in his 20s who lives far away from his parents. As such, he has a group of other young professionals with whom he spends holidays, birthdays, and the routines of his daily life. Because he goes to them when he wants to talk about the future, relies on them for help in times of emergency, and enjoys the support of these people throughout his various life stages, he often refers to them as family. He is even known as "Uncle Barry" to a couple of his friends' children, and he doesn't see any reason to correct their assumption that they are related. In a way, they are.

Mario is an employee at a local day care facility. Because of the insurance regulations that apply at his work, he is in charge of ensuring that only legal family members pick up the children under his care. As such, people must provide proof of adoption or a birth certificate or have been prescreened to prove their documented guardian status. Mario's employer is using a **sociolegal lens** to view family, which instead focuses on families as constituted by the laws and rules that apply to that family, based on the family's legal context. Under this definition, as long as government or civic law calls a person part of a family or recognizes him or her as such, that person is considered family. In his case, Mario is forced to define family by whatever the current legal definition of family is.

Finally, if you look at a family unit through a **biogenetic lens**, you are likely to simply define family according to reproductive success or the transmission of genetic material, like when people use the term *blood relationship*

Role Lens
The perspective that families are groups of people who feel and behave like a family, typically due to love, support, and/or attachment.

Sociolegal Lens
The perspective that families are groups of people that have been recognized as such through civic or governmental laws and regulations.

Biogenetic Lens
The perspective that families are groups of people who work toward reproductive success and share common genetic material.

BOX 10.1: **Commendable Connections**

Ethics and Nepotism[2]

As the first member of his family to continue his education past high school, Josh has worked relatively hard during his years in school. After a summer internship at a local newspaper, Josh is beginning to narrow his focus about what he wants to do. However, since he is still undecided about his future, he thinks he will simply take an entry-level position at his father's car dealership after graduation until he can figure out the types of jobs to which he will apply. He doesn't want to stay at Level One Autos, but it seems like decent money until he can figure out what he wants to do.

Frangine is also motivated in her marketing education. She hopes to get into sales. She has worked in promotions for a major car manufacturer and wants to get her foot in the door through one of the small dealerships in her hometown. Her job as an auto promoter has allowed her to make connections at all the local places, and when she found out that an employee was retiring at Level One Autos she allowed herself to get her hopes up. When she made an appointment to talk to the general manager, though, she found out that the position was going to be reserved for her classmate Josh until he decided on a career. Frangine was noticeably upset and left the dealership a deeper shade of red than when she had entered.

Josh's dad is engaging in **nepotism**, or the meritless favoring of family members for sought-after employment positions. Though not always illegal, it is a hotly argued topic in the business community. After all, from an evolutionary perspective it makes sense that people would want to bestow quality opportunities on their kin. However, many people argue that this practice is unfair, and in the public sector some of those nepotistic practices have been outlawed. Many people argue that impartial hiring is the best approach for industry. After all, there are laws against discrimination for other group memberships like race, sex, and religion, right?

INSTRUCTIONS: If you were Frangine, how would you feel? What if you were Josh's dad? Would you want the position to be given to your son? Consider all perspectives in this encounter. Could there also be some pressure on Josh to conform to his father's career path? Is the promise of a "backup job" not allowing Josh to strive for his full potential? What advice would you give to each of the three people in this situation?

to describe a member of the family. Jenna is getting married next week and has asked her biological father to walk her down the aisle, even though she admits disliking him. Although they have been estranged for years and have little to no actual relationship, Jenna's dad will be sitting in the front row as she exchanges her vows. When asked why she has invited her father to be in the wedding despite their history, Jenna simply replies, "Blood runs thicker than water, and he's family." Proponents of the use of this biogenetic lens

Nepotism
Favoring family members for sought-after positions of employment.

often point out that there is an evolutionary benefit to supporting our genetic relatives, to the point that we give them benefits and support that we may be unlikely to give others. Some argue we may even naturally be wired to tend to define family in this way.

Each of these three ways of viewing families would then influence or even change our understanding of what makes a family. Depending on your cultural or family background, you may be more or less inclined to adopt one of these perspectives, or even be predisposed toward some composite blending of them. Because of his father's background as a professional athlete, Jake and his five siblings had to move every few years when his father got traded to different teams. Because of this, Jake never had a close group of friends that he shared a history with. His girlfriend, Clarissa, grew up in a small town in a tight-knit group of friends and neighbors. Although she is able to see a technical difference between someone who shares the same ancestral heritage as herself, she considers all of her parents' friends as "second moms and dads" or "aunts and uncles." When Jake asks Clarissa to tell him about her family, Clarissa starts off with a story about her cousin Blaine who lives next door; halfway through the story, Jake experiences confusion as he realizes there is no biological connection between the two neighbors. To him, Blaine is simply her neighbor, someone who shares a fence but not much else and who is likely to change the next time circumstances arise. In order to encompass elements of the three different perspectives afforded by the lens approach to family, this text defines family rather broadly. Our working definition reflects the perspectives of many scholars, distilling the breadth of the field to define **family** as a multigenerational group of people with a shared history who constitute themselves as "family" through interpersonal attachment and involvement.[3,4,5,6]

Family
A multigenerational group of people with a shared history who constitute themselves as "family" through interpersonal interaction and attachment.

Families Are Multigenerational

Scholars have maintained that families are made up of people from all different generations.[7] From young children just starting out in life to grandparents and great-grandparents enjoying their golden years, the ages and experiences of family members are just as diverse as the individuals themselves. Not only do people differ in their biological age, but family members likely range across a variety of developmental stages as well, which increases the diversity of the multigenerational experience within the family unit.[8] Kyle and Brenda have just found out that they are six weeks pregnant and are excited and nervous at the prospect. Kyle immediately turns to his cousin Bill to ask general advice about financial stability as a young father, while Brenda quizzes her mother about the upcoming changes to her body that she should expect. Both Kyle and Brenda have enjoyed babysitting their two nieces, who served as ringbearers at Kyle and Brenda's commitment ceremony, so they feel prepared to begin learning about their future together. On hearing the news, Kyle's grandmother got out the family Bible and recorded the birth announcement in the front cover according to the family tradition. Each family member participated in the moment in her or his own unique way.

Families Have a Shared History

One thing that all families have in common is a shared past. Whether that commonality is related to an ancestral heritage or to a set of experiences gleaned from years spent living in close proximity, a key aspect of the definition includes a history that in some way links family members together. Jacob and David were cousins who grew up down the street from each other. Not only were their fathers siblings, but they also felt like brothers as they

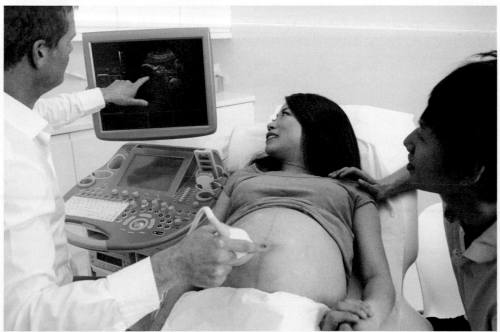

played in the cul-de-sac at the end of the street. While riding bikes, trying out for the same lacrosse team, or fighting over their first crushes, Jacob and David know intimate details of each other's lives. Now that they are attending rival colleges and are socially engaged, each man looks forward to the annual lacrosse game that will bring the two together. Once the evening starts flowing, old stories pour out to Jacob's and David's eventual embarrassment. It's all in good fun, though, because each has enough stories about the other to provide years of blackmail material. This winter's upcoming family Hanukkah celebration will likely provide an opportunity for even more stories to come out, as members of the extended family love to reminisce about the inseparable Jacob and David.

Families Constitute Themselves as "Family"

Constitutive
The ability of a person or group to create the existence of an abstract concept simply by naming it as a concept.

One key element of families that often gets overlooked is the **constitutive** nature of families. Language is powerful, and often giving a social condition a name actually creates a type of relationship. When Mike and Breck got engaged a few years ago, there was no formal legal process to facilitate that relationship definition; the fact that they called each other "fiancé" was in part what made that engagement real. Relatedly, the use of language to name a group of people as a "family" is quite powerful. That is, people have the power to use language that identifies each other as family, thereby *actually making* themselves a family. Sian's mother struggled with a drug dependency throughout Sian's formative years, and Sian's neighbors took her in and raised her as their own. Even though her mother lived in close proximity, Sian and her neighbors used the term *family* to describe their grouping. Because they felt like a family, behaved like a family, and called themselves a family, they *created* a family unit regardless of their lack of biological connections.

BOX 10.2: Communication Currents

Family Types in Current Television

Modern Family, Season 1, Episode 1, "Pilot," http://bit.ly/2n7RELh

One of the most popular television programs in our current media landscape, *Modern Family* depicts the new normal for much of Western culture: families composed of various types of people and their relationships. As such, the family in this situation comedy is composed of three generations, two different sexual orientations, multiple ethnic backgrounds, and the full spectrum of socioeconomic roots and cultural sensitivities.

As we watch this video clip, we are reminded of the diversity of family structures as Cameron dramatically reveals an adoption in the family. Cameron and his boyfriend have adopted an international baby despite the varying degrees of support from among the extended family.

INSTRUCTIONS: Watch the video again, paying careful attention to the diverse family members and the different ways of interacting. What is your initial reaction to each family unit? If you are familiar with the show, does this early clip remind you of the issues associated with varying definitions of "family"? Consider if you were one of the characters in the clip. How might you respond throughout this situation?

Families Have Interpersonal Interaction and Attachment

Possibly the most basic component of a family—yet one quite easily overlooked—is the idea that families are in part defined by their direct interaction with one another. This may flout our previous discussion of the biogenetic lens, as this implies that genetically related people who don't interact are not necessarily family. The importance of interaction highlights a key component of the essence of what makes a family different from just a group of interrelated people. Communication and social interaction are the basis for interpersonal relationships, and families inherently cannot exist without these relationship types.

Let's approach this with a tangential example. Rob and Mark were best friends in third grade but haven't seen each other in years. They haven't talked on the phone or kept up on Facebook or other social media, nor have they even sent messages through mutual friends or accidentally run into each other in the shopping center. Mark doesn't know that Rob had a hard time when his mother was diagnosed with cancer or that he recently thought of dropping out of school. Rob has no idea that Mark is thinking of getting engaged because he just found out that his girlfriend is pregnant. Are Mark and Rob friends? Sure, they spent formative years together and will always have fond memories of their youth, but are they really attached to one another? This same level of relationship analysis can come into play when we consider family. If we believe that Mark and Rob are not *really* friends, then why would we apply the term *family* to them because of simple genetics? If Mark and Rob were cousins, we may describe them as estranged because they are missing that special component that makes their connection familial.

From a biological perspective Mark and Rob would be clearly related if they were, in fact, cousins, but their lack of influence and interaction makes it difficult to call them a family. However, not all groups of people who do interact are family, either. In addition to interaction, there must be attachment. In Chapter 9, many different forms of attachment were discussed. Indeed, not all forms of attachment necessarily have positive outcomes or impacts on the individuals involved, but that attachment demonstrates the interdependence of individual lives lived together. Charmyn and her grandmother have been close since Charmyn was very young; it has gotten to the point that Charmyn calls her grandmother every day, and they can finish each other's sentences during a conversation. Katherine interacts with her uncle Doug, but a past history of enabling behaviors makes her hesitant to completely trust that Doug has her best interest in mind. Bryson and Derrick don't get to hang out that much anymore since Derrick took the job up north, but when the brothers grab a drink together in a particularly rough neighborhood bar they know that each one has the other's back if anything goes down.

TYPES OF FAMILY STRUCTURES

As highlighted in the introduction, families are as diverse as the individuals that comprise them. Very few families fit the old television sitcom model of a mother and a father with two perfect children and a golden retriever on mild sedatives. (And, even *those* seemingly perfect families experience the same relational difficulties as everyone else!) Just as we are often reticent to categorize individuals into groups and give them labels, it is sometimes difficult to come up with appropriate labels for the wide range of family types. However, scholars have come up with a few key terms that allow us to describe family structures in ways that make it easy for us to discuss and describe them. Scholars categorize family types using a variety of terms, and we present four of these types in this chapter.[9]

Two-Parent Biological Family

One term often thrown around is the **nuclear family**. With his mother and father married to each other and sharing the same household with him and his siblings, Paul's family fit the definition of this classical term. However, the nuances of family structure and legal definition can be much more complex, so a more modern phrase is increasingly used to describe this setup. Now, scholars tend to use the phrase **two-parent biological family** to describe Paul's family experience.[10] This terminology encompasses essentially the same situation but broadens the scope, allowing for Paul's parents to be either married or unmarried as a **cohabiting couple**.

Primary-Parent Family

Dan retained majority custody of his daughter when he and his wife, Marilyn, divorced six years ago. His friends often refer to him as having a **single-parent family**, because he oversees the daily experience of raising his child and is the primary guardian. However, Dan prefers to use slightly different terminology when he describes himself, because he is *not* the only parent and wants to acknowledge Marilyn's role in helping to shape the life of their daughter. His ex-wife's financial contribution and regular weekend mother–daughter "girls' nights" have been rather formative in their daughter's quality of life. Because of Marilyn's active role in the life of their child, Dan refers to himself as the **primary parent** but does not necessarily correct his coworkers' and friends' terminology.

Nuclear Family
A family unit that consists of cross-sex parents and their children, whether biological or adopted.

Two-Parent Biological Family
A family unit that consists of two parents who are biologically related to each of the one or more children living in the household.

Cohabiting Couple
Two unmarried adult individuals who have chosen to live together as romantic partners.

Single-Parent Family
A family unit that consists of one parent with sole parental duties for one or more children, whether biological or adopted.

Primary-Parent Family
A family unit that consists of one parent with primary (but not necessarily sole) parental duties for one or more children, whether biological or adopted.

Sean De Burca/Getty Images

Rob Hainer/Shutterstock.com

Blended Family

When a family unit composed of a legal and/or biological parent–child relationship becomes joined to another partner through marriage or cohabitation, that new family is referred to as a **blended family** or **stepfamily**. The variation in structure for a blended family is broad. It could consist of two long-term romantic partners, one of whom has a single biological child. Alternatively, that same term could apply to a widower with four children marrying a divorcée with five children, forming a new household of 11 individuals (not counting pets!). Add to the complexity the possibility of adoption and multigenerational individuals who live within the household, and a blended family can take almost any form. The terms used by members of the family in these scenarios may make it difficult for people outside the family to understand the complex living situation, as well, as some people may refer to a stepfamily member without using the prefix *step*– depending on the perception of the relationship or the age at which the family blending occurred.

Intergenerational Family

In our definition of family, we already discussed the idea that families are multigenerational, composed of parents and/or children, grandparents, aunts, uncles, cousins, and so on. When the family unit living together includes additional **extended family** beyond the traditional parent(s) and child(ren), that is more appropriately termed an **intergenerational family**. Ravinderpaul has a unique living situation. His parents, grandparents, and uncles all bought the houses at the end of a cul-de-sac, tearing down the fences between the houses and building one large fence around the entire complex. In his house, he lives with his mother, his father, his two siblings, and his grandmother on his mother's side. All together, there are over

Blended Family
A family unit that consists of adults and children, where at least one of the children is either biological or adopted and from a previous relationship.

Stepfamily
See Blended Family.

Extended Family
Those family members that exist out of the traditional parent/child unit.

Intergenerational Family
A family unit that consists of parent(s) and child(ren) and at least one additional layer of extended family.

30 family members spread among the many large, expensive, connected houses. Although Ravinderpaul knows that he is free to plan his future as he pleases, there is considerable family pressure for him to build a separate addition to one of the houses once he and his fiancée, Preet, get married. Preet likes the idea of a tight-knit family and grew up with her maternal grandmother living with her and her parents, but frankly his family intimidates her.

Committed Partners

Although these categories may help to more easily describe families and allow us to conceptualize the unique ways that they may look, the categories outlined are not an exhaustive list of possibilities, nor are the categories necessarily mutually exclusive. For example, Bill and Helen are **committed partners** who no longer believe in the institution of marriage but wanted to have a commitment ceremony to recognize their deep and lasting affection. Bill and Helen met through a mutual friend after one of them was widowed and the other was divorced. Bill brought his children from his previous marriage to the combined household, while Helen allowed her mother to move in since they had an extra room. After all, Helen felt an obligation to her mother, who raised her on her own since the moment Helen was born. If we're being technical, this family has characteristics of each of the four broad categories listed earlier.

Committed Partners
Two people who have developed a significant romantic relationship and intend to remain together, regardless of legal or marital status.

External Boundary Management
The process of using specific tactics to hide or share information about your family in order to present it in a desirable perspective to outsiders.

BOX 10.3: InterFace

Discussing Family with Diverse Others [11,12]

Family is complicated. No matter what your family background, every person you interact with—even your own siblings—will have had a different experience with her family of origin. For some people, remembrances of family are relatively positive, with a wide variety of pleasant experiences and memories of a supportive environment. Others' memories may be of a childhood with a mix of positive and negative moments, particularly if that person had significant factors influencing family structure like alcohol or drug dependency or even abuse. Still others may find that their family seems complicated just because of the family structure itself. Regardless of *why* a family looks different, questions about and especially challenges to the family identity are likely to cause points of tension or conflict between people who interact.

Because many people expect that others outside their family won't fully understand their family experiences, it is common to try to frame information about one's family using a process called **external boundary management**. In this process, an individual tries to manage the amount and type of information that he shares with other people in order to present himself in the most desirable light. The more different that one family looks from another, the more likely that the family member is going to want to manage these points of tension or conflict.

(Continued)

If you want to get to know someone and put her at ease in interacting about family-related concerns, there are a few things that you can do in an attempt to *not* put her on the defensive. Conversations that avoid the following behaviors will make it easier to interact with a range of people who come from diverse family backgrounds:

> **Avoid labeling others' families:** We naturally tend to apply labels to our own families, describing our family members as "my stepdad" or "my brother's first wife." However, when referring to another person's family members it is best to allow the other person to offer a label, rather than applying one ourselves. This helps to avoid the "made-for-TV mistake" of referring to a coworker's "dad" before finding out that the older man we are meeting is actually her husband, putting them both on the defensive.

> **Avoid pointed questions about discrepancies:** Often we have general ideas about how families should look, based on our own experiences. However, each person has family dynamics that may or may not be open topics for discussion. Instead of asking genuine questions that manage our own uncertainty but put others in an awkward position, determine whether it is actually necessary to know the answer to the question. Bryson and Alan are committed partners who adopted their friends' infant shortly after the couple died in a car accident. As an interracial black and white gay couple with an Asian baby, they sometimes feel like people are asking questions to satisfy their own curiosity rather than first interacting with them as people.

> **Avoid comments about relationship legitimacy:** We easily understand family according to traditional definitions, even though family is often much more complicated. If someone claims a relationship or a tie to someone else, don't attack the validity of that linkage. Sarah's first husband came from a loving family, and she grew very close to her mother-in-law, Winifred. Even after her marriage dissolved, Sarah spends time with Winifred and often drives her to medical appointments in their small town. It feels like a personal attack to both Sarah and Winifred when outsiders point out the lack of a biological or legal tie to one another.

INSTRUCTIONS Think about a time when you have been forced to defend your family from someone who had a different or unique perspective. How did that make you feel? How did it impact your relationship? What can you do to avoid these kinds of mistakes in your interactions with others?

FAMILY SYSTEMS THEORY

Fraternal twins Jad and Emma have experienced a lot of family change over the past year after their younger sister Kayin's leukemia diagnosis. As siblings, all three have been relatively involved in each other's lives, but with Emma receiving a partial scholarship to a prestigious four-year college, Jad made the decision to attend a local community college to be able to help

age fotostock/Alamy Stock Photo

his parents with Kayin's complex medical needs. Jad's decision allowed his mother to continue to work, and the combined income of his parents ensures that the family will be able to not only pay for Kayin's health care but also continue to pay their mortgage on the family home. Emma's upcoming semester break will be the first time that the family has been together since she left home, yet she brings a strange mixture of emotions as she packs her suitcase for the long drive. Guilt about leaving her family, excitement about the upcoming togetherness, and anxiety about leaving the relative escapism of college life with her new friends all combine to ensure a somewhat awkward reunion.

Families are incredibly complicated. Each member does not live in a vacuum, but rather, the actions or experiences of one person have a ripple effect throughout the family unit. What caused Emma's emotional schism? Is Kayin's health to blame or Jad's sacrificial choice? Should the family have cut back on monthly expenses, or should Emma have turned down the scholarship? In actuality, no single behavior directly influences a general family experience. **Family systems theory**[13] claims that families are systems, a complex set of interrelationships characterized by patterns of behavior wherein individual actions have chain effects through the family unit as a whole. Scholars have found seven key characteristics of families that lead to these interrelational patterns, briefly outlined here.

Interdependence in Systems

In Chapter 9, we introduced the concept of **interdependence**, where the thoughts and behaviors of one relational partner influence the thoughts and behaviors of the other partner, and vice versa. In a family system, this gets much more complicated. Although the number of affected people is

Family Systems Theory
A theoretical perspective of families as interrelated individuals, with the behaviors and interaction patterns of each individual influencing the experience of the family as a whole.

Interdependence
The thoughts and behaviors of one relational partner influence the thoughts and behaviors of the other partner(s) (from Chapter 9).

greater, a change in one individual still has the ability to change the dynamics of the family system as a whole. Arguably, Jad's decision to remain at home may have just as much influence on the family system as does Kayin's medical diagnosis. A change in one member leads to a change in all members.

Wholeness in Systems

Relational Synergy
The belief that the whole of an interpersonal network io moro complicated than the sum of the individual members of that network.

A family system is often described as having **relational synergy**, or a situation where the combination of individuals in the system create much greater complexity than each member brings to the family unit on his own. Jad often talks to Emma about how much they will miss her when she leaves for college, describing their family as an orchestra; while they are each individual instruments, the complexity and negotiation of the family interactions can create a complete musicality that would not wholly exist without any individual part. When families come together, as an outsider you can understand that system by not only looking at each individual within the system but also by looking at the social context and interactions that are created by the connections that emerge within the group.

Patterns/Regularities in Systems

Each person in a family has a variety of complex interactions. To make things casier, family members often fall into routine patterns of behavior and expression to facilitate feelings of familiarity that make relationships easy. Not only does Emma feel enmeshed with her mother, her father, and each of her two siblings, but she also behaves one way when she's with *just* her siblings

Jason_V/E+/Getty Images

and another way when she's with *just* her parents. When she is with her mom and her brother, she often playfully antagonizes Jad until her mother leaps to his defense. When she goes golfing with the "boys," Jad and her father pick on her for "swinging like a princess" but cater to her whims like royalty, nonetheless. In fact, each combination of family members invokes a different set of patterns. Although the longevity and influence of those patterns may vary, if one of those individuals changes patterns of interaction, the other family members are also in some way impacted.

Interactive Complexity in Systems

Family interactions necessarily involve the participation of multiple people within the system. For example, when difficulties emerge within a family system, it is fruitless to attempt to assign blame to only one participant. Jad and Emma often joke about their decade-old fights in the back of the car on long family road trips: Jad would tell his parents that Emma was sitting on him, and Emma would respond that it was because Jad was on her side. Which of the two children was most at fault for the argument? Clearly, both parties should accept *some* blame for the confrontation. Although family difficulties are often much more nuanced than this example, they are still the result of a negotiation between family partners. Patterns of interaction—including but not limited to conflict—can only occur when there are two parties willing to engage in that communication pattern, and the characteristics of the family as a system enable interactions to occur that lead to this complex behavior-response cycle.

Openness in Systems

Family systems are also influenced by outside events. No matter how isolated the family or how controlling the family system may seem, there is regular influence from the beliefs, ideas, or environment of the society and the institutions that exist outside of the specific family context. Although Jad and Emma's relationship will still be defined by the fact that they are twins who have grown up relatively close to one another, the influence of Emma's college experience and Jad's caretaking behaviors will necessarily allow them to experience a different side of their lives than they would have known previously. As such, the whole family will have to adapt to the ideas and influences that Jad and Emma each bring anew to the family system.

Complex Relationships

As we've discussed in earlier chapters, the smallest unit of interpersonal interaction is called a dyad. When we think of a family system, there are a variety of dyads within even the smallest families. Consider Jad's family: Jad and his father, Jad and his mother, Jad and his younger sister Kayin,

FIGURE 10.1
Complex Family Relationships

and Jad and his twin sister Emma. Similar linkages emerge for each of the members of the family, as shown in Figure 10.1. Add to that the group-level linkages, where Jad may interact with *more* than one other person, and it gets even more complicated: Jad and his parents, Jad and his siblings, Jad and his female family members, and so on. Each of these relational units has the aforementioned patterns that may occur within the system, as well as a variety of relational factors that influence interaction like power, sophistication, intimacy, communication scripts, and so on. Because the family interacts as a system, the relational style of one or more partnerships influences the entire family unit.

Equifinality

Families are often thought of as groups of people who come together to accomplish some goal or to function in some way. For Jad and Emma's family, the goals may include Kayin's health or Jad and Emma's college education. Although these goals are quite specific, there are myriad ways that the family could work together to accomplish those goals. Although their family has selected one path toward reaching those goals, a wide range of options are available to support Kayin, Jad, and Emma toward their desired future. Each one of these family goals or functions exhibits **equifinality,** or the characteristic of a goal being reached by the family system through a variety of means and processes. In the next section, we discuss the most important of the functions identified by scholars.

Equifinality
The ability of a family system to reach a goal or accomplish a function through a variety of means.

TYPES OF FAMILY FUNCTIONS

Jessica and Xiao Chen have a healthy partnership and are expecting their second child at the end of the month. With our current discussion of families and a brief snapshot of Jessica and Xiao Chen, we can label them as a two-parent biological family without really knowing the intricacies of what their daily life looks like. Creating a definition of a family and knowing a variety of common structures are characteristics that are important for the study of families, but they do not address the actual lived experience of the family system and each individual family member. Now, we turn our attention to what families actually accomplish for themselves. In unpacking the following six topics, we are looking at both central and ancillary ways that healthy families function, as well as identifying some of the ways that a **dysfunctional family** may fall short, including varying degrees of structure

Dysfunctional Family
A family that finds itself lacking the ability to successfully manage the tensions of at least one of the family functions, specifically including but not limited to growth and cohesion, being adaptable, creating a family identity, and communicating in a positive, affirming manner.

and emotional connectedness. Highly functioning families typically accomplish a wide range of the following outcomes and in doing so provide a model of prosocial behavior.[14,15]

Cohesion and Connection

One major function of a family is to find a healthy balance of **cohesion**, a complex combination of emotional bonding and life spent connected together. Much like our discussion of dialectic tensions in Chapter 7, families can comfortably exist along a range of the continuum of cohesion, but the family must work hard to avoid the extreme ends of that continuum. A **disengaged family** is one where family members are completely separate from one another and have no emotional connection, while an **enmeshed family** is one where family members cannot comprehend their own existence apart from one another and don't express any healthy individuality. Trisha's childhood family is now disengaged, with family time emerging only out of convenience, and feelings of obligation edging out feelings of closeness. Trisha's coworker Price has a family on the opposite end of the spectrum. Even though Price is in his mid-40s, he and his wife live at home with his parents and have an active social calendar involving the four of them. Trisha recently asked Price to attend an important work conference in the city, but Price commented that he would never leave his family for anything longer than his eight-hour workday. Although Price exhibits cohesion, his family's level of enmeshment does not allow him individuality. In actuality, the most productive function of a healthy family is to model appropriate connections as members struggle with the tension of closeness and autonomy, constantly striving toward a healthy balance.

Cohesion
An interpersonal experience of both emotional bonding and a connected life spent together.

Disengaged Family
A family with relatively little or no emotional connection, characterized by extreme individuality and separation.

Enmeshed Family
A family with relatively little individuality among members, characterized by extreme emotional attachment and even dependency.

Adaptability

A second major function of a family is to allow for family **adaptability**, which can be described as the tendency of a family to allow natural family changes in rules, roles, and family leadership structures over the collective life span. As these behaviors also lie along a continuum with healthy families finding a balance between the extremes, at polar ends we note **rigid families** that are unwilling to adapt to changes or personal growth among members as compared to **overly flexible** (or **chaotic**) **families** that do not provide structure within the family system, allowing for constant fluctuation. Beau grew up in a chaotic communal living situation, with biological parents who felt that children are better raised by an extended network of adults; as such, family rules varied depending on which adult figure he talked to within the commune, and he was unable to select a singular role model from among all the people trying to help him express his independence. Elijah had an opposite experience, with a rigid patriarchal structure in his family home. Even as a young adult attending college in his hometown, Elijah must obey his father and acts subservient around the household, obeying a strict 8:00 p.m. curfew.

Adaptability
The tendency of a family to allow natural changes in rules, roles, and family leadership structures over the collective life span.

Rigid Family
A family with an inflexible set of rules, roles, and leadership structures that do not change to fit personal growth among members.

Overly Flexible Family
A family with few to no rules, roles, or leadership structure, allowing for constant fluctuation and unclear expectations for members.

Chaotic Family
See Overly Flexible Family.

Zurijeta/Shutterstock.com

Communication

A third function of a family is communication, which facilitates the successful negotiation of all other family functions. Without communication, families could not accomplish any other goal or function; in fact, according to our earlier definition they would not even be *considered* family without communication. Scholars have highlighted the key components of quality family communication,[16] which are unsurprisingly not at all different from quality communication skills highlighted throughout the rest of this textbook. Functional families communicate with respect, speaking clearly and listening to one another, while also using self-disclosure to share personal information that is not readily available to outsiders. Ximena is surprised when she visits her roommate's family, because they have deep conversations regularly and seem to have intimate knowledge of each other's daily life and experiences. Ximena's family of origin rarely discusses topics that don't involve the daily functioning of the household, and Ximena wants her own family to communicate better in the future.

Establishing Boundaries

An important function of the family is to guide and direct the experiences of family members, particularly with regard to the daily experience of

Peter Dazeley/Photographer's Choice/Getty Images

youth. By setting up boundaries, families can clearly define the roles and expectations and interaction partners for the family. **Internal boundaries** are those limitations and expectations that help guide families toward an appropriate sense of relationship with one another. Although Cara's niece may not like the fact that Cara sometimes replies, "Because I'm your aunt, and I said so!" to an unhealthy or inappropriate request, Cara is setting clear boundaries: establishing the importance of a hierarchy because of her age and experience, as well as demonstrating the caretaker role that Cara has assumed within the family. **External boundaries**, on the other hand, help define for families the connections that members may have with the outside world, also clarifying the influence and manner of interaction that the outside world may have on the family system. William's family always set clear external boundaries when he was growing up, making it clear to him that all members of family should prioritize each other over nonfamily. In addition, the only adults that he and his siblings were allowed to interact with were coaches, teachers, and church leaders; all other adults fell into the realm of "stranger danger" and were considered off-limits.

Internal Boundaries
The limitations and expectations that help family members remain in appropriate relationships with one another.

External Boundaries
The limitations and expectations that define with whom and in what manner family members should interact as they approach the outside world.

Facilitating Growth

Over the course of the life span, one of the most visible family functions involves the facilitation of the growth of family members. Although the basics of raising children may include the obvious components of providing food, shelter, and adequate care for the health of each individual, there are

Africa Studio/Shutterstock.com

many aspects of cognitive and psychological health to which the family may contribute. Families help model and nurture a child's developing sense of self, both as an individual and as a member of a larger community. Families provide an understanding of gender identity and contribute to the attitudes about sexuality and sexual health that are formed at a young age. Families encourage (or discourage) the development of certain skills, characteristics, or a burgeoning sense of independence throughout the life of family members. Greg's preteen son Chance enjoys reading, and Greg has always encouraged him to explore a multitude of genres in order to expand and develop his understanding of the world around him. Recently, Chance has begun to read young adult fiction whose covers look like gothic romance novels. Greg's response to these book selections will undoubtedly influence Chance's understanding of himself as male and the way that he portrays himself. As individuals develop, the influence of family experiences can often be easily traced.

Creating a Family Identity (Generating Themes and Images)

A final family function that we discuss is the generation of a family identity. As discussed in Chapter 2, identity is incredibly important to the development of an individual, and allows for people to have greater understanding of themselves and how they relate to the world around them. Interestingly, our own views of our family are also developmentally essential, as we create a narrative of our lives that influences our understandings of our origins and our life trajectory. By generating images and themes to describe the family, members create a shared understanding about the goals and roles that are valued within the family system. Davis's parents always described their family, the Dicksons, as being like "the little engine that could." Using the metaphor regularly around the house, as well as buying toys and home decor that reinforced the theme, the Dicksons communicated the importance of hard work, drive, ambition, and resilience. Because of Davis's parents' own difficult family backgrounds, they wanted to instill the ability in their children to bounce back from whatever life may throw at them. Regardless of the challenges that may await him and his family members, Davis believes that he can respond well and meet most any difficulty with both hard work and enthusiasm.

McIninch/iStock/Getty Images

Each family interacts in different ways. One way to determine the type of communication patterns that emerge in a specific family unit is by using a survey like the one in Box 10.4. By asking questions about the content of family conversations—as well as looking at the acceptable senders and receivers of those messages—Ritchie and Fitzpatrick's Family Communication Patterns Scale[17] is an example of a way to better understand how family members engage one another. After taking the modified version in Box 10.4, do you think the scale accurately represents your family patterns?

BOX 10.4: Let's Get INTRApersonal

Family Communication Patterns Scale[18,19]

Have you ever stopped to think about the many ways that your family has influenced your life? Some scholars have found that even the way that your family approaches daily conversation may influence your tendency to process messages later in life, with concept-oriented conversations in the household likely to cause children to focus on information contained in a message rather than the way that message was delivered.

Regardless of impact, it is helpful to think about how your family converses. Use this self-assessment to think about your family interactions. This survey is a modified and shortened version of a survey created by the original researchers (Ritchie & Fitzpatrick) in 1990. It was used to look at how members of a family discuss topics.

INSTRUCTIONS: Think carefully about the way your family interacts. Then, write the number that shows how much you agree or disagree with the statements below. At the end, you'll be able to figure out your current family's communication pattern!

1	2	3	4	5	6	7
Strongly Disagree	Moderately Disagree	Slightly Disagree	Neither Agree Nor Disagree	Slightly Agree	Moderately Agree	Strongly Agree

_____ 1. In our family we often talk about our feelings and emotions.

_____ 2. In our home, my parents usually have the last word.

_____ 3. My family likes to hear my opinions, even when they don't agree with me.

_____ 4. If my family doesn't approve of it, they don't want to know about it.

_____ 5. We often talk as a family about things we have done during the day.

_____ 6. My parents often say something like "You'll know better when you grow up."

_____ 7. In our family we often talk about our plans and hopes for the future.

_____ 8. When I am at home, I am expected to obey my parents' rules.

_____ 9. I can tell my family almost anything.

_____ 10. When anything important is involved, my family expects me to behave without question.

Now, consider how you've answered the odd-numbered questions as compared to the even-numbered questions. Does one of these two sets of five questions seem to have higher scores? If the odd numbers are generally higher than the even numbers, it indicates that your family is more conversation oriented, with a focus on interacting. If the even numbers are generally higher, it indicates that your family is more focused on group membership and conforming to the norms of the family. What does this tell you about how your family interacts? How do you want your own family to interact in the future?

TYPES OF FAMILY CHALLENGES

In discussing the behaviors of functional families, it is easy to look at the list of positive interactions and forget that *every* family experiences its own challenges over the course of the life span. From minimal conflict over who gets to ride shotgun in the minivan to major stressors like the hospitalization, incarceration, or death of a family member, the family unit is subject to a variety of threats to the stability and the functionality of both the system and its individual members. Some challenges are common to almost every family and provide insight into the potential elasticity and adaptability of family systems.

All Families Experience Conflict

As we discussed in Chapter 7, conflict is a part of most every close relationship. Not all conflict is necessarily a transgression, either, as families may engage in conflict that helps them to further navigate and define the roles, rules, and leadership structures that must necessarily change within a family system as members move throughout the stages of the life span. One challenge that often occurs, however, is that close family members may actually avoid dealing with conflict issues in order to protect the relationships, which may counterintuitively lead to increased frustration and tension.[20] Until conflict is resolved, it can never be handled and moved beyond.[21] Celeste and Adam are cousins who spend time in the same larger social circle. After college, Celeste began dating her cousin Adam's best friend, Mark, until she found out that Mark already had another girlfriend. When Celeste confronted her cousin about the situation, Adam said his relationship with his best friend was more important than his relationship with his cousin and that he was taking Mark's side in the issue. As a result, any time that Celeste and Adam interact at family functions, the unresolved conflict makes social situations awkward, and Celeste finds herself unable to trust him or his side of the family anymore. Conflict can be a difficult experience. Conflict handled well, however, may model behaviors that allow children to be more successful in their own future relationships, both at handling conflict and at knowing that relationships can survive even those intense encounters.[22]

FPG/Archive Photos/Getty Images

All Families Experience Change

In Chapter 7, we discussed how to maintain relationships in times of change. Families are one of the relational contexts in which change is most apparent. In almost no other context do you experience the development of the individual as part of a larger system throughout the life span. Members of the family may leave the family system because of death or estrangement, and new partnerships may add new individuals through romantic relationships and/or the addition of children to the family. As roles change and new leadership structures are tested and reshuffled, a family can look significantly different after only a couple of years. Rebecca was

BOX 10.5: iPersonal

Family Monitoring and Technology[23,24,25]

As recently as 25 years ago, families would send their children off to school in the morning and hope that they returned safely, relying on dinnertime conversations as the sole source of information about what transpired in the daily lives of their children. Recent technological innovations allow for much greater connectivity, with cell phones made for youth and marketed to the parents of elementary school children, home security cameras designed to monitor both children and their nannies or caretakers from remote locations, and even devices that can be installed in cars to inform parents of both the route and the speed that the teens have traveled over the course of the day. In general, the opportunity for parents to monitor their children has been increased greatly by technological innovation.

A more active form of monitoring is often encouraged in the oversight of adolescent Internet usage, with research finding that parents who oversee their children's use of social media and other online activities are more likely to protect those children from interacting with potentially harmful strangers. Also, this form of parental monitoring may be able to allow parents to offer guidance in making choices about issues like body image, sexual behavior, and other areas in order to avoid long-term consequences. Parental monitoring doesn't necessarily protect children from harmful online interactions with the very same people who they also know in "real life," however, so parents should be vigilant about their online activities or engage regularly in conversations about bullying or abusive interactions with known others.

There is no question that a family can use this greater diversity of communication technologies to easily keep in touch in our modern age. Indeed, there is research to suggest that technology can lead to positive benefits within a family unit. However, simply increasing the amount of technology available is not helpful, and in fact many families find that the impact of increased technology in the home may actually lead to less quality time spent in person. Despite research suggesting greater connectivity between technologically networked families, too much technology can lead to perceptions of reduced intimacy or closeness. One suggestion for this problem is the monitoring of the amount of time spent using technology in the home for all family members.

INSTRUCTIONS: Think carefully about the costs and benefits of increased technology use in the home. What role do you think parents should play in monitoring their children's online usage? In your opinion, is there a specific age or life stage at which parents need to give their children greater privacy? At what point should monitoring cease among family members, if at all?

an only child to two parents who were each only children. Family Christmases were small, with only the three members of Rebecca's immediate family and one set of grandparents. Although her memories of Christmas were joyful and pleasant, she much prefers the chaos of her current family situation. Rebecca has gotten married to a man who already had two children, and together they had two more kids. Although Rebecca's grandparents are no longer living, her parents and her husband's parents play the role of doting grandparents at the family events that include her children's cousins and their parents. Because of the energy level of both sets of grandparents, Rebecca is the one "in charge" for the entire extended family. Each year she enjoys hosting almost 20 people at the family holiday celebration.

All Families Experience Stressors

Not all change is necessarily related to birth, death, maturation, or other life span issues, however. Stressors can lead to discomfort within a family system, regardless of the amount of change that occurs as a result of those stressors. Some common stressors include the loss of a job or getting relocated because of a career change or a military deployment. Perhaps an injury or hospitalization has complicated the shared daily experience, or the onset of a mental illness may stress the family structure. In times of economic difficulty or even when people are moving from one location to another, families have to deal with the additional burden of the stress and all the associated mental gymnastics that accompany a life difficulty. Morris thought that his family was invincible and always commented on the close relationships that he had with his siblings and parents. However, when Morris was involved in a car accident that put the other driver in the hospital, his underage consumption of alcohol left his family legally liable for the damages after the insurance companies refused to pay. Morris's older sibling could no longer afford to attend his upscale private university, as he didn't qualify for financial aid because of family income. Morris's younger sister had to quit her karate lessons, and both of his siblings treated him with open hostility despite their attempts to forgive him. Most disappointing during this time of transition was the lack of trust that Morris's parents bestowed on him. Once he was labeled as the family "screwup" the entire family system seemed to unravel. Will Morris's family make it through this stressful time? Certainly some distance from the immediacy of the situation will allow the family to move forward. However, until the stress is removed from the system and the relationships are repaired, the outlook is rather bleak for Morris's family interactions.

Monkey Business Images/Shutterstock.com

BOX 10.6: InterConnect

What Was Your Childhood Like? What Will Your Adulthood Be Like?

It is easy to spend time thinking about the past, worrying about issues from your childhood that have already happened and may never fully resolve. Indeed, some scholars have implied that we take our early childhood experiences and interact with other people based on our early perceptions about the world around us.[26] However, our childhood does not determine every single thing about our future relationships. Instead, our early experiences throughout childhood and adolescence help us to understand patterns and behaviors that people in general can easily fall into. A proactive critical thinker, however, can use these positive and negative experiences to influence her own life trajectory. For example,

> Carlton's father fell in love with his secretary and left the family, so Carlton is vigilant about keeping his workplace relationships professional and remaining faithful despite temptations.

> Erica's older brother brought home a case of beer when they were both in junior high, and after years of use, now Erica relies on Alcoholics Anonymous as a support group to help her from slipping back into the patterns she established at that early age.

> Alessandra's mother was a successful small-town politician, but she never let that interfere with the family's weekly Saturday morning pancake breakfast; Alessandra is careful to set aside time for her relationships despite a rigorous class schedule and a demanding internship.

> Ricardo has a close relationship with his father, but that only developed during high school when his father lost his job and spent more time involved in his children's lives; Ricardo is careful to not let work intrude into his own family time.

> Sylvie was the victim of sexual abuse from her second cousin and is now involved in a local advocacy group to help children avoid the situation in which Sylvie once found herself.

INSTRUCTIONS: Think carefully about the situations and relationships that influenced your youth. Some of them may be positive memories, while others may have been rather negative. Take out a separate sheet of paper and write down all those influences on the left, and then brainstorm your current and future reactions to these influences on the right-hand side of the page. How has each situation impacted you? How has each situation made you more able to navigate your own future? Are there any areas that you may want to discuss with someone like your campus counselor? The best way to recreate the positive moments for your own family—and avoid the negative ones—is to first become aware of the influences that each had on your own experience.

Chapter Summary

More than anything else, this chapter highlights the diversity of the family experience. Because families are as different as the individuals and interpersonal relationships that make up those families, there are many ways of viewing a family and defining what makes a group of people a family. Although family relationships are complicated for a variety of reasons, our own impressions about family often serve to influence our understandings of how families should look and what they are likely to accomplish in both the minutia of daily life and over the course of the life span. Regardless of the functioning of the family—or the richness of the day-to-day life that each family system may afford—the importance of communication within a larger family system cannot be overstated.

Interestingly, families behave as complete systems, with each individual part in some way influencing every other part as well as the family as a whole. As a result, inevitable challenges arise that may create points of tension within the larger family system. Highly functioning families can navigate the difficulties of stress, change, or conflict by using prosocial forms of communication and coming to a shared resolution. Regardless of family structure, issues of functionality, or even both the positive and negative features of one's family experience, the impact of family on daily life can be mitigated or accentuated through a variety of communication behaviors. After all, the constitutive nature of family means that a family is *truly* what we make of it.

MindTap®

First-Person Video

Visiting Mom at the Station

Apply what you've learned in this chapter by analyzing the "Visiting Mom at the Station" video, using the accompanying questions as a guide. This video and these questions are available online with your MindTap Speech for *Interconnections: Interpersonal Communication Foundations and Contexts.*

MindTap®

Key Terms

Use flashcards to learn key concepts and take a quiz to test your knowledge.

Adaptability	Constitutive	External Boundary
Biogenetic Lens	Disengaged Family	Management
Blended Family	Dysfunctional Family	Family
Chaotic Family	Enmeshed Family	Family Systems Theory
Cohabiting Couple	Equifinality	Interdependence
Cohesion	Extended Family	Intergenerational
Committed Partners	External Boundaries	Family

Internal Boundaries   **Relational Synergy**   **Stepfamily**
Nepotism   **Rigid Family**   **Two-Parent Biological**
Nuclear Family   **Role Lens**   **Family**
Overly Flexible Family   **Single-Parent Family**
Primary-Parent Family   **Sociolegal Lens**

Discussion Questions

1. Think about your family. How would you describe it? What terms do you use to explain your background that someone else might find confusing? Why?

2. Do you or any of your family members use technology to monitor the behavior of other family members? Have you ever been tempted to invade a family member's privacy using technology? What was the situation, and how did it unfold?

3. Think about your definition of family. Which lens of viewing family do you tend to use? Are you more likely to tend toward the biogenetic lens or the role lens? What is it about your background that makes you lean in this direction?

4. Discuss a time when you have faced a significant family challenge. How did members of your family system or of your larger support network influence your response to this challenge? What was the ultimate outcome?

5. Consider your expectations for the future of your family. What will it look like? What is your role? Will you be strategic in pursuing that family expectation?

Making Connections

Families are complicated. Our family relationships influence our self-identity (Chapter 2) and also our ability to maintain close relationships with friends and others. How has your family affected your ability to express yourself? When do you feel the impact of your family experience in your everyday life?

Chapter Quiz

1. Dante grew up as an only child, but his biological parents adopted a toddler when Dante was in high school. Which of the following terms now describes his household?

   a. Two-parent biologi-   d. Intergenerational
      cal family   family
   b. Nuclear family   e. None of the above
   c. Blended family

2. Lucy's father married Roxanne after he was widowed. Roxanne has two older children in college. Which of the following terms now describes her household?

   a. Two-parent biologi-   d. Intergenerational
   cal family   family
   b. Nuclear family   e. None of the above
   c. Blended family

3. Which of the following perspectives on family argues that families should be defined by the ways in which members of a group interact with one another?

   a. Biogenetic lens   d. Sociolegal lens
   b. Evolutionary lens   e. None of the above
   c. Role lens   f. All of the above

4. Which of the following perspectives on family argues that families should be defined by the ways in which civil society uses laws and regulations?

   a. Biogenetic lens   d. Sociolegal lens
   b. Evolutionary lens   e. None of the above
   c. Role lens   f. All of the above

5. Ade and her sisters are intelligent on their own, but when they come together to manage the family business they are able to create layers of meaning and shared understanding that they never could have accomplished as just three individuals working separately, and the resulting environment is fun and lively. According to family systems theory, Ade and her sisters are demonstrating which of the following?

   a. Dysfunction   d. Intergenerationality
   b. Equifinality   e. Commitment
   c. Relational synergy   f. None of the above

6. T/F If families work hard to isolate themselves, they can protect the family from all outside influence.

7. T/F Because Tai's grandmother Clarice lived with Tai's mother before Tai was born, Clarice is not considered extended family.

8. T/F One thing most all families have in common is a shared past.

9. T/F According to our discussion of family systems theory, it is possible for a family member to change a pattern of interaction without influencing the rest of the family system.

10. T/F Most people conceptualize family in a similar manner, regardless of cultural background.

Endnotes

1. Floyd, K., Mikkelson, A. C., & Judd, J. (2006). Defining the family through relationships. In L. H. Turner & R. West (Eds.), *The Family Communication Sourcebook* (pp. 21–39). Thousand Oaks, CA: Sage.

2. For an overview of nepotism and its impact, see Jones, R. G. (2012). *Nepotism in Organizations*. New York, NY: Routledge/ Taylor & Francis Group.

3. Galvin, K. M., Bylund, C. L., & Brommel, B. J. (2012). *Family Communication: Cohesion and Change* (8th ed.). Boston, MA: Allyn & Bacon.

4. Pearson, J. C. (1993). *Communication in the Family: Seeking Satisfaction in Changing Times* (2nd ed.). New York, NY: HarperCollins.

5. Turner, L. H., & West, R. (2012). *Perspectives on Family Communication* (4th ed.). Boston, MA: McGraw-Hill.

6. Yerby, J., Buerkel-Rothfuss, N. L., & Bochner, A. P. (1994). *Understanding Family Communication* (2nd ed.). Scottsdale, AZ: Gorsuch Scarisbrick.

7. Ibid.

8. For an overview, see Carter, B., & McGoldrick, M. (2005). *The Expanded Family Life Cycle: Individual, Family, and Social Perspectives* (3rd ed.). Boston, MA: Allyn & Bacon.

9. Galvin, K. M., Bylund, C. L., & Brommel, B. J. (2012). *Family Communication: Cohesion and Change* (8th ed.). Boston, MA: Allyn & Bacon.

10. For example, Hadfield, K., & Nixon, E. (2016). "He's had enough fathers": Mothers' and children's approaches to mothers' romantic relationships following the dissolution of previous partnerships. *Journal of Family Issues*, doi: 10.1177/0192513X16638385.

11. Galvin, K. M. (2006). Diversity's impact on the family: Discourse-dependence and identity. In L. H. Turner & R. West (Eds.), *The Family Communication Sourcebook* (pp. 3–19). Thousand Oaks, CA: Sage.

12. For example, see Ebersole, D. S., & Hernandez, R. A. (2016). "Taking good care of our health": Parent-adolescent perceptions of boundary management about health information. *Communication Quarterly, 64*(5), 1–23.

13. For an expansive overview and critique, see Galvin, K. M., Dickson, F. C., & Marrow, S. K. (2006). Systems theory: Patterns and (w)holes in family communication. In D. O. Braithwaite & L. A. Baxter (Eds.), *The Family Communication Sourcebook* (pp. 309–324). Thousand Oaks, CA: Sage.

14. For a review of models using *cohesion, adaptability,* and *communication,* see Olson, D. H., & Goran, D. M. (2003). Circumplex model of marital and family systems. In F. Walsh (Ed.), *Normal Family Processes: Growing Diversity and Complexity* (3rd ed., pp. 514–548). New York, NY: Guilford Press.

15. Hess, R. D., & Handel, G. (1959). *Family Worlds: A Psychosocial Approach to Family Life.* Oxford, England: University of Chicago Press.

16. Olson, D. H., & Goran, D. M. (2003). Circumplex model of marital and family systems. In F. Walsh (Ed.), *Normal Family Processes: Growing Diversity and Complexity* (3rd ed., pp. 514–548). New York, NY: Guilford Press.

17. Ritchie, L. D., & Fitzpatrick, M. A. (1990). Family communication patterns: Measuring intrapersonal perceptions of interpersonal relationships. *Communication Research, 17*(4), 523–544.

18. Ritchie, L. D., & Fitzpatrick, M. A. (1990). Family communication patterns: Measuring intrapersonal perceptions of interpersonal relationships. *Communication Research, 17*(4), 523–544.

19. McLeod, J. M., & Chaffee, S. H. (1972). The construction of social reality. In J. Tedeschi (Ed.), *The Social Influence Processes* (pp. 50–59). Chicago, IL: Aldine-Atherton.

20. Kielpikowski, M. M., & Pryor, J. E. (2008). Silent parental conflict: Parents' perspective. *Journal of Family Studies, 14,* 217–227. doi:10.5172/jfs.327.14.2-3.217

21. Galvin, K. M., Bylund, C. L., & Brommel, B. J. (2012). *Family Communication: Cohesion and Change* (8th ed.). Boston, MA: Allyn & Bacon.

22. Cox, M. J., & Harter, K. S. M. (2002). The road ahead for research on marital and family dynamics. In J. P. McHale & W. S. Grolnick (Eds.), *Retrospect and Prospect in the Psychological Study of Families* (pp. 167–188). Mahwah, NJ: Lawrence Erlbaum.

23. Williams, A. L., & Merten, M. J. (2011). iFamily: Internet and social media technology in the family context. *Family & Consumer Sciences Research Journal, 40*(2), 150–170, doi:10.1111/j.1552-3934.2011.02101.x

24. Kurz, D. (2009). 'I trust them but I don't trust them': Issues and dilemmas in montoring teenagers. In M. K. Nelson & A. I. Garey (Eds.), *Who's Watching? Daily Practices of Surveillance among Contemporary Families* (pp. 260–276). Nashville, TN: Vanderbilt University Press.

25. Taylor, E., & Rooney, T. (2016). *Surveillance Futures: Social and Ethical Implications of New Technologies for Children and Young People.* London: Routledge.

26. Bowlby, J. (1969). *Attachment and Loss: Vol. 1. Attachment.* New York, NY: Basic Books.

andresr/Getty Images

How do healthy interpersonal relationships exist in a workplace context?

What are the differences in boundaries between work and personal relationships?

Review the chapter's learning objectives and **start** with a quick warm-up activity.

Learning Objectives

After you finish reading this chapter, you will be able to:

Analyze the influence of humor, jargon, and storytelling in workplace culture.

Recognize different workplace structures and their relational impact.

Describe types of messaging that contribute to workplace tensions.

Use politeness theory to identify face threats in natural settings.

MindTap

Read, highlight, and take notes online.

Kristen is excited to start her new job at the advertising firm. After having quit her job in the restaurant industry 12 years ago to raise her daughter, Kristen found that she felt like an older sister to the other students in her classes when she returned to college last year to finish her degree. Now that she is finally graduating, Kristen looks forward to working with her new boss Bonnie, who is about the same age as Kristen. She expects that she will feel both eager anticipation and awkward nervousness the night before her first day, however, as she knows the kinds of thoughts that will run through her head: "How do I behave around Bonnie?" "Do I call her by her first name since we're the same age?" "What about my other coworkers? I've never worked in an office!" "Should I bring baked goods on my first day?" For her part, Bonnie has none of this nervousness; Bonnie manages a large team and hired Kristen because she was the most competent job candidate. As such, Bonnie hasn't even considered what their social interactions will look like and instead looks forward to the relief of filling an empty slot with a qualified new professional.

THE CULTURE OF WORK

How do healthy interpersonal relationships exist in a workplace context? What are the differences in boundaries between work and personal relationships? The workplace is a unique context within which all of us find ourselves at some point. Some

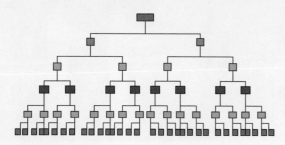

FIGURE 11.1

Tall Organizational Structure

Hierarchy
The leadership structure associated with a group of people, often with increasing power in the organization being distributed to decreasing numbers of individuals, such that a relative few hold the majority of the power.

Colleague
A person whom an individual works with, often in a formal professional business context.

Collegiality
The good-natured cooperation that exists among colleagues in a professional context.

may work in a boutique or an office or in a broader context like the military or police, while others may spend time in similar contexts as customers or citizens. Regardless, every single person reading this book has entered someone's workplace and interacted with an individual who earns his or her living by laboring in that context. From employees to customers, including superiors and their subordinates, the manner in which people interact in a workplace context affects not only the interpersonal interactions among workers but also the experience of the people who enter or patronize that unique environment.

Not all workplace environments are similar; in fact, news reports often highlight the different types of workplace cultures that people may experience.[1] A financial firm on Wall Street may encourage formal interaction, neckties or pantsuits, and a clear **hierarchy** like the one shown in Figure 11.1, where individuals report to one another in a clearly prescribed manner.

A new technology start-up in Silicon Valley may instead promote a casual atmosphere with sneakers and ironic T-shirts, with all employees having almost equal access to all members of the leadership team like the one shown in Figure 11.2.

A military unit deployed in a distant country may even have a unique combination of the two structures, with clear chains of command based on rank yet a communal spirit among men and women as they live and work with each other on base.[2] The ways that individuals work together may clearly influence the types of communication that they are able to have with one another.

Even more noteworthy, however, is the way that these types of communication interactions can influence and be influenced by the nature of the interpersonal relationships among **colleagues**, or people who work with one another. Typically, colleagues strive to have a cooperative and mutually beneficial relationship, exhibiting **collegiality** and support for one another. However, having close relationships with people at work can lead to unique situations where job duties and friendship seem at odds. Marian and Jacob have been friends since their first week on the job. Marian put in extra effort, though, and worked hard to exceed her job expectations during her first years on the job. As a result, Marian is now in a position of authority over Jacob although they have worked hard to maintain that closeness with one another. Now, however, their company needs to downsize an employee from Marian's unit, and she realizes that Jacob's job performance over the past quarter has been the lowest out of anyone in the division. Marian is faced with the tough choice of severing her professional ties with Jacob or

FIGURE 11.2

Flat Organizational Structure

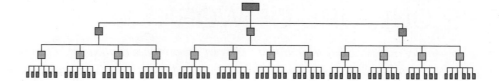

BOX 11.1: Let's Get INTRApersonal

Measuring "Liking" among Colleagues[3]

In workplace environments, individuals may have a wide variety of reactions to one another. One colleague may prove to be tough but fair, while another spends much of his or her time trying to make everyone feel good about him- or herself. Still another person might always do better than everyone else but be willing to share credit with the entire team. A variety of different characteristics may cause us to have an emotional or intellectual response to the behavior of another person. If you are curious about how much you like a coworker or want to be able to compare your feelings for various people, you can use this self-assessment to gain insight into your liking for another person. This is a modified and shortened version of the Liking Scale that was created by the original researcher (Zick Rubin) in 1970 to help distinguish among types of positive evaluations of other people.

INSTRUCTIONS: Think carefully about your relationship with a coworker or classmate with whom you regularly interact. What is your attitude toward them? How do you relate to them, and how do you imagine that they relate to others? This scale may help you think about your own experiences of workplace communication with those around you.

1	2	3	4	5	6	7
Strongly Disagree	Moderately Disagree	Slightly Disagree	Neither Agree Nor Disagree	Slightly Agree	Moderately Agree	Strongly Agree

_____ 1. I think that my coworker is one of those people who quickly wins respect.

_____ 2. I have great confidence in my coworker's judgment.

_____ 3. My coworker is one of the most likable people I know.

_____ 4. It seems to me that it is very easy for my coworker to gain admiration.

_____ 5. Most people would react very favorably to my coworker after a brief acquaintance.

_____ 6. My coworker is the sort of person whom I myself would like to be.

_____ 7. When I am with my coworker, we are almost always in the same mood.

_____ 8. I would highly recommend my coworker for a responsible job.

_____ 9. I think that my coworker is unusually well adjusted.

_____ 10. I would vote for my coworker in an office election.

Now, add up the total score. Is it high? Low? The highest score you can get is a 70, but it is rare for someone to score that high. What does it tell you about how positively you feel about your coworker? Are you surprised to find that you feel the way that you do about him or her? How does this influence your relationship with them?

sacrificing her integrity for the sake of a friend. Having a close relationship with coworkers brings both good and difficult experiences to the workplace; such relationships add a layer of complexity when the job requires difficult decisions, even though people are typically happier in their careers when they have better relationships with their coworkers.[4]

Workplace Structure and Politeness Theory

As aforementioned, people within organizations may find themselves in positions of power or authority over colleagues; most workplaces, regardless of structure, typically have *some* form of chain of command.[5] When Charley interacts with an individual who has power over him—whether that power includes the ability to bestow resources and recognition or punishments and even termination—Charley would describe that powerful person as his boss or his **superior**. When Charley has someone who works under him and looks to *him* as a supervisor or manager or superior, Charley would describe that person as a **subordinate**. These relationships are often difficult when friendship is involved, as a superior may need to require her subordinate to accomplish a task that the subordinate would prefer to avoid. Charley discovered this recently when his boss asked him to convert all the forms in the file cabinets into an easily accessible electronic system. Charley knew that this project would cause him to delay doing those things that he much preferred to do as part of his daily tasks.

Not only do superiors and subordinates have different abilities to assign both desirable and undesirable tasks to one another, but also they have different responsibilities in how they engage one another in their interpersonal relationships because of this difference in power and status. Researchers found that high-status people within a hierarchy typically feel much more

Superior
A person in a position of power or authority over another, occupying a higher level in a hierarchical organizational structure.

Subordinate
A person in a weaker position of power, occupying a lower level in a hierarchical organizational structure.

PJF Military Collection/Alamy Stock Photo

comfortable engaging in teasing or playful interactions, while low-status people are more often the target of such teasing and may not feel comfortable responding in a similar manner.[6] There are even differences in the display of relational behaviors, with subordinates typically feeling less comfortable or confident in their verbal or nonverbal ability to display closeness, such as a friendly touch on the shoulder.[7,8] Any time that differences in power are introduced into a relationship, that power has the ability to differentially impact each relational partner.

Politeness Theory

In order to better explain the difficulties associated with power differences among coworkers, it may be useful to apply a theory that takes into account both the evaluation processes associated with managing others and the inherent difficulties associated with assigning tasks to a subordinate. **Politeness theory** was developed by scholars Brown and Levinson to discuss each individual's motivation to present himself as he wants and have control over his own behavior.[9] This theory argues that a primary drive in our understanding of our own selves is that we want to be able to be perceived in the manner that we desire. We also want to be able to do those things that we like and to avoid those things that we dislike. The superior/subordinate relationship complicates these primary desires, as a superior will engage in regular workplace behaviors that impinge on these goals both intentionally and unwittingly, displaying a range of behaviors known as a **face threat**.

POSITIVE FACE   The first type of face threat that one can experience is a threat to one's **positive face**, or the ability to present oneself in a manner one feels is most desirable. Tessa, for example, wants to present herself as a competent, conscientious worker. Kaitlyn likes to be the life of the office, with a

Politeness Theory
Brown and Levinson's theory that people are motivated to present themselves in a desirable way and to avoid external impositions and constraint.

Face Threat
A behavior that lessens a person's ability to present oneself in a desired way or to avoid imposition and constraint.

Positive Face
A person's ability to present a favorable or desired image of one's self.

Sven Hagolani/Corbis/VCG/Corbis/Getty Images

quick joke and a smile for everyone. Chris prides himself on his dependability and skill in completing projects ahead of schedule. During their recent annual evaluations, though, their manager Valerie was forced to point out to Tessa that she had completely overlooked a major part of her job description. Valerie noted that Kaitlyn was spending too much time socializing and was not getting things done, and she highlighted how Chris was actually a month behind in a few key components of his computer programming goals. Even though Valerie was doing what she was supposed to do as a manager, she still threatened the positive face of her subordinates as she highlighted some areas requiring improvement. Although the feedback was intended to help her employees perform better and improve their workplace experience, each felt an undesirable emotional response to the performance evaluation.[10]

NEGATIVE FACE The other type of face threat has to do with a desire to be free from imposition or constraint, such that a person can do what she wants when she wants. Indeed, we experience such **negative face** threats on an almost constant basis, because society functions through social control and the regulation of behavior, even down to the simplest structures like traffic signals, which tell us when to go and stop. However, a superior/subordinate relationship often has many more of these negative face threats, as it is often the role of a manager or supervisor to assign tasks to others and to make them do things that they don't enjoy or to stop doing things that they do enjoy. Santiago recently had to tell the new intern Mikey that he needed to spend more time working on the social media campaign documents and less time drinking free coffee with the other interns in the break room.

Politeness theory argues that these threats to positive and negative face are a part of every human interaction as people try to display and manage their identities as they move through their daily lives. We already try to

Negative Face
One's perceived freedom to engage in desired activity and ability to refrain from imposition or constraint.

Response Latency
The amount of time — chronological or psychological—that passes before a person responds to the statement or query from another.

Chronological Time
The amount of time that passes, as measured in standardized units like seconds, minutes, hours, days, etc.

Psychological Time
The amount of time that passes, as described by individual or group perceptions like "a lot of time" or "relatively quickly."

Alex Veresovich/Shutterstock.com

BOX 11.2: iPersonal

Response Time and the Workplace[11,12,13]

Technology has greatly improved our ability to communicate quickly within an office environment. In previous generations, when someone wanted a response from a coworker she may have walked down the hall and asked that person face-to-face or even created a list of questions to refer to at a later meeting during that day or week. With each communication technology that is developed to make such interactions easier and quicker, the expected delay in a reply has gone down. Often, the more important that a sender seems, the more quickly we expect to respond to him or her; power influences the time it takes to interact with each other. Researchers call this time between a query or statement and its subsequent reply the **response latency**, which refers to the amount of time that passes between the two interactions.

Different types of communication technology may imply different response latencies. A text message may require a quick, short reply; a formal email, on the other hand, may suggest that the receiver can take some time to think before crafting a response. The time it takes to respond to someone may also impact a coworker's impression of you, depending on the amount of time and the nature of the relationship.

Interestingly, that response time can be measured in a variety of ways. **Chronological time** refers to the actual amount of time that passes between a query and a response (e.g., four minutes) while **psychological time** refers to the feelings that people may have about the amount of time that passes (e.g., a long time.) Both influence our perceptions of the time that passes—and our perceptions of each other—as we use technology to communicate interpersonally.

> ❯ Before leaving work on Friday, Brad emailed his boss Cheryl his final report for the fiscal year and was surprised to find that she already had feedback about it on Monday morning when he arrived at his desk.

> ❯ Stephanie tweeted about her company's new product line, and after getting a text message about a misspelling there was a new tweet within two minutes of the original one.

> ❯ Monica checks her voicemails and emails as soon as she gets to work each morning. Monica responds to the emails first, however, because she doesn't want to return phone calls too early in the morning.

Different communication mediums use technology in different ways, and some of these allow for instant access to one another. As coworkers, it becomes essential to clarify what forms of communication are acceptable, discussing the boundaries and limitations of each technology. It may also be helpful to consider how each form influences perceptions of power, perceptions of face and importance, and the imposition that it may cause on a wide variety of social interactions.

INSTRUCTIONS: How quickly do you reply to statements or requests from others? What makes you want to respond to people individually? How might you craft messages so that people respond to your requests in relatively short periods? Do you believe that different types of technology require different and/or quicker attention?

manage our identities with friends and families and romantic partners, as we tell parents that we are too old to do chores or we try to demonstrate to romantic partners that we are the best fit for one another because of our shared interests and similar looks. However, as these people confirm or disconfirm these assertions, we are constantly negotiating how we are perceived by those around us[14]; in the workplace, these threats may be magnified as they are often tied to performance evaluations, promotions, regular interactions, and the identities that people attach to achieving career success.

Verbal Tools for Creating Culture

Although people often speak of an "office culture," many people don't realize that they are coparticipants in the creation and establishment of that workplace culture. Just as each coffee shop has a different feel depending on the attitudes of the workers, so, too, do the workers in each office building or firehouse or landscaping team have a variety of ways that they can approach their job with one another. Although nonverbal interactions like smiling or frowning and nodding or shaking one's head may serve to confirm or disconfirm assertions about the culture of a workplace, there are a few key verbal tools that serve to highlight and create those assertions in the first place. Culture is not merely reflected by members of a workplace; culture is created through the communication that occurs between members of the group.

Stories

One important social function within a workplace is the storytelling that occurs by coworkers that helps to create and establish what is considered acceptable.[15] By highlighting both exemplar behavior as well as what

BOX 11.3: Commendable Connections

. . . .

Ethics *and* Hierarchical Leadership

In many organizational contexts, a goal of communication is to accomplish some task, often through convincing others of the merits of that task. In other situations, communication simply occurs to transmit a direct order or a command within a leadership structure. That hierarchy can cause people to be "forced" to engage in behaviors that they would not otherwise prefer to do. Whether through the threat of punishment, the promise of reward, or the use of a strong rhetorical argument (see Chapter 4), individuals lower on the hierarchy may find themselves engaging in work that they don't enjoy.

Even though some of these behaviors may simply be unpleasant (e.g., collating endless amounts of handouts to be stapled), some may actually go against the values or belief systems of an individual (e.g., convincing a client to purchase something that he doesn't actually need or want). Individuals may find it difficult to resist engaging in such behaviors, particularly when they have a close relationship with the person who is asking them to do it.

Recently, Jocelyn found out that she was supposed to be working on a project with her manager, Hank. Before she realized that she was supposed to have help from Hank, Jocelyn had already completed the project and received great feedback during an office-wide meeting; unfortunately, during that meeting both Jocelyn and Hank were praised for Jocelyn's work, and he whispered to her, "Just go with it." After the meeting, Jocelyn felt like she had been used by her boss and that he had taken unjustified credit.

Have you ever been asked to do something at work that you didn't want to do? What about something that you didn't think was morally or ethically justifiable? Because some ethical considerations are culture specific or a matter of personal belief, it can be difficult to explain why such a behavior is undesirable—or even detestable—to a coworker.

INSTRUCTIONS: Take a personal inventory of your workplace interactions. Have you ever been asked to do something that went against your personal code of conduct? Have you ever asked someone else to do something that she found morally wrong? People come from a wide range of ethical perspectives. What distinguishing features of your workplace can you use to meet your own ethical goals?

behavior is disallowed in a workplace, stories help individuals to see the **norms** and behaviors that others generally agree do or do not belong in the workplace. When Myles first started work at the local news station, his coworkers told him about the recently fired intern who would set press releases to be automatically sent from his email every morning so that people thought he was hard at work when he was really sleeping in; through this story, Myles quickly learned that punctuality and determination are essential parts of the job and that cleverness is admired when used appropriately and punished when not. Additional stories helped him understand what his new colleagues found interesting or noteworthy, and Myles quickly

Norm
Typical or usual patterns of behavior, often based on established social rules.

learned that he needed to keep up with college sports because it was a big part of that newsroom's regular discussion.

Humor

Although stories may give insight into what behaviors are prized or despised, humor is often used to correct poor performance or to demonstrate inclusion or exclusion from a social group.[16] When people make fun of behavior that they think is nonnormative, they are often offering subtle cues that something needs to be fixed or changed in order for someone to fit in with the rest of the group. When Bradley wore jeans to his new job as a hospital administrator, his coworkers made fun of his casual dress until he realized the unspoken rule that people in management positions needed to wear dress slacks and a tie. Diane was a new teacher who required her students to read much more than any other instructor at the high school where she taught; when she overheard students joking about how she shouldn't expect them to "read as much as her because she had no life," Diane was able to understand (albeit painfully) that this was a minor admonishment to her excessive reading expectations (which she chose to ignore) rather than a personal attack.

Jargon
Technical words and language used by professionals or members of an interest group (from Chapter 4).

Jargon

As mentioned in Chapter 4, the final verbal tool that allows us to draw a clear distinction between people who are members of the workplace culture and those who are outsiders is **jargon**, which is technical language that is not understood except by members of a particular culture. When Billy started work at the prison, he quickly realized that the use of terms like *newjack* and *SHU* and *cellie* were intentional ways for prisoners to distinguish themselves from the guards like him. Once he had worked there a while and was accepted as a member of the correctional complex, he too began to use terminology that made new employees quickly realize that they had a lesser status in the culture and a lack of knowledge about their environment.

TENSIONS IN WORKPLACE RELATIONSHIPS

Even though verbal language is a useful way to establish norms of desirable and undesirable behaviors within a workplace environment, the constant threat to positive and negative face inherently causes tensions to emerge as some people are ultimately proved to be more competent than others or find themselves having to engage in less desirable parts of their job. Collaborative or team-based workplaces allow for much more interaction to occur than in a traditional independent office environment, and as such tensions may begin to emerge among coworkers. Some of these tensions may simply be a result of group membership within the larger organization, while other tensions may result from the need to deliver bad news to a coworker.

In-Group/Out-Group Status

One reason that conflict may occur in interpersonal relationships in workplace environments has to do with something we discussed in depth in Chapter 3 when we talked about group membership. When coworkers view one another as members of the **in-group**, they are likely to see one another as similar and are willing to offer support, encouragement, and the sharing of resources. When a coworker sees a colleague as a member of the **out-group**, however, he is likely to behave in direct competition with him and avoid sharing resources equally. Such a perspective often causes competition to occur and can result in members of the same organization working actively to outperform or even sabotage the members of the out-group. As such, it may prove helpful to individuals and the team as a whole to collectively highlight similarities in both thought and behavior with one's coworkers and to bring attention to the shared goals of all employees within the larger organizational structure.

One scholar, Zick Rubin, was able to create a scale that measured the amount of liking that individuals have for one another.[17] Look at the items in Box 11.1 and try to imagine what the likely scores would be for members of an in-group, as compared to members of an out-group. How might they differ from one another? If you are employed and have taken the modified

In-Group
Perceived members of an interconnected group who appear similar in specific ways that group members see as important criteria for inclusion (from Chapter 3).

Out-Group
People who are perceived as *not* members of an interconnected group because those individuals are different in ways that group members see as important criteria for exclusion (from Chapter 3).

Image Source/Image Source/Getty Images

BOX 11.4: Communication Currents

· ·

Teams and Tensions in Current Television

***The Office*, Season 2, Episode 2, "Sexual Harassment,"** http://bit.ly/2n7Un7p

In the hugely successful television situation comedy *The Office*, a group of characters interact as they work together to sell paper products at a moderately sized company in mid-America. The group of misfits has difficulty navigating the office environment, as a sense of professionalism is not top priority in the workplace.

As we watch this clip, we see an office manager in open conflict with a team of executives and lawyers from corporate during a formal intervention about his inappropriate humor in the office environment. Michael expresses direct confrontation with his corporate supervisor, Jan, while also later attempting to publicly shame the visiting Dunder-Mifflin team in front of the entire office. By combining both passive and active forms of aggression, Michael makes it clear that he thinks his voice—and his particular sense of humor—should be heard.

INSTRUCTIONS: Watch the video again, noting the multiple forms of conflict that occur throughout the clip. How does each group deal with workplace tension? Consider your experiences working or dealing with others in a task capacity. How might each situation have been resolved in a more successful way? How would you respond if you were Michael's supervisor Jan, the victim of the most egregious disrespect?

version of Rubin's scale in Box 11.1, how did those scores describe how much you like your coworkers? We may have positive feelings toward people in work relationships who aren't necessarily in our in-group and we may dislike individuals with whom we feel closely connected.

Indirect Messaging in the Workplace

When delivering disappointing or bad news to a coworker in a workplace environment, people often rely on indirectness as a way to assuage the negative response from that coworker and to increase understanding.[18] When Cheryl thought that Eric's work at her bakery was substandard and decided not to give him the promotion to shift manager that he'd hoped for, indirect messaging proved the best way to negotiate the difficult interactions. Indeed, when situations that involve threatening someone's positive face or negative face arise, it may be best to use indirectness, as highlighted by Lesikar and Flatley:

- **Begin with a strategic buffer.** Start the delivery of bad news with a general rationale that does not directly identify the bad news that is about to come. Instead, consider highlighting the rationale behind the decision that was made. When she discussed Eric's productivity with him, Cheryl began her conversation with Eric by discussing the expectations of the job and highlighting the areas for improvement that Eric could consider.

- **Develop the strategy.** Use direct logical descriptions and a persuasive technique to highlight your understanding of the message recipient's viewpoint. Be specific when possible. In her case, Cheryl next pointed out that she knew that the low number of baked goods Eric produced was likely the result of the amount of time that he spent decorating each one, making each item cost more in labor than they were selling it for.

- **Present the bad news positively.** After having highlighted the rationale behind a decision, even a face-threatening statement should logically make sense to the receiver. Put a positive spin on the discussion while making sure that the negative message is not weakened, and do not diminish the importance of the bad news. Cheryl used her conversation to praise the visual quality of Eric's baked goods and to explain that their customers were interested in a high volume of cupcakes to be eaten in a fast-paced cafeteria environment. So his skills were needed for speed and efficiency rather than artistic merit.

- **End on a positive note.** Because all face-threatening encounters can leave the threatened individual feeling diminished or powerless in some way, it may be useful to try to insert some positive communication at the end of the message. Reassurances or encouragement may allow for the information to be less undesirable on receipt. Cheryl finally highlighted that she saw the dedication that Eric put into his job and that she knew that he could adapt to a different set of standards in order to justify another conversation at the end of the next fiscal quarter. By giving him specific steps to take to strengthen his position, Cheryl helped Eric leave the conversation thinking he could make some changes in how he approached his job.

BOX 11.5: InterFace

Group Cooperation with Diverse Others[19]

Sara and Wentian work for a large pharmaceutical firm, but while Sara lives in North America her colleague Wentian runs a laboratory conducting research in China. When Wentian visits Sara in her office during a North American visit, his gentle handshake causes Sara to assume that he is weak-willed, while her firm Western handshake causes Wentian to assume that she is trying to assert authority over him.

Alfred moved to the United States from Germany and accepted a job at the firm where Jake started working only a few months before. Jake comes from a culture that encourages colleagues of similar status to use first names when they interact, but this practice is offensive to Alfred. Jake doesn't realize that it is essential to ask a new colleague what he prefers to be called, particularly in this case where Alfred's cultural heritage utilizes more formal forms of address until people have established a relationship.

Brandon and Will are working on a team project, and in order to work well with his own schedule, Will has set their meetings at 5:30 p.m. when other work duties have ended for the day. Unfortunately, Will did not realize that Brandon is the primary caregiver for two children, and the schedule dramatically impacts the time that the kids are left at home alone with moderate supervision from a neighbor.

In our friendships and romantic relationships, often the interactions center around the process of getting to know one another. In workplace relationships, two people may spend great amounts of time working together without ever discussing information of a personal nature. So, how do you best engage a wide variety of diverse others within the workplace? Although it may seem strange at first, the brief conversations and introductions that occur in the workplace offer opportunities to gather helpful information that may give cues to interaction. Even more important, frank interactions and openness to correction may allow for healthy workplace interaction patterns to be developed, making the office environment more helpful for all.

INSTRUCTIONS: Do these scenarios remind you of any personal experiences? Have you ever worked on a project or a job without really getting to know your peers and/or coworkers? Consider your own preferences and desires. Would vocalizing those concerns or needs make your working life more successful in a complicated office culture?

POPULAR TEAM-BASED WORK CONTEXTS

Whether your coworkers are trying to get a large amount of food on the tables at a restaurant or to get a multimedia presentation done in time for an important product launch, often the most comprehensive approaches to work involve teams:

- **Decision-making teams.** Some work contexts require that multiple people contribute their unique expertise to a situation in order to get the most desirable result. This discussion of information can result in a decision that far surpasses one likely to be made by an individual alone.[20]

Matthew Horwood/Alamy Stock Photo

- **Division of labor.** By having individuals work on specific parts of a project, they can each become experts in their area. By distributing ownership and leadership of a large project to each member of a team, it is possible to have incredible oversight over a wide variety of specific work functions.[21]

- **Capitalizing on strengths.** Some people are great at interfacing with clients and can easily form close relationships with them.[22] Others are great at technical skills, able to accomplish in minutes what it may take others days to finish.

- **Sheer capacity.** Finally, some jobs may simply take a large number of people to be able to finish in a reasonable time frame. A landscaping crew at a major theme park is able to tidy and groom the entire resort every evening because of the sheer number of crew members; an online provider like Amazon.com can ship such a high volume of products to a large number of customers because of the many "pickers" that it uses to populate its supply chain.[23]

Because of the demands of a wide variety of industrial, military, educational, service, and professional careers, individuals are coming into contact with coworkers across a spectrum of interaction types. Naturally, working together with someone allows for interaction to occur. Interpersonal relationships can develop from among these regular workplace interactions, whether those individuals work face-to-face in an office environment or collaborate through technology across town or even internationally.

BOX 11.6: InterConnect
. . . .

Workplace Networks: Which Linkages Are Strongest?

As mentioned earlier in the chapter, it is relatively straightforward to create a chart of one's own work-related networks. Even though the sheer number of people in one's workplace network may appear relatively manageable, the addition of networking sites like LinkedIn or even professional usages of Facebook may make the creation of a comprehensive chart of work-related linkages—like the one seen in Figure 11.3—to be a daunting task.

Just like the various degrees of closeness that we experience among our own personal friendships or families, not every work relationship is necessarily a strong one. Indeed, some people who are "friends" on Facebook or "connections" on LinkedIn may actually have relatively little consequence in our daily working lives.

(Continued)

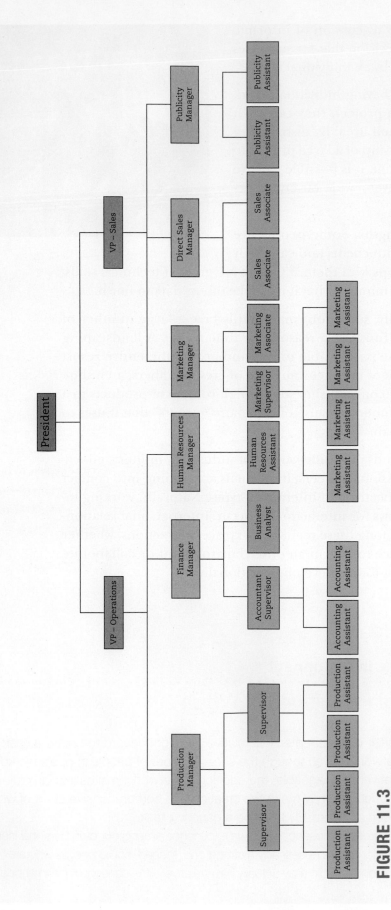

FIGURE 11.3
Workplace Network Chart

Consider the nature of the working relationships in the following examples.

> Matt and Enrique started a small business together years ago and sold the business last month for a large profit. They still talk daily because of their friendship, yet they currently have no financial ties to one another.

> Brent works the day shift at a local restaurant. When he is sick, he knows that he can text Max to cover his shift since Max put a note on the bulletin board expressing a desire to pick up extra hours.

> Madge and Marie were both hired as social media interns at a local minor-league baseball team. Marie typically handles the Twitter feed and YouTube account for the team, and Madge is the "guru" for both Facebook and Snapchat. Madge and Marie typically want consistency and collaboration across all four platforms.

> Andrew and his administrative assistant decide to celebrate one of the VP's upcoming anniversaries of working at the firm. Andrew's assistant calls her counterpart in the VP's office to find out what kind of cake he likes.

> Selah works from home but knows her boss because they went to high school together, decades ago. Any time Selah has a problem with something that she is working on, she texts her boss's mobile phone rather than calling his office and taking the time to deal with leaving a voicemail for a response.

INSTRUCTIONS: Think carefully about each of the relationships above. Each relationship represents a type of workplace connection, but it appears that there is great variety in the relational interactions between partners. How would you describe each relationship? Based on your knowledge of interpersonal communication, what style of interactions would you guess is most common in each scenario? Are each of these relationships appropriate for the workplace? Do you have similar experiences with people that you have worked or studied with?

Chapter Summary

Workplace interactions are among the most frequent interactions in some people's lives, yet we rarely consider the interpersonal nature of our interactions with our colleagues. Whether one telecommutes from home or shares an office location with a colleague 40 or more hours a week, both interpersonal skills and those of coworkers influence one's work experience. Because of the unique structures afforded by an office hierarchy, people may find themselves in deference to a person that they may have considered a peer in other contexts. As such, employees are constantly negotiating their face with one another as each presents him- or herself in a desired way; at the same time, those people are also attempting to accomplish both the tasks assigned to them while also assigning tasks to other people. This process of dealing with threats to both positive and negative faces causes the opportunity for much conflict to occur.

Not only do people often work on creating some tangible product or intellectual output, but also people are in the process of creating *culture* each day that they work in an organizational context with other people. From the stories and jokes that they tell to the use of insider language that only they know, each workplace environment has created a shared culture regardless of whether that context is in an office building, a firehouse, a sports team, or a deployed military unit. As part of that culture, people may find themselves similar to some other members and dissimilar from others. These experiences of group membership have significant impact on the daily interactions of each member as they use communication to accomplish their workplace tasks, affording the opportunity to negotiate both individual and collective interpersonal experiences.

MindTap

First-Person Video

His Presentation at Work

Apply what you've learned in this chapter by analyzing the "His Presentation at Work" video, using the accompanying questions as a guide. This video and these questions are available online with your MindTap Speech for *Interconnections: Interpersonal Communication Foundations and Contexts.*

MindTap

Key Terms

Use flashcards to learn key concepts and take a quiz to test your knowledge.

Chronological Time	Jargon	Psychological
Colleague	Negative Face	Time
Collegiality	Norm	Response Latency
Face Threat	Out-Group	Subordinate
Hierarchy	Politeness Theory	Superior
In-Group	Positive Face	

Discussion Questions

1. Think about media and film depictions of employer/employee relationships. Which interactions look most desirable to you? What difficulties might arise from those interactions?

2. Have you worked in groups or teams, whether in a job or in your education? How have you balanced the need to accomplish a task with the desire to form relationships with your group partners or teammates? How did that influence your ability to interact with members around you?

3. Think about your work relationships. How would you characterize or describe the nature of your interactions?

4. Discuss a time when you have felt like someone in a position of authority asked you to do something that you did not want to do. How did that make you feel? Do you still harbor resentment about that interaction?

5. Consider your current interactions with friendships. What types of face threats do you regularly experience with them? Are those threats meant as humor or as something else?

Making Connections

Workplace interactions often seem very different from other interpersonal relationships, likely because they are often rather involuntary. Although our friendships and our romantic relationships are typically much more voluntary, our family relationships can often also be characterized as involuntary. What similarities can you identify between workplace relationships and family relationships? What differences seem to emerge?

Chapter Quiz

1. Brandon shares a cubicle with Miranda, who tells him that he eats loudly. In terms of politeness theory, Miranda has most likely threatened Brandon's
   a. Negative face
   b. Positive face
   c. Both negative and positive face
   d. None of the above

2. In response, Brandon tells Miranda to put on some noise-canceling earphones. In terms of politeness theory, Brandon has most likely threatened Miranda's
   a. Negative face
   b. Positive face
   c. Both negative and positive face
   d. None of the above

3. Later in the day, when Miranda walks close to Brandon she holds her nose with a disgusted face and tells him to take a shower. In terms of politeness theory, Miranda has most likely threatened Brandon's
   a. Negative face
   b. Positive face
   c. Both negative and positive face
   d. None of the above

4. Clearly, Brandon and Miranda have problems working closely with one another. Even though Miranda's behavior is inappropriate, because they have the same job she is Brandon's
   a. Supervisor
   b. Manager
   c. Colleague
   d. Subordinate
   e. Employee
   f. None of the above

5. If Brandon gets a promotion, Miranda is now Brandon's
   a. Supervisor
   b. Manager
   c. Colleague
   d. Subordinate
   e. Employee
   f. Both C and D

6. T/F Because workplace communication involves messaging across and within levels of hierarchy, tensions never emerge among coworkers.

7. T/F It is relatively easy for people to pick up on the specialized language and jargon of a group without having to interact with members of that group.

8. T/F Humor can be an effective way to help someone learn about the workplace culture.

9. T/F Jack feels that he is very similar to his coworker and is willing to pick up slack on projects when his coworker makes mistakes. Jack likely sees his coworker as a member of his in group.

10. T/F Most businesses do not have a hierarchical structure in order to accomplish tasks.

Endnotes

1. Steward, J. B. (2013, March 16). At Google, a place to work and play. *The New York Times: Business Day*. Retrieved from http://www.nytimes.com/2013/03/16/business/at-google-a -place-to-work-and-play.html

2. For an overview of literature, see Clark, M. G., Jordan, J. D., & Clark, K. L. (2013). Motivating military families to thrive. *Family and Consumer Sciences Research Journal, 42*(2), 110–123.

3. Rubin, Z. (1970). Measurement of romantic love. *Journal of Personality and Social Psychology, 16*(1), 265–273.

4. Winstead, B. A., Derlega, V. J., Montgomery, M. J., & Pilkington, C. (1995). The quality of friendships at work and job satisfaction. *Journal of Social and Personal Relationships, 12*, 199–215.

5. Holmes, J., & Stubbe, M. (2015). *Power and Politeness in the Workplace: A Sociolinguistic Analysis of Talk at Work*. New York, NY: Routledge.

6. Keltner, D., Young, R. C., Heerey, E. A., Oemig, C., & Monarch, N. D. (1998). Teasing in hierarchical and intimate relations. *Journal of Personality and Social Psychology, 75*(5), 1231–1247.

7. For an overview, see Richmond, V. P., & McCroskey, J. C. (2000). The impact of supervisor and subordinate immediacy on relational and organizational outcomes. *Communication Monographs, 67*(1), 85–95.

8. For a review, see Bonaccio, S., O'Reilly, J., O'Sullivan, S. L., & Chiocchio, F. (2016). Nonverbal behavior and communication in the workplace: A review and an agenda for research. *Journal of Management, 42*(5), 1044–1074.

9. Brown, P., & Levinson, S. (1978). Universals in language use: Politeness phenomena. In E. N. Goody (Ed.), *Questions and Politeness: Strategies in Social Interaction*. Cambridge, UK: Cambridge University Press.

10. For an overview of responses to criticism, see Wilson, K. L., Lizzio, A. J., & Whicker, L. (2003). Effective assertive behavior in the workplace: Responding to unfair criticism. *Journal of Applied Social Psychology, 33*(2), 362–395.

11. Kalman, Y. M., & Rafaeli, S. (2011). Online pauses and silence: Chronemic expectancy violations in written computer-mediated communication. *Communication Research, 38*(1), 54–69.

12. Panteli, N., & Fineman, S. (2005). The sound of silence: The case of virtual team organising. *Behaviour & Information Technology, 24*(5), 347–352.

13. Barber, L. K., & Santuzzi, A. M. (2015). Please respond ASAP: Workplace telepressure and employee recovery. *Journal of Occupational Health Psychology, 20*(2), 172–189.

14. Cupach, W. R., & Carson, C. L. (2002). Characteristics and consequences of interpersonal complaints associated with perceived face threat. *Journal of Social and Personal Relationships, 19*(4), 443–462.

15. Driscoll, C., & McKee, M. (2007). Restorying a culture of ethical and spiritual values: A role for leader storytelling. *Journal of Business Ethics, 73*(2), 205–217.

16. Keltner, D., Young, R. C., Heerey, E. A., Oemig, C, & Monarch, N. D. (1998). Teasing in hierarchical and intimate relations. *Journal of Personality and Social Psychology, 75*(5), 1231–1247.

17. Rubin, Z. (1970). Measurement of romantic love. *Journal of Personality and Social Psychology, 16*(1), 265–273.

18. Lesikar, R. V., & Flatley, M. E. (2002). Indirectness in bad-news messages. *Basic Business Communication: Skills for Empowering the Internet Generation* (pp. 150–173). Boston, MA: McGraw-Hill.

19. Lesikar, R. V., & Flatley, M. E. (2002). Techniques of cross-cultural communication. *Basic Business Communication: Skills for Empowering the Internet Generation* (pp. 436–452). Boston, MA: McGraw-Hill.

20. Wittenbaum, G. M., & Bowman, J. M. (2004). A social validation explanation for mutual enhancement. *Journal of Experimental Social Psychology, 40*(2), 169–184.

21. Collinson, D. L., & Collinson, M. (2004). The power of time: Leadership, management, and gender. In C. Epstein & A. L. Kalleberg (Eds.), *Fighting for Time: Shifting Boundaries of Work and Social Life* (pp. 219–246). New York, NY: Russell Sage Foundation.

22. Gwinner, K. P., Gremler, D. D., & Bitner, M. J. (1998). Relational benefits in service industries: The customer's perspective. *Journal of the Academy of Marketing Science, 26*, 101–114.

23. Woolf, C. (Producer). (2013, November 29). For many Amazon pickers, you may have a job one day but be out of work the next. *PRI's The World*. Podcast retrieved from http://www.pri .org/stories/2013-11-29/many-amazon-pickers-you-may-have -job-one-day-be-out-work-next

Postscript

Interpersonal communication is a complex and interactive experience, shaping our lives as we interact with others and better understand ourselves. In this text, we have explored a variety of contexts and relationships that have shaped who we are and that will influence who we will become. At times insightful, and at other times challenging, the theories and concepts discussed here may help us become more open as individuals, connect us with one another, inspire us to participate in our communities, and empower us to think outside ourselves to our broader world.

From my first experience learning about interpersonal relationships as a college student at UC Davis decades ago, I have found that the field of communication studies provides deep insight into our family, friends, romantic partners, and coworkers in a variety of ways. As I continue to learn more and more about myself and about those people whom I hold dear, the theory and understanding of interpersonal communication continue to make me a better friend and colleague and family member each and every day. Although many textbooks cite statistics about how students of interpersonal communication are more successful or positive in their close relationships throughout their lives, I invite you to reflect and decide for yourself how life has been improved as a result of the new understandings of yourself and of your community.

—Jonathan M. Bowman

Glossary

Accent A catchall vocalic designation for a wide variety of linguistic factors that influence a pattern of ways that words may be spoken.

Accommodating Being cooperative yet unassertive with one's relationship partner, often ignoring one's own needs in order to satisfy the needs, goals, or desires of the relationship partner.

Action The fourth element of the listening process, this involves determining the type and scope of a response to a message.

Actionable A message that can or should be responded to with an in-kind message or behavior.

Actor–Observer Effect Assuming that negative experiences in one's own life are the result of external or contextual factors rather than caused by individual choice or personality.

Adaptability The tendency of a family to allow natural changes in rules, roles, and family leadership structures over the collective life span.

Adaptors A set of kinesic movements that indicate a person's internal state by releasing energy, often unintentionally encoded.

Affect Displays A set of kinesic movements displayed in the face that indicate the sender's emotional experience (i.e., facial expressions).

Affective Stage In this third stage of social penetration, relational partners begin to discuss personal issues or topics that they consider private, feeling sufficiently close to allow conflict to occur.

Agape The love style most characterized by nurturance and care.

Ambushing An attempt to listen aggressively with the sole goal of finding an opportunity to attack a conversational partner.

Analytic Listening The type of active listening in which one party seeks to analyze and/or critique the message and the implications of a communication interaction in order to determine the truth or veracity of the message.

Androgyny The norms associated with someone displaying approximately equal amounts of masculinity and femininity.

Anxious-Ambivalent *See* Preoccupied.

Appearance The communication code focused on nonverbal messages related to one's visual self-presentation.

Artifacts Items or objects carried or worn that have intentional or unintentional communicative value (e.g., a briefcase in a professional environment).

Assurances Relationship-maintaining behaviors wherein partners use either verbal or nonverbal messaging to express their commitment to one another.

Asynchronous A description of messages that are not sent or received in a timely fashion and do not afford either interaction partner the opportunity to create an immediate response.

Attachment Theory Bowlby's theory that early interpersonal experiences as a child influence the pattern of relying on relational partners for interdependence, security, and affection.

Attention The second element of the listening process, in which a receiver devotes mental energy and awareness to the sounds or sights received from a sender.

Attribution The process of assigning an explanation for an observed or enacted behavior.

Autonomy Independence associated with a desire to be seen as an individual within a relationship.

Avoiding (in conflict) With a low concern for self and a low concern for others, this conflict style focuses on ignoring the competing goals that led to relational conflict between interaction partners.

Avoiding (in relationship stages) The fourth stage of moving apart, this part of relational de-escalation is characterized by the complete cessation of all interaction with one's relational partner.

Betrayal A perceived relational state when one or both partners are unsupportive or even work against the goals or desires of the other partner.

Biogenetic Lens The perspective that families are groups of people who work toward reproductive success and share common genetic material.

Biological Sex The genetic continuum established at birth that includes genital, hormonal, and chromosomal displays of maleness and femaleness.

Blended Family A family unit that consists of adults and children, where at least one of the children is either biological or adopted and from a previous relationship.

Blind Quadrant This quadrant of the Johari Window can be used to describe information that we do not know about ourselves but of which others have awareness.

Body Image The perception that one has about the shape or attractiveness of one's own body, often in relation to a desired ideal.

Bonding The fifth stage of coming together, this part of relational development is characterized by both verbal and nonverbal demonstrations of the closeness shared with one's relational partner.

Booty-Call Sexual encounters between on-demand short-term sexual partners with no commitments to one another, which may recur over a long time.

Casual Relationship The relationship type where partners have no definitive obligation toward one another and are often free to date others.

Casual Sex *See* Short-Term Sex.

Centrifugal Perspective In order for a close relationship to continue, effort, energy, and other resources must be put into the maintenance of the partnership's desired state.

Centripetal Perspective People naturally tend toward one another, and the maintenance of a close relationship can be relatively effortless.

Channel Immediacy The degree to which the channel through which a message is conveyed can gain interest and attention.

Channel Richness The degree to which a communication attempt relies on a variety of channels in order to send a message.

Channel Synchronicity The degree to which the channel through which a message is conveyed can be received and responded to in real time.

Channel The mechanism through which a message is transmitted, whether using sight, sound, taste, touch, or smell.

Chaotic Family *See* Overly Flexible Family.

Chronological Time The amount of time that passes, as measured in standardized units like seconds, minutes, hours, days, etc.

Circumscribing The second stage of moving apart, this part of relational de-escalation is characterized by lessened intimacy and the restriction of self-disclosure shared with one's relational partner.

Closedness The withholding of private information from a romantic partner associated with a desire to be seen as mysterious or more interesting.

Cognition The process associated with thinking, learning, and applying logic to observations and experiences.

Cohabiting Couple Two unmarried adult individuals who have chosen to live together as romantic partners.

Cohesion An interpersonal experience of both emotional bonding and a connected life spent together.

Collaborating With a high concern for self and a high concern for others, this conflict style focuses on reaching a mutually beneficial solution with an interaction partner.

Colleague A person whom an individual works with, often in a formal professional business context.

Collectivism A cultural emphasis on the communal nature of groups within a social system.

Collegiality The good-natured cooperation that exists among colleagues in a professional context.

Colloquialism Informal words understood by individuals across broad communication cultures.

Commitment An attachment decision that motivates the continuation of a relationship with another person over time.

Committed Partners Two people who have developed a significant romantic relationship and intend to remain together, regardless of legal or marital status.

Committed Relationship The relationship type where couples have a clearly defined obligation toward one another and are monogamous.

Commonalities Information that people identify as held in common, whether attitudes, values, beliefs, experiences, or demographic characteristics, often resulting in perceptions of similarity.

Communication Accommodation Theory Giles's theory that people alter their use of vocalics in specific communication contexts, becoming more similar in their use of vocalics with desirable conversational partners (i.e., speech convergence) and less similar with undesirable conversational partners (i.e., speech divergence).

Communication Climate The tone of an interpersonal relationship, often discussed using emotive terms.

Communication Culture A large group of people who communicate similarly and have overlapping experiences of their social world.

Communicative Aggression Violence that uses implicit or explicit messages to intentionally cause psychological harm to a person.

Competence Interpersonal power that comes from possessing skills that lead to decision making, task accomplishment, topical discussions, or other desired outcomes.

Competing With a high concern for self and a low concern for others, this conflict style focuses on "winning" the conflict encounter at the expense of the interaction partner.

Competitive Interruption Active attempts to interrupt a conversational partner in order to gain control of the interaction.

Complementarity A difference in characteristic or interest from another person, often with one individual seen as having a strength where the other has a related weakness, or vice versa.

Compromising With a moderate concern for both self and others, this conflict style focuses on each interaction partner giving up some aspect of her competing goals in exchange for other(s).

Conflict The active process of navigating disagreement over access to resources, people, or opportunities in which one or more parties perceive incompatible goals.

Connection Interdependence associated with a desire to be seen as part of a dyad within a relationship.

Connotative Meaning: A culture-specific set of understandings or interpretations associated with the formal definition for a word.

Constitutive The ability of a person or group to create the existence of an abstract concept simply by naming it as a concept.

Contempt An obvious expression of disdain or the articulation of a belief that the other person is worthless.

Context The physical or conceptual environment in which a communication message is transmitted.

Conversational Narcissism Attempting to seek attention by shifting conversational topics to focus attention on the self.

Cooperation The dimension of conflict styles that involves the mutual consideration of the goals of both interaction partners.

Correspondence Bias Assuming that the behavior of others is due to individual choice or personality rather than external or contextual factors.

Critical Listening *See* Analytic Listening.

Criticism An expression of disapproval or a critique of another person.

Culture An accumulated pattern of values, beliefs, and behaviors shared by an identifiable group of people with a common history and verbal and nonverbal symbol system.

Cyberbullying Using computer-mediated forms of communicative aggression to harass or threaten someone intentionally.

Deception The deliberate attempt to cause a receiver to believe something that the communicator considers false.

Decode To interpret a sender's idea based on a verbal or nonverbal message (from Chapter 1).

Decoding To interpret a sender's idea based on a verbal or nonverbal message.

Defamation A statement that has a negative impact on an individual's reputation.

Defensiveness Warding off the complaints or criticisms of another without accepting responsibility for any of the expressed concerns.

Denotative Meaning: A formal definition for a word, like that found in a dictionary.

Depenetration The process of withdrawing from the depth of a relationship by decreasing self-disclosure and revealing less personal information.

Deviant An individual who engages in behaviors considered beyond the range of what is normal in a culture or context.

Dialect Region-specific rules or words that are not necessarily shared by the larger language community.

Dialectic Tensions *See* Relational Dialectics.

Dialogic Listening The type of active listening in which both parties seek to co-construct shared meaning and understand each other's thoughts and feelings through conversation and dialogue.

Differentiating The first stage of moving apart, this part of relational de-escalation is characterized by the development or accentuation of differences between one and one's relational partner.

Directness The dimension of conflict styles that involves the willingness to engage the process of conflict and to communicate openly about that conflict.

Disengaged Family A family with relatively little or no emotional connection, characterized by extreme individuality and separation.

Disfluency The disconnect between the intent of a message sender and the receiver's understanding of that message.

Dismissive The style of attachment that is characterized by high self-worth but no desire to turn to others to provide a sense of intimacy.

Distal Relationship *See* Long-Distance Relationship.

Dominance Controlling behavior intended to influence decisions or behavior.

Dyad Two people who interact.

Dyadic Communication The sending and receiving of messages between two people.

Dysfunctional Family A family that finds itself lacking the ability to successfully manage the tensions of at least one of the family functions, specifically including but not limited to growth and cohesion, being adaptable, creating a family identity, and communicating in a positive, affirming manner.

Ectomorphs A body shape characterized by a tall, slender shape with lean muscle mass.

Emblems A set of kinesic movements that have an agreed-on meaning within a culture.

Emoji A small graphic image used in text-based channels to nonverbally alter the meaning of a message (e.g., using ☺ to indicate happiness).

Emoticon A "nonverbal" symbol used in text-based channels to represent emotions or facial expressions (i.e., an emotion icon) or alter the meaning of a message (e.g., using ;) to indicate a wink).

Emotional Infidelity Forming a romantic attachment with someone other than your romantic partner.

Empathic Listening The type of active listening that focuses on adopting the perspective of one's conversational partner and interpreting the world through that perspective.

Encode To create a verbal or nonverbal message that represents the sender's idea (i.e., through language/expression/gesture; from Chapter 1).

Encoding Creating a verbal or nonverbal message that represents the sender's idea (i.e., through language/expression/gesture).

Enculturation The process of teaching someone how to think, behave, and interact using a system of both explicit and implicit rules and values.

Endomorphs A body shape characterized by a rounded shape, shorter height, and a large amount of subcutaneous body fat.

Enmeshed Family A family with relatively little individuality among members, characterized by extreme emotional attachment and even dependency.

Environmental Features The communication code focused on nonverbal messages that people derive from the physical layout or objects within a particular setting.

Envy A desire to have the relationship, the characteristics, or the access to resources of an outside party.

Equifinality The ability of a family system to reach a goal or accomplish a function through a variety of means.

Equivocation A type of deception that involves changing a topic or avoiding questions without appearing to have done so.

Eros The love style most characterized by passion, attraction, and sexual interest.

Ethnocentrism A bias in favor of your own group or culture.

Ethos The use of speaker characteristics like credibility and/or charisma in a message intended to influence an audience.

Euphemisms Words or phrases that ameliorate or soften the impact of otherwise blunt language or terminology.

Evaluation The third element of the listening process, this involves critically thinking about the various qualities of the messages that we have heard and making judgments about them.

Exaggeration A type of deception involving taking facts or ideas that are essentially true but then changing the specific details.

Expectancy Violation Theory Burgoon's theory that unexpected behaviors cause us to evaluate and assign valence to the nature of our relationship with interaction partners.

Experienced Power Interpersonal power that is derived from an individual's perception or feeling about his or her own influence over people or events.

Experimenting The second stage of coming together, this part of relational development is characterized by small talk and other attempts to discover relevant information about one's relational partner.

Explicit Rules Relational rules that are clearly stated by one or more parties within a relationship.

Exploratory-Affective Stage In this second stage of social penetration, partners begin to reveal themselves as conversations move toward attitudes about matters of public interest.

Extended Family Those family members that exist out of the traditional parent/child unit.

External Attribution Assigning responsibility for a specific behavior to the context in which an actor finds him- or herself.

External Boundaries The limitations and expectations that define with whom and in what manner family members should interact as they approach the outside world.

External Boundary Management The process of using specific tactics to hide or share information about your family in order to present it in a desirable perspective to outsiders.

Face Threat A behavior that lessens a person's ability to present oneself in a desired way or to avoid imposition and constraint.

Falsification A type of deception involving the fabrication of information and presenting it as truth.

Family A multigenerational group of people with a shared history who constitute themselves as "family" through interpersonal interaction and attachment.

Family Systems Theory A theoretical perspective of families as interrelated individuals, with the behaviors and interaction patterns of each individual influencing the experience of the family as a whole.

Fearful-Avoidant The style of attachment that is characterized by low self-worth and a belief that relational partners are unable to meet relational needs.

Feedback Verbal and nonverbal responses in reaction to a message that influence or alter future messaging pattern among or between people.

Femininity The culturally determined norms for the set of social roles associated with biological femaleness.

Freedom Restriction Monitoring another person and/or denying him or her the everyday autonomy afforded to other people.

Friends-with-Benefits Sexual encounters between friends who have little or no sexual commitment to one another.

Fundamental Attribution Error *See* Correspondence Bias.

Gaze An intentional form of eye contact that is steady and unbroken.

Gender Expression An individual's binary gender presentation as male or female based on social behaviors and/or external appearance.

Gender The cultural continua learned over time that include social, preferential, and constructed displays of masculinity and femininity.

Geographically Close Relationship A relationship with no significant perceived physical separation.

Gestalt A whole that is perceived as the combination of the sum of all parts.

Haptics The communication code focused on nonverbal messages related to touch or other forms of physical contact.

Hearing The biological process of passively perceiving sounds in one's environment.

Hearing-Impaired The inability of an individual to perceive some or all sounds across the spectrum of available sounds.

Hidden Quadrant This quadrant of the Johari Window can be used to describe information that we know about ourselves and of which others have no awareness.

Hierarchy The leadership structure associated with a group of people, often with increasing power in the organization being distributed to decreasing numbers of individuals, such that a relative few hold the majority of the power.

High Power-Distance A cultural belief that people are born with fundamental differences that influence each person's access to opportunities.

High-Context Culture A cultural manner of expression that encourages indirect expressions of emotion, opinion, and conflict through nonverbal means when interacting with a person of higher status.

Homophily The widespread bias that leads people to feel more comfortable around others who appear to share similar cultural experiences with themselves.

Hookups Brief sexual encounters between nominally acquainted people (strangers or casual acquaintances) who have little or no sexual commitment to one another, typically not lasting longer than one night.

Humiliation Degrading or mocking another person or revealing information about that person that they would prefer to remain private.

Hyperpersonal The evaluation of an online interaction as more desirable than interactions with that same person through other channels, often because of the ability of both parties to limit access to undesirable information.

Ideal Self The combination of characteristics and identities that represent who an individual desires to become.

Identity The relatively unchanging set of ideas and/or perceptions that one holds about oneself.

Idioms Words or phrases that have special meaning within a culture or large group.

Illustrators A set of kinesic movements that accompany speech and illustrate message content.

Impersonal Communication Messaging between two people that is not characterized by the reliance on a unique relationship.

Implicit Rules Relational rules that are implied rather than directly stated.

In-Group Perceived members of an interconnected group who appear similar in specific ways that group members see as important criteria for inclusion.

Individualism A cultural emphasis on the solidarity or uniqueness of each individual within a system.

Infidelity A situation in which one or both partners are unfaithful to the other in a close romantic relationship.

Information Overload Having received a large amount of knowledge, experience, or interaction through face-to-face and mediated means, this situation occurs when a person can no longer take in additional information.

Initiating The first stage of coming together, this part of relational development is characterized by the brief interaction and evaluation of one's relational partner.

Insecurity Induction Threatening a person's sense of well-being, whether through deception, acting secretive, or implying potential infidelity or an impending breakup.

Insider Language *See* Personal Idioms.

Instrumental Goals The desire to accomplish some task or get a benefit from another person.

Integrating The fourth stage of coming together, this part of relational development is characterized by both verbal and nonverbal demonstrations of the closeness shared with one's relational partner.

Intensifying The third stage of coming together, this part of relational development is characterized by increased emotional and physical intimacy with one's relational partner.

Interdependence The thoughts and behaviors of one relational partner influence the thoughts and behaviors of the other partner(s).

Intergenerational Family A family unit that consists of parent(s) and child(ren) and at least one additional layer of extended family.

Internal Attribution Assigning responsibility for a specific behavior to the decision making of an actor.

Internal Boundaries The limitations and expectations that help family members remain in appropriate relationships with one another.

Interpersonal Communication Messaging between two people who use knowledge they derived from their unique relationship to predict the impact of those messages.

Intimacy The sense of closeness, liking, and emotional connection to another person.

Intimate Distance A range of distance from one's body, typically 0 to 18 inches, that is reserved for very close interaction partners (i.e., family and romantic partners).

Involuntary Relationships Partnerships characterized by situation or obligation rather than self-selection and one's own volition.

Isolation Trying to break apart or restrict the social connections of another person.

Jargon Technical words and language used by professionals or members of an interest group.

Jealousy A desire to protect a relationship or a resource from an outside party.

Johari Window A graphic representation of the knowledge that we may access about ourselves, as well as the knowledge that others may access in evaluating us.

Kinesics The communication code focused on nonverbal messages related to motion-based forms of communication (i.e., gestures or facial expressions).

Language An agreed-on system of symbols that allow humans to communicate.

Libel A statement of defamation that is recorded in some written or otherwise permanent form.

Liking A positive attitude toward a person, object, or idea.

Linear Model of Communication The noninteractive process of sending and receiving messages from one person directly to one or more other persons.

Listening The process of actively receiving and attending to the potential meanings in messages.

Logos The use of logical argument in a message intended to influence an audience.

Long-Distance Relationship A relationship having a separation of psychologically significant physical space.

Long-Term Sex Sexual intimacy between people in relationships over a perceived significant period.

Looking-Glass Self The understanding of the self that is derived from testing and observing the reactions of others who view an identity portrayal.

Love Style An individual- and culture-specific way of approaching and experiencing love with one's romantic partner.

Loving A strong attitude toward another person composed of multiple components of interpersonal attraction.

Low Power-Distance A cultural belief that all people are equal and deserve to have the same opportunities as each other.

Low-Context Culture A cultural manner of expression that encourages direct expression of emotions and the open sharing of opinion regardless of status.

Ludus The love style most characterized by playfulness and a lack of commitment.

Mania The love style most characterized by control and a demand for loyalty.

Masculinity The culturally determined norms for what is considered the set of social roles associated with biological males.

Mere Exposure Effect An individual is more likely to be attracted to the people that he or she interacts with frequently, as compared to someone whom he or she rarely sees.

Mesomorphs A body shape characterized by an athletic build, average height, and a muscular, V-shaped torso.

Message The intentional and/or unintentional verbal and nonverbal content that is transmitted during a communication interaction.

Microexpression The unintentional brief "flash" of a person's emotional experience through facial expressions.

Multitasking Attempting to accomplish two or more distinct processes and/or interactions at the same time.

Name-Calling Using any negative names or offensive profanity.

Negative Face One's perceived freedom to engage in desired activity and ability to refrain from imposition or constraint.

Nepotism Favoring family members for sought-after positions of employment.

Networks Relationship-maintaining behaviors wherein partners intentionally overlap friend and family relationships.

Neutralization Compromising between the two poles of a relational dialectic so that each one is satisfied to some degree.

Noise A physical or psychological barrier to the process of perceiving a communication event.

Nonverbal Code A category of communicative behaviors that have been grouped by nonverbal characteristics that they share.

Nonverbal Communication Any communicative characteristic or behavior that intentionally or unintentionally conveys a message without the use of verbal language.

Norm Typical or usual patterns of behavior, often based on established social rules.

Novelty The enactment of various and/or new behaviors associated with a desire to be seen as spontaneous within a relationship.

Nuclear Family A family unit that consists of cross-sex parents and their children, whether biological or adopted.

Oculesics The communication code focused on nonverbal messages related to eye behavior (i.e., eye contact or gaze).

Omission A type of deception involving leaving something out of a testimony or story that should be conveyed.

Open Quadrant This quadrant of the Johari Window can be used to describe information that we know about ourselves and of which others also have awareness.

Openness The sharing of both broad and deep ranges of information with a romantic partner associated with a desire to be seen as fully known.

Orientation Stage In this first stage of social penetration, conversations are brief and focus on trivial matters.

Out-Group People who are perceived as *not* members of an interconnected group because those individuals are different in ways that group members see as important criteria for exclusion.

Overly Flexible Family A family with few to no rules, roles, or leadership structure, allowing for constant fluctuation and unclear expectations for members.

Paralanguage Nonverbal behaviors that modify or intensify the meaning of a verbal message.

Partner-Focused Motive The act of a speaker engaging in deception with the goal of a tangible or intangible benefit to the audience.

Passion The sense of excitement or arousal that drives people to take action.

Pathos The use of emotion and emotional engagement in a message intended to influence an audience.

Perceived Power Interpersonal power that comes from other people believing that a person has influence over people or events.

Personal Idioms Words or phrases that have a special meaning within a dyad or a small group of people.

Personal-Casual Distance A range of distance from one's body, typically 18 to 48 inches, that is reserved for friends and acquaintances.

Personality Dominance Interpersonal power displayed as a consequence of a person's individual yearning or predisposition toward demonstrating influence or control over others, regardless of position.

Perspective-Taking The attempt to look at a problem or situation from the point of view of the other person or persons who are involved in the same issue, regardless of one's level of agreement.

Physical Aggression Violence that uses real or perceived force to intentionally cause physical harm to a person.

Physical Attraction The type of attraction that comes from a positive evaluation of the appearance of another individual, whether based on platonic or sexual interest.

Physical Noise Any sound that stops someone from accurately perceiving the full extent of a verbal or nonverbal message.

Physiognomy Facial features derived from one's sex and racial heritage (i.e., skin color, eye shape, hair texture, etc.)

Physiological Noise Any physical state of being that stops someone from accurately perceiving the full extent of a verbal or nonverbal message.

Pitch The vocalic designation for the high or low sound of one's voice.

Loudness The vocalic designation for the ease/ability of one's voice to be heard at increasing distance.

Politeness Theory Brown and Levinson's theory that people are motivated to present themselves in a desirable way and to avoid external impositions and constraint.

Position Power Interpersonal power derived from one's role or title and the associated expectations.

Positive Face A person's ability to present a favorable or desired image of one's self.

Positivity Relationship-maintaining behaviors wherein partners affirm one another and mutually express positive emotions.

Power The ability of a group or individual to direct the people, events, or behaviors within a defined system.

Pragma The love style most characterized by practicality, logic, and relational problem solving.

Predictability The enactment of regular patterns of behavior associated with a desire to be seen as having routines within a relationship.

Preoccupied The style of attachment that is characterized by low self-worth and a belief that others are able to fulfill their relational needs but will likely not.

Primary-Parent Family A family unit that consists of one parent with primary (but not necessarily sole) parental duties for one or more children, whether biological or adopted.

Proxemics The communication code focused on nonverbal messages related to personal space and interpersonal distance.

Proximal Relationship *See* Geographically Close Relationship.

Proximity A physical closeness to another person, whether geographically or in actual interaction.

Pseudolistening Pretending to pay attention to a conversational partner while actually giving most or all attention to something else entirely.

Psychological Noise Any mental state of being that stops someone from accurately perceiving the full extent of a verbal or nonverbal message.

Psychological Time The amount of time that passes, as described by individual or group perceptions like "a lot of time" or "relatively quickly."

Public Distance A range of distance from one's body, typically beyond 8 feet, wherein personal interaction is not necessary and unknown others are given access.

Rate The vocalic designation for the speed at which a person speaks.

Receiver The recipient of a verbal or nonverbal message.

Reception The most basic element of the listening process, in which sounds or sights can be seen or heard and are made available for cognition.

Reframing Changing the conversation about relational dialectics in order to remove any seeming tension between the two poles.

Regulators A set of kinesic movements that aid in the regulation of conversational turn-taking.

Relational De-Escalation The process of decreasing perceptions of closeness, intimacy, and interaction as one moves apart from one's relational partner.

Relational Development The process of two people increasing in intimacy and perceptions of closeness with one another.

Relational Dialectics The opposing forces or tensions of relationships wherein partners struggle to find a balance between competing relational goals.

Relational Goals The desire to pursue individuals because of the belief that a relationship with them would be satisfying in some way.

Relational Maintenance Working to keep a relationship in a specific desired state or condition.

Relational Rule A norm or standard for interpersonal behavior that is assumed to be agreed on within a specific relationship.

Relational Synergy The belief that the whole of an interpersonal network is more complicated than the sum of the individual members of that network.

Relational Turning Points The events or experiences that facilitate moments of change within relationships.

Relationship Talks Relationship-maintaining behaviors wherein partners discuss the current state of their partnership and any plans or ideas about the future of their relationship together.

Relationship-Focused Motive The act of a speaker engaging in deception with the goal of either mutual benefit or the preservation of the connection between the speaker and the audience.

Relationship-Maintaining Behaviors Communication or action enacted with an intent of maintaining or increasing the strength of an interpersonal relationship.

Religiosity The degree of adherence to the teachings of a particular religious tradition.

Response Latency The amount of time — chronological or psychological—that passes before a person responds to the statement or query from another.

Retention The final element of the listening process, an effective listener typically attempts to actively remember information about the message that was sent.

Rhetorical theory The understanding of how humans use symbols to engage the communication process and influence an audience.

Rhythm The vocalic designation for the cadence or musicality of one's voice.

Rigid Family A family with an inflexible set of rules, roles, and leadership structures that do not change to fit personal growth among members.

Role Lens The perspective that families are groups of people who feel and behave like a family, typically due to love, support, and/or attachment.

Sapir-Whorf Hypothesis *See* Theory of Linguistic Relativity.

Schemata The mental framework of experience, consisting of defining characteristics used to understand and quickly process new information.

Secure The style of attachment that is characterized by high self-worth and an ability to rely on others for relational needs.

Selection Choosing one pole of a relational dialectic at the expense of the other.

Selective Listening Attending only to those parts of a message that are interesting or important to the receiver, ignoring other message content.

Self-Concept *See* Identity.

Self-Disclosure Revealing personal information about the self that cannot otherwise be discovered through observation or casual interaction.

Self-Esteem The positive or negative evaluation that each individual forms about his own identity.

Self-Focused Motive The act of a speaker engaging in deception with the goal of a tangible or intangible benefit to that speaker.

Self-Fulfilling Prophecy A set of strongly held beliefs about one's self-concept that cause someone to interact in ways that make those beliefs come true.

Self-Monitoring Paying attention to the set of auditory, visual, and social messages that one gives off in social interactions, as well as to the feedback and reactions of the intended audience.

Self-Presentation Goals The desire to pay special attention to how other people view us and to work hard to present an image of ourselves that we want those people to see.

Semantic Noise Any word choices or pronunciations that stop someone from accurately perceiving the full extent of a verbal or nonverbal message.

Sender The originator (or creator) of a verbal or nonverbal message.

Separation Relegating one pole of a relational dialectic to certain contexts/periods and the other extreme to yet other contexts/periods.

Sexual Infidelity Erotic or sexual activity with someone other than your romantic partner.

Short-Term Sex Sexual encounters between two people who do not have an emotionally close relationship.

Similarity A resemblance to another person, or having a variety of things in common with that person.

Single-Parent Family A family unit that consists of one parent with sole parental duties for one or more children, whether biological or adopted.

Slander An impermanent statement of defamation that is spoken in an interpersonal or public context.

Slang Informal words created by a subculture that distinguish users from a larger group.

Social Attraction The type of attraction that comes from the belief that a person would be fun to hang out with or would get along well with one's current friends.

Social Identity Theory The idea that people often form an understanding of the self based on the group memberships in which they select or find themselves.

Social Information Processing Theory Joseph Walther's theory that computer-mediated communication can share the same characteristics and depth as face-to-face communication, given enough time.

Social Penetration Theory Altman and Taylor's theory highlighting increasing relational depth as people move toward increasingly intimate conversational content.

Social Validation An individual is likely to respond positively toward others who appear or behave similarly, because that similarity seems to affirm the choices and/or preferences of that individual.

Social-Consultative Distance A range of distance from one's body, typically 4 to 8 feet, that is where most interaction with unknown others occurs.

Sociolegal Lens The perspective that families are groups of people that have been recognized as such through civic or governmental laws and regulations.

Speech Convergence The conscious or subconscious alteration of vocal characteristics to make speech more similar to that of desirable conversational partners.

Speech Divergence The conscious or subconscious alteration of vocal characteristics to make speech less similar to undesirable conversational partners.

Stable Stage In this final stage of social penetration, conversations are deep and personal, and partners have intimate knowledge of the thoughts and emotions of one another.

Stage Hogs Individuals whose goal is to be the primary or majority speaker in an interpersonal or small-group interaction.

Stagnating The third stage of moving apart, this part of relational de-escalation is characterized by relational inactivity and little to no communication with one's relational partner.

Status Interpersonal power derived from one's membership in a social group.

Stepfamily *See* Blended Family.

Stonewalling Ceasing all significant interaction with a relational partner.

Storge The love style most characterized by friendship, intimacy, and commitment.

Structural Power *See* Position Power.

Subculture A portion of a larger culture that shares one or more characteristics that distinguish it from the larger group.

Subordinate A person in a weaker position of power, occupying a lower level in a hierarchical organizational structure.

Superior A person in a position of power or authority over another, occupying a higher level in a hierarchical organizational structure.

Symbols Words or items that are used to represent or substitute for concrete things or abstract ideas.

Task Attraction The type of attraction that comes from the belief that a person can assist in the completion of an otherwise difficult goal.

Tasking Relationship-maintaining behaviors wherein partners balance the work within the relationship by each accomplishing mutually beneficial tasks.

Terminating The fifth stage of moving apart, this part of relational de-escalation is the formal ending of the relationship with one's former relational partner.

Theory of Linguistic Relativity As we use language to describe and understand our social world, that social world is shaped by and interpreted through the verbal skills of the individual or culture.

Transactional Model of Communication The interactive process of creating meaning and shared understanding among two or more people.

Transgender The experience of not completely identifying with one's own culturally proscribed gender roles.

Transgression Any behavior or experience where one relational partner feels that the other partner has violated a relational rule.

Transsexual The experience of identifying completely with the opposite biological sex.

Triangular Theory of Love Sternberg's theory that love is composed of three primary components—passion, intimacy, and commitment—each of which may be expressed to varying degrees within a relationship.

Turning Points Analysis The method of charting variation in relational commitment as associated with significant events or experiences.

Two-Parent Biological Family A family unit that consists of two parents who are biologically related to each of the one or more children living in the household.

Uncertainty An inability to understand or predict the attitudes and/or behaviors of an interaction partner.

Uncertainty Reduction Theory Berger and Calabrese's theory highlighting a desire to understand or predict attitudes and behaviors as a primary motivator in human communication.

Understanding Relationship-maintaining behaviors wherein partners provide acceptance and engage in perspective taking with one another.

Unidirectional A communication pattern in which messages only flow in one direction, from a sender to a receiver, with no feedback to that original sender from his or her audience.

Uniqueness A relational characteristic demonstrated by treating a relational partner differently than other individuals.

Unknown Quadrant This quadrant of the Johari Window can be used to describe information that we do not know about ourselves and of which others have no awareness.

Valence The degree of positivity or negativity that we assign to a particular person or relationship.

Verbal Aggression Screaming at another person or using an offensive tone of voice during an interaction.

Verbal Communication Any communicative behavior that conveys an intentional or unintentional message using symbolic language.

Vocal Fillers The vocalic designation for sounds used to fill pauses or empty spaces by a speaker (i.e., vocal segregates or vocalized pauses).

Vocal Segregates See Vocal Fillers.

Vocalics The communication code focused on nonverbal messages related to vocal variation (i.e., loudness, tone, pitch, etc.).

Vocalized Pauses See Vocal Fillers.

Voluntary Relationships Partnerships characterized by self-selection and one's own volition rather than by forces outside the relationship pairing.

Withdrawal Intentionally neglecting a relationship or ignoring the other person.

Index

Featured content in every chapter demonstrates the relevance of interpersonal concepts and skills.

 Communication Currents: This feature uses current electronic media clips to further expand on chapter content. These media selections briefly illustrate key theories or concepts in an accessible, student-centered way. Embedded links in the e-book on MindTap allow one-click access to short clips from these television episodes.

 Let's Get INTRApersonal: These scholarly questionnaires provide an opportunity for students to use the scales and measures associated with key interpersonal research to gain insight into their own personal experiences. These reflective self-assessments allow for students to get unbiased behavioral data about themselves that they can then process at their leisure or during class discussion.

 InterConnect: These lay prompts allow qualitatively inclined students to journal and reflect on their communication patterns and behaviors. By presenting introspective topics for journaling, an engaged student can consider the topic of each chapter through a more personal lens.

 iPersonal: Highlighting the role of technology in shaping our interpersonal interactions, this boxed feature selects an innovative communication technology and discusses the implications of that technology on human interaction in an increasingly mediated social environment.

 Commendable Connections: The role of ethics in communication is widely known yet rarely discussed in a modern classroom context. This boxed feature provides an extended example of an interpersonal communication dilemma, asking probing questions to encourage the exploration of ethical communication.

 InterFace: This feature focuses on specific praxis-based behaviors that can be applied directly to interactions with diverse others, combining scholarship and practical advice to highlight some of the common challenges that an engaged student may face in an increasingly complex social world.

Unique first-person videos in every chapter in MindTap provide everyday scenarios for analysis.

"Coming Home for the Holidays"	"Mom and Dad Fighting"	"Selfies to Remember"
"An Awkward Blind Date"	"Friends of the Roommate Meet"	"Visiting Mom at the Station"
"Chatty Tourists Abroad"	"Long-Distance Partners Skype"	"His Presentation at Work"
"Birthday Party Confusion"	"The Couple with the Ailing Parent"